De jure maritimo et navali: or a treatise of affairs maritime, and of commerce. In two volumes. ... The tenth edition, with many valuable additions, brought down to the present time. By Charles Molloy, ... Volume 1 of 2

Charles Molloy

PRINT EDITIONS

Gale ECCO Print Editions

Relive history with *Eighteenth Century Collections Online*, now available in print for the independent historian and collector. This series includes the most significant English-language and foreign-language works printed in Great Britain during the eighteenth century, and is organized in seven different subject areas including literature and language; medicine, science, and technology; and religion and philosophy. The collection also includes thousands of important works from the Americas.

The eighteenth century has been called "The Age of Enlightenment." It was a period of rapid advance in print culture and publishing, in world exploration, and in the rapid growth of science and technology – all of which had a profound impact on the political and cultural landscape. At the end of the century the American Revolution, French Revolution and Industrial Revolution, perhaps three of the most significant events in modern history, set in motion developments that eventually dominated world political, economic, and social life.

In a groundbreaking effort, Gale initiated a revolution of its own: digitization of epic proportions to preserve these invaluable works in the largest online archive of its kind. Contributions from major world libraries constitute over 175,000 original printed works. Scanned images of the actual pages, rather than transcriptions, recreate the works *as they first appeared.*

Now for the first time, these high-quality digital scans of original works are available via print-on-demand, making them readily accessible to libraries, students, independent scholars, and readers of all ages.

For our initial release we have created seven robust collections to form one the world's most comprehensive catalogs of 18th century works.

Initial Gale ECCO Print Editions collections include:

History and Geography
Rich in titles on English life and social history, this collection spans the world as it was known to eighteenth-century historians and explorers. Titles include a wealth of travel accounts and diaries, histories of nations from throughout the world, and maps and charts of a world that was still being discovered. Students of the War of American Independence will find fascinating accounts from the British side of conflict.

Social Science

Delve into what it was like to live during the eighteenth century by reading the first-hand accounts of everyday people, including city dwellers and farmers, businessmen and bankers, artisans and merchants, artists and their patrons, politicians and their constituents. Original texts make the American, French, and Industrial revolutions vividly contemporary.

Medicine, Science and Technology

Medical theory and practice of the 1700s developed rapidly, as is evidenced by the extensive collection, which includes descriptions of diseases, their conditions, and treatments. Books on science and technology, agriculture, military technology, natural philosophy, even cookbooks, are all contained here.

Literature and Language

Western literary study flows out of eighteenth-century works by Alexander Pope, Daniel Defoe, Henry Fielding, Frances Burney, Denis Diderot, Johann Gottfried Herder, Johann Wolfgang von Goethe, and others. Experience the birth of the modern novel, or compare the development of language using dictionaries and grammar discourses.

Religion and Philosophy

The Age of Enlightenment profoundly enriched religious and philosophical understanding and continues to influence present-day thinking. Works collected here include masterpieces by David Hume, Immanuel Kant, and Jean-Jacques Rousseau, as well as religious sermons and moral debates on the issues of the day, such as the slave trade. The Age of Reason saw conflict between Protestantism and Catholicism transformed into one between faith and logic -- a debate that continues in the twenty-first century.

Law and Reference

This collection reveals the history of English common law and Empire law in a vastly changing world of British expansion. Dominating the legal field is the *Commentaries of the Law of England* by Sir William Blackstone, which first appeared in 1765. Reference works such as almanacs and catalogues continue to educate us by revealing the day-to-day workings of society.

Fine Arts

The eighteenth-century fascination with Greek and Roman antiquity followed the systematic excavation of the ruins at Pompeii and Herculaneum in southern Italy; and after 1750 a neoclassical style dominated all artistic fields. The titles here trace developments in mostly English-language works on painting, sculpture, architecture, music, theater, and other disciplines. Instructional works on musical instruments, catalogs of art objects, comic operas, and more are also included.

old books. new life.

The BiblioLife Network

This project was made possible in part by the BiblioLife Network (BLN), a project aimed at addressing some of the huge challenges facing book preservationists around the world. The BLN includes libraries, library networks, archives, subject matter experts, online communities and library service providers. We believe every book ever published should be available as a high-quality print reproduction; printed on-demand anywhere in the world. This insures the ongoing accessibility of the content and helps generate sustainable revenue for the libraries and organizations that work to preserve these important materials.

The following book is in the "public domain" and represents an authentic reproduction of the text as printed by the original publisher. While we have attempted to accurately maintain the integrity of the original work, there are sometimes problems with the original work or the micro-film from which the books were digitized. This can result in minor errors in reproduction. Possible imperfections include missing and blurred pages, poor pictures, markings and other reproduction issues beyond our control. Because this work is culturally important, we have made it available as part of our commitment to protecting, preserving, and promoting the world's literature.

GUIDE TO FOLD-OUTS MAPS and OVERSIZED IMAGES

The book you are reading was digitized from microfilm captured over the past thirty to forty years. Years after the creation of the original microfilm, the book was converted to digital files and made available in an online database.

In an online database, page images do not need to conform to the size restrictions found in a printed book. When converting these images back into a printed bound book, the page sizes are standardized in ways that maintain the detail of the original. For large images, such as fold-out maps, the original page image is split into two or more pages

Guidelines used to determine how to split the page image follows:

• Some images are split vertically; large images require vertical and horizontal splits.
• For horizontal splits, the content is split left to right.
• For vertical splits, the content is split from top to bottom.
• For both vertical and horizontal splits, the image is processed from top left to bottom right.

D E

JURE MARITIMO

E T

NAVALI:

OR A

TREATISE

OF

AFFAIRS MARITIME,

AND OF

COMMERCE.

In TWO VOLUMES.

VOL. I.

The TENTH EDITION, with many valuable Additions, brought down to the prefent Time.

By *CHARLES MOLLOY*, late Barrifter at Law.

LONDON.
Printed for T. WHIELDON and T. WALLER, oppofite Fetter-Lane, Fleet-Street.
MDCCLXXVIII.

Rec Dec 7, 1904.

TO THE

READER.

THE Wisdom of God is highly to be admired, who hath not endowed the other living Creatures with that Sovereign Perfection of *Wisdom*, but hath secured and provided for them by natural Muniments from Assault and Peril, and other Necessities : But Man he formed naked and frail, because of furnishing him with Wisdom, Understanding, Memory, and Sense, to govern his Actions; endowing him with that pious Affection of desiring Society, whereby one is inclined to defend, love, cherish, and afford mutual Aid to each other : Nor hath he in no less wonder- *Lactantius,* ful manner (infinitely transcending all *lib.* 9. human Wisdom and Understanding) created the material World to be subservient to his Being and Well-being : Yet without human Understanding and Reason did he not build a Ship, raise a Fort, make Bread or Cloth; but these came to pass only by human Arts and Indus-

try,

try, in which by the Revolutions of the Celeftial-Bodies, Times and Seafons, Materials and other Neceffaries are brought forth, by the Alteration of which, Men in their proper Seafons reap the Fruits of their Labour; fo that there is no Society, Nation, Country, or Kingdom, but ftands in need of another. Hence it is, that Men knowing each others Neceffaries, are invited to *Traffick* and *Commerce* in the different Parts and Immenfities of this vaft World to fupply each others Neceffities, and adorn the Conveniencies of human Life.

Seneca 4. de Beneficiis, cap. 18.

And as God hath fo ordered this wonderful Dependance of his Creatures on each other, fo hath he by a Law immutable provided a Rule for Men in all their Actions, obliging each other to the Performance of that which is right, not only to Juftice, but likewife to all other moral Virtues; the which is no more *but the Dictate of right Reafon founded in the Soul of Man, fhewing the Neceffity to be in fome Act by its Convenience and Difconvenience in the rational Nature in Man, and confequently that it is either forbidden or commanded by the Author of Nature, who is the eternal Creator of all Things.* And as God hath imprinted this univerfal Law in the Minds of all Men, fo hath he given Men Power fociety being admitted) to eftablifh other

Leg at vim D de juft & ur c 7, & 8.

other Laws, which proceed from the Will, the which is drawn from the Civil Power, that is, from him or them that rule the Commonwealth, or Society of Freemen united for their common Benefit, (which is called the *Laws of Nations*) and which by the Will of all or many Nations, hath received Force to oblige; and is proved by a continued *Vasquez 2* Use and Testimony of authentick Me- *Controv 54* morials of learned or skilful Men. *4.*

Now by the Laws of Nature every Man is bound to profit another in what he can, nor is the same only lawful but commendable; so true was that saying, *Florentius* *Nothing is more serviceable to Man than* *part tit 22.* *Man:* But if Man shall neglect this im- *Sect 5* mutable Law in the aiding and assisting *Leg Servius* his Fellow Citizen, and inquire and dis- *D de serv* pute why God hath laid this Necessity *export* upon him; and when Opportunity gives *Cicero Offic.,* leave to take the Benefit of Wind or *lib. 11 ae* Tide (in order to his furnishing himself *Panetio.* or Neighbour with those things that adorn human Life) to dispute the Causes of their Flux and Reflux, and how they vary and change; he not only offends the Laws of Nature, but assumes a Power of destroying Society, and consequently becomes (at the least) a wilful Transgressor of the Laws of Nations.

And though the Eternal Power hath so established this Necessity in Mankind,

that

that every Man ſhall ſtand in ſeed of a-
nother Man, yet ſo great a Providence
is over induſtrious Men, that ſcarce any
Man not diſabled by Nature or Accident,
Sickneſs, Impotency, and the like; but
by his Induſtry and Pains may earn more
than would ſupply his Neceſſities; and
ſo much as any Man gets by being truly
induſtrious above what ſupplies his Neceſſities, is ſo much beneficial to himſelf and Family, as alſo an enriching to
that Kingdom or State where he reſides:
From whence it is, that all Mankind
(preſent or to come) are either Traders
by themſelves or others; and the Ends
deſigned by Trade and Commerce, are
Strength, Wealth and Imployment for
all ſorts of People, (where the ſame doth
Coke 2. Inſt: moſt flouriſh) the End tending to the
fol: 28. Advancement, Opulency and Greatneſs
of ſuch a Kingdom or State.

Anno 1453. *Conſtantinople* (the Throne once of
Vide Knowles Chriſtendom) having been ſacked by
Hiſtory of the
Monarchy *Mahomet* the Second, became a Place of
Deſolation as well as Horror, yet he by
granting a free Trade and Religion,
ſoon after repeopled that great (but unhappy) Spot. Nor did *Silemus* tread a-
miſs in following the Steps of his victorious Predeceſſor, when having the
like Succeſs on *Tauris* and *Grand Cairo,*
he tranſlated the *Perſian* and *Egyptian*
Artificers and Traders to that repeopled
City,

City, following the Example of the *Ro-*
man Virtues. Nor did our victorious
Third *Edward* deem it an Act unbe-
feeming his great Wifdom, when he
brought in the *Walloons*, whofe Induftry
foon eftablifhed the Woollen Manufac-
ture, he vouchfafing to give no lefs a
Security for the enjoying their then
granted Immunities and Privileges, than
his own Royal Perfon. Nor did that
politick Princefs fhut her Ears from em-
bracing the Offer of thofe diftreffed *Bur-*
gundians (after the Example of her Great
and Royal Predeceffor) who fought Refuge in her Dominions from the rigid
Severity of the long-bearded *Alva*, who
planting themfelves by her Appointment
at *Norwich, Colchefter, Canterbury,* and
other Towns, have of thofe Places (then
only Habitations for Beggars) raifed
them now in Competition with (if not
excelling) all, or moft of the Cities in
England, for Riches, Plenty, and Trade.
Nor need we run into the Hiftory of
earlier Times to give an Account of the
many Kingdoms and States that have
rifen by Induftry and Commerce; 'tis
enough, if we caft our Eyes on our
Neighbour, the *Hollander*, a Place by
relation of *Ortellius*, not much bigger
than *Yorkfhire*, and fuch a Spot, as if
God had referved it as a Place only to
dig Turf out of, for the accommodating

Mirror, c. 5.
Sect. 2.
11 Ed 3. c 3.

Vide Cam-
den's Q Eli-
zabeth, An.
1568
A E Meteran.
Piftor Belg.
lib 3.

A 4   thofe

thofe Countries wherein he hoards up
the Miferies of Winter, it affording naturally not any one Commodity of ufe;
yet by Commerce and Trade (the
Daughters of Induftry) it is now become the Store-houfe of all thofe Merchandizes that may be collected from
the rifing to the fetting of the Sun, and
gives thofe People a Name as large and
high as the greateft Monarch this Day
on Earth: Nor need we pafs out of
Chriftendom to find Examples of the
like, when *Venice, Genoua, Lubeck,
Embden,* and the reft of the *Hanfiatick*
Towns, once the Marts of the World,
till Sloth, Luxury, and Ambition, got
within their Walls, and drove it to Ports
of Induftry that have fince kiffed and
embraced it, the which this Ifle, by the
Influence of his Royal Majefty, hath
been no fmall Sharer in.

Hence it is, that Trade and Commerce
are now become the only Object and
Care of all Princes and Potentates, its
Dominion not being acquired by the
ruful Face of War, whofe Footfteps
leave behind them the deep Impreffion
of Mifery, Devaftation and Poverty,
they knowing the Return of Commerce
is Riches, and Plenty of all things con-
ducing to the Benefit of human Life,
and fortifying their Countries with Reputation and Strength.

It

It was Trade that gave occasion to the *Anno* 1666. bringing of thofe Mighty Fleets to Sea, 1672, 1673. as if God had left it to them to decide by Force, (wherein no Age or Time can witnefs the like) the Empire of the World . Hence it was, (the Advantages being found which arife by Commerce) that *Navigation* got its Birth into the World, reducing the feveral Nations on the Earth by that means to be even as one common Family ; and when in this Ifle we were even in the State of Canibals, it brought in a People that inftruc- ted us in Arts, Policies and Manners, *Camden.* and taught us Actions no lefs virtuous than thofe themfelves followed, And altho' long and difficult it was before that mighty People could be brought *Quæftus omnis* over to have Thoughts of the Advanta- *indecorus pa-* ges arifing from *Commerce* and *Naviga-* *Livy, lib.* I. *tion* (they only propounding to them- *Dec.* 3. felves Blood, Slaughter, Conqueft, the Riches and Spoils of Nations;) yet Though they when they entered into the *Carthaginian* had 100 Ships Wai, a Quarrel with a People not lies under worth the Oppofition of a Tribune (as *Caius Duillus* they thought) finding that neither *Tri-* legue, as *Po-* *bune* nor *Conful*, no nor the Flower of *lybius* ob- the *Roman* Army was able to withftand ferves. them, or to prevent the Invafion of their Country, and they in the very Bowels of the fame, put it to the Queftion, *Rome* or *Carthage* Miftrefs of the Wolld ;

World; they began to confider whence and from what Caufes thofe unknown *Africans* fhould withftand the *Confcript Fathers* and Power of *Rome*, and fhould dare to difpute with thofe that had led fo many captivated Kings in Triumph, and brought fo many haughty Nations to truckle under their victorious Eagles; at laft they found it was *Commerce* and *Navigation* that gave Power and Force to that mighty People; then it was that *Rome* began to know *that* Rome *could not be* Rome *without a naval Force*; the which, and to redeem their bleeding Honour, they foon haftened and equipt, great as their Competitors; afterwards *Argentum* being won, *Carthage* became no more impregnable; after which with Peace they plowed the neighbouring Streights to *Tinges*, * *Gades*, and the *Herculean Streights*; nor could any thing be too difficult afterwards, till they arrived on the *Britifh* Shore, where beholding her ample Bays, Harbours, Rivers, Shores, and Stations, the Jewels and Ornaments of that Spot, and having made a Conqueft of the fame) they foon cultivated into our rude Natures the Spirit of *Commerce*, teaching and inftructing us in thofe polite Ways that fortify a Kingdom by Naval Force, *as the Standard and undeniable Marks of Empire*, and by aiding and teaching us

in

* Now the important City of *Tangier*.

in the driving on a continued and peaceable Tract of *Commerce*, we have fathomed the unknown Depth of the *Indian* Shores, uniting, as it were, Extremes, made the Poles to kiss each other, teaching us thereby, that it was not the vast immensities of Earth that created Empire, but Situation accompanied with *Industry*, *Commerce*, and *Navigation*, that would enable a People to give Laws to the World: In the Pursuit of whose Virtues, this Nation hath not been wanting; and of following their great Directions in the enlarging our Fleet; for they, when they advanced their *Eagles* on the *British* Shore, found us not then without Ships of Force, Time having not been so envious to this Island, as to eat out those Records wherein mention is made, that the *Britains* accompanied the *Cymbrians* Strabo, lib 3. and *Gauls* in their memorable Expedition to *Greece*, long before the Incarnation of the World's Saviour; and it was from that Center that the mighty *Cæsar* first drew his Line, and took Thoughts of plowing the Ocean to find out that warlike People to face his victorious Legions; when having landed, and finding a Place adorned by Nature beyond any thing that could be called great, taught us to maintain the Superiority of Dominion, that no neighbour-

ing

ing Nation fhould frequent our peaceable Shores, and thofe Merchants that came were affigned Places to drive their Commerce and Traffick, jealous that any neighbouring Rival fhould kifs his beloved *Britannia* but a *Roman*, and for whom he fetched fo long and tedious a March; thus in our Infancy, teaching us both Defence and Commerce. And when that mighty Empire began to decline, and thofe remaining *Romans*, began to moulter and mix among the Natives, and to become as one People again, then Sloth, Luxury, and Idlenefs (the Forerunners of Ruin) invaded our Shores by a fatal Stupidity, which fuffered our floating Caftles (Bulwarks of the Kingdom) to rot in their neglected Brine, and our Ports to be furveyed by Foreign People; which fupine Negligence foon fubjected us a Prey to our ambitious Neighbours, who no fooner finifhed their Conquefts, and fheathed their devouring Swords, but each (as if infpired by the very Genius of the Place) equip'd out Fleets great as their Competitors, to fecure what they had fo dearly won, of whom Story makes mention of the mighty *Arthur*, no lefs famous in his warlike Atchievements, than in leading his Squadrons as far as *Iceland*, bringing thofe Northern People to pay Obeifance to his victorious

Stand-

Gauls Towns near Yarmouth the Mart for thofe neighbouringMerchants.

Abrahamus Whelochus de prifcis Anglorum legibus, written originally by Mr. Lambard.

Standard, and acknowledge him as their fupreme Lord, even from the *Britifh* to the *Ruffian* Tracts, and by him left to famous *Edgar*, who no fooner found his undoubted Right, but refolved to vindicate that Dominion which his Royal Predeceffor had with fo much Glory acquired, and with fo great Care communicated and remitted down to his Succeffor : With no lefs a Number than four hundred Sail of Ships did that mighty Prince at once cover the neighbouring Ocean, making them the *Portcullis* of this Ifle and the adjacent Seas, by which he vindicated his Dominions on the Waters, and gave Laws in the Chambers of his Empire : Nor did his Succeffors *Canutus* (whom Record makes mention, that having laid that ancient Tribute, called *Danegeld*, for the guarding of the Seas, and Sovereignty of them, was emblematically expreffed, fitting on the Shore in his Royal Chair, while the Sea was flowing, fpeaking, " *Tu meæ ditionis es, & terra in qua fedeo eft, &c."* *Egbert, Althred, Ethelfred,* forget the Affertion of their great Predeceffors Dominion and Sovereignty of the fame, under no lower a Style, than " *Supreme Lords and Governors of the Ocean furrounding the Britifh Shore,"* never fo much as contefted by any Nation whatfoever, unlefs by thofe that

attempted

Inferted in Leges Edwardi, *and afterwards confirmed by the* Norman *Conqueror* Mr Selden's Mare Claufum, lib. 2 cap. 10, to 16.

Matth Weft Anno 1035. fol 409 Selden's Mare Claufum, lib. 2 cap 11.

attempted the Conqueſt of the entire
Empire, in which that became ſubject
to Fate as well as the other of the Land:
Nor did the ſucceeding Princes alſo of
the *Norman* Race ſtart or wave that
mighty Advantage in their ſucceſſive
Claims, and maintaining their Right to
the adjacent Sea; as appeared not long
after, by that famous Accord, made
between *Edward* the Firſt, and the
French King *Philip the Fair,* calling him
to an Account for Piracies committed

Coke 4. Inſt.
fol. 142.

within the *Britiſh* Seas; the Submiſſion
of the *Flemings* in open Parliament in
the Second *Edward*'s Reign; and the
Honour or *Duty of the Flag,* which the
politick King *John* had above four hundred Years ſince challenged by that me-

Inter Leges
Marinas ſub
fine anni Regni
Regis Johan
2.

morable Ordinance at *Haſting,* there
decreed to take Place univerſally, not
barely as a *Civility,* but as a *Right,* to
be paid *cum debita reverentia,* and Perſons refuſing to be aſſaulted and taken as
Enemies, the ſame not only to be paid
to whole Fleets bearing the Royal Standard, but to thoſe Ships of Privilege
that wear the Prince's Enſigns or Colours of Service: Nor was this, barely
a Decree written, but nobly aſſerted by
a *Fleet* of no leſs than 500 Sail in a
Voyage Royal of his, wherein he ſailed
for *Ireland,* in his way commanding all
Veſſels which he met in the eight cir-
cumfluent

cumfluent Seas to pay that Duty and Acknowledgment. Nor was the Third *Edward* flow in following the Steps of his wife Predeceffors, when he equip'd out a *Fleet* of no lefs than 700 (though on another Occafion) with 200 of which he vanquifhed a *Fleet* of twice the Number before *Calais*, to the Lofs of 30,000 *French*. Nor did our victorious Conqueror of the Sepulchre, the Great *Richard*, in his Return from the *Holy Land*, want a Naval Royal to attend him home, by the Force of which he took and deftroyed near 100 more Ships of the *French*. And look we but into the mighty Actions of the fucceeding Princes, we fhall find that all that ever defigned Empire were zealous in the Encouragement of Navigation, looking on that Axiom as undeniable, *Qui Mare tenet,* *Cic ad Attic.* *eum neceffe effe rerum potiri,* and that *l.* 10 *Ep.* 7. without which the *Britifh* Sovereignty is but an empty Title.

Nor ought alone the Praifes of thofe great Monarchs, whofe mighty Care had always been to preferve the Reputation of their Empire in their Maritime Preparations, to be remembered, but alfo thofe of our Inhabitants, who always have been as induftrious to follow the Encouragement of thofe Princes under whom they flourifhed, and who with no lefs Glory and timely Applica-

tion

tion in Traffick, did conftantly follow the Examples of thofe of *Genoa, Portugal, Spaniards, Caftil·ans,* and *Venetians,* whofe Fame in Matters of Commerce ought to be enrolled in Letters of Gold, fince the Ages to come, as well as prefent, having been doubly obliged to their Memory, the third of which making ufe of a difcontented Native of this Ifle, the famous *Columbus,* who, prompted by that Genius that naturally follows a native wife Man, difcovered a new World, in whofe Expedition he fathomed unknown Paths, and detected the *Antilles, Cuba,* and *Jamaica,* &c. and the *Terra Firma* of the *American* Shore, who taking his Conjectures from the fpiring of certain Winds from the *Weftern* Points by ftrong Impulfe, accompanied with that Philofophy he attained to, concluded fome Continent muft needs be hid in thofe unknown Parts; his Service being firft offered to his Prince, and refufed, he was foon after entertained, purely on the Faith of that noble Princefs *Ifabella* of *Spain,* who for 17,000 Crowns (for which fhe engaged her *Jewels*) received not long after, as many Tuns of Treafure, and to her Hufband's own ufe, in eight or nine Years Time came above fitteen hundred thoufand of Silver, and three hundred and fixty Tuns of Gold.

Thus

Born in England, but Refident at Genoa.

Her. 7.

Campanel. Hift Hifpar

'Thus Ingenuity encouraged, though in one fingle Perfon, hath occafioned Wonders, and from a fmall Kingdom (as *Spain*) it hath fince raifed its Head, in a Condition of bringing all thofe many Kingdoms, and vaft Immenfities of Earth which they poffefs, under their Protection; putting them once on Thoughts of no lefs than an UNIVERSAL MONARCHY. We need only mention *Sebaftion Chabot*, a Native of *Briftol*, who difcovered *Florida*, and the Shores of *Virginia*, dedicated to that Virgin Princefs *Elizabeth*, *Thorn*, *Elliot*, *Owen*, *Gwyned*, *Hawkins*, *Cavendifh*, *Furbifher*, *Davis*, *Stadfon*, *Ralegh*, and the incomparable *Drake*, who was the firft (agreed univerfally) of any Mortal to whom God vouchfafed the ftupendous Atchievments of incompaffing not this New World alone, but New and Old together, twice embraced by that mighty Man, who firft making up to *Nombre de Dios*, got Sight (with Tears of Joy) of the *Southern* Seas, the which in five Years after he accomplifhed, paffing through the *Magellan Streights* towards the other *Indies*, and doubling the famous Promontory, he circumnavigated the whole Earth.

Nor ought that truly worthy Captain Sir *John Narborough* be precluded from having Place after the mighty *Drake*,

he having not long fince paffed and re-
paffed the *Magellan Streights*, by which
that worthy Perfon hath performed that
Atchievment, which was never done
by any Mortal before. To reckon up
the particular Actions of *John Oxenham*
(a Sharer in that mighty Performance
of *Drake* who drawing his Veffel up
to Land, and covering the fame with
Boughs, paffed the unknown Paths of
Land from *Nombre de Dios* to the *South*
Sea, and there building a Pinance, enters the Ifle of *Pearls*, and from the
Spaniards takes a Treafure almoft beyond Credit, of the undefatigable Di-
ligence of *Willoughby*, *Burroughs*, *Chanceler*, *Buffin*, *Furbifher*, *James Middle-
ton*, *Gilbert Cumberland*, who plowed up
the *North-Eaft* and *North-weft Catha-
ian* and *China* Paffage; of *Jones* and
Smith, whofe Fortune and Courage was
great in thofe Parts, of *Poole*, who
found the Whale Fifhing; of Captain
Bennet, the firft Difcoverer of *Cherry-
land*; of *Gillian* and of *Pett*, and *Jack-
man* that paffed the *Vaigates*, *Scythian*
Ices, and the River of *Ob*, as far as
Nova Zembla; nor of the famous *Da-
vies* and *Wood*, who had penetrated to
86 Degrees of Latitude, and almoft fet
their Feet on the *Northern* Pole, and
for truly valiant the famous *Monk*, *Blake*,
Lawfon, *Mines*, *Sandwich*, *Offory*, and
the

the never-to-be-forgotten *Spragg*, and
living his Royal Highnefs *York's* victorious Duke, and the brave *Rupert*, Men
whofe Courage and glorious Actions as
well in Battles as in the atchieving of
Difcoveries, and pointing out to Places
for an immenfe Improvement in Navigation and Commerce, ought to be inrolled in the Temple of Fame as Mo-
numents to fucceeding Ages, of their
mighty and laborious Travails and Induftry. The Confideration of all which
gives fome Sparks of Encouragement to
the writing the enfuing Tract, efpecially when reflecting, that among all Nations, there is a Common Law which
governs the mighty Thing of Navigation and Commerce; I had fome Impul-
fes more than ordinary to induce me to
the fame, efpecially at a time when Navigation and Commerce were never
(from the Erection by Divine Inftinct
of that mighty Prototype, the Ark to
this prefent Age) in greater Efteem than
now, and by which we have found vaft
and great Eafements and Difcharges
from thofe loyal and juft Rights and
Dues, which now and of old were juftly
due to thofe that governed this Empire;
therefore ought by all Ways and Means
to be fortified and encouraged, be it
by whatfoever Art, Science or Thing,
that does in the leaft point out towards

the fame.   Nor was it then wanting in Thoughts to promote and incite the Profeffors of the Law, raifing and ftirring up their Genius to the Advancement of the Law in this Point; and though I believe many have wifhed that fuch a thing might be, yet none that I can find have ever yet attempted the fame : Nor is it poffible, unlefs thofe things which are by Law *conftituted and known*, be rightly feparated from thofe that are *natural*; for natural Law is immutably and always the fame, therefore may eafily be collected into Art. But things that come from Conftitution, becaufe they often vary and change, and are divers in divers Places, are put without Art, as other Precepts of Laws pofitive or municipal; hence it was that the Conftitutions and Laws of *Rhodes*, for their Juftice and Equity, got footing amongft the *Romans*, as well as amongft other the bordering People on the *Mediterranean, Rhodiorum ufq, rerum memoriam difciplinæ Navalis & gloria remanfit*; yet when they, as well as the *Romans*, became fubject to Fate, they then remained only as Examples of Juftice and Reafon for others to imitate and follow : An obfequious Adorer of which was the great *Juftinian*, who caufed them to be inferted into the Civil Law; and though they obtained a

Place

Maml. pro Orat Leg.

And M. Serjeant *Callis* muft be fo underftood of the ancient Civil and Modern

Place amongſt others of the Ancient *Romans* as well as the Modern, yet have they not all received by Cuſtom ſuch a Force as may make them Laws, but remain only as they have the Authority in Shew of Reaſon, which binds not always alike, but varies according to Circumſtances of Time, Place, State, Age, and what other Conveniences or Inconveniences meet with it; nor have thoſe Laws, inſtituted at *Oleron*, obtained any other or greater Force than thoſe of *Rhodes* or Imperial, conſidered only from the Reaſon the which are not become Laws by any particular Cuſtom or Conſtitution, but only eſteemed and valued by the Reaſons found in them, and applied to the Caſe emergent.

Roman Law reduced into one, and they are not now two Laws, one Civil, and the other Imperial, but only one, that is, the Imperial *Vide* his reading on the Statute of Sewers, *Sect.* 1 *fol* 31. The Article of Enquiry annexed to them in 12 *Ed* 3 The Inquiſition at *Quinſborough*, 49 *E* 3. *Anno* 1375 Statutes of Enquiry tranſlated by *Roughton.*

'Tis true, that in *Rome,* and ſome other Parts of *Italy* and *Germany,* and the Kingdom of *Portugal,* in all thoſe Caſes wherein the municipal Ordinances of thoſe Countries have failed in providing, the Imperial Laws (if the Caſe be ſuch as that it *non Tragua peccado,* or be not ſpiritual) is there made of Force; but there is no other Nation, State or Republic can be named, where any Part of the Body of thoſe Imperial Laws hath obtained the juſt Force of a Law, otherwiſe than as Cuſtom hath particularly induced it, and where no ſuch

    ſettled

settled Custom hath made it a Law, there, it hath Force only according to the Strength of Reason and Circumstance joined with it, or as it shews the Opinion and Judgment of those that made it, but not at all as if it had any commanding Power of Obedience, that is, *valet pro ratione, non pro inducto jure; pro ratione quantum Reges, Dynastæ & Reipublicæ intra potestatis suæ fines valere patiuntur:* And for *Spain* it is observed, *Hispani duplex habent Jus, solum Cononicum scilicet & Regium; Civile enim* (meaning the Imperial Laws) *non habet vim Legis, sed rationis.* And since this Kingdom, as well as most others, being free from all Subjection to the Empire, having a constituted or known Law of its own, excludes all Imperial Power and Laws, otherwise than as Custom hath variously made some Admission, I applied myself to the Collection of such Matters, according to my Inconsiderable Judgment, as are either constituted by the Supreme Authority of the Three Estates, or that which hath in some measure obtained by continued Custom the Force of Law in reference to Matters Maritime, and of Commerce, as well in Cases publick as private.

By the first Part of which I thought it necessary, since Nature by Traffick

hath

Selden's Titles of Honour, lib ult cap ult.

hath made us all Kinfmen, to confider and examine upon what Grounds, and in what manner, *Commerce* was firft procured and eftablifhed, which is by the Laws of Leagues, Embaffies, and the like, which is a thing fit to be known; fo likewife of what may interrupt the fame, and likewife of thofe that have any reference to Seafaring Caufes in Matters Civil.

In the Profecution of this Work, I have taken care to refer thofe things, which pertain to the *Laws of Nature,* unto Notions fo certain, that no Man, without offering of Violence to himfelf, may deny them; and to afcertain the Truth of fuch, I have ufed the Teftimonies of fuch Authority, as in my weak Judgment are of Credit to evince the fame; and as to that Law, which we call the Law of Will, or Common Confent, or the Law of Nations, for that which cannot by fure Confequence be deduced out of fure Principles, and yet appears every where obferved, muft needs have its Rife from free Will and Confent, which is that which is called the *Law of Nations*; both which (as much as poffible) hath been endeavoured to be kept afunder where the Matter hath required it. And for the Civil Law, I have afcertained the feveral Au-

thorities

thorities which I have made ufe of, that
is of the *Romans* into three forts, the
Pandects, the *C des* of *Theodofius* and
Juftinian. *the Novel Conftitutions*, and
thefe moft excellent *Jurifconfults*, that
have by their Profoundnefs of Judgment
illuftrated the obfcure Paths of the fame
Law; the third thofe moft excellent
Perfons who joined Policy to Law, as
Grotius, *Ralegh*, *Bacon*, *Selden*, and the
like. Of other Pieces, that of *Shar-
dius*, intituled, *Leges Navales Rhodiorum*, *& felectæ Rhodiorum*, *Petrus Pe-
kius* the *Zealander*, *Locinius*, *Vinius*,
that of *Oleron* collected by *Garafias*,
alias *Ferrand* and *Cleriack*.

As to thofe Matters that have paffed
the Pikes at the *Rommon Law*, I have
as carefully as poffible referred to their
feveral Authorities.   In the whole
Work I have no where medled with the
Admiralty or its Jurifdiction (unlefs by
the by, as incidently falling in with
other Matters) knowing well, that it
would have been impertinent and faucy
in me to enter into the Debate of *Imperium merum*, *Imperium mixtum*, *Jurif-
dictio fimplex*, and the like, and of the
bounding out of Jurifdictions, which
in effect tends to queftion the Government, and trip up the Power that gives
Laws and Protection to us, fince all
that

It is called
Internum, be-
caufe it pro-
ceeds from the
Authority of
the Judge, and
not from any
right inherer:

that can be said, as well on the one side as the other, hath been so fully and learnedly handled and treated of by several worthy Persons (that have indeed said all that can be said) but more especially in that famous Dispute, not long since before His Sacred Majesty in Council, where all the most elaborate and ingenious Reasons that could be drawn by the Skill of a learned Civilian, were there asserted in vindicating the Admiralties Jurisdiction, by the Judge of the same, Sir *Leoline Jenkins,* in Answer of whom was produced that *Great Good Man* the Lord Chief Justice *Hale,* who as well by Law positive as other his great Reasons, soon put a Period to that Question, which during his Days slept, and it may modestly be presumed will hardly (if ever) be awaked.

in the Party.
Leg 1 §. *de Const Princip.* Coke *lib.* 10 *fol* 73 *in le Case del Marshalsea.*

He that hath never so little to do with the Compass, though he sits still in his Place, does as much or more than all the other necessary Noise in the Ship; the Comparison is quit of Arrogance, for it holdeth in the Design, it is not meant of the Performance.

And though I well know, that those that spend their Time in brewing of Books, are by *Seneca* compared to petty Painters, that busy themselves in copy-

ing

ing out Originals, having this half
Verfe of *Horace* often thrown in their
Teeth.

———*O imitatores fervum pecus!*

Yet I have this Hope left, that my
Faults and Flaws, like thofe found in
the Cuts of Diamonds, may at this
Time the eafier efcape under the Excellency of their Subject, or at leaft under
that of your Charity.

Charles Molloy.

T H E

THE
CONTENTS
OF THE
FIRST BOOK.

The

The CONTENTS,

The CONTENTS of the Second Book.

CHAP. I.

Of Dominion or Property in general, and of the Causes changing the same by War.

B

I. NO sooner had the Eternal Power created Man, but he bestowed on him a Right over the things of this inferior Nature, nor was his Goodness lessened upon the Reparation of the World after the Flood (*all things being then undivided and common to all, as if all had one Patrimony*) since every Man might then take to his use what he pleased, and make consumption of what he thought good in his own Eyes, which use of the universal Right was then instead of Property · For what any one had so taken another could not without Injury take away from him.

Just n, l.b 43.

A Theatre is common, yet the place possessed by any one, may be rightly called his own

II. Nor was it impossible for that State to have continued, if Men through *great Simplicity* or *mutual Charity* had lived together,

and

and this is instanced in those *Americans*, who through many Ages have lived in that Community and Custom, and the other of *Charity*, which the *Essenes* of old practised, and then the *Christians* who were first at *Jerusalem*, and at this Day not a few that lead an ascetick Life The Simplicity of our first Parents was demonstrated by their Nakedness, there being in them rather an *ignorance of Vice, than a knowledge of Virtue*, their only Business being the Worship of God. living easily on those things, which the Earth of her own accord brought forth without labour.

Just n, lib 2 Ut de Scythis loqui ur Trogus Primum inter Homines man nescia & ad uc astutiae inexperta simplicitas

III. Yet in this simple and innocent way of Life, all Men persisted not, but some applied their Minds to various *Arts*, the most antient of which were *Agriculture* and *Pasture*, appearing in the *first Brothers*, not without some distribution of Estates, and then from the diversity of each Man's Actions arose *Emulation*, and then *Slaughter*, and at length, when the Good were infected with the Bad, *a gigantick Kind of Life*, that is, *violent*, but the World being washed by the *Flood*, instead of that fierce Life, succeeded the desire of *Pleasure*, whereunto *Wine* was subservient, and thence arose *unlawful Loves*, but by *that more general Vice Ambition*, Concord was chiefly broken, after which Men parted asunder, and severally possessed several parts of the earth; yet afterwards there remained amongst Neighbours a communion not of cattle, but of Pastures, because in the small number of Men, so great was the Latitude of Land, that without any incommodity it might suffice to the uses of many, until the number of Men, so of Cattle

Seneca Naturalium. 3 in fine.

Ne insignare quidem aut par ire limite campos Fas erat.

tle increasing, Lands every where began to
be divided, not among Nations as before,
but among Families, an instance of which
we have hourly before our Eyes in those vast
immensities that are daily appropriating and
planting in *America*: From hence we learn
what was the cause for which Men departed
from the primitive communion of things,
first of *moveables*, and then of *immoveables*
also; to wit, because when not content to
feed upon that which grew of itself, and the
Earth singly brought forth, to dwell in *Caves*,
to go naked, or clad with rinds of Trees, or
skins of Beasts, they had chosen a more exqui-
site kind of Life, there was need of Industry,
and using of Art in those matters, which
they should give themselves up to, so likewise from hence we learn, that Men not content to live in that innocent state of community, how things went into Property, not
only by the act of the Mind (for they could
not know the thoughts of one another, what
every one would have to be his own, that
they might abstain from it, and many might
desire the same thing) but by a certain *Cove-*
nant, either *express* as by division, or *tacit*
as by *occupation*. For so soon as Communion
did not please them, and division was not
made, it ought to be supposed an agreement
amongst all, that every one should have proper to himself what he seized on, * *for every*
one might prefer himself before another, in get-
ting those things useful for the accommodating of
human Life, Nature not being repugnant to
the same

IV And

Bodin lib 3
cap 7.

Grotius de Ma-
ri libero, cap
15

* *Cic offic 1*
Addendum il-
lud Quint La-
w, S hæc con-
dito est, ut
quicquid in u-
sum hominis
cessit, propri-
um sit habertis, profecto quicquid jure possidetur, injuria aufertur   Ma
crobius Saturn l 3 c 12.

IV. And though Property may feem to have fwallowed up all that right which arofe from the common ftate of things, yet that is not fo, for in *the Law of Dominion, extreme neceffities* feem excepted. Hence it is that in Navigation, if at any time Victuals fail, what every one hath, ought to be brought forth for the common ufe. And fo in a Fire, I may pull down or blow up my Neighbour's Houfe to fave mine; deftroy the Suburbs, to raife Lines or Forts to preferve the City thereby, dig in any Man's Ground for Salt *Leg 2 § cum* Petre, cut in pieces the Tackling or Nets *in eadem D ad* upon which my Ship is driven, if it cannot *Leg. Rhod* be difintangled by other means All which *Quo non fragm.* are not introduced neither by the *Civil Law*, *§ Quod ait* not the *Municipal Laws* of Countries, but *Quemadmo-* are expounded by them, with their proper *dum § item, D* diverfities. *ad l Aquilam, 12 Ed. 3 tit*

diftreff 170. 11 *H* 7 5 Reniger & Fogaffa, Plowden *fol* 1 *to* 10. Coke 3 *Inftit fol* 83.

V. Nor is Property fo far inftated in Man, *Bald lib 3* but the fame may again be divefted by fuch *de rerum di-* means as ftand with the Law of *Nature* and *verfarum,* *Nations*, and firft by War, the Caufes of *feems to have* which are affigned to be three, *Defence, Re-* *been of opi-* *covery*, and *Revenge*. *nion, that*
by the Laws
of Nations

one may take Arms to abate the growing Power of his Neighbours. *Sed ut vim pati poffe ad vim inferendam Jus tribuat, ab omni æquitatis ratione abhorret* But that a poffibility of fuffering Force, fhould give a right of offering of Force, this is far from all Equity, fays the excellent *Grotius, lib 2. cap 1. fect. 27 Ralegh's* Hiftory of the World, *p. 678 Grot de jure belli & pacis, l. 3. c. 6 Sect 11, 12, 13, 14*

But then fuch War muft be juft, and he that undertakes it muft be a *Sovereign* The juft caufes to make a War are our *Prince's* or *Country's* defence, and that of our Allies, the Satisfaction of our Injuries, or

B 3 theirs,

theirs; our juft-Pretenfions to an Eftate or Right, Divines have added another, not only the Defence of Religion, but its Advancement and Propagation, by the way of Arms, and fome the extirpation and rooting up a contrary   Certainly War is too rough a Hand, too bad a Means, to plant Piety; *Sicut non Martyrem pœna, fic nec fortem pugna, fed caufa*, As it is not the punifhment that makes the Martyr, fo it is not fighting that declares a valiant Man, but fighting in a juft caufe, in which whofo fhall refolvedly end his Life valiantly, in refpect of the caufe, that is, in the Defence of his Prince, Religion, or Country, *ought to be numbered among the Martys of God*

Ralegh, 630 [left margin note beside "na, fed caufa"]

VI Publick War is either *Solemn* by the Laws of Nations, or elfe lefs *Solemn*   What we here call Solemn is commonly called Juft, in the fame fenfe as a juft Teftament is oppofed to *Codicils*, not that it is not lawful for him that pleafes to make Codicils, but becaufe a Solemn Teftament hath by the Civil Law fome peculiar effects, and this difference is worth Obfervation, feeing many mifunderftanding the Word juft conceive all Wars to be condemned as unjuft and unlawful, whereunto this appellation of Juft is not agreeable.

Ia ntr cizes crant quædam a r minia nea jufia, non juft. l Lert Paul S_nt l.t 2 tit. 19 [left margin note]

VI That the foregoing Section, we think it may be of ufe to abftract Lord Chief Juftice *Hale's* fenfe of this matter as follows,——Our Wars with foreign Countries have been either fpecial or general   1 Special, ufual, called *Marque or Reprifal*, and thefe either particular, i e granted to fome particular Perfons on particular Occafions to right themfelves vid *Stat 2 H 5. 7* Or, 2 general *Marque* or *Reprifal*, which though it hath the effect of a War, yet differs in thefe two inftances, 1 regularly no Perfon may by aggreffion take the Ship or Goods of the adverfe Party, without a Commiffion, 2 the two Nations are not therefore in a perfect State of Hoftility, though

For the more clear underftanding of [left margin note]

though they mutually take from each other as Enemies; and many times these general Reprisals grow into a formed War. Such was the *Dutch* War 1664 *Hale's Hist Pl Cr.* 162

A general War is either solemnly denounced, or not solemnly denounced, the former when War is solemnly declared or proclaimed by our King against another State. Such was the *Dutch* War 1671, (and the late War with *Spain*) An unsolemn War is when two Nations slip into a War without any solemnity, and ordinarily happeneth among us Again, if a foreign Prince invades our Coasts, or sets upon the King's Navy at Sea, hereupon a real, though not a solemn, War may, and hath formerly arisen Such was the *Spanish* Invasion in 1588 So that a State of War may be between two Kingdoms without any Proclamation or Indiction thereof, or other matter of Record to prove it *Idem* 164

VII That War, according to the Law of Nations, may be Solemn, two things are requisite · First, That it be waged on both sides by his Authority who hath the highest Power in the Commonwealth Secondly, That certain Rights be used (of which we shall speak in due place) one of these without the other (because they are both required) doth not suffice Publick War less Solemn may want those Rites, and be waged against private Persons, and have for the Author any Magistrate. And according to the opinion of most Civilians, if the matter be considered without Civil Laws, it seemeth that every Magistrate hath right to wage War, as for the defence of the People committed to his Charge, so for the Exercise of Jurisdiction, if he be opposed by Force · But because by War the whole Commonwealth is endangered; therefore by the Laws of all Nations that War be not undertaken without the Authority of him whose Power in the Commonwealth is the highest, there is extant such a Law of *Plato's*, and in the Roman Law it is called Treason in him who, without the Command of the Prince, hath *Ult de Leg l 3. D ad leg Jul maj.*

B 4 waged

waged War, or lifted Soldiers, or raifed an
Army ; in the *Cornelian* Law brought in by

Fol. 9 *Le Roy*
doit de droit
faver & de-
fende for
Realm vers
Enemies, &c
F N. B 113
a
L Cornelius Sylla it was, *without the Command
of the People*; in *Juftinian*'s Code is extant a
Conftitution of *Valentinian* and *Valens, None
have leave to take any Arms without our knowledge and direction.* And my Lord *Coke* in
his Third Inftitutes obferves, That by the
Common Law of this Realm it was High-
* See i *Hale*'s
Hift Pl Cr p
230, &c. and
to the end of
Chap 14 for
much good
matter on this
Point It muft
be a levying
Treafon * to levy War without Authority
from the King, for to him it belongeth only And the Reafon why it fhould be fo
fubjected is, becaufe that natural Order for
preferving of peace among Men requires
that an Authority and Council in undertaking of War fhould remain in Princes
War *againft the King*, by the Statute ; and it muft be *in his Realm.*
Therefore private Quarrels, tho' carried on *more guerrino* among the
great Men, did not amount to the levying of War.

The Realm of *England* comprehends the narrow Seas *Idem.* p 154.

VIII. But as all Laws muft be interpreted
by Equity, fo muft this Law, and therefore
there is no Queftion but that 'tis lawful for
one having Jurifdiction, by force of thofe
which we call a peaceable Guard or Power,
viz. Conftable, Serjeants, Watchmen, *&c.*
to conftrain a few difobedient Perfons as oft
as there's no need of greater Power to that
purpofe, and no imminent danger to the
Commonwealth Again, if it be fo prefent
a danger, that time will not admit of Con-
fultation with him who hath Supreme Power,
here alfo neceffity affordeth another Exception ; and therefore in Garrifons, if the
Townfmen fhould endeavour to fall over to
an Enemy, they may be dealt withal as Enemies by the Governor of the Garrifon, and
by that Right *L Pinarius*, Governor of
Enna, a Garrifon in *Sicily*, having information

tion that the Townſmen were falling off to
the *Carthaginians*, making ſlaughter of them
kept the Town And the reaſon why ſuch
extraordinary Force is called War, is, for
that the ſame is commenced by the right of
the Magiſtrate, in which caſe the War is
ſuppoſed to be made by the higheſt Power,
becauſe every one is judged Author of that
which he giveth another Commiſſion to do;
beſides the univerſal reaſon which warrants
the act, requires that all Dangers, Rebel-
lions, and Inſurrections be withſtood and
checkt in the very bud, and tho' this is Our Author
called War, yet this ſtrictly is not properly would be un-
War, tho' the parties who ſuppreſs or puniſh derſtood here
are impune. of War with-
in the Realm.
But War ſolemn or unſolemn with Enemies out of the Realm, are
both equally War   *See* 1 *Hale's Hiſt.* 163. ſhewed above, *Sect.* 6.

IX But War properly by the Laws of
this Realm or *Solemn*, is, when the Courts of
Juſtice are ſhut up, and the Judges and Miniſters of the ſame cannot protect Men from
violence, nor diſtribute Juſtice . So when by
Invaſion, Inſurrection, Rebellion, or the like,
the current of Juſtice is ſtopt and ſhut up,
Et ſilent leges inter arma, then it is ſaid to 14 *Ed* 3. *tit.*
be time of War, and the Trial of this is by *Scire facias*
Records and Judges of the Courts of Juſ- 122 *inter Mor-*
tice, and not by a Jury   So likewiſe War *timer* and the
by the Laws of *England* is when the King's *caſter.*
Standard and Hoſt enter the Realm of another Prince or State, and hath been there
by the ſpace of Forty Days, for till then *Trin* 7 *Ed* 3.
the War is not properly ſaid to be begun. *fol.* 29

X Wars, though undertaken by publick *Grot. de jure*
Authority, muſt have the Effects of Law, *belli et pa. lib.*
that is, there muſt be a juſt cauſe for the 2 *c.* 1. §. 1
undertaking the ſame, ſo that *Alexander,*
for

for that without caufe he warred upon the
Perfians and other Nations, is by the *Scy-*
Seneca de bene- *thians* in *Curtius* and by *Seneca* too deferved-
fic. l c 13 ly called a Robber. For take away Juftice,
and what are Kingdoms but great Robberies ?
Therefore the juft caufe of taking Arms
muft be the Iniquity, or, as we underftand
it, the Injury of the adverfe Party, according to the Words ufed in the antient Denun-
* Ego vos te- ciation of the Roman Heralds, ** I call you*
ftor, Populum *to witnefs, that People is unjuft, and doth not*
illum injuftum *perform what is Right*   Now that is unjuft
effe, neque jus which hath a neceffary repugnance to the
perfolvere. rational and focial nature.   Now amongft the
firft principles of Nature there is nothing neceffarily repugnant to War, there is much in
favour of it, for the end of War, the con-
fervation of Life and Members, and the
keeping or acquiring of things ufeful unto
Life is moft agreeable unto thofe Principles :
And if need be, to ufe Force to that purpofe is not difagreeable, fince every thing
hath by the Gift of Nature ftrength, to the
end it may be able to defend and help itfelf, and therefore *he is by Nature fitted for*
Peace and War ; though coming into the World
unarmed, yet he hath a Hand fit to provide
and handle Arms   Moreover right Reafon
and the Nature of Society inhibits not all
Force, but what is repugnant to Society,
that is, which depriveth another of his Right,
for the end of Society is, that by mutual Aid
every one may enjoy his own   And this
were fo, although the Dominion and Propriety of Poffeffions had not been introduced ; for Life, Members, Liberty would
yet be proper to every one, and therefore
could not without Injury be invaded by
another,

another, and to make ufe of what is common, and to fpend as much as may fuffice Nature, would be the right of the occupant, which right none without Injury could take away · And that is made evident, fince by Law and Ufe, Dominion is eftablifhed, and that appears by the Orator, *Ut fi unumquod- que membrum fenfum fuum haberet, ut poffe putaret fe valere fi proximi membri valetudinem ad fe traduxiffet debilitari & interrire totum corpus neceffe eft* · And applying that, fays, *So if every one of us fnatch unto himfelf the commodities of other Men, and draw away from every one what he can to advantage himfelf, human Society cannot ftand, Nature gives leave to every man, in the acquifition of things ufeful, to fupply himfelf before another* · *But by the Spoils of another to increafe his own Store, that Nature doth not permit.* It is not then againft Society to provide for one's felf, fo that another's right be not diminifhed, nor is that violence unjuft which doth not violate the Right of another. Of the two kinds, Contention by debate and by force, the one agreeing to Men, the other more becoming Beafts, we muft fly unto the latter when the former would not ferve The incomparable *Ulpian* fays, *Caffius writes that it is by Nature lawful to repel Force by Force, and Arms by Arms.* And this is further proved out of Sacred Hiftory; for when *Abraham* having armed his Servants and Friends, purfued the four Kings that fpoiled *Sodom,* and returned with Victory and Spoil of the Enemy, God by his Prieft *Melchifedeck* approved his Action, *Bleffed be the moft High God,* faid *Melchifedeck, who hath delivered thine Enemies into thine Hand* Abraham, as appears by the Story, had taken

Arms

Tully's Offic 3.

Leg 1 *fect vim vi D de vi, & vi arma. a.*

Gen xiv. 18

Arms without any special Commission from
God, therefore the Law of Nature was his
Warrant, whose Wisdom was no less eminent
than his Sanctity, nay, God himself hath pre-
scribed to his People general and perpetual
Laws of waging War, thereby shewing that
Wars may be just, even without his special
Mandate; for he doth plainly distinguish the
Cause of the seven Nations (in which God
gave a special Mandate for the destroying of
them, which is properly called the Wars of
God, and not of human Counsel) from the
Cause of other People, and prescribing nothing about the just Causes of entering into
War, thereby shews them to be manifest
enough by the Light of Nature, as the cause
of the defending of the Frontiers in the Wars
of *Jephtha* against the *Ammonites*, and the
cause of Embassadors violated in the Wars of
David against the same People.

XII. By the Law of Nature, in War those
things are acquired to us, which are either
equal to that, which being due unto us, we
cannot otherwise obtain, or else is such a
mark as does infer Damage to the guilty
party by a fit measure of Punishment, and
by the Laws of Nations, not only he that
wages War on a just Cause, but every one in
solemn War, and without end and measure,
is Master of all he taketh from the Enemy in
that Sense, that by all Nations, both himself
and they that have Title from him, are to
be maintained in the Possession of them,
which as to external Effect we may call Dominion, *Cyrus*, in *Xenophon*, *it is an everlasting
Law among Men, that the Enemies City being
taken, their Goods and Money should be the Conquerors*, for the Law in that matter is a common

Xenoph.; de Instit Cyri.

mon Agreement, whereby the things taken *Arist. 1. Polit.*
in War become the Takers From the Ene-
my are judged to be taken away those things
also which are taken away from the Subjects
of the Enemy, and Goods so taken, cannot
by the *Law of Nations* be properly said ta- *Hujusmodi res*
ken, but when the same are *out of all proba-* *non tam capta*
ble hopes of recovery, that is, as *Pomponius* *quam recepta*
observes, *brought within the bounds or guards* *intelligitur,*
of the Enemy, For, says he, *such is a Person* *Pomponius &*
taken in War, whom the Enemies have taken *Leg in Bello*
out of our, and brought within their Guards, *Parag Si quis*
for till then he remains a Citizen   And as the *servum in par.*
Law of Nations is the same reason of a Man, *post*
so likewise of a thing, and therefore Goods
and Merchandize are properly said to be the
Captor's, when they are carried *Infra Præ-*
sidia of that Prince or State, by whose Sub-
jects the same were taken, or *into the Fleet, or* 1 *Hale's Hist.*
into a Haven, or some other place where the *Pl C 1 p* 163.
Navy of the Enemy rides · For then it is that
the recovery seems to be past all hope.   And
therefore the *common Law* of this Realm calls
such a taking a *Legalis Captio in Jure Belli,* 2 *R* 3 *fol* 3
and in 7 *R* 2. an Action of Trespass was 7 *R* 2 *Tres-*
brought for a Ship, and certain Merchandize *pass Stathan.,*
taken away, the Defendant pleaded that he *Pl* 54
did take them in *le haut Mere ou les Normans*
queut sont Enemies le Roy   And it was adjudged that the same Plea was good.   And,
in the year 1610, a Merchant had a Ship and
Merchandize taken by a *Spaniard,* being an
Enemy, a Month after a Merchant Man,
with a *Ship* called *The little Richard,* retakes M 8 *Jac B*
her from the *Spaniard*   It was adjudged, that *R* 2 *Brown-*
such a possession of the Enemy, divested the *low* 11 7 *Ed*
Owner of his interest, and the retaking af- 4 14 *a* 24
terwards in *Battle,* gained the Captors a Pro- *Ed* 3 16, 17
perty *Lucas,* 79.

XIII

XIII. 'Tis true, the Civilians do hold, That it is not every Poffeffion that qualifies fuch a Caption, and makes it become the Captor's; but a firm poffeffion (that is) when the Prize doth *pernoctare* with the E- nemy, or remain in his poffeffion by the fpace of 24 Hours; but as this is a new * Law, fo it is conceived to be againft the antient Judgments of the Civil Law, as well as the modern Practice of common Law: For the Party in the antient Precedents doth not mention by his Plea, that the Prize did *per- noctere* with the Enemy, but generally, that the fame was gained by Battle of the Enemy

XIV This right of changing of Dominion or Property by force of Arms, is fo odious, that in the taking of Goods, if by any poffi- bility the right Owners may have reftitution, the fame hath been done And although a larger time than 24 Hours happens between the capture and recapture, and fo it may *pernoctare* with the Captor, yet reftitution may be made ; and therefore if one Enemy takes the Ship and Merchandize of another Enemy, and brings her into the Ports or Havens of a *Neuter Nation*, the Owners may feize her, and the *Admiral* of that *Neuter Nation* may in fome cafes reftore the Ship and Goods to their Owners, and the Perfons captive to their former liberty, the reafon is, for that the fame ought to have been brought *infra Præfidia* (a) of that Prince or State by whofe Subject fhe was taken

A *Dunkirker* having feized a *Frenchman's* Veffel, *fuper altum Mare*, fold the fame with her lading at *Weymouth*, whither it had been driven before fhe was brought *infra Præfid Dom. Reg. Hifpaniæ*. The *Frenchman* coming

into

1 *Hale's Hift Pl Cr. p.* 163

* *Confulatu Maris, c.* 283 287. *Conftit. Gallicæ, l.* 20 *tit* 13. *art.* 24 7 *R.* 2 *Tref- pafs Statham, Pl* 54.

(a)*Res quæ in- tra præfidia perductæ non- dum funt, quan- quam ab hofti- bus occupatæ, Dominum non mutârunt ex Gentium jure Grotius de jure Bell ac Pacis, l* 3 *c* 9 ♦ 16

into Port, there claims the benefit of the
Laws of Nations, the King of *England* being then in amity with both their Princes,
and that restitution be made ; in which case
it was resolved by all the Judges, (b) That
if there be a Caption by Letters of *Marque*
or *Piracy*, and the Vessel and Goods are not
brought *infra Præsidia* of that Prince or
State, by whose Subject the same was taken,
the same will not divest the Property out of
the Owner , with this agrees the Law Civil,
and restitution may be made. For this is
not an absolute property immediately vested
in the Captor upon the taking , but a conditional property to answer the original Debt
or Damage, which cannot be done without
a judicial Adjudication, the opportunity of
which he hath lost by bringing the Prize into
the Country of another Prince For, as to
private War, their Countries are as an
Asylum

(b) *March,*
110.

Per leg libertas, & de leg Jur

XV. But if the Ships of War of Nations
in enmity meet at Sea, and there be a caption,
if there be that which is called *a firm possession*,
the *Neuter Nation* cannot re-deliver or make
restitution of the thing so acquired And so
it was adjudged, where *Samuel Pellagu*, with a
Ship of War of the Emperor of *Morocco*, took
a *Spanish* Ship, and brought the same into
England, that he could no ways be questioned
for the same *criminaliter*, or restitution to be
made *civiliter* , for that the King of *Spain*
and the *Morocco* Emperor were Enemies, and
the King of *England* in Amity with both,
and that such a caption is not called *Spoliatio,*
sed legalis captio, in which there can be no
restitution made, upon neither of the Statutes
of 31 *H* 6. *cap*. 4 or 27 *Ed*. 3 *cap*. 13 for

See Chap x.
S xix

1 *Re Rep* 175.
3 *Bulstrod* 28
The getting
of Letters of
Reprisal a-
gainst a Nati-
on, does not
make a War
between both
States , nor
can they be
said to be at
Enmity
22 *E* 3 *fol* 13
Coram Rege &

he

Concilio suo in
Camera Stella-
rum Michael.
2 R 3 fol 2 A
he that will sue to have restitution in *England*
for Goods taken at Sea, must prove, *That
the Sovereign of the Party was in amity with
the King of* England.   Secondly, *That he that
took the Goods, his Prince was at the time of
the taking in amity with the Sovereign of him
whose Goods were taken.*   For if he which
took them, was in enmity with the Sovereign
of him whose Goods were taken, then the
same will not amount unto a depredation or
robbery, but a lawful taking, as every Enemy
might take of another

A *Spanish* Merchant, before the King and
his Council, *in Camera Scaccarii*, brought a
7 E 4. 14.
13 E. 4 9
22 E 3. fol
23 2 R 3
fol 2
Bill against divers *Englishmen*, wherein setting
forth *quod deprædatus & spoliatus fuit*, upon
the Sea, *juxta partes Britanniæ per quendam
Virum Bellicosum de Britannia, de quadam Navi*,
and of divers Merchandizes therein, which
were brought into *England*, and came into
the Hands of divers *Englishmen*, naming them,
and so prayed process against them, who
came in, and pleaded, that in regard this
depredation was done by a Stranger, and not
27 E 3 c. 13
31 H 6 c 4.
3 Bul. 28
1 Ro. Rep. 175
by the Subjects of the King of *England*, they
ought not to answer.   It was there resolved,
Quod quisquis extraneus, who brings his Bill
upon this Statute to have restitution, *debet
probare quod tempore captionis fuit de amicitia
Domini Regis*, and also, *quod ipse qui eum
ceperit, & spoliavit, fuit etiam sub obedientia
Regis, vel de amicitia Domini Regis, sive Principis quærentis, tempore spoliationis, & non Im-
micus Domini Regis, sive Principis quærentis ·
Quia si fuerit inimicus, & sic ceperit bona, tunc
non fuit spoliatio, nec depredatio, sed legalis
captio, prout quilibet inimicus capit super unum
& alterum.*

But

But if the King of *England* is in enmity *Hujufmodi res* with the *States of Holland*, and one of their *non tam capta,* *Ships of War* takes a Merchant-Man of the *quàm recepta* *intelligitur* King of *England's*, and afterwards another *per D Leg* *Ship of War* of *England* meets the *Dutchman* *Pomponius, &* and his Prize, and in *aperto prælio*, regains *per Leg inBel-* the Prize, there restitution is commonly made, *fervum in pr.* the Owners paying the *Salvage* So where the *deCap & poft.* Prize is recovered by a *Friend in amity*, or comes into his *Ports*, restitution is likewise made ; but when such Goods become a lawful and just prize to the Captor, then should the *Admiral* have a tenth part, following the *Per Leg poft-* religious example of *Abraham*, after his *limini, Par* Victory over the five *Kings* *Poftlimini de* *Cap & poftb.*

Boyce & Cole, verf Claxton, Hill 26, *& 27 Car 2 in B R* Restitution made formerly by a *French-Man*, who had regained an *Eng-lifh* Prize out of the Hands of a *Dutch* Man of War.

XVI. He that is an Enemy, may every where be affaulted, according to the Laws of Nations. Enemies may therefore be attacked or flain on our Ground, on our Enemies, or on the Sea, but to affault, kill, or fpoil him in a *Haven* or *peaceable Port*, is not lawful ; but that proceeds not from their Perfons, but from his right that hath *Empire* there, for Civil Societies have provided that no force be used in their Countries againft Men, but that of Law, and where that is open the right of hurting ceafeth The *Carthaginian Fleet* was *Sir Walter* at Anchor, in *Syphax* Port, who at that time *Raleigh, l 5* was at Peace with the *Romans* and *Carthag-* *c 3 § 17* *nians*, *Scipio* unawares fell into the fame Haven, the *Carthaginian Fleet* being the ftronger, might eafily have deftroyed the *Romans*, but yet they durft not fight them The like did the *Venetian*, who hindered the *Greeks* from affaulting the *Turkifh Fleet*, who

C rid

rid at Anchor in a Haven, then under the Government of that *Republick*; so when the *Venetian* and *Turkish Fleet* met at *Tunis*, though that very Port acknowledges the *Ottoman* Emperor; yet in regard they are in the nature of a *Free Port* to themselves, and those that come there, they would provide for the peace of the same, and interdicted any hostile attempt to be made there.

The *Corsairs* having been in the *Gulph*, put into the Port of *Vallona*, which is subject to the Turk; whereupon *Capello*, Proveditor-General for the *Venetian*, and Captain of the Gulph, having notice of the same, made into the Port, and though the *Ottoman Port* had by Treaty permitted the *Venetian* to pursue the Pirates in all Places, and forbad their Commanders to protect or shew them any Favour, yet the Castle interdicted, and forbad the *Venetian* General with Cannon to attack them; for it was nevertheless intended by the Treaty that the Peace of Ports must be preserved.

History of the Republick of *Venice* in *Anno* 1638 and *sol* 447

And the same Republick having War with those of *Genoa*, met, at *Tyre*, *Reinerius Zenus* Duke of *Venice* with the united Power of the *Venetians* and *Pisans*, counting no fewer Number than 74 Vessels well provided, and would have engaged in the very Haven, but were there interdicted by the Governor, but yet with this Proviso, that if by consent they would go out of the Protection of the Port, and at open Sea decide the cause, they had then freedom. And accordingly they sailed forth and engaged. The like not long since happened between *Cornelius de Wit*, Commander of a Ship of War of the *States General*, and Captain *Harman*, Commander of one

Fuller's Holy War, *l.* 4. *c* 23.

one of His Majesty's Frigates at *Cales*, a Challenge being made in that Port by the first, and as briskly accepted by the latter, but both were interdicted the execution of the same in the Port, but out of the protection of the same they might decide the Question, *Jan Anno 1672* the which they did to the no small Fame of the last, for in that dispute, of 380 Men then aboard the *States* Man of War, there were scarce 100 whole Men in her, and *Harman* having entered and taken her, brought her at his stern in Triumph to the Port again

But they of *Hamburgh* were not so kind to the *English*, when the *Dutch Fleet* fell into their Road, where rid at the same time some *Anno 1665,* *English* Merchant-Men, whom they assaulted, *1666 Bell* took, burnt, and spoiled, for which Action, *Angl cum Ba-* and not preserving the Peace of their Port, *tav* they were by the *Law of Nations* adjudged to answer the damage, and I think have paid most or all of it since But Enemies in their own *Ports* may be assaulted, burnt, or de- *This is Jus* stroyed by the Laws of Arms. *belli, & in Republica*

maxime conservanda sunt Jura Belli Reg fol 129 *Arrest fact super* *bonis Mercator alienig*

XVII. If the Ships of any Nation happen to arrive in any of the King of *England*'s *Grot de Jure* Ports, and afterwards, and before their de- *belli & pacis* parture, a War breaks out, they may be se- *lib 3 c 11.* cured, privileged without harm of Body or *Sect 12.* Goods, but under this limitation, till it be *Some of old have held that* known to the King, how the Prince or Re- *Clericus, Agri-* publick of those, whose Subjects the Parties *cola & Merca-* are, have *used and treated those of our Nation* *tor tempore bel-* *in their Ports.* But if any should be so bold *li ut colat, com-* as to visit our Ports after a War is begun, *muiet, ereque* *pace fruuntur* they are to be dealt with as Enemies *Co 2 Instit.* *fol 58.*

C 2   XVIII By

XVIII By the Laws of Nations generally all things are the Captor's which he takes from his Enemy, or which his Enemies gained from another by Force of Arms, so likewise all those Goods that he shall find in his Enemies custody But then it must be apparently manifest, and evidently proved, that it is really the Enemies; for if an *English-Man* should have Goods in the custody of a *Dutch Factor* at *Cales,* and a War should break out between that *Prince* and that *Republick,* yet are not the Goods of the *English-Man* subject to the seizure of the *Spaniard,* it being apparent, that the Owner is not a Subject of their Enemies · So likewise if the Goods of *Friends* are found in the Ships of *Enemies,* this does not *ipso facto* subject the same to be *prize* by the Laws of Nations, though it be a violent presumption, and may justly bear a legal examination, till which there may be a securing of the prize, till adjudication shall pass So on the other hand, if the Ships of *Friends* shall be freighted out to carry the Goods of *Enemies,* this may subject them to be *prize,* especially if the Goods shall be laden aboard *by the consent or privity of the Master or Skipper,* though in *France* they have subjected and involved the innocent with the nocent, and made both of them *prize* In the late *Flemish* Wars with *England,* the *Ostenders* became obsequiously serviceable with their Ships to the Traffick and Commerce of both Nations. Memorable was the Action, when the War was between the two Republicks, *Venice* and *Genoa,* the *Grecian* Ships being then employed, (as those of *Ostend)* were searched, and the Enemies pulled out, but no other matter done However it is most certain,

Consul Mare c. 273

Hostis sit ille, &c. quicunquæ præsed a prin. Let him be our Enemy, and the that is within his Guards Let his pass Et chi passa

Grot. l b 9

certain, let the *Commiffion* or *Protection* of
fuch Ships be what they will, if Men will
venture to trade under fuch a Cloak, it behoves them, that the *Skipper* and his *Crew*
be entirely ignorant; for it is his action that
will go far in the freeing, or making abfolute the Prize, and Goods fo made prize,
the property is immediately gone and changed,
be the Owner who he will, he never can
claim the fame, for the Laws of Nations
made the Enemies firft Mafters by External Do-
minion, and then by Conqueft gave the property
to the Captor · Following that Judgment of
the *Romans, Whatfoever they got of their Ene-*
mies by Valour, they would tranfmit to their
Pofterity by Right.

Romaninos ho-
neftiffimas eas·
atque juftiffi-
mas credimus poffeffiones quas Belli Lege captas habemus , neque verò in-
duci poffimus ut ftulta facilitate deleamus virtutis monumenta, fi eas illis
reddamus, quibus femel perierunt Imo vero tales poffeffiones, ron tantum
cum his qui nunc vivunt civibus noftris communicandas , fed & pofteris
relinquendas cenfemus Tantum abeft ut parta relinquendo in nos ipfos ea
conftituamus, quæ in Hoftes conftitui folent Titus Largus his opinion in
the Senate of Reftitution We *Roman.* believe thofe poffeffions to be
moft honourable and juft, which we have taken by the Law of War,
nor can we be induced by a foolifh Facility to part with the Monuments of our Valour, and reftore them to thofe that were not able
to keep them , nor do we judge fuch poffeffions to be communicated
only to our Country-Men now living, but to be left to our Pofterity.
So far are we from relinquifhing what we have got, and dealing with
ourfelves, as if we were our own Enemies *De Veri idem in Romula*
narrat Plutarchus

XIX. 'Tis not againft Nature to fpoil the
Goods of him, *whom it is lawful to kill ,* and
by the Laws of Nations it is permitted that
the Goods of Enemies may be as well fpoiled
as taken , and *Polibius* obferves, That all
things of the Enemies may be fpoiled, their
Ships, Goods, Forts, &c.

Hift 5
Grot de jur
bel i & facit
lib 3 . 12
§ 1

XX. And though it may happen fometimes that a War may break out, and there

may be no publick denouncing or proclaiming the fame, that if a Friend or Neuter fhould affift an Enemy with *Contraband Goods*, that is, Arms, &c. whether upon fuch a caption the Goods may be made prize, the refolution of which will depend on thefe Confiderations

First, By natural Law, *where either force offered, is repelled, or punifhment exacted of one that hath offended, and is denied*, there needs no denunciation, for Princes are not to ftand debating with Words and Arguments, being injured beyond Words. *For War undertaken to refift violence, is proclaimed not by an Herald, but by Nature.* For it is no more than the invading of one for another, or taking of the Goods of the Debtor, to anfwer the Creditor's damage.

Secondly, *Interpellation* is introduced by the Laws of Nations, whereby Princes or Republics having received injuries, may apparently fhew that they had no other way to recover their own, or that which is due to them for fuch *Interpellation* following after injuries committed, conftitutes that Prince or State in a fault *that fhall not render fatisfaction.*

Thirdly, Admitting that *Interpellation* hath gone, and fatisfaction hath been required for the damage, and no fatisfactory return hath been made, whether then the Ships or Territories of the enemy may be affaulted And for that it has been conceived they may, for denunciation is no more but to fignify that the Parties, againft whom the fame is commenced, *are unjuft and will not do right, and therefore Wars begun by the Supreme Power.* Now Princes or Republicks having done that which

by

Marginal notes:

Ower, 45 but *quære* of the Cafe

Gro. 1. lib 3. cap 3 §. 2, 3

Vid Maria-nam 27. 13 1 Hale's Hift. Pl Cr p 161, 162, &c

Denunciation is either conditionate or pure· Conditionate where it is joined with remanding of things, and in the name of, or refpect to the Heralds Law, called *Ju fecial*, compre-

the Law of Nature they were not obliged
to do, that is, after a wrong done, abftained
from War by Friendly demanding of Satif-
faction or Reparation (which is required only
by the Laws of Nations) and public Juftice
being denied them, there remains no other
or further obligation on the State, the fame
amounting to, and indeed is an apparent *de-*
fiance, and *Proclamation* is no other

hended not
only vindica-
tion by right
of Dominion,
but alfo the
profecution
of that which
is due upon
a civil or cri-
minal caufe.

Severus

XXI True it is, that while the *Romans*
were uncorrupted in their Difcipline, they

—— *ad 10*
Æn explains
it rightly,

thence was that in the Forms *to be rendered, to be fatisfied, to be*
yielded, where to be yielded, as we have faid elfewhere is to be underftood, unlefs they that are called upon will rather punifh the guilty
themfelves This requiring of things *Pliny* teftifies was named Cla-
rigation, *lib* 8

were religioufly fcrupulous in beginning a
War, for they never fent forth their Armies
till they had fought for Juftice in the tracts
of Peace, and after the publick promulga-
tion of their intent. Such alfo was the integrity of the *Achæans*, before they had fore-
warned the enemy to a defence. *Machiavel*
commends the fimplicity of the antient *Flo-*
rentines, that enterprized no hoftility on their
neighbours till they had, by ringing a Bell for
the fpace of a whole month, fummoned them
to a peaceable fatisfaction or a brave refiftance But thefe Cuftoms and Inftitutions
are only of fome Countries, not from the
Law of Nations The white Rod among
the *Greeks,* the Turfs and Bloody Spear among
the *Equicolæ,* renunciation of Friendfhip and
Society (if there had been any) thirty folemn
days after fatisfaction demanded, * are rather introduced by that which we call the
Cuftom or Law of particular Kingdoms and

* The throw-
ing of the
Spear, and
fuch fort of
Cuftoms

C 4   States; which did

States, for there may be War no Queftion introduced, without any folemn Proclamation, as the violation of Ambaffadors, by approbation of publick Authority is an open denunciation of War, and upon the fame Reafon *Guftavus Adolphus* invaded † the *German* Empire, without ever declaring War, to revenge the contumelious ufage of his Ambaffadors at *Lubeck* The form of denunciation of War is either conditional, or abfolute, Conditional, when reftitution or fatisfaction is demanded at the fame time that the War is denounced A pure or abfolute denunciation, is that which efpecially is called an Indiction or Proclamation, which is either when the other Party hath already begun the War, or when he himfelf hath committed that which deferves to be punifhed *See Examples, Grot lib.* 3 c 3, 8, 7.

XXII But if War be indicted, or is begun, againft him who hath the higheft power over the people, it is fuppofed to be proclaimed againft all his, not only Subjects, but thofe who will join themfelves unto him, as being an acceffion to his party And this is that which the Law interprets, *the Prince being defied, his adherents alfo are defied*; for to proclaim a War is to defy, which is to be underftood of that fame War which is waged againft him to whom it is indicted, as when War was denounced againft *Antiochus*, they were not pleafed to denounce it againft the *Ætolians* apart, becaufe they had openly joined themfelves with *Antiochus* The Heralds anfwered, *Ætolians have declared War of their own accord againft themfelves*; but that War being ended, if another People or King, for

supply

supply of Aids, is to be warred againft, that the effects of the Laws of Nations may follow, there will be need of a new Indiction, for now he is not looked upon as acceffary, but principal: Wherefore it is rightly faid, That by the Law of Nations, neither the War of *Manlius* upon the *Gallo-Greeks*, nor of *Cæfar* upon *Arioviftus* was lawful. For they were not affaulted now as an acceffion of a Neighbour's War, but principally To which purpofe, as by the Law of Nations Indiction, fo by the Roman Law a new Command of the Roman People was neceffary. For what was faid in the propofal againft *Antiochus* · *Was it their Will that War fhould be entered with King* Antiochus *and thofe that followed his Party* (which was obferved alfo in the Decree againft King *Perfeus*) feems truly underftood fo long as the War continued with King *Antiochus* or *Perfeus*, and thofe that really immixed themfelves in that War.

Idem dici poteft de bello fociorum Ulyffis in Cyconas Priamo quondam auxiliatos, de quibus Hom. Odyff 1 *& ibi Didymus.*

Livius, lib. 36, 42

XXIII Now the true Reafon wherefore Nations required Denunciation to that War which was faid to be juft by the Law of Nations, was not that Force fhould not be offered privily, or carried on by deceit, for that pertains more to the excellency of their Valour than to ftrict Right; (for fome Nations (as we have read) have appointed their Enemy the time and place of Battle) but that it might certainly appear the War was not waged by a private undertaking, but by the will of either people or their heads *Servius Honoratus* when he had deduced the Original of the Heralds Law from *Ancus Manlius*, and further from the *Equicolæ*, faith, *That if at any time Men or Beafts were by any Nation taken from the People of* Rome, *the*

Pater

Pater Patratus *went with the Heralds* (that is, Priests) *who have Authority in making Leagues, and standing before the Bounds, with a loud voice pronounced the cause of the War;* and *if they would not restore the things taken, or deliver up the Authors of the Injury, he threw a Spear, which was the beginning of the fight,* and thenceforth it was lawful, after the manner of War, to take the Spoil.

Tum certare o-
diis, tum res
rapuisse lice-
bit.

XXIV. War is not only lawful against those that are our Enemies, but likewise against those that supply them, but yet we must distinguish of the things themselves For some things there are that have use only in War, as Arms Some that have no use in War, as those that serve for pleasure: Some that have use both in War and out of War, as Money, Corn, Victuals, Ships and things belonging thereto.

1. It is plain, that by the first he is my Enemy that supplies my Enemies with things necessary for the War.

2. But by the second he is not, according to that of *Seneca · I will not help him to Monies to pay his Guards, but if he shall desire Marbles and Robes, such things hurt not others, only they minister to his Luxury · Soldiers and Arms I will not supply him with; if he shall seek for Players and Recreations to soften his fierceness, I will gladly offer to him Ships of War I will not send him, but such as are for Pleasure and Ostentation of Princes sporting in the Sea* I will deny to give to one that purposes the destruction of another's Country those things that are essential, for it is a bounty not to be allowed of.

French and
Dutch in en-
mity, and the
English neu-
ter with both,
the latter per-
mitted the
French King
to build a Ves-
sel of Pleasure
at Portsmouth,
which was
sent into
France, and
was no breach
of the Neu-
trality, Anno
1676

3 But in the third, which is a doubtful use, there the state of the War is to be considered · For if I cannot defend myself un-

less

lefs I intercept the things fent, neceffity will then give right, but with the Burden of Reftitution *, except fome other caufe accede ; but if the apportation of thofe things hinders the execution of my right, and he could know fo much who brought them, as if I had driven the Enemies fleet into a Port or Haven, or had ftraitened a Town with a Siege or Blockade, and were now in expectation of their yielding or compounding, there is no queftion but he that fhall in fuch cafe fuccour my Enemy, ought in Juftice be made liable for the Damage I have fuftained thro' his means. Like a Goaler that fhall wilfully fuffer my Prifoner to efcape; or one that hath refcued my Debtor juftly detained by me for my damage, whereby I am injured, and according to the meafure of my Lofs his Goods alfo may be feized and brought into fuch a ftate, to the end I may obtain a juft fatisfaction But if he hath not yet done any damage, but hath been willing to do it, there will be a right by retention or ftaying of the Ship and Goods to compel him to give caution for the future; but if my Enemies injuftice towards me be moft evident, and a Nation that ought to be Neuter confirm him in that moft unjuft War, in that cafe it will not only Civilly be liable, but Criminally as one that refcues a Pirate manifeftly guilty from the Judge at the very Bar, and therefore it will be lawful to determine againft him by fuch meafures as are neceffary and meet for his Offence Wherefore within thofe rules, he may be fpoiled of Ship and Lading, and that is the true reafon why Indiction or publick Proclamation by internal right ought to be denounced, that fo other Nations may fee they have a juft caufe who com-

menced

*Grotius in jure belli & pacis, lib. 3. c 1. §. 5.

The *English* drive the *Dutch Eaft-India* Fleet into *Bergen*, and the *Dane* there protected them againft the League and the Laws of Nations, for which the enfuing War was accounted juft on the King of *Britain's* part *Sylv. in verb. Reftitut* p. 3 §. 12.

menced the War, and that they ought not to be impeded in the acquiring due satisfaction.

And though Neuters are not compellable, by the rigour of War, to afford Assistance to either Party without the Will of the other, yet such may the emergency of the case be, that if enforced, they may lawfully declare, though to the damage of the weaker. Such was the case, when the *Venetians* had so far prevailed against the *Turks* in *Candia*, that *Canea*, which they then besieged by Sea and Land, was brought to that extremity, that in all human probability it must then have been speedily surrendred, the *English* Ships being then at *Smyrna*, and pressed by the *Turk* to assist the *Grand Signior* in the relief of that City. If the Persons whom the *English* had thus assisted, had been Christians, there is no question this Auxiliary Aid had been well, but to assist an Enemy of Christianity against Christians themselves hath seemed doubtful: But surely there seems little reason for such an Ambiguity; for if it be lawful to make League with those that are Aliens from the true Religion by the Law of Nature, then there can be no doubt but they may be aided. Now by the Law of Nature they may be entered into by Christians with such, for that Law is so common to all Men, that it admitteth not any Difference of Religion: Nor was the same universally forbidden by the *Hebrew* Law, as appears by *Abraham*'s

Laus eorum in aiding the wicked *Sodomites* with his Arms; *Thargum* and that which was very remarkable, that the *Asmonæans*, being exceedingly skilful in the *Vid Carolum* Law, and great Observers of the *Hebrew Molin tract* Rites, yet made Leagues with the *Lacedæ-* *2 disput 112 monians* and *Romans* by the consent of the Priests;

Priefts and People, yea and publickly offered Sacrifice for their fafety. Nor were they
forbidden by the Evangelical Law, accord-
ing to that of *Tertullian*, who obferves, That *Lib 7. c. 3.*
fo long as *Ifrael* was only his People, God
did juftly command mercy towards their Brethren alone, but after that, he gave unto
Chrift the Nations for his inheritance, and the
ends of the Earth for his poffeffion, and that
began to be paid which was promifed in *Ho-*
fea, They that were not my People fhall be my
People, and the Nations that had not obtained
mercy fhall obtain mercy, From that time
Chrift hath extended unto all the Law of
fraternal benignity, excluding none from our
Compaffion, no more than from his Voca- *Vide* the Cafe
tion : From whence it follows, that the ac- at large in the
tion of thofe Captains being then in the pow- end of this
er of the *Turk*, was lawful in the affifting Chapter.
them againft the *Venetians*.

XXV. And altho' the Goods of Friends, *Jus feciale.*
according to the circumftance of the cafe,
may be preferved by adjudication, and reftored to their owner, yet all manner of
Goods have not that privilege. For though
the *Freedom of Trade* preferves the Goods of
Friends, againft the *rigor of War*, yet it does
not *thofe Goods that fupply the Enemy* for War, *Vide* Treaty
as *Money, Victuals, Ships, Arms, and other* 1 Dec at Lor-
things belonging thereto. For to fupply an *don* 1674.
Enemy that invades our right, or feeks the Art the
deftruction of our Countries, is a liberality third, what
not to be allowed of, and it certainly ftands is meant by
with neceffity, that *if I cannot fafely defend* Goods con-
myfelf, or endamage my Enemy without inter- traband or
cepting the things fent, it may juftly be done prohibited
But when fuch goods are feized, whether Merchan-
they give the Captor a right of Property, or dize

right

right by Retention, to compel that neuter
Nation to give Caution for the future, by
Hoftages or *Pledges*, not to fupply the Enemy,
may be a queftion. The *Romans* who had
*Cambder vide
Ann.* 1589.
1595. brought Victuals to the Enemies of *Carthage*,
were taken by the *Carthaginians*, and again
rendered upon requeft, the *Hollanders* in the
heat of the War between *Sweden* and *Poland*,
never fuffered themfelves to be interdicted
with either Nation, the fame State when
they had War with *Spain*, intercepted the
French Ships, paffing to or from *Spain*, but
reftored them.

Plutarch. And *Pompey*, in the Hiftory of the *Mithri-
datick* War, fet a Guard on the *Bofphorus*, to
obferve if any Merchant failed in thither;
whofoever did, and was taken, was furely
put to Death, fo *Demetrius* when he poffeffed *Attica* with his Army, having blockt
up *Athens*, hanged up both the Mafter and
Commander of a Ship, who attempted to
Meurfius in his
Danifh Hift
I part 2 bring in Corn · The *Hollanders* having blockt
up *Dunkirk*, fome *Englifh* Merchants Ships
did attempt to enter, but were denied by the
Hollanders

Moft certain, if a *Neuter Nation* had had
notice of the War, and Caution given them
(as is ufual) not to fupply the Enemy with
the Counterband Goods, as they call them,
Vide Tit Cu-
ftoms. if fuch be the cafe, the prize is become abfolutely the Captor's. So Queen *Elizabeth*
did when fhe feized on the 60 Sail of the *Hanfiatick Towns*, who were carrying of Goods,
ropas contrebanda, to the *Spaniard* her Enemy,
fhe condemned them, and made them abfolute prize; *For as neuters are not compellable
by the rigour of War, to give any thing againft
their Will, fo muft they not againft the Will of*
each

each Party afford such things as may damage one Owen, 45.
another For Perfons or Nations having had
notice of the War, which is done, and Caution given fometimes by *Proclamation*, or fome
other publick Edict, fignifying the right of
their Caufe, and fhall afterwards gather to,
and affift the Enemy, whether Affociates, *Bald ad l 2.*
Neuters, or Subjects, the fame yields *a right,* *c de Seven 70.*
fo far as to them, not only to the charge and Under the
damage that may fall thereby, by making Name of Contraband may
them prize ; but may make them obnoxious be compre-
to punifhment : *For it is the Duty of thofe that* hended Arms
abftain from War to do nothing for the ftrength- only, as pie-
ning of him who maintains a bad Caufe, whereby ces of Ord-
nance, with
the motions of him that wageth a juft War may all Imple-
be retarded ; and where the caufe is doubtful ments be-
they ought to fhew themfelves equal to both, longing to
permitting paffage, baking, dreffing, and af- them, Fire-
Balls, Pow-
fording Provifion for each Army or Navy. der, Matches,
Bullets, Pikes, Swords, Lances, Spears, Halberts, Guns, Mortar-
Pieces, Petards, Granadoes, Mufket-refts, Bandaliers, Salt-petre,
Mufkets, Mufket-fhot. Helmets, Corflets, Breaft-plates, Coats of
Mail, and the like kinds of Armature, fo for Horfes and other
Warlike Inftruments *Vide Marine* Treaty between *England* and
Holland, December 1, 1674 *Art* 3 *Vide* the Attempt made by
John Burrough, to trade with the *Swede* exprefly againft the Inter-
diction of the *Danifh* King Sir *Walter Raleigh ,* l. 5 c 1 § 10

    L. Æmelius Prætor accufed the *Tejans* for So likewife
victualling the Enemy's Navy, promifing Ships Mafts,
and whatfo-
them Wine, adding, That unlefs they would ever fhall be
do the like for the Navy of the *Romans*, he thought or
would account them as Enemies , but com- afcertained
mon Experience hath taught Nations and capable of
Kingdoms, when they declare Neutrality, to arming an
Enemy
make Provifion by way of League with both *Bartol l nul-*
the Nations at War, that when it fhould hap- *lus nunc lib. 2.*
pen the Armies of both, or any draw towards *de Judeis Cœ-*
their Territories, it might be lawful for them *licolis.*

to exhibit the *Common Offices of Humanity* to both.

It happened that about seven stout Merchant Men rode in the Port at *Smyrna*, the General of the *Venetians*, being jealous of their joining with the *Turkish* Armado, desired to know their Minds, who answered, they would prove Neuter in the Dispute, but afterwards (though at first the Captains all refused) upon the threatning of the *Grand Signior*, to lay an Embargo on all the Goods of the *English* Nation in his Dominion, and to make Slaves of their Persons, those Captains were forced to join with the *Turkish* Forces, who beat the *Venetians* from before *Canea*, and so reliev'd it, the *Venetian* Ambassador complained to the then Powers in *England*, but could have no Relief, being answered, *That those Ships being in the Turks Power, were subject to it*, the accident being such as made the Action lawful, as we have afore remembred

Anno 1650, or 1651 *unde R Cooke* of the church's state in equal danger with the Trade

Leagues may be made with Infidels, by the Law of Nature, and likewise by that of Religion, which is so equally indulgent to all Men, that it will not admit of any Difference upon the score of Religion, *Vid* Examples and Cautions *Grot de jure belli & pacis, lib.* 2 *Cap.* 15 § 8, 9, 10, 11, 12.

CHAP.

C H A P. II.

Of Letters of Marque and Reprizal.

 XVII. *Re-*

Grot de Jure Belli c. Pacis, l 3 c 2 § 4, 5

I. REprisals, known to us by the Word *Reprisalia,* or *Letters of Marque,* in Law have other Appellations, as *Pignoratio, Clarigatio,* and *Androlepsia,* &c in Imitation of that *Androlepsia,* among the *Greeks,* to seize the three next Citizens of that Place, whither the Murderer had fled, and was always given to him who required revenge of the Offender, the word *(Reprisals)* is from the *French* reprendre and *Reprise, i e resumptio,* that is, to retake or take again one thing for another, like our *Saxon* Withernam. Though the Act

Act is now become lawful by the Law (indeed *consent*) of *Nations*, yet must it have its Standard mark, for the same cannot be done by any private Authority, but only by the power of that Prince or Republick, whole Subject the injured Person is, nor is the same grantable by Authority, but where the Party injured has *Justice denied him*, or the same *illegally delayed*.

Reprizals are all one, both in the Common and Civil Law, Reprisal a est potestas pignorandi contra quemlibet, de terra debitoris dria creditori pro injuriis &

damnis acceptis vocabular. utriusque Juris 27 E 3 Stat 2 cap 17. 2 Inst 204, 205.

II. By the *Law of Nature* no Man is bound for another's Act, but only the Succeffor of his Estate, for that Goods and Estate should pass with their *Burthens*, was introduced together with the *Dominion* of Things; hence it is, that the Son cannot be molested for the debt of his Father, * neither the Wife for the debt of the Husband, nor the Husband for the debt of the Wife, the same being against natural equity, that one should be troubled for the debt of another

*Leg unica, c. ut null ex vicanis c ne uxor pro mar & ne fil pro patre. totis tit

So it is, that no particular Men owe, or are obliged for the debt which the *Community* owes, that is, if the *Community* have any Goods, but if Money be lent to a *Community*, each Particular is naturally bound, as they are a part of the whole, if the Stock publick be wanting If one lends my Country Money (says *Seneca*,) *I will not call myself his Debtor, yet will I pay my share* And again, *Being one of the People, I will not pay as for myself, but contribute as for my Country* Naturally, nay, by the very *Roman Law*, * one Village was not bound for the other, nor one Man's Possessions charged for another, no not so much as with the Debts publick, the reason being

Ulpian Leg ficut fect quod cuique urivers nom Et singuli debebunt non tanquam proprium fed tonquam publicam publici parten Seneca, lib 6. de Benefic c 20 & cap 19

* Leg nullam, c de Execut. & Exactionibus

added,

added, *That it was against reason for one to be charged with the debt of another.*

III And though by the *Law of Nature* one Man's Goods are not tied for the debts of another, no nor for those of the *Publick*, yet by the voluntary Law of Nations, the same might be introduced and brought in, and the same may stand well with the *Laws of Nature*, for that might be introduced by Custom and tacit Consent, when even Sureties, without any Cause, may subject and make liable their Goods and Estates for the Debts of a Stranger So likewise that for any Debt, which any *Civil Society*, or the *Head* thereof ought to make good, or because the *Sovereign* or *Head* hath not done right in another's Debt, but hath made himself liable to render Satisfaction; such a *Society* may oblige and make liable all their Goods corporeal or incorporeal, for the Reddition of Satisfaction. Hence it was, as the great *Justinian* observes,

In Nov Just 52 134 c. unico de injuriis in sexto Just Inst de Jure Na

That this Custom was constituted by the *Nations*, grounded on the Urgency of human Needs, asserted with the greatest of Necessities · Since without this, great Licence would be given and tollerated for the committing of Depredations and Injuries; especially if only the Goods of Rulers were made liable, who seldom possess any thing, that, for Satisfaction, the injured may easily come by; whereas those private Men, whose Commerces are various, may be catcht for recompence, sometimes with the greatest ease, and

Baldus 3 cons 58 Bartol de repress q 5 ad ter num 9

freest from Danger Besides, the Owners of such Prize being Members of the same *Society*, might more easily obtain mutual right for satisfaction of the injur'd, and their own future indemnity than Foreigners could, who

without

without fuch a Tye would be very little regarded.

IV. Befides, the Benefit of this Obligation was common to all Nations, fo that they which were one Time grieved with it, another time might be eafed by the fame   Moreover that this Cuftom was received, appears not only out of full Wars which Nations wage againft Nations (for in thefe what is obferved may be feen in the Forms of the ancient Denunciations.   *Populis prifcorum La-* Liv lib 1. *tinorum, hominibufque, prifcis Latinis bellum indico facioque*   So likewife in the Propofal · *Vellent, juberent Philippo Regi, Macedonibufque* Lib 31. *qui fub regno ejus effent, bellum indici*   And in the very Decree or Proclamation itfelf. *Populus Romanus cum populo Hermundulo homi-* Gellius, lib 16. *nibufque Hermundulis bellum juffit*) but alfo cap 4 where Wars are not come to that fulnefs of War, yet there is need of a certain violent Execution of Right, that is, imperfect War. *Agefilaus* of old faid to *Pharnabazus*, a Subject to the King of *Perfia.   We*, O Pharna- Plutarch Age- bazus, *when we were the King's Friends, car-* fil. *ried ourfelves like Friends towards all his, and being now become his Enemies, we carry ourfelves like Enemies, wherefore feeing you will be one of the things that are his, we do juftly oppofe him in you*   A fpecies of this fort of Execution by Reprizal was that which the *Athenians* called apprehenfion of Men, of which the Attick Law (as Mr. *Rous* obferves) Archæologiæ *If one have force offered him and die, his Kinf-* Atticæ. *men and Friends may apprehend Men, till either the Manflayer be duly punifhed or yielded, but it is lawful to apprehend three Men and no more.*   By which it plainly appears, that for the debt of the City, which is bound to punish her Subjects that have hurt others, is

tied a certain incorporeal right of the Subjects, that is, the liberty of taking whom they please, and doing what they will. So that such Persons so taken by that Law, might be made Slaves, until the City did that which by Law she was obliged to perform. In like manner to recover a Citizen taken Captive by manifest Injury, are the Citizens of that City, where the Injury was done, retained by Reprize. Wherefore at *Carthage*

they would not suffer *Ariston* the *Tyrian* to be taken, for, said they, *the same will befal the Carthaginians at* Tyre, *and in other Towns of Trade, whereto they often resort.*

V A due Administration of Justice is not the least sense, wherein Princes are stiled Gods. To deny or delay Justice is Injustice; Justice is every Man's right, who hath not forfeited what he might claim by the *Jus Gentium.*

If therefore the Party cannot obtain his Definitive *Sentence* or *Judgment,* within a fit time against the Person of whom he complains, or if there be a Judgment given against *apparent Right* and Law, yet if no Relief can be had, the Bodies and Moveables of his Subjects, who renders not right, may be taken.

VI. In the Prosecution of which there must be,

1. The Oath of the Party injured, or other sufficient proof, touching the pretended Injury, and of the certain Loss and Damage thereby sustained.

2. A Proof of the due Prosecution for the obtaining of Satisfaction in a legal way.

3. Protelation or denial of Justice

4. A Com-

4. A Complaint to his own Prince or State.

5. Requisition of Justice by him or them, made to the Supreme Head or State, where Justice in the ordinary course was denied.

6. Persistency still in the denial of Justice

All which being done, Letters of Reprizal under such cautions, restrictions and limitations as are consonant to Law, and as the special case may require, may issue not only by the *Jus Gentium* and *Civile*, but by the antient and municipal Laws of the Kingdom*.

* *Magna Charta C* 30. the latter part 2 *dorf.*

Clause *Clauf* 7 *Johan Reg m* 22 *Pat* 15. E 3 48 *Pat* 23 *H* 6 *part* 2 *dorf* 14, 15

VII. The *Reprizals* grantable by the Laws of *England*, are of two sorts, *Ordinary* and *Extraordinary*. The *Ordinary* are either within the Realm or without, and are always granted where any *English* Merchants or their Goods are spoiled, or taken from them, in parts beyond the Sea by Merchants Strangers, and cannot upon Suit, or the King's demanding of Justice for him, obtain the same, he shall have upon Testimony of such prosecution, a Writ out of the *Chancery* to arrest the Merchants Strangers of that Nation their Goods here in *England*, the which is grantable to the Subject oppressed of *Common Right*, by the *Chancellor* or *Keeper* of *England*, who always in such case hath the approbation of the King or Council, or both, for his so doing, the other, which is for satisfaction out of the Realm, is always under the Great Seal.

Fitz. H. N. Bre 114. *Reg.* 129 *Pat Rolls* 14. 14 *H* 6 *par.* 1. *dorf* 15 17. 22 & *M* 5. 6. 7. *par* 2. *dorf* 18 22 *b* 4. *par* 2. *M* 25. *dorf* 2 & 4 *Inft* 124. 125. 137. *Lex Mercat* 120 1 *Hale's Hift Pl Cr p* 162 They are either, 1 Particular to par-

ticular Persons upon particular Occasions, or, 2. General, which hath in a great Degree the Effect of a War, though it is not a regular War. *See* for more Matter the Place cited, or above, *Chap.* I. *Sect* 6

VIII. But Letters of Reprizal granted in the *Ordinary* way for reparation out of the

Realm, which are always under the Great
Seal of *England*, cannot be revoked, (though
perhaps in point of State there may be a sus-
pending the Execution of them for reason
grounded on the publick good) and the reason wherefore they cannot be annulled or revoked is, because after the Person injured

Leg qui resti-
tuere de rei
vindic.

hath petitioned, and hath according to Law
made out by proof his loss, and Letters of
Request have gone, and no reparation made,
then the Letters Patents of Reprizal being
sealed, the same does immediately create and
vest a National Debt in the Grantee, to be satisfied in such manner and by such means, as
the same Letters Patents do direct out of the
Goods and Estates of his Subjects, who re-

Vide Treaty
1666. *Breda,*
Art. 5

fuses or protelates to do right (however, as
the King hath the Legislative power of Peace
and War in a publick Treaty for the Nation's
good, they may be mortified, and then revoked by the Great Seal in pursuance of that
Treaty)

    Nor do I see it an act unjust internal to deny
the Execution of such Letters Patents, according to that of St *Paul, All things are lawful*
for me, but all things are not expedient. Now
to the true Interpretation of the word *lawful*
strictly, it is to do a thing without violating
the Rules of Piety and Charity. Now there
are many things amongst men which are not
internally just, and cannot be done without
violating the Laws of Charity, yet are lawful

Quintilian

to be done, as in the Law of the *XII Tables,*
the Creditors might divide the Debtor's Body
amongst them So in acquiring satisfaction for Damages, the Lives and Goods of
Innocents may be involved in Death and Destruction, whose peaceable Tract in Com-
meice

merce never gave them knowledge of this *privatum Bellum*, nor were they Actors in the Injury original. 'Tis true externally, according to that of *Lucan*, *That Prince or State that denies me right, gives me all.* But the incomparable *Cicero* obferves, *That there are fome Offices to be done to them from whom you have receiv'd an Injury, for revenge and punifhment muft have a meafure.* Now if the fupreme Power does think that the Execution of fuch Letters of Reprizal cannot well be effected without endangering the Peace of both Eftates, there may be a juft caufe to refpite the Execution till a time more convenient may occur, for that the Lives and Eftates of thoufands may be involved in the repairing of one Injury, private and peculiar · Nor do I fee the fame to appear repugnant to the Laws pofitive that have been made for the awarding thofe Commiffions 'Tis very true the † Statute reciting, " That at the " grievous Complaints of the Commons of " *England*, who had fuffered many Wrongs " and Injuries in the Lofs of their Ships and " Goods upon the main Sea againft Leagues, " fafe-Conducts, and Truces which were " broken by the Subjects of other Nations, " the fame Parliament reciting their willing- " nefs to provide Remedy and Relief for the " grieved, by fpoil and injuries done unto " them beyond the Seas, upon Complaint " to the Keeper of the Privy-Seal (on full " evidence fhewn) he fhall fign Letters of " Requeft to demand reftitution and repara- " tion to the Parties grieved · Which if not " made in convenient time, then the Lord " Chancellor of *England* fhall grant Letters " of Reprizal in due Form of Law for the In- " demnity

Omnia dat qui jufta negat. Orat. pro Balbo.

Eft enim aliquid quod non oporteat, etiam fi licet Idem pro Milone.

†4 Hen. 5. c. 7.

" demnity of the Perfons interefted and in-
" jured " Yet this does in no refpect reftrain the King's Prerogative and Authority,
which he had at the Common Law in the
judging the conveniency and time, when to
be executed Nor does the fubfequent Sta-

†14 Ed 4 c 4. tute †, reciting, " Whereas divers great
" Offences were often committed againft
" Leagues, Truces and Amities between the
" King and other Princes or States, againft
" fafe-Conducts and Licences, and againft
" the Laws and Statutes of the Realm (in
" that cafe made and provided) to the great
" flander of our Sovereign Lord the King,
" and the Damages of the good Subjects the
" Commons of *England*. It was therefore
" Ordained, Eftablifhed, Enacted, and Con-
" firmed by the Confent of the Lords Spi-
" ritual and Temporal, and Commons af-
" fembled in Parliament, That all Statutes
" and Ordinances againft the Offenders of
" Leagues, Truces, fafe-Conducts, and Ami-
" ties fhall be in full force, excepting the
" Claufe in the Act which made it High
" Treafon in the Second Year of *Hen* V."
Therefore it is plain, there were Statutes
made for the more effectual providing for the
Subject, and Letters of Reprizals, they be-
† Johan Reg ing granted long † before the Statutes, and
memb 22
Pat 15 Ed. 3
part.2.dorf 48 the King's Prerogative not the leaft diminifhed, but remaining at the Common Law
to judge when expedient.

IX And fince the granting of Letters of
Reprizal does not, in the ordinary way for
particular fatisfaction, amount to a breach of
the Peace, I have thought fit for the excellency and care that is had in the compofing
and framing of them, to recommend one that
was

granted upon Solemn Advice, and for the *Vide* §. 15. Reasons therein mentioned. *postea.*

X The *Extraordinary* are by Letters of *Marque*, for reparation at Sea, or any place out of the Realm, grantable by the *Secretaries* of State, with the like approbation, of the King or Council, or both, but they are only during the King's Pleasure, and to weaken the Enemy during the time of War, and may at any time be revoked

XI. As Princes by the Laws of *Nations* are *Machiavel on* responsible for injuries *publick*, so should they *his Tit. Liv. C.* by the most prudent ways imaginable prevent A Prince in those that are *private*, not suffering Foreign- this latter Age ers, if possible, to receive wrongs in their lost his Coun- Countries: For, as the *Florentine* observes, try but for a *If a Man be exceedingly offended, either by the* Sheep-Skins. *publick, or by any other private hand, in a* *Philip Comines* *Foreign Nation, and cannot obtain reparation* *in vita Caroli* *according to Justice, he will never leave blow-* *Ducis Bur-* *ing the Coals, or cease promoting the injury, till* *gund.* *the flame break out into War, in which he* *cares not if he see the ruin of that Kingdom or* *State, where he received his wrongs.*

Nor should the Prince or State of the Per- son injured, value his Misfortune at so low a Rate as to deny him Letters of Request, for that were to heap up injury upon injury, *Leg. qui resti-* but likewise, if Justice be denied after such *tuere de rei* request, to arm him with power to take sa- *vindicat.* tisfaction by reprise, *vi, manu & militari.*

Generally there always proceed Letters of Request, two or three, more or less; and according to the satisfaction, sufficient or in- sufficient, returned in answer to the same, Commissions are awarded

XII. *Subjects* cannot by force hinder the *Res judic. pro* Execution even of an unjust Judgment, or *veritate habe-* lawfully

lawfully purfue their right by force, by reafon of the *efficacy* of the power over them : But *Foreigners* have a right to compel, which yet they cannot ufe lawfully, fo long as they may obtain fatisfaction by Judgment But if that ceafes, then Reprizal is let in.

XIII. Now Judgment is obtained either in the *Ordinary* Courfe, by way of *Profecution*, or *Suit*, or *Appeal* from the fame, after Sentence, or Judgment given, to a higher Court, or elfe in the *Extraordinary* way, which is by way of Supplication, or Petition to the *Supreme Power*, but we muft underftand that to be, when the matter *in controverfy* is, *tam quoad merita quam quoad modum procedendi*; not doubtful, for in doubtful matters the prefumption is ever for the Judge or Court.

But the Reprizal muft be grounded on wrong Judgment given in matters *not doubtful*, which might have been redreffed one, way or other; either by the ordinary or extraordinary power of the Country or Place, and the which was apparently *perverted* or *denied*

But if the matter be doubtful, then otherwife, for in Caufes dubious or difficult, there is a prefumption always that Juftice was truly Adminiftred by them who were duly Elected to publick Judgments.

XIV. And yet in this latter Cafe, fome * are of Opinion, that if the Cafe were dubious, and if the Judgment were againft apparent Right, the Stranger oppreffed is let into his fatisfaction; and the reafon is, becaufe the Judge's Authority is not the fame over *Foreigners* as over *Subjects*, for the reafon abovementioned

If an *Englifh* Merchant fhall profecute a Suit in the Ordinary Courts of the Law be-yond Seas, and Sentence or Judgment fhall pafs againft him, from which he appeals to the *Supreme Judgment*, and there the firft Judgment or Sentence is affirmed, though the Complainant hath received a Judgment againft the *real Right* of the Caufe, yet this will be no caufe for Letters of Reprizal, though perhaps it may occafion Letters of *Requeft* (if there be ftrong circumftances for the fame) to have a rehearing of the Caufe

But if an *Englifh* Man fhall recover a Debt there, and then the Officer having the Debtor in Cuftody, will wilfully let the Pri-foner efcape, and then become infolvent, the fame may perhaps occafion Reprizal.

In *England*, If a Foreigner bring an Action Perfonal againft *I. S* and the matter is found *fpecial* or *general*, and the Party prays Judg-ment, and the Court refufes it, and then the Defendant dies, and with him the Action, (the nature of it being fuch) the Party is here without Remedy, the fame may occafion Letters of Reprizal, if it be accompanied with thofe Circumftances that evince an ap-parent denial of Juftice, *i e.* as putting it off from *Term* or *Term* without caufe.

Nulli vende-mus, nulli ne-gabimus, aut deferemus juftitiam, Grand Char-ter, *Coke* 2 *Inft* 56.

An *Englifh* Man purfues his Right in the legal Courts beyond Seas, and the Military Governor oppofes the profecution, and by force conveys away the Debtor and his Goods, the Sentence or Judgment is obtained: its ultimate end being *Execution*, being thus fruftrated, may occafion Letters of Reprizal.

XV Perfons murder'd, fpoil'd, or other-wife damnified in hoftile manner, in the Ter-ritories or places belonging to that King, to whom

Cafe of Slaughter, *Lee* againft the Governor of

Legborn, upon the Petition of *Gould* and *Canham* merchants, in *Nov* 1670, on which two Letters of Request were sent to the great Duke of *Tuscany*, for redress

whom Letters of Request are issued forth, if no satisfaction be returned, Letters of Reprizal may issue forth; and the Parties Petitioners are not in such cases compelled to resort to the Ordinary prosecution But the Prince of that Country, against whom the same are awarded, must repair the damage out of his or their Estates, who committed the injuries, and if that proves deficient, it must then fall as a common Debt on his Country

т After the Massacre at *Amboyna*, and the other depredations

Such Letters of Request generally allot a time † certain for Damages to be repaired, if not, Reprizals to issue forth A singular Example of which you will find hereunder.

committed by the *Flemings* on the *English*, his Majesty in 1625, issued forth his Letters of Request to the States of *Holland*, for Satisfaction within 18 Months, otherwise Letters of Reprizal *Vide* Journals of that Year, and *Leo Aitzma*, *p* 48 13 41 82 So likewise Letters of Request went to the King of *Spain*, requiring Satisfaction for the depredation committed on the Ship and Goods of Mr *Stampe*, who was spoiled and murdered at the *Havanna*, *Anno* 1674, *Vide* the Proclamation 1675, of Reward promised by his Majesty for apprehending the Offenders dead or alive

A Copy of Letters Patents, for especial Reprizals from the King of *Great Britain*, (under the Great Seal of *England*) against the States-General and their Subjects, inrolled in the High Court of Chancery, 19 Mart, 15 Car 2

CHARLES the Second, by the Grace of God, of England, Scotland, France, and Ireland, King, Defender of the Faith, &c To all Christian People, to whom these Presents shall come, GREETING. WHEREAS our loving Subject *William Courten*, Esq, deceased, and his Partners, Anno 1643, by the depredation and hostile act of one *Gailand*, Commander in chief of Two Ships belonging to the East-India Company of the *Netherlands*, was between *Goa* and *Macceo* in the Straights of *Malacca*, deprived and most injuriously spoiled of a certain Ship named the *Bona Esperanze*, and of her Tackling, Apparel, and Furniture, and all the Goods and Lading in her, upon a very hopeful trading Voyage to *China*,

China, which were carried to *Batavia*, and there all *de facto* without due Proceſs of Law confiſcated And that alſo in the ſame Year another laden Ship of Our ſaid Subject, called the *Henry Bonadventure*, being come on ground near the Iſland *Mauritius*, was there both Ship and Goods ſeized upon by ſome of the Officers and Miniſters, and others under the Command of the ſaid Eaſt-India Company, and utterly detained from the right Owners. *AND WHEREAS* the ſaid *William Courten*, and his Aſſigns in his Life-time, uſed all poſſible endeavours to recover the ſaid Ships and Goods, and to procure further Juſtice againſt the Malefactors, and yet could obtain no Reſtitution or Satisfaction, whereby they became much to be diſtreſſed and utterly undone in their Eſtate and Credit And that thereupon, and upon the moſt humble Supplications and Addreſſes of *Francis* Earl of *Shrewſbury*, and *William Courten*, Eſq, Grand-Child and Heir of the ſaid *Sir William*, deceaſed, *Sir John Ayton* and *Sir Edmond Turner*, Knights, *George Carew* and *Charles Whitaker*, Eſquires, on the behalf of themſelves, and divers others intereſted in the ſaid two Ships *Bona Eſperanza* and *Henry Bonadventure*, and in the Eſtates of the ſaid *Sir William Courten*, deceaſed, *Sir Edward Littleton*, Baronet, and *Sir Paul Pindar*, Knight, deceaſed, that We would take their Caſe into our Princely conſideration *WE OUT OF A JUST SENSE* We then had, and ſtill have, of their unjuſt *SUFFERINGS* in that buſineſs, both by Our own Letters under *OUR SIGN* Manual to the *States-General* of the *United Provinces*, and by *Sir George Downing*, Knight and Baronet, Our Envoy Extraordinary,

Extraordinary, to whom We gave especial Command so to do, required satisfaction to be made according to the Rules of Justice, and the Amity and good correspondence, which We then desired to conserve with them firm and inviolable *AND WHEREAS* after several Addresses made to the said *States-General* by our said Envoy, and nothing granted effectual for Relief of Our said Subjects, (whom we take Ourselves in Honour and Justice, concerned to see satisfied and repaid) We lately commanded the said *Sir George Downing* to intimate and signify to the said *States*, that we expected their final Answer, concerning satisfaction to be made for the said Ships and Goods by a time then prefixed and since elapsed, that We might so govern Ourselves thereupon, that our aforesaid Subjects might be relieved according to Right and Justice, and yet no satisfactory Answer hath been given, so that We cannot but apprehend it to be, not only a fruitless Endeavour, but a prostituting of Our Honour and Dignity, to make further Application after so many denials and slightings *AND WHEREAS John Exton*, Doctor of Laws, Judge of our High Admiralty Court of *England*, upon our Command, to certify to Us the Value of the Losses and Damages sustained by the said *William Courten* and Partners, whose Interest is now vested in our loving Subjects, *Sir Edmond Turner*, Knight, and *George Carew*, Esq, and Partners, hath upon full Examination, and Proofs thereof made by Witnesses in Our High Court of Admiralty, reported and certified under his Hand, that the same do amount to the Sum

of

of One Hundred fifty one Thoufand fix Hundred and twelve Pounds.

NOW KNOW YE, That for a full reftitution to be made to them for their Ships, Goods and Merchandizes, of which the faid *William Courten*, and the Affigns of the faid *William Courten* and Partners, were fo defpoiled as aforefaid, with all fuch Cofts and Charges, as they fhall be at for the recovery of the fame, We by the Advice of our Privy Council have thought fit, and by thefe Prefents do grant Licence and Authority under Our Great Seal of *England*, unto our faid Subjects, *Sir Edmond Turner* and *George Carew*, their Executors, Adminiftrators and Affigns, for and on the behalf of themfelves, and other Perfons interefted as aforefaid, to equip, victual, furnifh, and to fet to Sea, from time to time, fuch and fo many Ships and Pinaces as they fhall think fit. *PROVIDED* always, that there be an Entry made and recorded in the Admiralty Court, of the Names of all Ships and Veffels, and of their Burden and Ammunition, and for how long time they are victualled. And alfo of the Name of the Commander thereof, before the fame or any of them be fet forth to Sea, and with the faid Ships and Pinaces by force of Arms to fet upon, take and apprehend any of the Ships, Goods, Monies and Merchandizes of the *States General*, or any of the Subjects inhabiting within any their Dominions or Territories, wherefoever the fame fhall be found, and not in any Port or Harbour in *England* or *Ireland*, unlefs it be the Ships and Goods of the Parties that did the Wrong. And the faid Ships and Goods, Monies and Merchandizes, being fo taken and brought

E   into

into some Port of Our Realms and Domi-
n.ons, an Inventory thereof shall be taken by
Authority of Our Court of Admiralty, by
the Judge or Judges thereof, for the time
being, upon Proof made before him or them,
that the said Ships, Goods, Wares, Merchandizes or Money, did belong to the *States
General*, or any of the Subjects as aforesaid.
That they shall be lawful Prize to the said
Sir Edmond Turner and *George Carew*, their
Executors, Administrators and Assigns, as
aforesaid, to retain and keep in their or any
of their Possessions, and to make sale and dif-
pose thereof in open Market, or howsoever
else, to their and every of their best Advantage and Benefit, in as ample manner, as at
any time heretorore hath been accustomed by
way of Reprizal, and to have and enjoy the
same as lawful Prize, and as their own proper
Goods *SO THAT* " *NEITHER* Captain,
" Master, nor any of the Company, that
" shall serve in his own person, or shall pro-
" mote and advance the said enterprise in
" manner and form aforesaid, shall in any
" manner of wise be reputed or challenged
" for any Offender against any of our Laws.
" And that also it shall be lawful for all man-
" ner of persons, as well our Subjects, as any
" other, to buy the said Ships, Goods, and
" Merchandizes so taken and apprehended
" by the said Captains, Masters and others,
" and adjudged as aforesaid, without any
" Damage, Loss, Hindrance, Trouble, or
" molestation, or incumbrance, to befal the
" said Buyers, or any of them, in as ample
" and lawful manner, as if the Ships, Goods,
" Wares, and Merchandize, had been come
" and gotten by the lawful Traffick of Merchants,

" chants, or of juft Prizes in the Time of
" open War." *PROVIDED* always, that
all Ships, Goods, and Merchandize, taken
by virtue of this Our Commiffion, fhall be
kept in fafety, and no part of them wafted,
fpoiled or diminifhed, or the Bulk thereof broken, until Judgment have firft paft as aforefaid, that they are the Ships and Merchandizes of the *States General*, or fome of their
Subjects as aforefaid. And if by colour of
this our Commiffion, there fhall be taken any
Ships, Goods, or Merchandizes of any of our
loving Subjects, or the Subjects of any Prince,
or State in good League, or Amity with Us
(except the *States General*) or their Subjects
as aforefaid, and the Goods therein laden,
fold and embezzeled, or diminifhed, or the
Bulk thereof broken in any place before they
fhall be adjudged to belong to the *States General*, or fome of their Subjects as aforefaid,
that then this Commiffion fhall be of no fufficient Authority to take the faid Ships,
Goods, and Merchandizes, or to warrant,
or fave harmlefs fuch as fhall receive, buy,
or intermeddle therein, but that both the
prizes fo taken, and the faid Ship of War,
fhall be confifcated to our Ufe. " *AND*
" *FURTHER*, We do hereby declare, that
" it is our Will and Pleafure, that this Our
" Commiffion fhall remain in full force and
" power, to all intents and purpofes, until
" the faid *Sir Edmond Turner* and *George Ca-*
" *rew*, their Executors, Adminiftrators, and
" Affigns, as aforefaid, fhall by virtue thereof
" have by force of Arms apprehended,
" taken, feized, recovered, and received from
" the faid *States General*, or their Subjects,
" one hundred fifty one thoufand fix hundred

" and twelve Pounds, according to the Ap-
" praifement to be made by fufficient Apprai-
" fers, upon Oath nominated and authorized
" in Our faid Court of Admiralty, of all fuch
" Ships, Goods, Wares, and Merchandizes,
" as fhall be taken from the faid *States Gene-*
" *ral*, or any of their Subjects, by virtue of
" this Commiffion, or fhall otherways receive
" fatisfaction of the Debt aforefaid, by Com-
" pofition to be made between thofe of the
" Eaft-India Company of the *Netherlands*,
" and the faid *Sir Edmond Turner* and *George*
" *Carew*, their Executors, Adminiftrators
" and Affigns as aforefaid. *NOTWITH-*
" *STANDING* it fo happen, the prefent
" Difference between Us and the *States Ge-*
" *neral*, depending upon general Reprifals,
" may be agreed and compofed, and that in
" the Interim a Peace and good Correfpon-
" dence may be renewed between Us and
" the *States-General: In which Cafe never-*
" *thelefs*, It is Our Will and Pleafure that in
" the Execution of this Our Commiffion, no
" Violence fhall be done to the Perfons of
" the faid Subjects of the faid *States-General*,
" but only in Cafe of Refiftance, and that
" after in cold Blood, the Subjects of the faid
" *States-General*, if hurt or wounded, fhall
" be ufed with all convenient office of huma-
" nity and kindnefs. *AND FURTHER*,
" Our Will and Pleafure is, That although
" it fhall happen that all hoftility between
" Us and the *States-General*, and Our refpec-
" tive Subjects fhall ceafe, yet this Our Com-
" miffion fhall remain, and be in full Force
" and Power, to the faid *Sir Edmond Turner*
" and *George Carew*, their Executors, Ad-
" miniftrators and Affigns, as aforefaid, by
                                    " virtue

" virtue thereof to apprehend, take and
" feize, by Force and Arms, fo many more
" of the faid Ships and Goods of the *States-*
" *General,* or any of their faid Subjects, as
" befides the faid Sum before-mentioned,
" fhall countervail, fatisfy, and pay all fuch
" Cofts and Charges as the faid *Sir Edmond*
" *Turner,* and *George Carew,* their Executors,
" Adminiftrators, or Affigns, as aforefaid,
" fhall from time to time make proof to have
" difburfed, and paid towards the equipping,
" manning, paying, furnifhing, and victual-
" ling of the faid Ships, fo licenfed and au-
" thorized as aforefaid, by this our faid Com-
" miffion, to be equipped, manned, furnifh-
" ed, and victualled, by the faid *Sir Edmond*
" *Turner* and *George Carew,* their Executors,
" Adminiftrators, and Affigns, as aforefaid,
" for the Purpofe aforefaid " *AND OUR*
WILL and Pleafure is, and we do hereby
require Our Judge or Judges of Our High
Court of Admiralty, for the Time being, and
all other Officers of the Admiralty, and all
other our Judge or Judges, Officers, Minifters, and Subjects whatfoever, to be aiding
and affifting to the faid *Sir Edmond Turner*
and *George Carew,* their Executors, Adminiftrators, and Affigns as aforefaid, in all
Points in the due Execution of this Our Royal
Commiffion, and to proceed to Adjudications,
and adjudge all Ships, Merchandizes, Monies,
and Goods, by Virtue thereof to be taken,
according to our Princely Intention, hereby
fignified and expreffed, and to take Care that
this Our Royal Commiffion to be duly executed, and favourably interpreted and conftrued
in all refpects, to the Benefit and beft Advantage of the faid *Sir Edmond Turner* and

E 3   *George*

George Carew, their Executors, Administrators, and Assigns, as aforesaid. *IN WITNESS* whereof, We have caused these Our Letters to be made Patents   Witness Ourself at *Westminster*, the 19th Day of *May*, in the Seventeeth Year of Our Reign

BY THE KING.

XVI. It is not the place of any Man's *Nativity*, but his *Domicil*; not of his *Origination* but of his *Habitation*, that subjects him to *Reprize* The Law doth not consider so much where he was born, as where he lives, not so much where he came into the World, as where he improves the World

If therefore Letters of Reprizal should be awarded against the Subjects of the *Duke of Florence*, and a Native of *Florence*, (but denizened or naturalized in *England*) should have a Ship in a Voyage for *Leghorn*, if a Caption should be made, the same is not lawful, nor can the same be made Prize. Yet by the Laws of *England*, a natural born Subject cannot divest himself of his Allegiance, tho' he happens to be commorant in the Enemy's Country

XVII It doth not any where appear, that *Reprizals* can be granted on Misfortunes happening to Persons or their Goods, residing or being in Foreign parts in time of War there; for if any Misfortune happens, or is occasioned to their Effects, or to their Persons, then they must be contented to sit down under the Loss; it being their own fault, they would not fly or relinquish the place, when they foresaw the Country was subject to the spoil of the Soldiers, and devastation of the Conqueror

The

The Factions of the *Guelfs* and *Gibellins* in *Florence*, warring against each other. The *Guelfs* obtaining the Victory, and thrusting the *Gibellins* out of it, after they had taken the City, *Domum cujusdam Hugonis de Papi in hoc Regno Angliæ demorantis diruerunt*, and plundered his Goods therein, *qui Hugo supplicavit Dominæ Regi, ut Inde Itali Mercatores* (of that Faction and City then in *England*) *emendas hic sibi facerent*, upon which *adjudicatum fuit, quod dicti Mercatores dicto Hugoni satisfaciant pro damnis susceptis, & destructione domus suæ* upon which a Writ of Error was brought, and the Judgment was reversed in these words; *Quòd non est consuetudo Angliæ de aliqua transgressione facta in aliena Regione, tempore Guerræ, vel alio modo —— consideratum est, quod totus processus & ejus effectus revocentur, &c.*

XVIII. By right (for so it is now called, of rendring like for like) there are many persons exempted, and those whose Persons are so privileged, have also protection for their Goods, some by the *Laws of Nations*, some by the *Civil Law*, others by the *Common Law*, among which *Ambassadors* by the Laws of Nations, their Retinue and Goods are exempt, coming from him who awarded the Reprize, the Laws of Nations not only provided for the Dignity of him that sends, but likewise the secure going and coming of him that is sent

Nor against those that travel for Religion, nor on Students, Scholars, or their Books, nor on Women or Children by the *Civil Law*. nor those that travel through a Country, staying but a little while there, for they are only subject to the Law of the place.

Mich 5. E 1. Rot. 53. (in Thesaur Recept Regis in Scac) coram Rege Florentiæ

Vide Ror Vascontiæ, 28 E 3. Rot 7. pro Rob. Draper & aliis Civibus Corke in Hibernia.

Rex facitne to Regium Nuntium Populi Romani Quærit. vasa comitesque meos The Ambassadors of the *Romans* being ill used by the *Carthaginians*, and *Scipio's* Army having surprized the Ambassadors of the *Carthaginians*, was demanded what should be done to them, answered, not as the

E 4   By

By the *Canon Law* Ecclesiastical Persons are expresly exempt from Reprizals.

A Merchant of another place than that against which *Reprizals* are granted, albeit the Factor of such Goods were of that place, is not subject to Reprizals.

XIX Ships driven into Port by storm or stress of weather, have an exemption from the Law of Reprizals, according to the *Jus Commune*, but by the Law of *England* otherwise, unless expresly provided for in the Writ, or Commission.

But if such Ship flies from his own Country to avoid Confiscation, or some other Fault, and is driven in by stress of Weather, she may then become subject to be prize.

But it is not lawful to make seizure in any Ports, but in his who awarded the Reprizal, or his against whom the same issued, for the Ports of other Princes or States the *Peace of them* are to be maintained.

Vita autem subditorum innocentium, ut ex tali causa obligatur, forte cred'tum fuit apud aliquos populos, eo nimirum quod crederent unicuique hominum jus vitæ
XX Ships attacked by those that have Letters of Reprize, and refused to be yielded up, may be assaulted and entred, and though it may fall out, not by intention, but by accident, that some of those that so resist, may happen to be slain, yet the Fault will lie at their own Doors, for hindring the Execution of right, and that which the Law most justy approves of.

plenum esse in se, & ad rem publicam potuisse transferri, quod minime est probabile, nec sanctiori Theologiæ consentaneum Grotius *de Jure b.*, *lib.* 3 *c* 2 § 4 And seems to be of opinion by the Law of Charity, that the Prosecution of right for a Man's Goods, which inevitably must be by the Life of Man, ought to be omitted *Lib.* 2. *cap* 10 *Liv lib* 2

XXI This right of changing of *Dominion* is so odious, that in the taking of Goods, if by any possibility the right Owners may have Restitution,

Reſtitution, the ſame hath been done, and though a larger time than 24 Hours may happen between the capture and recapture, and ſo may *pernoctare* with the Captor, yet Reſtitution may be made.

If a Ship be Prize or not, this ſhall be tried in the Admiralty, and no Prohibition ſhall be granted. The Caſe was, there being War between us and *Denmark*, a Privateer of *Scotland* took a Ship as Prize being a *Daniſh* Ship, and ſhe was condemned as Prize by the Admiralty in *Scotland*, and brought her upon the Land, and S libelled in the Admiralty of *England*, and ſuggeſted that ſhe was not a *Daniſh* but a Ship of *London*, *per* Curiam, in as much that the matter is Prize or not Prize no Prohibition *Tompſon* and *Smith*, 1 *Sid.* 320. 2 *Keeble* 158 *&* 176.

One who had Letters of Marque in the late Wars with the *Dutch*, took an *Oſtender* for a *Dutch* Ship, and brought her into an Haven, and libelled againſt her as Prize, and the *Oſtender* libelled in the Admiralty againſt the Captor for damage ſuſtained, for the hurt the Ship ſuſtained in the Port, and a Prohibition was prayed, for this that the Suit is for damage done in the Port, for which an Action lies at the Common Law, but the Prohibition was denied, becauſe the Original being a Caption at Sea, and the bringing her into Port in order to have her condemned as Prize, is but a conſequent of it, not only the Original, but alſo the conſequences ſhall be tried there *Turner* and *Cary* con: *Neeles* 1 1 *Lev.* 243 1 *Sid* 367 2 *Keble* 360. 364. 1 *Vent* · · *Redly* and *Delbow* con. *Eglesfield* ·· · hital 2 *Keble* 828. and 2 *Lev* 25 2 *Saun.* 259. *Cr. Car.* 97. *Skin.* 59 2 *Show.* 232

Prize or not Prize is of Admiral Juriſdiction.

Brown and *Burton, v. Franklyn, Carth* 474.

A Ship taken at Sea as Prize ſhall be tried in the Admiralty

Raymond 473, *Hughs* againſt *Cornelius & al*

Thermolin v Sands, Carth 423. *Comb* 462

Barthol in Leg ſi quid

And

BelloD de cap.
Ang. & Salic
in Leg. ab
hoftibus, C de
Capt Conf
Gall. 20 in
13 Art. 24.
Conful Maris
287.

And therefore if he, who hath Letters of *Marque* or *Reprizal*, takes the Ships and Goods of that Nation, againſt whom the ſame are awarded, and brings the ſame into a *Newter-Nation*, the Owners may there ſeize her, or there the *Admiral* may make Reſtitution by Law, as well of the Ship's Goods to the Owners, as the Perſons captives to their former Liberty, for that the ſame ought firſt to have been brought *infra Præſidia* of that Prince or State, by whoſe Subjects the ſame was taken.

March 110
2 Keble 441.
Morris v Ber-
cley Res quæ
infra Præſidia
perductæ non-
dum ſunt,
quanquam ab
hoſtibus occu-
patæ, Domi-
num non muta-
runt, ex Gen-
tium jure.

And with this agrees the *Common Law*, for a *Dunkirker* having taken a *French* Veſſel, ſold the ſame at *Weymouth*, whither it had been driven before it was brought *infra Præſidia Dom Regis Hiſp* it was in ſuch caſe ruled, that if a Ship be taken by Piracy, or Letters of *Marque* and *Reprizal*, and is not brought *infra Præſidia* of that Prince or State, by whoſe Subject the ſame was taken, the ſame could not become lawful Prize, nor were the Owners by ſuch a Caption diveſted of their Property.

But if the Caption be by Ships of War, the Property will be immediately in the Captors, and never diveſted, unleſs afterwards *vi, manu & forti* it be in Battle regained

Vide 6 A c 13
§ 6, 7, 8.

XXII Upon the ſharing the *Spoil* of the captivated Ships, regard is had to the Ships preſent, not the Captors only, (for his Reward muſt be the Encouragement of his Prince, like the *Roman Corona's*, of which there were various, according to the Atchievement of the Conqueror,) for the Profits of Prizes are to be equally divided amongſt the Ships preſent, and not ſolely to the Captor, therefore if Letters of Reprizal are granted to

two

two Ships, and they happen both of them at Sea to meet a Prize, and the one attacks and enters her, by means of which she becomes *absolutely* the Conqueror, yet the other hath right to an equal distribution with the Captor both in Ship and Goods, although he did nothing in the Conquest: the reason is, *That although he missed the opportunity of taking of her, yet the presence of his Vessel armed and prepared for Battle, at the time of taking, became a Terror to the Ship that was so conquered.* And by the Law presumed *sine ejus*, that the other Ship would not or could not be so taken, which Law hath passed the current, and approbation of the *Common Law*, as reasonable, just, and equitable, and may be pretended or surmised to entitle the Party Captor to the making Restitution of a Moiety to his Companion then present

Mich 32 Eliz Somers and Sir Rich Bulkley's C Leonard 2. part 182.

XXIII But if it should happen, that those to whom Letters of *Marque* are granted, should instead of taking the Ships and Goods of that Nation against whom the same were awarded, wilfully take or spoil the Goods of another Nation in amity, this would amount to a downright *Piracy* And the Persons offenders would for such fault create a Forfeiture of their Vessel, and the Owners must be for ever concluded by the same, notwithstanding such *Commission*.

Rolls Abr-dg. fol 530 Moor 776

XXIV But that must be understood where such a Caption is done in a Pyratical manner, for most certainly, if Letters of Reprizal are granted to a Man, and then he devolves the power to another, and the Party to whom the power is consigned, takes the Ship and Goods of another Nation than against whom the same were awarded, but

upon

upon a violent prefumption that he made a right Caption, for that he found the Colours of feveral Nations in the Ship, the Mariners of feveral Countries, the Ship of the Built of that Country againft whom the Letters of Reprizal were awarded, though perhaps upon a Judicial hearing the Parties are reftored to their Ship and Goods, yet the Captors are not to be punifhed *Criminaliter*, nor the Grantee of the Letters Patents *Civiliter* · And the reafon wherefore it was no injury in the Captors to take, did arife from the probable caufe which will excufe the Captors from punifhment (though perhaps it will not from anfwering of the damage;) but it is clear the Grantees are excufed from both, unlefs privy to the Caption, and the reafon is this, for the Letters Patents do not only veft the debt in the Party, but do likewife give Power to the Party to recover, and is a judicial procefs to obtain fatisfaction, *vi, manu & forti* from the Subjects of that Prince or State againft whom the fame are awarded · So then it will be no more than if the Creditor deliver procefs to the Officer to take his Debtor, and he takes a wrong Perfon without the Knowledge of the Creditor, this may fubject the Officer to anfwer Damage to the Party taken, but not the Creditor.

Stat. 4 H. 5 c. 7. 14 H. 4 c. 4.

XXV Therefore Letters of *Marque* or *Reprizal* iffue not without good and fufficient Caution firft given for the due obfervance thereof according to Law, the Tranfgreffion of which creates a Forfeiture of the fame.

And therefore having taken a Prize, and brought the fame *infra Præfidia*, the Captor muft exhibit all the Ship-papers, and captivated Mariners to be examined, in order to adjudication,

adjudication, till when Bulk ought not to be broken without *Commiſſion*, nor may the Captain of the Captor ſuffer an embezzlement of the lading, or ſell, barter or diſpoſe of any part without *Commiſſion*, for the King hath a proportion in all Prizes. *3 Eliz cap. 5*

Such Goods ſo brought in are not ſubject to pay Cuſtoms *12 Car II. called the Act of Naviga- tion*

XXVI By the Law of *Nations, ipſo facto,* the Dominion of the things taken by thoſe to whom Letters of *Marque* are granted, become the Captors, till the Debt and Coſts, that is, the original Damage and ſubſequent charges are ſatisfied, which being done, the reſidue ought to be reſtored : So the *Venetians* uſed their equity, having taken the Ships of *Genoa*, did not ſpoil any of the lading, but preſerved the ſame very carefully, till the Debt was paid, which done, reſtitution was made of the things entirely, without diminution. *Greg lib. 9.*

XXVII. When for the fault perhaps of a few, a debt becomes *National*, by reaſon of which the Goods of the innocent become liable (if taken for ſatisfaction) whether by the Law of *England*, the party ought to have Contribution, is a queſtion moſt certain by the *Common Law*, where more are bound to one thing, and yet one is put to the whole Burden, the Party may have proceſs called *Contributione' facienda* for his Relief but when a debt becomes Univerſal or National, it ſeems otherwiſe For if one lends my Country Money, I will not call myſelf debtor, yet I will pay my ſhare * So it may ſeem equitable by the Laws of Charity, though not compellable by the Laws of the Land *Fitz. N. B. fol 162 Ola N Bre 103. Reg Orig fol 176.*

So it may ſeem equitable *Seneca Benef cap. 19*

XXVIII. Yet when depredations have happened to Foreign Merchants, and complaint

                              hath

hath been made, the Kings of *England* have often iſſued forth Commiſſions to enquire of the ſame: and ſo it was done upon the Petition of ſome Merchants of *Genoa,* who complained againſt the Inhabitants of the Iſle of *Guernſey* for a depredation, in taking away and detaining their Merchandize and Goods, to the value of many thouſands of Pounds, out of a Ship wrecked by tempeſt near that Iſle, by which the Commiſſioners were empowered *to puniſh the offenders, and to make reſtitution and ſatisfaction for the damages.*

Pat 26 E 3 pars 1 M 16. Dorſo

The like complaint was made by the Merchants of the Duke of *Britain,* of certain depredations committed by the Subjects of the King of *England,* who iſſued forth the like Commiſſion, and to give them reparation and damages for the ſame, ſo that if the Subjects of the King of *England* have had their Goods taken by way of Reprize for the ſatisfaction of ſuch debt or damage, they may have the Benefit of the like Commiſſions to lick themſelves whole out of the Eſtates of the Offenders.

Pat de An 6 H 5. pars 1. M 9 Dorſo De Cæteris perſonis arreſt & capiend.

CHAP.

C H A P. III.

Of Privateers or Capers.

I. **N**Aturally every one may vindicate his own Right, therefore were our Hands given us, but to profit another in what we can, is not only lawful, but commendable, fince nothing is more ferviceable to Man than Man. Now there are divers obligations between Men, which engage them to mutual Aid, for Kinfmen affemble and bring

Leg fervus. D. de Serv. export. DD ad Leg. fi quis in fervitutem D de fur. Leg prohib. c. de Jure Fifci.

bring help, and Neighbours are called upon, and fellow *Citizens*; for it behoves every one either to take Arms for himself, if he hath received Injury, or for his Kindred, or for his Benefactors, or to help his Fellows if they be wronged. And *Solon* taught, *That Commonwealths would be happy when ein every one would think another's injuries to be his own* But when War is denounced, it matters not what obligations are wanting, it is enough the Nation is *injured in general*; for in that every individual is wronged, and all participate in the Indignities and publick Damages of his Country, to revenge or prevent which, is the Duty of every Member of the same.

Barthol. in Leg ut vim D. de Just & Jure, n 7. &8

II. Since therefore it is not against the *Law of Nature, to spoil him whom it is lawful to kill,* no wonder that the Laws of Nations permitted the Goods and Ships of Enemies to be spoiled, when it suffered their Persons to be slain.

Cicero Offic. 3.

III. The approbation of which in the Wars of later Ages, hath given occasion to Princes to issue forth Commissions to endamage the Enemy in their Commerce, and to prevent such Supplies as might strengthen or lengthen out War, to persons to whom the prize or caption become absolutely the Captors, and that to prevent the spare of Ships of Force to be absent from their respective Squadrons or Fleets.

The Son of *Ca.e Censorinus* having served as a private Soldier of pay under *Pompilius*, the Legion being disbanded, the young man was resolved to remain with the Army, tho' but a Volunteer; *Cato*

By those of *Holland* they were termed *Capers*, by the *Spaniard* they had their denomination from their respective parts, as *Ostenders, Dunkirkers,* and the like, in *England* called *Privateers*, how far the Actions of those, as in relation to the attacking and killing of the Enemy, or spoiling of their

Ships

Ships and Goods are lawful, not being com-manded nor hired thereto, may be a queſtion.

wrote to Pom-pilius the Ge-neral, that he ſhould give him an Oath the ſecond time, giving this Reaſon, *Qua priore amiſſo, jure cum hoſtibus pugnare n n poterat* Cicero ſets do\ n the very Words of *Cato* to his Son, whereby he admoniſheth him not to enter into Battle, *Neque enim jus eſſe qui miles non ſit pugnare cum hoſte.* Cic Offic 1

IV. By the Laws of Nations (as hath been ſaid) it is lawful for every Subject of that Nation in War, to ſeize upon the Enemy's Goods and Ships, as alſo to kill them, for they are, after War denounced by Law, looked upon as of no account, and if reſpect be had to natural and internal Right, it ſeems granted to every one in a juſt War to do thoſe Things, which he is confident within the juſt meaſure of warring, to be advanta-geous to the innocent party but though there may be ſuch authority given, yet what title can they claim or appropriate to them-ſelves of the Ships or Goods of Enemies, (for ſurely there is nothing owing to ſuch, nor are they lawfully called to the ſame; unleſs they can ſhrowd themſelves under the Pro-tection of this, that what they do, is only to exact puniſhment from the Enemy by the common right of men

V Commiſſions to kill or ſpoil the Enemy are in two reſpects, either general or ſpecial ·General as in a tumult, among the *Romans* the *Conſul* ſaid, *Whoſoever would have the Commonwealth ſafe, let him follow me*; and to all particular ſubjects is ſometimes granted a Right of killing in ſelf-defence, when it is publickly expedient, as on a ſudden occaſion, and the like.

VI Special Commiſſions are ſuch as are *Leg. Deferto-rem D de re milit.* granted to thoſe that take Pay, and are under Orders; the not obeying of which may be

F　　puniſhed

punished with Death, though the act succeeds well.

*C. Quando
licear unicui-
que Leg. 1
& 2*

Others to repair a particular damage by way of *Reprize*, the original damage being turned into a National debt, but that satisfied, the other determines. or else to those who receive no pay, but go to War at their own charge, and that which is more, administer at their own costs a part of a War, by providing Ships of Force, and all other military provisions to endamage the Enemy or their Confederates, the which are termed *Privateers*, &c. as above, to whom instead of pay is granted leave to keep what they can take from the Enemy; and though such Licence is granted them, yet may they not convert of their own Heads to their private use those Prizes, before the same have been by Law adjudged lawful to the Captors

VII. Nor may such Privateers attempt any thing against the Laws of Nations, as to assault or endamage an Enemy in the Port or Haven, under the protection of any Prince or Republick, be he Friend, Ally, or Neuter, for the peace of such places must be kept inviolably

Sir *Kenelm Digby* having obtained a Commission against the *French*, being in the *Straights*, was every where honoured as a *Cavalier* whom the King of *Great-Britain* favoured, in his Voyage he took some Prizes, and coming to *Algier* redeemed several Captives, whom he took aboard, and placed in the several Vessels he had made prize of: the which he so effected, that in a short time he became *Illustrissimo* of six Ships of War, coming to *Cape Congare*, ten leagues from *Scanderoon*, and having sent a Boat to descry

the

the road, word being brought that there were in the road two *Venetian* Galeasses, with two other Galleons, two *English* Ships, and several *French* Ships, Sir *Kenelm* being satisfied of the Prize, resolved to attack them the next morning, although the Admiral of the *Venetians* had declared himself Protector of the *French*, and that he would destroy all the *English* Ships of War that he should meet, either in that *Republick*'s or *Grand Signior*'s Seas Sir *Kenelm* notwithstanding resolved to engage them, and accordingly bore up to them, and the *Venetian* General weighed Anchor to meet him, Sir *Kenelm* before he fired, sent a *Settee* to inform the *Venetian* of his Quality, and of his Commission, *being only to endeavour to make prize of the French*, and giving him all the assurance possible of his friendship and respect to the Republick, but before the *Settee* was answered, the engagement was begun by the *English*, *French*, and *Venetian* This Action of Sir *Kenelm Digby* was questioned by the *Turk*, for that Hostility had been committed by the *English*, in the *Grand Signior*'s Road, and thereupon the *Bassa* of *Aleppo* and *Cady* of *Scanderoon* made an *Avania* or *Embargue* on the *English* Merchants, till reparation was made, for the breaking the Peace of the Port

The matter was highly debated at the Council-Board on the complaint of *Lonci*, then Ambassador for that Republic at *London, Anno* 16 9 *Vide Hist. Republic. Venet. fol* 170

VIII In the granting of such private Commissions there is always great care to be had and taken by caution, to preserve the Leagues of our Allies, Neuters and Friends, according to their various and several Treaties; and therefore at this day by the late Treaty between his Majesty and the *States* of *Holland* at *London*, before any *Privateer* or *Caper* can receive Commission, the Commander is obliged

liged

ligeo to enter before a competent Judge, good and sufficient security by able and responsible Men, who have no part or interest in such Ship, in 1500*l* *Sterling*, or 15,500 *Gilders*, and when they have above an hundred and fifty Men, then in 3000*l* or 33000 *Gilders*, that they will give full satisfaction for any damage or injuries, which they shall commit in their courses at Sea, contrary to that Treaty, or any other Treaty made between His Majesty and that *State*, and upon pain of Revocation and Annullity of their Commissions, and for answering of such damage or injuries, as they shall do, the Ship is made liable

‡ It is a Declaration that in the Commission must always be mentioned that they have given such security

The is a Provision to the like Effect between us and the *French* on the last Peace

IX If a Suit be commenced between the *Captor* of a Prize and the *Claimer*, and there is a Sentence or a *Decree* given for the party reclaiming, such Sentence or Decree (upon security given) shall be put in execution, notwithstanding the Appeal made by him that took the Prize, which shall not be observed in case the Sentence shall be given against the Claimers, if torture, cruelty, or barbarous use happens after a Caption, to be done to the Persons taken in the Prize, the same shall *ipso facto* discharge such a Prize, although she was lawful, and the Captains shall lose their Commissions, and both they and the Offenders be subjected to punishment

art 13

These Articles for their excellency are not to be a Standard to all the Nations of Europe, art 14.

X Such sorts of Instruments having made a caption of Ships bound for an Enemy from Nations Neuter, or in amity with both the warring States, the lading, in order to be made Prize is reduced to these three several heads

First,

First, those Goods that are fit to be used in War, under which are included Powder, Shot, Guns, Pikes, Swords, and all other instruments and provisions of Armature fit to be used in the Field or at Sea

The second are those things that may be used in time of War, and out of War, as Money, Corn, Victuals, Ships, and the like.

And the last, are those Goods that are only fit for luxury and pleasure

XI The first are accounted Prize without controversy, *He is to be accounted an Enemy that supplies an Enemy with things necessary for the War.*

The second is to be governed according to the state and condition of the war, for if a Prince cannot well defend himself, or, endamage the Enemy, without intercepting of such things, necessity will then give a right to the condemnation   And so Queen *Elizabeth* did the *Hansiatick* Fleet taken, laden with Corn for *Lisbon*, upon consideration of the state of the War, the same became prize not upon any account be called prohibited, nor subject to a condemnation, except carried to places besieged, *Art.* 4   See *John Meursius* his *Danish* History concerning the prohibiting of Goods by those Northern States   *Vide postea*, the Grand Prize condemned by Q *Elizabeth* in tit Customs, and *vide* tit Ships of War, §. 24

The last become free, and (as we have before-mentioned) according to that of *Seneca*; *I will not help him to Money to pay his Guards, but if he shall desire Marbles and Robes, such things hurt not others, only they minister to his luxury Soldiers and Arms I will not supply him with, if he shall seek for Players and recreations to soften his fierceness, I will gladly offer to him Ships of War I would not send him,*

Consultat Maris editus est lingua Italica, in quem relatæ sunt constitutiones Imperatorum Græciæ, &c cujus libri tit. 276.

Cambden Ann. 1591 By the fourth Article of the Treaty at *Lond* 1674. those Goods that may be used out of War as in War (except Ships) may

F 3   but

but such as are for pleasure and ostentation of
Princes sporting in the Sea, I will not deny

And Persons so attempting to relieve an Enemy may in some cases be punished; but if the same be done by necessity of obedience, though the parties are much to be blamed, they yet are not to be punished; and so it was with those which relieved Sir *John Oldcastle* with provisions, who being taken, were discharged.

XII If a Privateer take a Ship laden wholly with counterband Goods, both Ships and Goods may be subjected, and made prize

But if part be prohibited Goods, and the other part is not prohibited, but such as according to the necessity of the War shall be so deemed, the same may draw a consequential condemnation of Ships, as well as lading.

By the eventh Article in the *Treaty at London,* if the Skipper will deliver out the prohibited Goods, the Ship may proceed with the rest in their Voyage or Course, as they please, and the Ship shall not be brought into Port.

If part of the lading is prohibited, and the other part is merely luxurious and for pleasure, only the Goods prohibited become prize, and the Ships and the remainder become free, and not subject to infection.

XIII If such Ships shall be attacked in order to an examination, and shall refuse, they may be assaulted, as a house supposed to have Thieves or Pirates in it, which refuses to yield up their persons, may be broken up by the Officer, and the Persons resisters may be slain.

Nec reus est mortis alienae, inquit *Augustinus qui jure possessioni suorum arbitium circumduxit. si aliquis ex ipsorum usu percussus intereat. Publ. Epist.* 154.

XIV But if any of these Privateers wilfully commit any spoil, depredations, or any other injuries, either on the Ships of our Friends or Neuters, or on the Ships or Goods of our own Subjects, they will, notwithstanding they are not in pay, be subjected in some cases to Death and other punishments, according to the demerits of their crimes, and perhaps may subject their vessel to Forfeiture

Leg. 5 de Na-to 6 1 C Lib 3 Tit. 3 Jac. in B R R.'s Abridg I 530

And

And though by the Law of Nature the Goods of Enemies are to be spoiled as well as their Persons slain, yet some Goods and things seem exempted, and ought not to be spoiled, and therefore it is not lawful to land on the Territories of our Enemies, to spoil places dedicated to God: Though *Pomponius* observes, when places are taken by the Enemy, all things cease to be Sacred, the reason given is, because the things which are called Sacred, yet are they not indeed exempted from humane uses, but are publick. *The Townsmen, saith Tacitus, opening their gates, submitted themselves and all they had to the* Romans, *themselves were spared, the Town was fired.* Pompey *entred the Temple by the right of Victory, not as a supplicant, but as a Conqueror* and though that privilege may seem right by the Law of War to a Sovereign, or a General, that intends a conquest, yet that power may not seem devolved to him, whose Commission is cautionally to endamage the Enemy only, as in reference to his commerce and provisions of enabling them to withstand the War Certainly that conquest is poor, whose Trophies and Triumphs are made up with Roofs, Pillars, Posts, Pulpits, and Pews, and the spoil of Agriculture. Hence it is, that at this day the king of *France* in *Germany* and the *Netherlands* accepts of Contributions, by which the Cities and Churches are not only spared, but even the Countrymen plough and sow as quietly as if there were no Armies in their Territories at all   F 4   XV. Most

Pompon. Leg cum loca D. de Religiosis.

Tacit. Annal 13.

Wars and Victories for the most part consist in taking and overthrowing Cities, which work is not done without injury of the Goods, the walls of Cities and Temples of the Gods partake in

the same ruin, the Citizens and Priests equally slaughtered, nor is the rapine of sacred riches and prophane unlike so many are the Sacrileges of the *Romans* as their Trophies, so many are their Triumphs over Gods and Nations, and then goes further, *Tot manubiæ quot manent adhuc simulachra captivorum deorum* Mox & bene, *Quod si quid adver.*

adverſi Urbibus accidit, eadem clades Templorum quæ & mænium jument.

Then upon the ſame Reaſon, that the Inſtruments of Huſbandmen are not to be taken for a pledge by the Civil or Common Law *Leg. e. cunt. C. quæ res pign.* Coke on Littleton 47

XV Moſt certain, thoſe ſorts of Capers or Privateers, being Inſtruments found out but of later Ages, and 'tis well known by whom, it were well they were reſtrained by conſent of all Princes, ſince all good Men account them but one remove from Pirates, who without any reſpect to the cauſe, or having any injury done them, or ſo much as hired for the Service, ſpoil Men and Goods, making even a Trade and Calling of it, amidſt the calamities of a War, and driving a commerce and mart with the ſpoil, and that with as much peace and content, as if they had never heard of Tears, Blood, Wounds, or Death, or any ſuch things ſuch to expoſe their lives againſt Ships of the like kind, were both honourable and juſt, or thoſe that ſhould aid the Enemy with Goods prohibited as afore, ſuch Prizes were poſſeſſions moſt noble, but the Goods, Ships and Lives of the innocent peaceable Traders to be expoſed to rapine and ſpoil, renders them worſe than the *Roman* Lictors, by how much 'tis to kill without cauſe, Headſmen executing the guilty, they the guiltleſs.

It was a high neceſſity that enforced the *Engliſh* to commiſſionate ſuch, the number of her then Enemies covering the Sea, like the *Egyptian* Locuſts, it were well they were rejected by conſent, or if allowed of, not ſubject to Quarter, when taken by Ships of War: A Trade that St *Paul* never heard of, when ‡ Cor iv. 7. he ſaid, *Who goeth to War at his own charge?*

CHAP.

CHAP. IV.
Of Piracy.

the

the party injured may proceed *Criminaliter* for *pu-nishment*, and *Civiliter* for *restitution*.

XVI. *Pirates take Men, and no part of the Lading, if Piracy.*

XVII. *Where a Master may commit Piracy of those things that are committed to his charge, and where not.*

XVIII *Where Piracy may be, though there be no-thing taken : and where Goods are taken out of a Ship, and nobody in it*

XIX. *The Captain and Crew of a vessel having a Commission of Reprize commit Piracy, whether those that employed them ought to answer the Da-mage.*

XX. *Where Goods taken at Sea amount not to Pi-racy.*

XXI *Goods taken and retaken by a Friend, whether the Property of the Prize is altered.*

XXII. *Of Restitution of Goods taken by Piracy by the Laws of* England.

XXIII. *Of Restitution refused by the Laws of Eng-land. Justifications in this by a Warrant from the Admiralty. The Admralty must allow the Statute of Limitation if pleaded.*

XXIV *Of Piracy as in reference to matters Cri-minal, and how punishable at this Day by the Laws of* England.

XXV. *The Statute of 28 H. 8. how it operates in cases of Piracy.*

XXVI. *Of Pardons in cases of Piracy, Forfeitures, Corruption of Blood, and Clergy*

XXVII. *Whether a Depredation committed in a Port within this Realm remains Robbery, at the Common Law, or Piracy by the Law Marine.*

XXVIII. *Whether Clergy is allowable for a Depreda-tion in a Port, and if Pardons extend thereto.*

XXIX *A Pirate arraigned and standing mute shall have Judgment of Pain, Fort and Dure.*

XXX. *Of the Operation of the Attainder in cases of Piracy.*

XXXI. *Of Goods taken at Sea and brought to Land, whether the Party is punishable by our Law,*
                                                              Stat.

I. A *Pirate* is a Sea-Thief, or *Hostis humani generis*, who to enrich himself, either by surprise or open force, sets upon Merchants and others trading by sea, ever spoiling their Lading, if by any possibility he can get the mastery, sometimes bereaving them of their Lives, and sinking their Ships; the Actors where n, *Tully* calls Enemies to all, *with whom neither Faith nor Oath is to be kept* Against Pirates and such as live by Robbery at Sea, any Prince hath power to make War, tho' they are not subject to his Government *Grot. de jure belli & pacis. lib.* c. cap 20 §. 40.

II. By the Laws of Nature, Princes and States are responsible for their neglect if they do not provide Ships of War, and other remedies for the restraining of those sort of *Robbers*; but how far they are bound, either by the *Civil Law* or *Common Law* of this Kingdom, may be some question, for it is agreed, they are not the cause of the unjust spoil that is committed by them, nor do they partake in any part of the plunder, but if a Prince or State should send forth *Ships of War*, or Commissions for reprise, and those instead of taking prizes from the Enemy, turn Pirates and spoil

If the offenders could be found, they ought to be yielded up to Justice; and if they have any Estate, the same ought to go towards the reparation of the damage.

the

the Subjects of other Friends, there has been some doubt, whether they ought not to make satisfaction to the Parties injured, in case the offenders should prove unable. Surely there is no more reason for this latter than the first; seeing Princes and States may give all their subjects power to spoil the Enemy, nor is such a Permission any cause why damage was done to our Friends, when even *Private* Men without any such permission, might send forth *Ships of War*; besides, it is impossible that *Princes* or *States* should foresee, whether they would prove such or not, nor can it be avoided, but we must employ such, otherwise no *Army* or *Fleet* could be prepared, neither are Kings to be accused if their Soldiers or Mariners wrong their Confederates, contrary to their commands, though they are obliged to punish and yield up the Offenders, and to see that legal Reparation be made out of the Estate of the Pirates. If *Letters of Marque* or *Reprizal* be granted out to a Merchant, and he furnishes out a Ship with a Captain and Mariners, and they instead of taking the Goods or Ships of that Nation against whom their *Commission* is awarded, take the Ships and Goods of a Friend, this is *Piracy**, and if the Ships arrive in *England*, or in any other of his Majesty's Dominions, the same shall be seized, and the Owners for ever lose their Vessel†.

Caution is commonly taken upon the giving forth of such Commission to prevent the same, if possible They are generally restrained by Proclamation when a War breaks forth, and commanded that none presume to set forth without a Commission *Constit. Galliæ tom 3 tit 3 Constitutione Anni 1583. cap 44 Vide etiam tom constit 3 tit. 2 constit Anni 1543 cap 44 Vide 21 Article at the Treaty at

Breda between *England* and *Holland*, and the 15th Article in the Marine Treaty at *London* 1674   † 1 *Rolls Abr* 530 776.

From hence it is, that Princes and States are very cautious upon this we call *Jure Belli privati*, how they engage themselves, or those who seek reparation for wrongs before received, for the Person *injured* governs not the action,

action, but devolves the power to some other
hired for that particular use, whose Law is
no more than this, *There is moſt right wheie
is moſt pay or prize*   Unhappy ſtate of man,
whoſe ſupport and living is maintained only
by expoſing himſelf to Death, a Calling that
nothing can make honeſt, but the higheſt neceſſity or pious charity   And therefore thoſe
that iſſue forth ſuch ſort of *Commiſſions*, generally take Caution for their returning within
a convenient Time, and not to wander in that
unhappy condition.

III. Though Pirates are called Enemies, *Leg Hoſtes de*
yet are they not properly ſo termed : *For he, veib ſiginf.*
is an Enemy*, ſays *Cicero*, *who hath a Commonwealth, a Court, a Treaſury, Conſent and
Concord of Citizens, and ſome way, if occaſion
be, of Peace, and League*, and therefore a
Company of *Pirates* or *Freebooters* are not a
Commonwealth, tho' perhaps they may keep
a kind of *equality* among themſelves, without
which no Company is able to conſiſt, and
though it is ſeldom they are without fault, yet *Leg Hoſtis de*
they hold ſociety to maintain *right*, and they *Captivis.*
do right to others, if not in all Things according to the *Law of Nature* (which among many
people is in part obliteiated, at leaſt, according
to *agreements* made with many other Nations,
or according to Cuſtom · So the *Greeks*, at
what Time it was accounted lawful to take
ſpoil at Sea, abſtained from ſlaughter and
depopulations, and from ſtealing Oxen that
plowed, as the *Scholiaſt* upon *Thucydides* ob-
ſerves ; and other Nations living alſo upon
the ſpoil when they were come home from
Sea, ſent unto the Owners to redeem (if they
pleaſed at an equal rate) what they were robbed of at Sea and at this day, if a Ship hath
                                              the

the Emperor of *Barbary*'s protection, the Pirates of that Nation (if they feize) will reftore, and if there be no protection, yet if taken within *fight* of their Caftles, the Prize is not abfolute; but if refiftance is made, and there be a Caption, fhe then becomes the Captor's for ever, *as the price of Blood.*

Grot. de Jure bell. & pacis, lib 2. c 18. §. 2.

IV. Again, Pirates that have reduced themfelves into a Government or State as thofe of *A'gier, Sallee, Tripoli, Tunis,* and the like, fome d conceive ought not to obtain the Rights or Solemnities of War as other Towns or places, for though they acknowledge the Supremacy of the * *Porte,* yet all the power of it cannot impofe on them more than their own Wills voluntarily confent to. The famous *Carthage* having yielded to the victorious *Scipio,* did in fome refpect continue, and began to raife up her drooping Towers, 'till the knowing *Cato* gave Counfel for the total extirpation, out of the Ruins of which arofe *Tunis,* the revenging Ghoft of that famous City, who now, what open Hoftility denied, by Thieving and Piracy continue, as ftinking Elders fpring from thofe places where noble Oaks have been fell'd, and in their Art are become fuch Mafters, and to that degree, as to difturb the mightieft Nations of the Weftern Empire, and though the fame is fmall in bignefs, yet it is great in mifchief, the confideration of which put fire in the Breaft of the aged *Lewis* IX. to burn up this neft of Wafps, who having equipt out a Fleet in his way for *Paleftine,* refolved to befiege it: Whereupon a Council of War being called, the queftion was, Whether the fame fhould be fummoned? and carried, it fhould not, *for it was not fit the folemn Ceremonies of War fhould*

* *Conftantinople,* generally fo called.

Fuller's Holy War; lib 4. cap 27.

should be lavished away on a company of Thieves and Pirates. - Notwithstanding this *Tunis* and *Tripoli*, and their Sister *Algier* do at this day (though nests of Pirates) obtain the right of Legation, and Sir *John Lawson* did conclude a Peace between his Majesty by the Name of the most Serene and Mighty Prince Charles the *Second, by the Grace of God King of* Great Britain, France *and* Ireland, *Defender of the Faith, &c. and the most Excellent Signors* Mahomet Bashaw, the Divan of the Noble City of Tunis; Hagge Mustapha Dei, Morat Bei, *and the rest of the Soldiers in the Kingdom of* Tunis, and with them of *Tripoli* by Sir *John Narborough* * *by the Name of* Halil Bashaw, Ibrahim Dey, Aga, Divan, *and Governors of the Noble City and Kingdom of* Tripoli *in* Barbary So that now (though indeed Pirates) yet having acquired the Reputation of a Government, they cannot properly be esteemed Pirates but Enemies.

V. Pirates and Robbers that make not a Society, *i. e.* such a Society as the Law of Nations accounts lawful, are not to have any succour by the Law of Nations. *Tiberius,* when *Tacfarinas* had sent Legates to him, he was displeased, that both a Traitor and a Pirate should use the manner of an Enemy, as *Tacitus* hath it; yet sometimes such men (Faith being given them) obtain the right of Legation, as the Fugitives in the *Pyrenean* Forest, and the *Banditti* at *Naples*; and *Solyman* the Magnificent, having entertained *Barbarossa* the famous Pirate, sent word to the *Venetians, that they should use him and esteem*

Octob 5 *Anno* 1662 But by the *Turk* in these words, confirmed and sealed in the presence of Almighty God, in our House, in the noble City of *Tunis*, the last day of the Moon *Delcad*, and the year of *Hegira* 1085.

* *March* 5, 1675-6, and (afterwards, *May* 1, 1676, by the *Turks*) being the 26th day of the Moon *Zaphire*, and the year of the *Hegira*, 1087.

Tacit Annal. 3 *Cæsar, lib.* 3. *de Bello Civ.*

Hist. Republ Venet fol 91.

esteem him no more as a Pirate, but one of their own Port

ff. ad Legem Rhod de jactu. l 2 § si navis à Piratis redempta

VI.   If a Ship is assaulted by a Pirate, for redemption of which the Master becomes a Slave to the Captors, by the Law Marine, the * Ship and Lading are tacitly obliged for his redemption by a general Contribution. But if a Pirate shall feign himself stranded, and to decoy the Merchant-Man for his relief, shall fire his Guns, or wave his Colours, who accordingly varies his Course for his Assistance, and the Pirate enters him, for redemption of which he becomes a Slave to the Pirate, there contribution shall not be made, because it was his folly to be so decoyed.

* The same Point, and also in Case of Capture by an Enemy, Lord Raymond 933 To know whether the Proceedings in such Matter be legal, the Party must wait till the Promovent has libelled, before he can move for a Prohibition. *Ibid.* 934.

VII   By the *Civil Law* a Ransom promised to a Pirate, if not complied with, creates no wrong; and the reason given is, for that the Law of Arms is not communicated to such, neither are they cabable of enjoying that privilege which lawful enemies may challenge in the Caption of another however this hath its measure, for a Pirate may have a lawful possession, the which he cannot be denied (if injury or wrong be done him) to claim the benefit of Law   But the reason of that springs from a more noble Fountain, which is his taking a legal course, for by that he hath submitted to the Magistrate, and paid obedience to the Laws in demanding Justice, besides, the same is not done so much in favour of the Pirate, as in Hatred of him who first commits the wrong   *Augustus* the Emperor proclaimed a reward of ten Sesterces to be given him that should bring in *Coracotas*, the

Butler l 1 c 1

famous

famous *Spanish pirate*, who having notice of
the fame, voluntarily comes and prefents himfelf before the Emperor, and demands the
promifed reward and the queftion was, whether death or the Sefterces were to be his reward. The Emperor gave Judgment, that the
fum promifed, fhould be paid him, for
otherwife in taking away his life he fhould
deceive him of the fum promifed, which
would, in effect, violate the publick Faith
given to him, who of himfelf offered himfelf
upon the trial of Juftice

A Pirate attacks a Merchant-Man, and
enters her, for redemption of which the Mafter gives his Oath, at a time and place to
pay the Pirate a fum certain, by fome it
hath been held, that the Mafter commits not
perjury, if the price promifed for redemption
be not brought according to the Oath; becaufe a Pirate is not a determinate, but a
common Enemy of all, with whom neither
Faith nor Oath is to be kept. but that is no *Leg bona fide*
reafon for the affoiling of the Vow, for *D hapof.*
though the Perfon be deficient, yet the Juft
God is concerned, nor can that perfon that
hath promifed a thing, fatisfy his Confcience
after he hath once delivered it to him, to recover it back again, for the words in an
Oath, as to God, are to be underftood moft
fimply, and with effect, and therefore he
that returned fecretly to the Enemy, and
again departed, made not good his Oath concerning his Return

VIII. If an *Englifh Man* commit Piracy, be
it upon the Subject of any Prince or Republick in amity with the Crown of *England,* he
is within the purview of the *Stat* of 28 *H* 8.
and fo it was held where one *Winterfen. Smith,*

G   and

On a Com-
miffion
grounded on
the Stat a-
warded,
Rott Adr
28 *Eliz. m* 23

and others, had robbed a Ship of one *Matu-
rine Gautier,* belonging to *Bourdeaux,* and
bound from thence with *French* Wines for
England, and that the fame was Felony by the
Law Marine, and the parties were convicted
of the fame

IX. And fo if the Subject of any other
Nation or Kingdom, being in Amity with the
King of *England,* commit Piracy on the Ships
or Goods of the *English,* the fame is Felony,
and punishable by virtue of the *Stat* and fo
it was adjudged, where one *Carelefs,* Captain of a *French Man* of War of about 40
Tuns, and divers others, fetting upon four
Merchant-Men going from the Port of *Briftol*

*Rott Adm
anno* 28 *Eliz
m* 24.

to *Caermarthen,* did rob them of about 1000*l.*
for which he and the reft were arraigned and
found guilty of the *Piracy.*

Normandy was
loft by King
John, and out
of the ligc-
ance of the
King of Eng-
land, and they
were as now
accounted
Aliens, 42
Aff. plea 1
25 *per Srard
and* 2 H 5
cap 6

But before the *Stat.* of 25 *Ed* 3 if the
fubjects of a foreign Nation and fome *English*
had joined together, and had committed Piracy, it had been Treafon in the *English,* and
Felony in the Foreigners. And fo it was faid
by *Shard,* where a *Norman* being Commander of a Ship, had together with fome *English,*
committed Robberies on the Sea, being taken,
they were arraigned and found guilty, the
Norman of Felony, and the *English* of Treafon, who accordingly were drawn and hanged.
But now at this day they both receive Judgment as Felons by the Laws Marine

X If the Subjects in enmity with the
Crown of *England* be Sailors aboard an *English*
Pirate with other *English,* and then a robbery
is committed by them, and afterwards are
taken, it is Felony without controverfy in the
English, but not in the *Strangers,* for they
cannot be tried by virtue of the Commiffion
upon

upon the *Statute*, for it was no Piracy in them, but the Depredation of an Enemy, for which they shall receive a Trial by Martial Law, and Judgment accordingly

XI. Piracy committed by the Subjects of the *French* King, or of any other Prince or Republick, in amity with the Crown of *England* upon the *British* Seas, is punishable properly by the Crown of *England* only, for the Kings of the same have *istud regimen & dominium exclusive* of the Kings of *France*, and all other Princes and States whatsoever

Selden Mare Clauf. lib. 1 cap. 27 Cafe of Reginor Grinbald in temp. Ed. 1 Cited in 4 Inst. fol. 142 in c. of the Admiralty

XII. If Piracy be committed on the *Ocean*, and the Pirates in the Attempt there happen to be overcome, the Captors are not obliged to bring them to any port, but may expose them immediately to punishment, by hanging them up at the Main-yard end before a Departure, for the old natural liberty remains in places where are no Judgments

Injicere manum parcæ traxerunt debitum fibi, & fermone ufus eft juris, nam manus injectio dicitur, quoties nulla judicis auctoritate, rem nobis debita n vindicamus Serv. Æn. 11

And therefore at this Day, if a Ship shall be on a Voyage to the *West-Indies*, or on a Discovery of those parts of the unknown World, and in her Way be assaulted by a Pirate, but in the Attempt overcomes the Pirate by the Laws Marine, the Vessel is become the Captors, and they may execute such *Beasts of Prey* immediately, without any Solemnity of Condemnation. If we respect expletory Justice, it cannot be denied, but for the Conservation of Ship and Goods, a Pirate invading may be slain, for the inequality between these things and life is made up in favour of the innocent, and by hatred to the injurious. Whence it follows, if we regard only that Right, that a Pirate running away with stolen Goods, if they cannot otherwise be recovered, may be funk. *Demosthenes* said, *It was very*

Oratione in Ariftocratem

G 2 *hard*

hard and unjust, and contrary both to the written Laws and the common Rules amongst Men, not to be suffered to use Force against him who in a hostile manner hath taken my Goods

Leg ex'at D. quod metus.

XIII So likewise, if a Ship shall be assaulted by Pirates, and in the Attempt the Pirates shall be overcome, if the Captors bring them to the next port, and the Judge openly rejects the Trial, or the Captors cannot wait for the Judge without certain peril and loss, Justice may be done upon them by the Law of Nature, and the same may be there executed by the Captors

Honorii & Theodosii, ideirco Judiciorum vigor Jurisque publici tutela in medio constituta, ne quisquam sibi ipsi permittere valeat ultionem Leg nulli C de Judæis

Caius Cæsar being but a private Man pursued the Pirates, by whom he formerly had been taken and spoiled, and making up to them with such a Fleet as he possibly in haste could get ready, attacked, burnt, and destroyed their Ships, and the Men he brought back to an Anchor, where repairing to the *Proconsul* to do Justice, and he neglecting, himself turned back, and there hanged them up.

Plutarch in Cæsar

XIV If a Pirate at Sea assault a Ship, but by force is prevented entering her, and in the attempt the Pirate happens to slay a person in the other Ship, they are all *Principals* in such a Murder, if the *Common Law* hath Jurisdiction of the cause but by the Law Marine, if the parties are known, they who gave the wound only shall be *principals*, and the rest *accessories* [*] ; and where they have cognizance of the principal, the Courts at *Common Law* will send them their accessory, if he comes before them [†].

* *Ralph Williams indicted for the murder of one John Terrey; and Brudge, Black, and others as Accessories M 21*   † *Molloy fol 134, 135*   *Rot Almir 28 Eliz.*

XV. If

XV. If a *Spaniard* robs a *French* Man on the High Sea, both their Princes being then in amity, and they likewise with the King of *England*, and the Ship is brought into the ports of the King of *England*, the *French* Man may proceed *Criminaliter* against the *Spaniard* to punish him, and *Civiliter* to have Restitution of his Vessel: but if the Vessel is carried *infra Præsidia* * of that Prince, by whose subject the same was taken, there can be no proceeding *Civiliter*, and doubted if *Criminaliter*, but the *French* Man † must resort into the Captor's or Pirate's own Country, or where he carried the Ships, and there proceed

Res quæ intra Præsidia perductæ nondum sunt quanquam ab hostibus occupatæ, dominum non mutârunt ex Gentium jure Grotius de Jure belli ac Pacis c 9 § 16

* *March's* Reports 110

† *Leg Hostes & Leg Latrones D. de Cap. Leg postlim à Piratis eod Tit*

A *Dutchman*, but naturalized by the Duke of *Savoy*, and living at *Villa Franca*, in his Dominions, procures a *Commission* from the States of *Holland*, and coming to *Leghorn*, there rid with the Colours and Ensigns of the Duke of *Savoy*, the Ship *Diamond* being then in Port, and having received her Lading, was afterwards in her Voyage home surprised by that Caper, and brought into *Villa Franca*, and there condemned and sold to one *Poleman*, which Ship afterwards coming for *England*, the Plaintiffs having Notice, made a seizure, and upon Trial, Adjudication passed for the Plaintiffs, the original Proprietors. For tho' the Ship of War and the Captors were of *Savoy*, and carried thither, yet being taken by virtue of a *Dutch Commission* by the *Law Marine*, she must be carried *infra Præsidia* of that Prince or State by virtue of whose *Commission* she was taken. Nor can such carrying of the Ensigns or Colours of the Duke of *Savoy*, who was then in amity with the Crown of *England*, or the *Commander*, though

The Caption was in 1665 Adjudication passed *May* 13, 1670 upon which there was an Appeal to the Duke of *York*; but nothing came of it

Ro't Admir in An supra dict

G 3   a subject

a subject of that Prince, make him a Pirate, or subject them or those to whom they have transferred their interest of the prize, any ways to be questioned for the same *Criminaliter*, for that the original *quoad* the taking was lawful, * as one Enemy might take from another, but *Civiliter* the same might be, for that the Captor had not entituled himself to a firm possession † And therefore in all cases where a Ship is taken by *Letters of Marque or Piracy* *, if the same is not carried *infra Præsidia* of that Prince or State by whose Subject the same was taken, the Owners are not divested of their Property, but may reseize wheresoever they meet with their Vessels.

* 3 Bulstrode 28
† Grotius, Lib 3 cap 9 § 15 & 16.
* 2 Brownl. 11 Weston's Case

XVI. If a Pirate attacks a Ship, and only takes away some of the Men, in order to the selling them for slaves, this is Piracy by the Law Marine, but if a Man takes away a *Villain* or *Ward*, or any other Subject, and sells them for slaves, yet this is no robbery by the *Common Law*

C 2 Inst 109 Ib 8 fol 32 5 Calvin's C but Blackmail and such sorts of taking in Cumberland, Northumberland, and Westmoreland was made Felony 43 Eliz cap 13

XVII If a Bale or Pack of Merchandize be delivered to a Master to carry over Sea to such a Port, and he goes away with the whole Pack or Bale to another Port, and there sells and disposes of the same, * the same is no Felony, but if he opens the Bale or Pack, and take any thing out, *animo furandi*, the the same may amount to such a Larceny, as he may be indicted in the *Admiralty*, though it amounts not to a Piracy Yet if such a Master of a Ship shall carry the Lading to the Port appointed, and after retakes the whole Pack or Bale back again, this may amount to
                                        a Piracy,

* 5 Nautæ Caup l 1 sect 3 Si b. (Item l 16 10 cap 13 13 Ed 4 9 Nautæ Caup 5 cb lib sect 7. sct recept Co 3 Inst 107, 108

a Piracy, for he being in the nature of a
Common Carrier, the delivery had taken its
effect, and the Privity of the Bailment is determined

XVIII If a Pirate shall attack a Ship, and 44 E 3 14
the Master for the Redemption shall give his 4 H 4 2.
Oath to pay a Sum certain, though there be §. ad Leg
no taking, yet is the same Piracy by the *Law* Rhod de jact.
Marine, but by the *Common Law* there must I 2 § si
be an actual taking, though it be but to the navis à Pira-
value of a Penny, as to a Robbery on the tis redempta-
Highway fit
14 E 3 115

If a Ship shall ride at Anchor, and the Mariners shall be part in their Ship-boat, and
the rest on the shore, and none shall be in the
Ship, yet if a Pirate shall attack her and rob
her the same is Piracy

XIX. A Merchant procures Letters of Tr in 7 Jac in
Marque or *Reprise*, and then delivers the B R Rolls
Commissions to persons to endeavour a satis- Abridg 530.
faction, if such Persons commit Piracy, the
Vessel is forfeited without controversy. But Constit Galliæ
the Merchant is no ways liable to make satis- tom 3 tit 3.
faction; for though the Superior shall answer Const anni
for the Actions of his Ministers or Servants, 1583 c 44.
yet that is introduced by the *Civil Law*; but
this question must be decided by the *Law of* Vide Moor's
Nations, by virtue of which such *Commissions* Reports 776
are awarded or granted, the which does ex-
empt any Man to answer for the Damages of
his Servants, unless he foreknew that they
would commit such a Piracy or Spoliation,
or any way have abetted or consented to the
same, which right may be forfeited, and the
Civil Law let in to acquire satisfaction. And
yet in the Case of Sir *Edmond Turner* and Mr Vid. the very
George Carew, who having Letters of Repr- Letters of Re-
sal against the *Dutch*, Mr. *Carew* by Indors- prizal, ante
fol 34.
G 4 ment

ment on the back-fide of the Letters Patents did nominate and appoint one *Tyrence Byrne* to execute and perform all such acts and things as by force of the Letters Patents he might lawfully do. *Tyrence Byrne* provides Ship and Crew, and being at Sea takes a certain Ship belonging to *Bruges* called the *Godelife*, and there was some probable cause of suspicion, yet not enough to warrant a Condemnation: Whereupon the Owners, having had sentence of Restitution, libell'd in the *Admiralty* against Sir *Edmond Turner*, Mr *Carew* and *Byrne*, for Damages, upon which a Sentence was given against the Defendants, who Appealing, the Delegates confirmed the first Sentence

Hill 30, 31. Car. 2 at Ser- jeants-Inn.

XX But if a Ship shall be at Sea and in necessity, if she attacks another Ship, and takes out some Victuals, Cables, Ropes, Anchors or Sails, (especially if that other Ship may spare them) this is not *Piracy*; but then the Party must pay ready Money for such things, or give a Note or Bill for the payment of the value, if on this side the *Straits* of *Morocco*, within four Months, if beyond within twelve Months

Leg 2 sect. cum in eadem D. ad l Rhod Leg quo rau- frag § quod ait D deince Leg. quemad- medum, sect. item D ad Leg. Aqu liam 27 H 8 cap 4 § 1 Per L g Pem- pon. u. de argu rer dam

XXI By the *Law Marine*, if Goods are taken by a Pirate, and afterwards the Pirate attacks another Ship, but in the Attempt is conquered, the *Prize* becomes absolutely the Captor's, saving the account to be rendered to the *Admiral* And it is accounted in Law a just Caption of whatsoever may be got or taken from such *Beasts of Prey*, be the same in their own or in their Successors Possession But then an account ought to be rendered to the *Admiral*, who may (if they happen to be the Goods of the Fellow-Subject of the Captors,

Per Leg Mul- er, eod cap & post

tors, or of Nations in amity with his own
Sovereign) make restitution to the Owner, the
costs and charges, and what other things,
in equity shall be decreed to the Captor, first
considered and deducted.

XXII. By the *Statute* of 27 *Edw.* 3 cap. *Bul* 28, 29.
13. if a Merchant lose his Goods at Sea by *March* 110.
Piracy or Tempest (not being wrecked) and
they afterwards come to Land, if he can
make proof they are his Goods, they shall be
restored to him in places *Guildable*, by the
King's Officers, and six Men of the Country,
and in other places by the Lords there and
their Officers, and six Men of the Country:
If a Pirate takes Goods upon the Sea, and
fell them, the Property is not thereby changed, no more than if a Thief upon the Land
steals them and sells them. *Godb* 193 *Barber*'s Case

This Law hath a very near relation to that
of the *Romans*, called *De Usu-Captione* or the
Atinian Law, for *Atinius* Enacted, That the
Plea of Prescription or long possession, should
not avail in things that had been stolen, but
the Interest which the right Owners had
should remain perpetual, the words of the *Sigonius de*
Law are these, *Quod surreptum est, ejus rei* *Jure Rom.*
æterna auctoritas esset, where by *Auctoritas* is *l 1 c 11.*
meant *Jus Domini*

XXIII Yet by the *Common Law of Eng-* *Bingly's Case*
land, it has been held, That if a Man com- *1 Roll's*
mit Piracy upon the Subjects of another *Abridgment,*
Prince or Republick (though in League with *fol 530 Lit*
us) and brings the Goods into *England*, and *C 4*
fells them in a Market *Overt*, the same shall *Grotius, lib 3*
bind, and the owners are for ever concluded, *c 9 sect 16.*
and if they should go about in the *Admiralty*

to queſtion the Property in order to Reſtitution, they will be prohibited (a) Hob. 79.

In Trover for Goods of 400l. value, Motion was for a Trial at Bar, the Goods being
taken by a *Spanifh* Caper, and brought into
Plymouth, and from thence fhipped away
without Condemnation, becaufe tho' *Br. Property* 38 fays, the Property is altered by the
Enemy's poffeffion above 24 hours, which is
good when they are brought into fafe Port of
an Enemy's Country, yet the conftant Opinion of the *Civilians* and the Practice at *Guild-
hall* in the *Dutch* War, is, that if fuch Goods
be brought into a Neutral Port, or, as thefe
were, into a Friend's, the Property is not altered till Condemnation, and thefe Goods
were taken from a *French* Man in League
with us, which is ftronger; and this being
matter of Evidence, tho' the Defendant was
only a Factor in *England*, could not condemn
the Goods, but the condemnation was in *Holland*, whither they were fhipped, yet the
Trial at Bar was granted. 3 *Keble* 397.
Verdale con Marten. Like Cafe *Radley* and
Delbow againft *Eglesfield & al* 2 *Sand.* 259
1 *Vent.* 173.

Several Perfons were Owners of a Ship,
which they fent to the *Indies* to merchandize,
upon the High Sea the Mariners and Refidue
commit Piracy. Upon the Return of this
Ship to the River of *Thames* the Admiral
feized her, as *Bona Pyratorum*, the Merchants
took the Sails and tackle out of the Ship
The Admiral fhall not have the Goods ftolen
from other Men, but the Owner fhall have
them, 1 *Rol Rep* 285 the Cafe of *Hildebrand*
and others.

XXIV. This

XXIV. This offence was not punishable by the *Common Law*, as appears by the Preamble of the *Stat.* of 28 *H* 8. *cap* 15, but the same was determined and judged by the *Admiral*, after the course of the *Civil Law*, but by force of the said *Act*, the same is inquired of, heard, and determined according to the course of the *Common Law*, as if the offence had been committed on *Land*.

But by Lord *Hale*, in *Hist. Pl. Cr Vol* 2. *p.* 14, 15. The Court of *King's-Bench* had certainly a concurrent Jurisdiction with the Admiralty, in Cases of Felonies done upon the narrow Seas or Coast; though it were High Sea, because within the King's Realm of *England* But this Jurisdiction of the *Common Law* Courts was interrupted by a special Order of the King and Council, 35 *Ed* 3. And since 38 *Ed* 3 it does not appear, that the *Common-Law* Courts took Cognizance of Crimes committed upon the High Seas

Stat 11 and 12 *W* 3 *cap* 7. All Piracies, Felonies, and Robberies committed in or upon the Sea, or in any Haven, River, Creeks, or Place where the Admiral hath Jurisdiction, may be tried at Sea, or upon the Land, in any of his Majesty's Islands, Plantations, Colonies, &c appointed for that purpose by Commission under the Great Seal of *England*, or Seal of the Admiralty, directed to such Commissioners as his Majesty shall think fit, who may commit such Offenders and call a Court of Admiralty thereupon, to consist of seven Persons at the least.

And for want of seven, then any three of the Commissioners may call others as therein is mentioned.

Trial of Piracy.

The

The Perfons fo affembled may proceed according to the courfe of the Admiralty, and give Sentence of Death and award execution of the Offenders, who fhall thereupon fuffer Lofs of Lands, Goods and Chattels

The Regifter of the Court, or if none be, the Prefident to take Minutes of the Proceedings, and tranfmit the fame to the Admiralty Court in *England*

If any natural born Subjects or Denizens of *England* commit Piracy or any act of Hoftility, againft any of his Majefty's Subjects at Sea, under Colour of a Commiffion or Authority from any Foreign Prince or State or Perfon whatfoever, fuch Offenders fhall be adjudged Pirates.

If any Commander or Mafter of a Ship, or Sea-man or Mariner, turn Pirate, or give up his Ship, &c. to Pirates, or combine to yield up, or run away with any Ship, or lay violent Hands on his Commander, or endeavour to make a Revolt in the Ship, he fhall be adjudged a Pirate and fuffer accordingly.

All Perfons who after the 29th of *September* 1700, fhall fet forth any Pirate (or be aiding and affifting to any fuch Piracy) committing Piracy on Land or Sea, or fhall conceal fuch Pirate, or fhall receive any Veffel or Goods, Piratically taken, fhall be adjudged acceffory to fuch Piracy, and fuffer as Principals, according to the Statute of 28 *H* 8. which is hereby declared to be in force

When any *Englifh* Ship fhall have been defended by Fight againft Pirates, and any of the Officers or Seamen killed or wounded, the Judge of the Admiralty or his Surrogate in *London*, or the Major or chief Officer in the Out-Ports, affifted by four fubftantial Merchants,

chants, may by Procefs out of the faid Court
levy upon the Owners of fuch Ships, &c. a
Sum not exceeding 2*l* *per Cent* of the Value of the Freight, Ship and Goods fo defended, to be diftributed among the Officers
and Seamen of the faid Ships, or Widows
and Children of the flain.

A Reward of 10*l.* for every Veffel of 100
Tons or under, and 15*l.* for every Veffel of
a greater Burden, fhall be paid by the Captain, Commander or Mafter, to the firft Difcoverer of any combination for running away
with, or deftroying any fuch Ship at the Port
where the Wages are to be paid

The Commiffioners aforefaid fhall after the
29th of *September* 1700, have the fole power
of trying the faid Crimes, and Offences within
the Colonies and Plantations in *America*, governed by Proprietors, or under Grants or
Charters from the Crown, and may iffue their
Warrants for apprehending fuch Pirates, &c.
and their Acceffories in order to their being
tried there, or fent into *England*

Commiffions for the Trial of the faid Offences fent to any Place within the Jurifdic
tion of the Cinque Ports, fhall be directed to
the Lord Warden of the Cinque Ports, or
his Lieutenant, and fuch Perfons as the Lord
Chancellor fhall appoint, and the Trial to be
by the Inhabitants of the Cinque Ports

All Seamen, Officers and Sailors, who fhall
defert the Ships or Veffels, wherein they are
hired for a Voyage, fhall forfeit their Wages

If any Mafter of a Merchant Ship or Veffel
fhall after the 29th of *September* 1700, during
his being abroad, force any Man afhore, or
wilfully leave him behind, or refufe to bring
all his Men home again, who are in a Condition

- dition to return, he fhall fuffer three Months Imprifonment

The above Act 11 and 12 *W* 3 *ch* 7 was continued by 1 *Geo* 1. *ch.* 25 for five Years, *&c.* and was made perpetual by 6 *Geo.* 1 *ch.* 19 And 'tis enacted by 4 *Geo* 1. *ch.* 11. *fec.* 7. That all Perfons who fhall commit any Offence for which they ought to be adjudged Pirates, Felons, or Robbers, by 11 and 12 *W* 3 may be tried and judged for every fuch Offence, according to 28 *H.* 8 and fhall be excluded from their Clergy

By *Stat.* 8 *Geo. ch* 24. *Sect.* 1. perpetuated by 2 *Geo* 2 *c.* 28. If any Commander of a Ship, or other Perfon, fhall any wife trade with any Pirate, or fhall furnifh any Pirate with Ammunition or Stores, or fit out any Ship with fuch defign, or confederate or correfpond with any Pirate, knowing him to be fuch, fuch Perfon fhall be adjudged guilty of piracy, and fhall be tried according to *Stat* 28 *H* 8 *ch* 15 and *Stat* 11 and 12 *W* 3 *ch* 7 and being convicted fhall fuffer as a Pirate And perfons belonging to any Ship, who fhall upon meeting any Merchantman upon the High Seas, forcibly board fuch Ship, and though they do not carry off fuch Ships, fhall throw overboard or deftroy any part of her Goods, fhall be punifhed as Pirates

And *ibid fec* 2 Every Ship fitted out with defign to trade with, or fupply any Pirate, and all the Goods put on board fuch Ship, fhall be *ipfo facto* forfeited, one Moiety to the King, and the other to the Informer, to be recovered in the High Court of *Admiralty*

And

And *ibid. fec.* 3 All perfons declared Acceffories by 11 and 12 *W.* 3. are hereby declared principal Offenders.

And by *fec.* 4. Offenders convicted on this Act are excluded Clergy

By *Stat.* 18 *Geo.* 2 *c.* 30 *Sect.* 1 All Perfons being natural-born Subjects or Denizens, who during the prefent or any future Wars fhall commit any Hoftilities upon the Sea, or in any Place where the Admirals have Jurifdiction, againft his Majefty's Subjects, under colour of any Commiffion from any of His Majefty's Enemies, or fhall be any otherways adherent to his Majefty's Enemies upon the Sea, or where the Admirals have Jurifdiction, may be tried as Pirates, Felons, and Robbers, in the Court of Admiralty, on Ship-board, or upon the Land, and being convicted fhall fuffer fuch Pains of Death, Lofs of Lands and Goods, as any other Pirates ought by 11 *W.* 3 *cap* 7 or any other Act

By *fect.* 2. Any Perfon tried and acquitted, or convicted according to this Act, fhall not be liable to be profecuted or tried again in *Great Britain* or elfe where for the fact, as High-Treafon

By *fect* 3 Provided that nothing in this Act fhall prevent any Perfons guilty of any of the faid Crimes, who fhall not be tried according to this Act, from being tried for High-Treafon within this Realm, according to the 28 *Hen* 8 *cap* 15

Piracies and Robberies on the Seas are excepted out of the General Pardon by *Stat* 20 *Geo* 2 *c* 52 *Sect* 13

XXV. The Act 11 and 12 *W* 3 *ch* 7. does not alter the Offence, or make the Offence

fence Felony, but leaves the Offence as it
was before this Act, *viz.* Felony only by the
Civil Law, but giveth a mean of Trial by
the *Common Law*, and inflicteth pains of
death, as if they had been attainted of any
Felony done upon the Land. The Indictment must mention the same to be done
upon the High Sea

Coke 3. Instit Tit. Admir.

Note, By 2 *Geo* 2 *ch* 21 If any Person
be feloniously stricken, or poisoned upon the
Sea, or at any place out of *England*, and
dies in *England*, or stricken or poisoned in
England, and dies on the Sea, or out of
England, the Fact is triable in any Coun-
ty, according to the Course of the Common
Law, except Challenges for the Hundred

Moore 756, Dy 308 But if the Party be attainted before the Admiral, and not before the Com-missioners, then there is no corrup-tion of Blood or forfeiture of Lands, *quod nota.* 1 *Inst* 391. *vid postea* § 30.

XXVI A pardon of all Felonies does not
extend to Piracy, but the same ought *especially*
to be named, and though there be a Forfeiture
of Lands and Goods, yet there is no *corruption* of Blood, nor can there be an *Accessory*
of this offence, tired by virtue of this *Statute*,
but if there be an Accessory upon the Sea to
a Piracy, he must be tried by the *Civil Law*.

The *Statute* of 35 *H* 8 *cap* 2 taketh not
away the *Statute for Treasons* done upon the
Sea, nor is *Clergy* allowable to the Party on
the *Statute* 28 *H* 8. *vide* 14 *Jac. in B R.
Moore* 756 *plcc* 1044 3 *Inst* 112

XXVII Though a Port be *Locus publicus
uti pars Oceani*, yet it hath been resolved more
than once, that all Ports, not only the Town,
but the Water is *infra corpus Comitatus*

Hide and o-thers robbed the Ship of Captain *Slue*, of the Mer-chandize of one Mr. *Mos*,

If a Pirate enters into a Port or Haven of
this Kingdom, and a Merchant being at Anchor there, the Pirate assaults him and robs
him, this is not *Piracy*, because the same is
not done *super altum Mare*, but this is a down
right

right Robbery at the *Common Law*, for that a Merchant in
the Act is *infra corpus Comitatus*, and was in- *London*, and
quirable and punishable by the *Common Law*, they were in-
before the *Statute* of 28 *H*. 8. *cap.* 15. dicted for it
at the Com-
monLaw, and
were found guilty of the same, *Anno* 22 *Car* 2 at the *Old-Bailey*

XXVIII. So if such a *Piracy* or Robbery *Moore* 756
be made in a *Creek* or *Port*, in such cases it 1 *Jac Par.*
has been conceived, that *Clergy* is allowable 1044
upon the *Statute* of 28 *H*. 8 but if it be done And the same
super altum Mare, there no *Clergy* is allowable, was so ruled
howbeit, if such a Robbery be committed on by the opi-
great Rivers within the Realm, which are nion of Sir
look'd upon as common Highways, there *Lyonel Jen-*
perhaps *Clergy* may not be granted , and so *kins*, and the
it was rul'd in the aforesaid Case of *Hyde*, who rest of the
with a parcel of Men came one Night in a Boat Judges, upon
in the River of *Thames*, and under the colour of the Piracy
Press-Masters, boarded the Ship of one Cap- committed by
tain *Slue*, and robb'd her, for which being *Cusack* and o-
taken and tried at the *Old-Baily*, by the great- thers , and he
er opinion of the Judges there present, 22 was executed
Car 2 *Clergy* was denied him By the Pardon *Anno* 1674
of all Felonies, at the *Common Law*, or by vide 19 *E* 3,
the *Statute-Law*, *Felony super altum Mare* is 124
not pardonable , for though the King may 9 *H* 4 2.
pardon this Offence, yet being no Felony in *Mo* 756 1
the eye of the Law of this Realm, but only *Inst* 191. *Dy.*
by the *Civil Law*, the Pardon of all Felonies 308
generally extends not to it , for this is a special
Offence, and ought especially to be mentioned

XXIX One *Cobham* was arraigned in
Southwark, before the Commissioners of Oyer
and Terminer, for a Piracy and Robbery
committed on a *Spaniard*, *& stetit mutuus &*
noluit directe respondere And it being moved

by the Attorney-General, whether he ought to have the Judgment of *pain fort & dure* in this Cafe, *Saunders*, Chief Baron, *Brown* and *Dyer* were of Opinion he fhould, and that by the Words and reafonable Intendment of the Statute of 28 *H.* 8 *c.* 15 and according to the Opinion *fupra*, the Judgment was given by *Carus* Serjeant   *Dy.* 241. *pl* 49.

9 E. 4. 28 cited in Coke's 3 Inftit fol 112.

XXX. A Man attainted by virtue of that Statute, forfeits his Lands and Goods, yet there works *no corruption* of blood, by virtue of that Attainder, nor can there be any Acceffory of Piracy by the Law of this Realm; but if it falls out that there is an Acceffory upon the Sea, fuch Acceffory may be punifhed by the *Civil Law*, before the Lord *Admiral*, but he cannot be punifhed by virtue of this Act, becaufe it extends not to Acceffories, nor makes the Offence Felony

28 Eliz. Butler's Cafe cited, 3 Inftit fol 113

XXXI. If one fteal Goods in one County, and brings them into another, the Party may be indicted in either County, but if one commits Piracy at Sea, and brings the Goods into a County in *England*, yet he cannot be indicted upon the Statute, for that the original taking was not Felony, whereof the *Common Law* took Cognizance

Marfh's Cafe, 13 Jac in B R 3 Bulftrod 27. 1 Rol Rep 175 ┬ Irft 152

XXXII If a Man is taken on fufpicion of *Piracy*, and a Bill is preferred againft him, and the *Jury* find *Ignoramus*, if the Court of *Admiralty* will not difcharge him, the Court of *King's-Bench* will grant a *Habeas Corpus*, and if there be good Caufe, difcharge him, or at leaft take Bail for him But if the Court fufpects that the Party is guilty, perhaps they may remand him, and therefore

fore in all cafes, where the *Admiralty* legally have an original, or a concurrent Jurifdiction, the Courts above will be well informed before they will meddle.

Trefpafs for breaking a Ship, and taking away the Sails, the Defendant juftified by warrant out of the Admiralty, by which he entered the Ship, and took away the Sails. Objection, The breaking is not anfwered, *per Curiam* its good enough, for the entry is a breaking in Law, as *Claufum fregit*, &c. And that he may carry away the Sails, becaufe this is the manner of their proceedings, and grounded upon Reafon, becaufe the Ship cannot be kept fafe, if the Sails be not carried away. *Creamer* againft *Tokely*, *Latch* 188.

Juftification in Tref by warrant of the Admiralty.

Suit in the Admiralty, the Defendant pleaded the Statute of Limitation, if that Court deny the Plea, Prohibition will be granted, or if they do receive the Plea, but will not give Sentence accordingly, Prohibition will go *Hardres* 502. *Berkly* and *Morris*.

Statute of Limitation pleadable there.

If a Man be in cuftody for Piracy, if any aids or affifts him in his Efcape, though that matter is an Offence at Land, yet the *Admiralty* having Jurifdiction to punifh the principal, may have likewife power to punifh fuch an Offender, who is looked upon *quafi* an Acceffory to the Piracy, but to refcue a Prifoner from an Officer of theirs, they may examine the caufe, but they cannot proceed criminally againft the Offender.

Yelverton 134, 135. Cro El 685. Cro Jac 269. Stiles 171, 340.

The Exemplification of the Sentence of the Court of *Admiralty*, under their Seal, is conclufive Evidence in a Court of *Common Law*. 2 Lord *Raymond*, 893

50 Eliz. 3
par. 2 Dorf
24. de audiend
& terminand.
Mercatoribus
super mare de-
prædatis.
Pat. 6. E. 1.
m. 24. Dorf
the Cafe of
Will. de Dun-
ftaple, a Citi-
zen of Win-
ton. Pat 32
E. 1 m. 4 Dorf. pro Wilhelmo Perin & Domengo Perez Mercatoribus.

XXXIII. Antiently when any Merchants were robbed at Sea, or spoiled of their Goods, the King usually issued out *Commissions* under the *Great Seal* of *England*, to enquire of such depredations and robberies, and to punish the Parties; and for frauds in Contracts, to give Damages to the Parties, and proceed therein *secundum Legem & consuetudinem Angliæ, secundum Legem Mercatoriam, & Legem Maritimam*; all three Laws included in the Commissions.

3 Bulstrode 27

XXXIV. The Courts of *Westminster* have a Sovereign power to enquire after the Liberty of every Man, and that he should not be deprived of the same without just cause, and therefore as in other capital Causes, so likewise in this they may send their *Habeas Corpus* to remove the Body of any committed upon such an account, and if they see a just cause, they may either bail, or discharge, or remand, as the matter shall seem just before them

Coke, 3 Instit
fol. 113

And altho' the Statute of 28 *H* 8 *c* 15. does not alter the offence, or make the offence felony, but leaveth the offence as it was before that Statute, (*viz*) Felony only by the *Civil Law*, and gives a mean of Trial by the *Common Law*, and inflicted such pains of death as if they had been attainted of any

* Seff Admir.
Feb 18, 1680.
Cafe of Comp-
tor Gwyther
& al.

Felony, yet it was resolved * by all the Judges, and the rest of the Commissioners then present, that his Majesty having granted Letters of Reprizal to Sir *Edmond Turner* and *George Carew*, against the Subjects of the *States General* of the *United Provinces*,

and

and that afterwards that Grant was called in by Proclamation, then mortified in the Treaty of *Breda*, and afterwards superseded under the Great Seal: That *Carew*, (without *Turner*) having deputed several to put in Execution the said Commission, who accordingly did, and being indicted for Piracy, the same was not a felonious and a piratical Spoliation in them, but a Caption in order to an Adjudication; and though the Authority was deficient, yet not being done by the Captain and his Mariners, *animo deprædandi*, they were acquitted.

CHAP. V.

The Right of the Flag, as to the acknowledging the Dominion of the British Seas.

I. *Confiderations general as in reference to the fame.*

II *Whether Princes may have an exclusive Property in the Sea.*

III *That fuch an exclusive Dominion may be, proved.*

IV. *Of the Sea, whether capable of Division as the Land*

V. *Confiderations general, in reference to Maritime Cities touching Sea Dominion*

VI *Of the Sea, by reafon of its instability, whether capable of subjection.*

VII. *Of the Dominion of the British Sea afferted long before, and ever fince the Conquest of this Ifle by the Romans.*

VIII. *The Duty of the Flag, but a confecutive Acknowledgment of that Right. And of the Ordinance of* Haftings *declaring that Customary Obeisance.*

IX. *Confiderations had on fome Treaties, in reference to afferting the Duty of the Flag.*

X. *Of the extent how far that duty is required and payable.*

XI *Of the duty of the Flag, not a bare Honorary Salute, but a Right.*

XII *Of the importance and value of the fame, as well in Nations Foreign, as in* England

XIII. *Of the effects of fuch a Right and Sovereignty. Of the extent of this Dominion by the Laws of* England

XIV. *Of the Duty of the Flag not regarded as a Civility, but commanded as a Duty*

XV *Of the importance of that acknowledgment.*

I AFTER the Writings of the Illuftrious *Selden*, certainly 'tis impoffible to find any *Prince* or *Republick*, or fingle Perfon

endued

endued with Reafon or Senfe, that *doubts* the *Dominion* of the *Britifh Sea*, to be entirely fubject to that *Imperial Diadem*, or the *duty* or *right* of the *Flag*, which indeed is but a *confecutive* Acknowledgment of that ancient *Superiority* · Yet there have not been wanting fome, who though they have not queftioned the former, have highly difputed the latter

But there are fome fatal Periods amongft our *Northern Regions*, when the Inhabitants do become fo brutal and prejudicate, that no obligation of Reafon, Prudence, Confcience or Religion can prevail over their Paffions, efpecially if they become the devoted *Merce-naries* of an implacable *Faction* †, in oppofi- † *Lovefein.* tion to all that can be called either juft or honourable, we need not rip up the Carriage of that late infolent Son of a *Tallow-Chandler*, whofe Deportments made him no lefs infup-portable at home, than he was amongft *Fo-reign Princes*, the teftimonies of his greateft Parts and Abilities being no other than Mo-numents of his *Malice* aad *Hatred* to this Na-tion, and Records of his own *folly* But Princes are not to be wrangled out of their ancient *Right* and *Regalties* by the fubtil Ar-guments of *Wit* and *Sophiftry*, nor are they to be fupplanted or overthrown by Malice or Arms, fo long as God and good Men will affift, in which his facred Majefty did not want, when he afferted his Right with the Blood and Lives of fo many Thoufands that fell in the difpute

II That Princes may have an *exclufive pro-perty in the Sovereignty of the feveral parts of the Sea, and in the paffage, Fifhing and Shores,* is fo evidently true by way of fact, as no man that is not defperately impudent can deny it;

H 4 the

the Confiderations of the general *practice* in
all Maritime Countries, the neceffity of *order*
in mutual Commerce, and the *Safety* of mens
perfons, goods, and lives, hath taught even
the moft *Barbarous Nations* to know by the
Light of *human Reafon*, that *Laws* are as
equally neceffary for the Government and
Prefervation of the Sea, as thofe that negotiate and trade on the firm Land, and that
to make *Laws*, and to give them the *Life* of
Execution, muft of neceffity require a *fupream
Authority*; for to leave every part of the Sea
and Shores to an *arbitrary and promifcuous
Ufe*, without a correcting and fecuring Power
in cafe of wrong or danger, is to make Men
in the like Condition with the Fifhes, where
the greater devour and fwallow the lefs

III. And though the Sea is as the *Highway*,
and common to all; yet it is as other *Highways* by Land or great Rivers are, which
See that Plea though *common* and *free*, are not to be ufurped
of *Chiozzola* by private Perfons to their own entire Service,
for the *Vene-* but remain to the ufe of every one   Not that
tian Sove-
reignty of the their Freedom is fuch, as they fhould be
Adriatick Sea, *without Protection or Government* of fome
at the end of Prince or Republick, but rather not *exclude*
Mr. *Selden.* the fame, for the true enfign of Liberty and
Freedom is *Protection from thofe that maintain
it in liberty*

IV. And as the Sea is capable of Protection and Government, fo is the fame no lefs
than the Land fubject to be divided amongft
Men, and *appropriated to Cities and Potentates*,
which long fince was ordained of *God* as a
thing moft natural, whence it was that *Ariftotle* faid, *That unto Maritime Cities the Sea is
the Territory, becaufe from thence they take their
fuftenance and defence*; a thing which cannot be,
unlefs

unless part of it might be *appropriated* in the like manner as the *Land* is, which is divided betwixt Cities and Governments, not by equal Parts, or according to their greatness, but according as they *are able to rule, govern, and defend them*, *Berne* is not the greatest City of *Switzerland*, yet she hath as large a Territory as all the rest of the twelve *Cantons* put together The Cities of *Noremberg* and *Genoa* are very rich and great, yet their Territories hardly exceed their Walls, and *Venice*, the Mistress and Queen of the *Mediterranean*, was known for many Years to be without any manner of Possession on the firm Land

V Again on the Sea, certain Cities of great Force have possessed large quantities thereof, others of little Force have been contented with the next Waters

Neither are there wanting Examples of such, as notwithstanding they are Maritime, yet having fertile Lands lying on the back of them, have been contented *therewith* without ever attempting to *gain any Sea-Dominion*, others who being *awed* by their more mighty Neighbours, have been constrained to *forbear* any such attempt, for which two causes a City or Republick, though it be *Maritime*, yet it may remain without any *possession of the Sea*. God hath instituted *Principalities* for the maintenance of Justice to the benefit of Mankind, which is necessary to be executed as well by Sea as by Land St *Paul* saith, that for this cause there were due to Princes, *Customs and Contributions*

It

The substance of what was alledged by the Hansatique Towns, at the Venetians asserting of the Sovereignty of the Adriatick, Inter res communes, uti ipse Imperator numerat mare, & ideo nemo in mari piscari; aut navigare prohibetur, & adversus inhibentem competit actio injuriarum, l 10

si quis in mare, l injuriarum, sect ult de injuriis Sin littora quoque communia sunt l 2 re diversi Quia accessorium sunt maris, & accessorium sequitur naturam Principalis, l 2 de peculio legat c accessorium de reg jur. in 6. Ad latus maris igitur accidere quivis potest, non piscandi

cardi tartum gratia, sed etiam ædificandi & occupandi causa quod in tit.
de acquirend Dom. l in litt ff. ne quid in loc pub Jo Angelius J C.
de repub. Hanfiat. par. 6 fol. 85 Edit Francof An Dom 1641 But
these arguments were easily answered by the *Venetian* Lawyers , *Quem-*
admodum communio littorum reftringitur ad populum, à quo occupata funt,
lib 3 fect littora. D. de quid in loc pub Ita etiam communio maris ·
adeo ut per mare à nemine occupatum navigatio fit omnino libera per mare
autem occupatum ab aliquo Principe ii liberam habeant navigationem qui
funt .lii Principi fubjecti ; alii verò eatenus, quatenus idem Princeps per-
mittit Julius Pacius de Dom maris Adriatici

It would be a great abfurdity to praife the
well Government and Defence of the Land,
and to condemn that of the *Sea* , nor doth it
follow, becaufe of the vaftnefs of the *Sea,*
that it is not poffible to be governed and protected , but that proceeds from a *defect in*
Mankind ; for Defarts, though part of Kingdoms, are impoffible to be governed and protected, witnefs the many Defarts in *Africk,*
and the immenfe vaftities of the *New World.*

VI As it is a gift of God, that a *Land* by
the Laws and publick Power be ruled, protected, and governed ; fo the fame happens
† *Grotius mare* to the *Sea,* and thofe † are deceived by a grofs
liberum Com- equivocation, who aver that the *Land,* by
munio parit reafon of its *ftability,* ought to be fubjected,
difcordiam . but not the *Sea,* for being an unconftant *Ele-*
quod commun- *ment,* no more than *Air ,* forafmuch as they
ter poffide'ur, intend by the *Sea* and the *Air* all the parts of
vitio natural. the fluid *Elements,* it is a moft certain thing
xeglig.'ur that they cannot be brought under *Subjection*
Habet commu- and *Government,* becaufe whilft a Man ferves
nio rerum ge- himfelf with any one part of them, the other
rendarum diffi- efcapes out of his *power ,* but this chanceth
culta.em Leg alfo to *Rivers,* which cannot be detained , but
pater §. dul- when one is faid to rule over a *Sea* or *River,*
-iffime Leg 2 it is underftood not of the *Element,* but of the
Site where they are placed The Waters of
the *Adriatick* and *British Seas* continually run
out thereof, and yet it is the fame *Sea* , as the
Tyber,

Tyber, *Poe*, *Rhyne*, *Thames*, or *Severn*, are the same *Rivers* they were a Thousand Years since, and this is that which is subject to Princes by way of *Protection* and *Government*.

Again, it would seem ridiculous if any Man would assert that the Sea, ought to be left without Protection, so that any one might do therein well or ill, robbing, spoiling, and making it unnavigable, or whatsoever should seem fitting in their Eyes, from all which it is apparent, that the *Sea ought to be governed* by those to whom it most properly appertains by the Divine Disposition

VII When * *Julius Cæsar* first undertook the Invasion of this *Isle*, he summoned the neighbouring *Gauls* to inform him of the Shores, *Ports*, *Havens*, and other things convenient that might accelerate his intended *Conquest*, but from them nothing could be had, they answering, All Commerce and Traffick, and visiting their Ports, was *interdicted to all Nations before licence had*, nor could any but Merchants visit the same, and then had they places † assigned them whither they should come, nor was this Dominion that the *Britains* then used, commanded without a *Naval Force*, the sight of which when *Cæsar* saw, he preferred them before those of the *Romans*. For upon that occasion it was that *Cæsar*, having seen those *Auxiliary Squadrons*, which the *Britains* sent the *Gauls* in their Expeditions against the *Romans*, took occasion to find out that Warlike People, whose bare Auxiliary Aid shook the Flower of the *Roman Squadrons*.

ces of Mart or Commerce for the *Gauls*

tibus noftris inde fulmin ftiata auxilia intelligebat.

* *Qui omnia fere Gallis erant incognita, neque enim temere piætor mercatores adit ad illos quisquam, neque eis ipsis quidquampræter oi am maritimam atque eas regiones quæ sunt contra Galliam notumest.Com. Gall. Bell lib. 4 fol 72.m 8*

† *Gauls* Town near *Yarmouth* being then, as is conceived, one of the common places

Quod omnibus fire Galli hostibus

And

And when the *Romans* became *Conquerors* of this *Isle*, the same *Right* or *Dominion* was during all their time supported and maintained, when they sailed round their new atchieved *Conquests* in the time of *Domitian*, *Tacit. in vita Agricola* giving terror to all the neighbouring *Agricol.* *Nations*

But when that *Mighty Empire* became subject to Fate, and this *Nation*, by the continual supply of Men, which went out of the Kingdom to fill up the Contingencies of the *Roman* Legions, became at last so enfeebled as to render us a Prey to the *Saxons*, which *Empire* having settled Peace with their *Danish* Neighbours, and quieted their own homebred Quarrels, and having reduced the several petty Kingdoms of their *Heptarchy* under one *Diadem*, they forgot not to assume their antient *Right and Dominion of the Seas*, as did

† Altitonantis the most Noble *Edgar* †, who kept no less a
Dei largiflua Number than 400 *Sail of Ships*, to vindicate
clementia qui and ascertain his *Dominion*, giving Protection
est Rex Re- to the peaceable, and punishment to the of-
gum; Ego fenders: Nor did his Successors *Etheldred*,
Edgarus An- *Canutus*, *Edmond*, and others that followed
glorum Basi- of the *Danish Race*, any ways wave, relinquish
leus, omnium- or lose that Royalty, but obsequiously main-
que regum tained the same down to the *Conqueror*, and
Infularum Oc- from him since for upwards of 1200 years in
ceani, quæ Bri- a quiet and peaceable Possession.
tanniam cir-
cum jacent,
cunctarumque

Nationum quæ infra eam includuntur, Imperator & Dominus   Ex Chart
fundam Ecclef. Wigor. *Sir* John Burroughs, *fol* 12   *Idem quoque*
Edgarus 400 *Naves congregavit, ex quibus omni anno post Festum Paf-*
chale 100. *Naves ad quamlibet Angliæ partem statuit, sic æstate Infulam*
circumnavigavit   hyeme verò judicia in Provincia exercuit   Ex Ra-
nulph Ceftrenf *fol* 22 *J B*

To mention the antient *Commissions*, and Exercise of this Sovereign Power, *Safe-Con-* *duct*, *Writs of Seizure*, *Arrests*, *Records of* *Grants*,

Grants, and *Licences* to pass through the Sea and to fish, *Parliament Rolls*, and the like, † would make a Volume ; in a word, if *Right of Prescription*, *succession of Inheritance*, *continual Claim*, *matter of Fact*, *consent of History* and *Confessions*, even from the Mouths and Pens of *adversaries*, be of any moment to the asserting of a Title, his Sacred Majesty may be presumed to have as good a Title to that, as the most absolute Monarch this day on Earth, hath to whatever he can claim or does enjoy 1 *Rol. Ab.* 528. *pl* 2

† So fully proved by Mr *Selden*, that it would be impertinent in this Tract to rehearse the authorities he vouches *Vide Jac Uſſer Armach. Epiſ Hiberniæ Sylloge, p* 121, 163

VIII Now the Duty of the Flag is no more but a consecutive acknowledgment that the *Right* and *Dominion* of the *British Seas* (not as a bare *Honorary Salute* or *Ceremony*, but as an *absolute Sign* of the Right and *Sovereignty* of those *Seas* where they are obliged to strike Sail; are in him to whose *Flag* they veil, and pay that duty to, and in substance is no more, but that the King grants a general Licence for Ships to pass through his Seas, that are his Friends, paying that obeisance and duty, like those services when Lords grant out Estates, reserving a *Rose* or *Pepper-Corn*, the value of which is not regarded, but the remembrance and acknowledgment of their *Benefactor's Right* and *Dominion*

The Duty of the *Flag* or Salutation, is to be paid not only by Foreigners, but also by natural-born Subjects, and such who refuse to pay the same, may be brought to the *Flag* to answer that Contempt

To be paid by Natives as well as Foreigners

That this hath been an *Antient Custom*, always waiting on that Sovereignty, appears by that memorable Record upwards of 500 years since made, where it is declared by King *John*

whit

what the *Antient Custom* was, in these Words;

InterLeg Marinas sub fine anni regni Regis Johanni secundi Entitled, Le Ordinance al Hastings

" That if a Lieutenant in any Voyage, being ordained by Common Council of the Kingdom, do encounter upon the Sea any Ships or Vessels, laden or unladen, that will not strike and veil their Bonnets at the Commandment of the Lieutenant of the King, but will fight against them of the Fleet, that if they can be taken, they be reputed as Enemies, and their Ships, Vessels, and Goods taken and forfeited as the Goods of Enemies, although the Masters or Possessors of the same would come afterwards and alledge, that they are the Ships, Vessels, and Goods of those that are Friends to our Lord the King, and that the common People in the same be chastised by Imprisonment of their Bodies for their Rebellion, by discretion "

Thus this *Immemorial Custom* was by that prudent Prince affirmed, the which hath been always before, and ever since (without interruption) by all Nations constantly paid to the *Ships of War*, bearing the *Royal Standard*, and other of his Majesty's *Ships*, wearing his *Colours* and *Ensigns of Service*, he knowing that

Leon Lessius de justic & jur l 2 c 2 dub. 19

undoubted Maxim of State, *That Kingdoms are preserved by reputation, which is as well their strongest support in Peace, as their chiefest safety in time of War, when once they grow despised, they are either subject to Foreign Invasions, or Domestick Troubles*, the which (if possible) that Prince would have prevented, but he lived when those Celestial Bodies, which govern the actions of *Princes*, seemed to frown on the most Virtuous and Wise

IX. And as there is no Nation in the World more tender and jealous of their Honour than the *English*, so none more impatiently tolerate the

the diminution thereof. Hence it was that in all Treaties, before any thing was ascertained, the *Dominion of the Seas*, and *striking the Top-sail*, was always first provided for.

In the Year 1653, after the *Dutch* had measured the length of their Swords with those of this Nation, and being sensible of the odds, had by their four *Ambassadors* most humbly besought Peace, this very Duty of the *Flag* was demanded by the 15th *Article* in these words.

" That the Ships and Vessels of the said United Provinces, as well Men of War as others, be they in single Ships, or in Fleets, meeting at Sea with any of the Ships of this State of *England*, or in their service, and wearing the Flag, shall strike the Flag, and lower their Top-sail, until they passed by, and shall likewise submit themselves to be visited if thereto required, and perform all other respects due to the said Commonwealth of *England*, to whom the Dominion and Sovereignty of the *British* Seas belong." *Note, That Cromwell was the first that ever inserted any such Article into any Treaty Our Right and Dominion over the British Sea having never been disputed before, but by an immemorial prescription and possession transmitted to us, and supposed as unquestionable by all Princes.*

This was so peremptorily demanded, that without the *solemn acknowledgment of the Sovereignty over the* British *Seas*, there was no Peace to be had. As to the *acknowledging of the Sovereignty* and the *Flag*, they were willing to continue the *Antient Custom*, but that of *Visiting* was somewhat hard, 'tis true, the latter Clause was by the *Usurper* waved, for *Leo ab Aitzma, fol. 847* Reasons standing with his private Interest, but the first was (with the addition of these words ——— " in such manner as the same hath been formerly observed in any times whatsoever") made absolute by the 13th *Article* between
tween

tween *Him* and that *Republick*, in these words : *Item quod Naves & Navigia dictarum Fœderatarum Provinciarum, tam bellica & ad Hostium vim propulsandam instructa, quàm alia, quæ alicui è Navibus bellicis hujus Reipublicæ in maribus Britannicis obviam dederint, vexillum suum è mali vertice detrahent, & supremum velum demittent, eo modo, quo ullis retrò temporibus, sub quocunque anteriori regimine unquam observatum fuit,* and from thence it

Sept. 14, 1662

was transcribed into the 10th *Article* at *Whitehall*, and afterwards into the 19th *Article* at *Breda*, and from thence into the 6th *Article* made last at *Westminster*, and that Clause of searching of each others Ships made reciprocate, by the 5th *Article* made in

Dec 18, 1674. S V.

the Marine Treaty at *London*, but that extends not to Ships of War, but only to the Ships of Subjects

X By the *British Seas* in the *Article* about the *Flag* are meant the four *Seas*, and not the *Channel* only ; for in the 16th *Article* of the

* But now by the last treaty at *Westminster*

Treaty in 1653, they did express what was meant by the *British Seas* *.

the dominion is ascertained from Cape *Finisterre* to the middle point of the Land *Van Stater* in *Norway*, Feb 9, 1674¼

Les mers qui entourent les Isles Britanniques, was the Language proposed by the *French* Ministers at the Treaty of *Utrecht* · but the *British* Ministers insisted on *Maribus Bri*

" That the Inhabitants and Subjects of the United Provinces may with their Ships and Vessels furnished as Merchant-Men, freely use their Navigation, sail, pass and repass, in the Seas of *Great-Britain* and *Ireland*, and the Isles within the same, commonly called the *British Seas*, without any wrong or injury to be offered them by the Ships or People of this Commonwealth , but on the contrary shall be treated with all love and friendly offices, and may likewise with their Men

of

of War—not exceeding such a Number as *tanmcis*, and shall be agreed upon—fail, pass and repass had it accordthrough the said Seas, to and from the Coun- ingly. tries and Ports beyond them, but in case the said *States General* shall have occasion to pass through the said Seas with a great number of Men of War, they shall give three Months notice of their intention to the Commonwealth, and obtain their consent for the passing of such a Fleet, for preventing of jealousy and misunderstanding betwixt the *States* by means thereof "

The first part of this Article doth plainly set out the extent of the *British Seas*, and that it is not the bare *Channel* alone that comprehends the same, but the four *Seas*; and the same is further explained in the Great Case of *Constable*'s, where the *Dominion* of the *Queen Hill 29 Eliz.* (before the Union) as to the Seas, did extend *B. R.* the mid-way between *England* and *Spain*, but Queen and entirely between *England* and *France*, the Sir *John Con-French* never had any right or claim to the *Leonard* 3. *British Seas*, for in the Wars between *Edward part 72 the First* and *Philip the Fair*, (all Commerce on both sides being agreed to be free, so that to all Merchants whatsoever there should be *induciæ*, which were called *fufferantia Guerræ*, *Selden de Dom* and Judges on both sides were appointed to *Maris l 2 c* take cognizance of all things done against 14 27 28. these *Truces*, and should exercise *Judicium fe-cundum Legem Mercatoriam & formam fuffe-* *Rolls Abridg rantiæ*) it was contained in the first provision 2 *part* 174. of that League, that they should defend each others Rights against all others, this afterwards occasioned the introducing that Judgment in the same King's time, (before those *Coke* 4 *Instit,* Judges, chosen by both the said *Princes* by 142. the *Proctors* of the *Prelates, Nobility,* and

VOL. I.   I   *High*

High Admiral of *England*, and all the Cities,
Towns, and Subjects of *England*, &c. unto
which were joined the suffrages of the most
Maritime *Nations*, as *Genoa, Catalonia, Spain,
Almain, Zealand, Holland, Friezeland, Denmark* and *Norway,* and divers other Subjects
of the *Roman Empire*) against *Reginer Grimbald,* then *Admiral* of *France,* for that there
being Wars between *Philip of France* and *Guy
Earl of Flanders,* he had taken Merchants
upon those Seas, in their Voyage to *Flanders,*
and despoiled them of their Goods, whereas
the Kings of *England* and their Predecessors
(as they all jointly do declare and affirm)
without all controversy beyond the memory
of Man, have had the *Supreme Government of
the English Seas, and the Islands thereof.*

1 *Ro. Ab.*
528 pl 2.   *Præscribendo scilicet Leges, Statuta atque interdicta armorum, naviumque alio ac Mercato-
riis armamentis instructarum, causationes exi-
gendo, tutelam præbendo, ubicunque opus esset,
atque alia constituendo quæcunque fuerint neces-
saria ad pacem, jus & æquitatem conservandam*

An universal
consent of all
Nations *inter omnimodas rates tam externas quam in Imperio Anglicano comprehensas quæ per illud tran-
sierint; supremam iisdem item fuisse atque esse
tutelam; merum mixtum Imperium in juredi-
cendo secundum dictas Leges, Statuta, præscripta
& interdicta, aliisque in rebus quæ ad summum
Imperium attinent in locis adjudicatis*

4. *Instit.* 142
Selden cap 27
Mare clausum Which memorable Record apparently
shews, that the Kings of *England* have had
istud regimen & dominium exclusivè of the King
of *France,* bordering upon the same Seas, and
of all other Kings and Princes whatsoever;
and it was there adjudged, that *Grimbald*'s Pa-

Sir *John Bur-*
roughs, fol 42. tent was an usurpation on the King of *England*'s Dominion, and he adjudged to make
satisfaction,

fatisfaction, or if he proved unable, then the King his Mafter fhould, and that after fatisfaction he be rendered to punifhment.

And as the fecond part of the *Articles* of giving notice, it was but an Act of common Prudence, their late unexpected Vifit, which they then gave, put the *Englifh* to fome furprife, but they facing the *Batavians*, foon made them know that they were as capable of beating them *home*, as they were then daring in coming out, and were not to be braved out of a *Dominion* and *Right*, which their Anceftors had with fo much Glory acquired and afferted.

XI. By the *Article* of the Offenfive and *Anno 1635.* Defenfive League between *France* and the *United Provinces*, it was agreed, That if at any time the *Dutch Fleet* (———which were to *Leo ab Aitz-* fcour the *French Coafts* in the *Mediterranean maH ft Tract.* from *Pirates*) fhould at any time meet the *pacis Belg* *French*, the *Admiral* of the *Dutch* was to *ftrike pag 177* *his Flag and lower his Top-fail* at his firft ap- *Edit Lugdum* proach to the *French Fleet*, and to falute the *Bata:ve:* *Admiral* of *France* with Guns, who was to re- *quarto 1654.* turn the faid Salute by Guns alfo, *as was ufual when the* Dutch *and* Englifh *Fleet did meet*.

Only in this the Right of the *Flag* of *England* differs from that claimed by the *French*, for if there had been a failure on the part of the *Dutch*, of paying that refpect to the *French*, the fame would have amounted to no more but a breach of the *League*, but the not ftriking to the King of *England*'s Flag, *is open Rebellion*, and the *Article* does fo fignify, for it is there mentioned as a *Right* and *Sovereignty*, not a bare *Dominion* only, like that of *Jerufalem* to the King of *Spain* 'Tis very true, the refufing of it is an abfolute annulling

I 2   of

of the Treaty; for though in the League with *England* it is mentioned, yet there is nothing of any conceſſion granted by the ſame, but only recognized there as a Fundamental of the Crown and Dignity of the Kings of *England*; nor was the ſame ever ſo much as mentioned in any former Treaty before *Cromwell*'s time, as we have already mentioned, but it was always a Clauſe in the Inſtructions of the *Admiral* and the Commanders under him   That in caſe they met with any Ships whatſoever on the *Britiſh* Seas that refuſed to ſtrike Sail at the Command of the King's *Admiral* or his Lieutenants, that then they ſhould repute them as Enemies (without expecting any declared War) and deſtroy them and their Ships, or otherwiſe ſeize and confiſcate their Ships and Goods, and theſe Inſtructions amongſt others continue to this day.   The like are given by the *Venetians* to their Captains in reference to the *Adriatick* Sea, and by ſeveral other Princes.

XII The Duty of the *Flag*, that had been ſo conſtantly paid to our *Anceſtors*, is of ſuch advantage to the continuing the Renown of this Nation, that it ſerveth to imprint *new Reverence* in *Foreigners* that render it, and adds new Courage to thoſe of our *Seamen* that exact it   And ſince we know how much it imports a State that it be *reverenced abroad*, and that *Repute* is the principal Support of any *Government*, it equally influenceth the Subjects at *Home* and *Foreign Allies* Abroad.   And as there is no Nation in the World more tender of their Honour than the *Engliſh*, ſo none more impatiently tolerate the diminution thereof.   With what reſentments would not only the more *Generous* and *Noble*, but even
the

the *popular* and *vulgar Seamen* deteſt this or any ſucceeding Age, ſhould they remit or loſe that *Regality*, thoſe Acknowledgments which their Predeceſſors with ſo much Glory aſſerted, and the Neglect whereof was always puniſhed as open *Rebellion?* The indignity of ſuch an Action being ſufficient to enflame the whole Kingdom The conſideration of which, beſides his Sacred Majeſty's own Royal Inclination to the ſame, and his evident teſtimonies never to abandon a Ceremony of ſo high a concernment, witneſs the expoſing the one half of his own heart, his *Royal Highneſs*, in the aſſerting the ſame, with ſuch *Fleets* and in ſuch *Battles*, that no age or time can ſhew a Memorial of the like, are cauſes ſufficient to create in us new flames of Love to thoſe *Royal Patriots* and Defenders of our *Rights* *Private Perſons* move in another Sphere, and act by other Rules than *Sovereign Powers*, the regard of Credit with them may oftentimes yield to thoſe of utility or other motives, the It is no policy *Publick* receives little injury thereby, nor is to attempt their Wiſdom queſtioned for ſuch punctilio's, the change of if they relinquiſh them for other emoluments old Cuſtoms or peace ſake, but Sovereigns cannot ſo tranſ- and Uſages, act, their Subjects the People participate in even errors their Honour and indignities, they have a and abuſes Property, a direct *Right* in the former *, *So-* are upon ſuch *vereigns* cannot alienate or ſuffer their Ho- an account nours to be impaired, becauſe it is not *really* legally tole- *theirs*, it appertains *to the Nation* univerſally, rated *In*

omnibus rebus vetuſtas ipſa plurimum

I 3 and habet dignita-

tis ita ut Maſſalienſes quorum præſtantiſſima creditur fuiſſe Reſpublica, laudentur eo nomine quod gladio ad puniendos fontes uſi ſint eadem à condita Urbe, quo indicarent in minimis quoque rebus antiquæ conſuetudinis momenta ſervanda Proxime enim ad Deum accedit Antiquitas, æternitatis quadam indagine Grot de Antiq Reipub Batav in Præfat

* *Vide* the Earl of *Shafteſbury*'s Speech to the Parliament, 1672

Cæteri

Cæteris mortalibus in eo stare confilia, quid fibi conducere putent Principum diverfam effe fortem, quibus præcipua rerum ad fummam dirigenda. Tacit. Annal lib 4. Si fama tua videtur neceffaria, rectam muneris tui adminiftrationem non poteft condonare. Leffius de Inft l 2 c 11. dub 24 § 26

and they are all effectually injured by such Tranfactions, either becaufe the indignity really extends *to them*, or becaufe the *Government* and *Authority* is thereupon *weakened* and prejudiced, which is the greateft of *Civil detriments* that can befal a People, tho' *ordinarily* they are not aware thereof.

As Prudence doth thus diftinguifh betwixt the Demeanor of *private* and *publick* Perfons, fo doth *Charity* itfelf; for though the *Gofpel* precepts do oblige particular Perfons to bear Injuries and Contumelies with patience, and to furrender even the *Coat* as well as the *Cloak*; yet is not this fo to be conftrued, as if even private *Chriftians* were to yield up their *Civil Rights* to every infolent one that would incroach upon, and ufurp them, or that they were to *deprive* themfelves of thofe *Reparations*, which the *Law* and *Government* affords them; neither is it fo to be underftood, as if the *Civil Magiftrate* in *Chriftendom* might not fecure himfelf of that Obedience and Reverence, which is due unto Dignity, but *bear the Sword in vain*.

XIII This being the *value* which this Nation did always place upon the *Right of the Flag*, the which they never did regard only as a Civility and Refpect, but as a principal Teftimony of the unqueftionable Right of this Nation to the Dominion and Superiority of the adjacent Seas, acknowledged generally by all the Neighbour *States* and *Princes of Europe*, and muft be paid and acknowledged

by

by all *Princes* in the *World*, that shall be, or pass on the same

The Effects of this *Dominion Universal*, or *Sovereignty* which accrue to a *Prince* are these :

1. Not only the Regality of the fishing for Pearl, Coral, Amber, &c. but likewise the Advantage of all Fish Royal, as Whales, Sturgeon, &c. and not only those, but also the direction and disposal of all other Fish, according, as they shall seem to deserve the regards of the Publick, as in *Spain, Portugal,* &c. is used. *Joan. Palatius de Dom Maris, lib.* 1. *c.* 11 5 *Coke* 107

2 The prescribing of Laws and Rules for Navigation, not only to his own Subjects, but unto others Strangers, whether they be Princes of equal strength and dignity with himself, or any way inferior   Thus the *Romans* did confine the *Carthaginians* to equip out no Fleets , and forbade *Antiochus* to build any more than twelve Ships of War   And if Tradition informs me right, Queen *Elizabeth* inderdicted the then *French* King to build any other or more Ships of War than what they then had, without her leave first obtained   The *Athenians* prohibited all *Median* Ships of War to come within their Seas, and prescribed to the *Lacedæmonians* with what manner of Vessels they should sail   All Histories are full of such Precedents, which Princes have enacted, either upon Agreements enforced upon the Conquered, or Capitulations betwixt them and others (their equals or inferiors) for mutual Conveniences. *Grotius de Jure Belli l* 2. *c.* 3. § 15.

3. The Power of imposing Customs, Gabels, and Taxes upon those that navigate in their Seas, or otherwise fish therein , which they do upon several rightful Claims, as protecting them from Pirates, and all other Acts of Hostilities, or assisting them with Lights *Joan. Palatius ubi supra Julius Paucius de Dom Maris Adriatici.*

I 4   and

and Seamarks, for which advantages common
13 H 3 fol
14. 5 Coke 63. Equity obligeth thofe that reap benefit thereby, to repay it with fome acknowledgment,
which ought to be proportioned according
to the favour received, and the Expence which
the Prince is at to continue it unto them.

4. As it is incumbent on a Prince duly to
execute Juftice in his Kingdoms by Land, fo
the Sea being his Territory, it is requifite
and a necessary effect of his Dominion, that
he caufe Juftice to be adminiftred in cafe of
Maritime Delinquencies

5. That in Cafe any Ships navigate in
thofe Seas, they fhall falute his floating Caftles, the Ships of War, by *lowering the Top-
fail, ftriking the Flag* (thofe are the moft ufual
Courfes) in like manner as they do his Forts
upon Land, by which fort of Submiffions
they are put in remembrance, that they are
come into a Territory, wherein they are to
own a Sovereign Power and Jurifdiction, and
receive Protection from it

Thefe are the proper Effects of a real and
abfolute Sovereignty over the Seas, which how
they are poffeffed by the *Venetians*, this
enfuing Account will declare

The Gulph of *Venice* is nothing elfe but a
large Bay or Inlet of the Sea, which entring
in betwixt two Lands, and fevering them for
many Miles continuance, in the end receives
a ftop or interruption of further Paffage by
an oppofite Shore, which joins both the oppofite Shores together. It is called the
Gulph of *Venice*, from the City of *Venice*,
fituate upon certain broken Iflands near unto
the bottom thereof, it is alfo called the
Adriatick Sea, from the ancient City *Adria*,
lying not far diftant from the former, from
the

the Entrance thereof unto the Bottom it contains about fix hundred *Italian* Miles, where it is broadeft it is an hundred and fixty Miles over, in others but eighty, and in moft an hundred. The South-Weft Shore is bounded with the Provinces of *Puglia* and *Abruzzo* in the Kingdom of *Naples*, the Marquifate of *Ancona* and *Romagnia* in the Pope's State; and the Marquifate of *Trevifana* in the *Venetian* State The North-part of it, or Bottom, hath *Friuli* for its bounds, the North-Eaft is limited by *Iftria, Dalmatia, Albania*, and *Epirus*, whereof *Iftria* doth not fo entirely belong to the *Venetians*, but that the Emperor, as Arch-Duke of *Gratz*, doth poffefs divers Maritime Towns therein, in *Dalmatia*, faving *Zara, Spalato* and *Cataro*, they have nothing of importance, the reft belonging to *Ragufa* and the *Turks* · In *Albania* and *Epirus* they poffefs nothing at all, it being entirely the *Turks*, fo that he who fhall examine the circuit of the Sea, which muft contain about twelve hundred Miles, fhall find the Shores of the *Venetian* Signory, not to take up two hundred of them, omitting fome fcattered Towns and difperfed Iflands lying on the *Turkifh* fide of the *Adriatick* Shore.

'Tis very true of late by the great Conduct and good Fortune of the Generals *Morofini* and *Coningfmarke*, they have now got *Alba Regalis*, and almoft the principal parts of the *Morea*

For the fecuring hereof from the depredations of Pirates, and the pretences of divers potent Princes, as the Pope, Emperor, King of *Spain*, and the Great *Turk*, who each of them have large Territories, lying thereupon; alfo to caufe all Ships which navigate the fame to go to *Venice*, and there to pay Cuftom and other Duties, the Republick maintains continually in action a great number of Ships, Gallies, and Galliots, whereto alfo they add more, as there may be occafion, whereof
fome

some lie about the bottom of the Gulph in *Istria*, others about the Islands of *Dalmatia*, to clear those parts of Pirates, who have much infested those Seas, and others, and those of most force, have their station in the Island of *Corfu* and *Standia*; in the first of which commonly resides the Captain of the *Gulph*, whose Office is to secure the Navigation of the *Gulph*, not only from the *Corsairs*, but provide, that neither the Gallies or Ships of the Pope or King of *Spain*, nor Great *Turk*, do so much as enter the same, without permission of the Signiory, and upon such conditions as best please them, which they are so careful to effect, that in the Year 1638 the *Turkish* Fleet entring the *Gulph* without Licence, was assailed by the *Venetian* General, who sunk divers of their Vessels, and compelling the rest to fly into *Valona*, he held them there besieged, although the same City and Port whereon it stands, be under the Jurisdiction of the *Grand Signior*, and notwithstanding that a great and dangerous War was likely to ensue thereupon betwixt the *Grand Signior* and the *Republick*, because the *Venetian* General being not content to have chased them into their own Ports, did moreover sink their Vessels, and landing his Men slew divers of their Mariners, who had escaped his fury at Sea, yet after that a very honourable Peace was concluded again betwixt them, wherein amongst other Things it was agreed, That it should be lawful for the *Venetians*, as often as any *Turkish* Vessels did *without their licence enter the Gulph*, to seize upon them by force, if they would not otherwise obey And that it should likewise be lawful for them so to do, within any Haven,

Baptista Nani his History of Venice, lib 11. fol. 446, 447, 448

Haven, or under any Fort of the *Grand Signior's*, bordering on any part of the *Venetian
Gulph*. So jealous hath this Republick been
in all times to permit any to fail the *Gulph*,
that in the Year 1630, (as *Palatius* relates) *De Dom Ma-*
Mary, Sister to the King of *Spain*, being *ris, l 2 c 6*
espoused to the Emperor's Son *Ferdinand*,
King of *Hungary*, the *Spaniards* designed to
transport her from *Naples* in a Fleet of their
own.   The *Venetians* suspected that they had
an intention hereby to intrench upon, and
privily to undermine, by this specious Precedent, that Dominion of the Sea, which the
Signiory had continued inviolate *Time out of
mind*, and that they took this Opportunity
when *Venice* was involved with a War abroad,
and infested with the Plague at home, and
therefore not in a condition to oppose their
Progress The *Spanish* Ambassador acquainted
the State, that his Master's Fleet was to
convoy the Queen of *Hungary*, being his
Sister, from *Naples* to *Trieste* The Duke
replied, That her Majesty should not pass
but in the Gallies of the Republick; the
Spaniard repined thereat, pretending that
they were infected with the Plague The
Senate being consulted, came to this Resolution, That the Sister of his Catholick Majesty should not be transported to *Trieste* any
other way, than by embarking in the *Venetian*
Gallies, according to the usual manner of the
Gulph, and that, if the Ambassador would
acquiesce therein, her Majesty should be at-
tended and used with all that respect and de-
ference which became her Quality *But if
she proceeded any other way, the Republick
would by force assert her proper Rights, and
attack the* Spanish *Navy as if they were declared*
Ene-

Enemies, and in hostile manner invaded them.
Whereupon the *Spaniard* was compelled to
desire the favour of them to transport the
Queen in their Gallies, which *Antonio Pisani*
did perform with much State and Ceremony,
and the Courtesy was acknowledged by
solemn Thanks from the Courts of the Emperor, and of *Spain*

XIV. The *Maritime Dominion* by the *Laws*
of *England* were always accounted the *Four
Seas*, such as are born thereon are not *Aliens*,
and to be within them is to be within the
Ligeance of the *King* and *Realm* of *England*

The Records in the days of *Edward the
Third* and *Henry the Fifth* proclaim it, that
those Kings and their *Progenitors* had ever
been *Lords of the Sea*; and amongst those
many great Instances of proving the *Sovereignty* of the same, is that famous Record of
Edward the First and *Philip the Fair* of *France*,
in which were the *Procurators* of most Nations bordering upon the Sea, throughout
Europe, as the *Genoeses*, *Catalonians*, *Almaines*,
Zelanders, *Hollanders*, *Friezelanders*, *Danes*,
and *Norwygians*, besides others under the
Dominion of the *Roman German Empire*,
where all jointly declare, " That the Kings
of *England*, by right of the said Kingdom
from time to time, whereof there is no memorial to the contrary, have been in peaceable possession of the Sovereign Lordship of
the Seas of *England*, and of the Isles within
the same, with power of making and establishing Laws, Statutes, and Prohibitions of
Arms, and of Ships otherwise furnished than
Merchant-Men use to be, and of taking surety, and affording safeguard in all cases where
need shall require, and of ordering all things
necef-

*Selden Mare
Clauf. l 2 c
21 Fitzherb
protection, tit
46*

*Seld ibid. c
23 Coke 4.
Instit. fol
142*

*1 Ro Alb. 528.
pl. 2.*

necessary for the maintaining of Peace, Right *Vide* part of and Equity, among all manner of People, the Record. as well of other Dominions as their own, passing through the said Seas, and the Sovereign Guard thereof."

By which it plainly appears, That the King of *England* had then been in peaceable possession of the said *Dominion* by immemorial Prescription, that the Sovereignty belongeth And the Case unto them, not because they were *Domini* 27 *Eliz in utriusque ripæ*, when they had both *England* B R. \Sir and *Normandy*, and were Lords of both *John Constable's, Leonard,* Shores; (for *Edward the First* at that time had 3 *par* 72. not *Normandy*) but that it is inseparably ap- The reason of pendant and annexed to the Kingdom of *Eng-* the opinion *land*, our Kings being *superiour Lords of the* taken, for the *said Seas*, by reason (as the very Record rightunto the mentions) of the said Kingdom, and since Sea ariseth that the Sovereignty of the Sea did always possession of appertain unto the *English King*, not in any for the Sea *other Right than that of the Kingdom of* Eng- and Land land, no Prince or Republick ought or can make distinct doubt the Title by which our present Claim Territories, is deduced, 'tis in right of *Britannia*, that laws of *Eng-* the same is challenged, 'twas in that right the *land*, the *Romans* held it. Land is called the Realm,

but the Sea the Dominion, and as the loss of one Province doth not infer that the Prince must resign up the rest, so the loss of the Land Territory doth not by Concomitancy argue the loss of the adjacent Seas It is no more necessary that every Sea Town should command an hundred Miles at Sea, than that each City should command an hundred Miles by Land *Julius Paucius de Domin Maris Adriatici*

The claim justified *Edward the Third* and his *Rose Noble*, though there are other reasons regarding the *Lancastrian* Line, which yield a Colour for the use of *Port-cullis* in the *Royal Banners* of *England*, yet as in reference to the *Maritime Dominion*, *Henry the Eighth* did embellish his *Navy Royal* therewith, and

Queen

Queen Elizabeth ftamped it upon thofe *Dollars* which fhe defigned for the *Eaft India* Trade, fignifying her power of fhutting up the Seas if fhe thought fit (as by a *Port-cullis*) with the *Navy Royal*, this *Dominion* of the *Britifh Seas* did authenticate the Proclamation of King *James*, ordaining the *Flemifh* at *London* and *Edinburgh* to take Licence to fifh. This juftified the like Proclamation by King *Charles* I and warranted by the *Earl of Northumberland* in his Naval Expedition.

Anno Domini 1600

Anno Domini 1609

Anno Domini 1636

Will Fulbeck's Paudeas of the Law of Nations, *cap* 4.

     That *Prefcription* is valid againft the *Claims* of Sovereign Princes cannot be denied, by any who regard the *Holy Scripture, Reafon*, the *practice* and *tranquillity* of the World. And that true it is, the modern *Dutch* have pretended, if not dared, to challenge the Freedom to fifh in the *Britifh Seas*, by *Prefcription*, but it is likewife as true, that *Prefcription* depends not upon the *Corporeal* but the *Civil* Poffeffion, and that is retained, if *claim* be but made fo often as to *barr* the *Prefcription*, the which hath been always made evident, firft by frequent *Medals*, next by punifhing thofe that refufed it as Rebels, by guarding of it, and laftly by giving Laws time out of mind on it, which evidently proves, that the civil Poffeffion is not relinquifhed; and our Kings conftantly claiming the Dominion of the fame, none elfe pretending, all Nations acknowledging it to be in them, and the fame never queftioned, 'till thofe modern *Dutch* (of yefterday) arofe.

The King againft Sir *John Byron*. *Bridgman, fol* 23, 24, 25.

     XV. The Importance of the Dominion of the Sea unto this Nation, is very great, for on that alone depends our Security, our Wealth, our Glory, from hence it is, that *England* hath a Right to all thofe Advantages and

and Emoluments, which the *Venetian* Republick draws from the *Adriatick* Sea, where the Ships of the *Grand Signior*, of the *Emperor*, King of *Spain*, and *Pope* pay Cuftoms, to maintain thofe *Fleets*, which give Laws to them within the *Gulph*, 'tis hereby that the *Englifh* can fhut up or open thefe Seas for Ships or Fleets to pafs or repafs them, whereto Queen *Elizabeth* had fo fpecial a regard, that when the King of *Denmark* and the *Hanfiatick* Towns follicited her Majefty to permit them free paffage, they tranfporting Corn into *Spain*, fhe refufed them; and when a *Proteftant Fleet of Hamburgers* and others, had prefumed to do fo, notwithftanding her prohibition, fhe caufed her *Naval Royal* to feize, take, burn, and fpoil them, when they were paffed her Maritime Territory, within fight of *Lifbon*; yielding this reafon for her juftification, That they not only relieved her enemy with provifions, but " had prefumptuoufly made ufe of her Seas, without obtaining her Royal Permiffion for fo doing." 'Tis from hence, that the Crown of *England* can juftly demand an account of any Ship or Ships occurring in thofe Seas, what their Bufinefs, and what their Intentions are; and prohibit any Prince or Republick to enter there with potent Fleets, without pre-acquainting his Majefty, and obtaining his Royal Permiffion, without which Dominion and Sovereignty, *England* can never live fecure on fhore; it being eafy for any Foreign Fleets to amufe us with fpecious pretences, and in their paffage to invade and furprife us. Thus while the *Turk* pretended to fail for *Malta*, he occafionally poffeffed himfelf of *Canea*, in the Ifle of *Candia*,

Vide poftea in Cap of Cuftoms *June* 30 *Anno* 1598

Selden, *lib* 1. *cap.* 11

dia, and after having tasted the sweet of that place, never forsook it, till he made himself Master of the whole. Many such Precedents do occur in History And in fear of such Surprizal, the *Athenians* (being Lords at Sea) did exclude the *Persian* Monarchs from sending any Ships of War into any part of the *Ægean, Rhodian, Carpathian,* and *Lydian* Seas, and that which tends to the *West,* towards *Athens,* the like caution was used by the *Romans* against *Antiochus* and the *Carthaginians,* and the *Turk* prohibits all Nations, saving his Vassals, to enter the *Black Sea* or *Pontus Euxinus,* and also the *Red Sea;* and 'tis by virtue and force of this Right, that the *British Nation* can drive on their own Commerce, navigate themselves, and permit others securely to trade with them 'Tis true, that the *Dutch* have presumed some years since, to *violate* the security of the *British Seas,* by attacking the Allies of *England,* not only within the *British Seas,* but in her *Harbours,* attempting to pursue a *French* Vessel up almost to *London,* and have more than once * attacked the *Spanish* Fleets in her Roads, under the protection of her Castles, and that against the *Laws of Nations,* and the *Peace of Ports,* in which for the time they seemed to cloud the *Honour* of the *Nation,* but satisfaction for Indignities of that nature, though *slow,* yet are *sure,* and should such as those have been longer tolerated, beloved *Britannia* must become a prostitute, by a confederation of those *States,* or take *Pass-ports* for her Commerce, but the *Royal Martyr's* Goodness was no longer to be trod on, his Heart and his Cause were good, and though those unhappy Times (which were crooked

to

Alberi Gentil. Hisp. Advocat. l 1 c.14. *Vide* Mr Secretary *Cook's* Letter to Sir *Will. Boswel,* April 16, 1635.

* The fight of the *Dutch* with the *Spanish* Fleet in the *Downs,* 1639 *Scilicet hoc factum Hollandorum est contra justitiam omnem pro certo & contra reverentiam quæ partibus & territoriis debetur alienis* Alb Gent.

to whatsoever seemed streight) did hinder the
accomplishment of his entire intention for *Sa-*
tisfaction, yet those whom the just *God of*
Heaven was pleased for a time to permit as a
punishment to this Nation to rule, did not
want in the *fulfilling*; for so soon as he was
pleased to stay the fury of the *Intestine Sword,*
their Hearts took *fire* from those *flames* that
had formerly been kindled in that *Royal*
Breast, and having prepared a Fleet, in order to the treating as Soldiers with Swords
in their Hands, they were in the like manner assaulted in their Territories in the *Downs*
(but the *Dutch* found then what it was (tho'
two for one) to assault a *British Lion* at the
mouth of his *Den*) intending, if possible, to
have destroyed the *English Power*, but were
frustrated in their design, being severely
beaten home to their own doors, and afterwards those that then had got the *English*
Sword in their hands, begun to consider that
the *Victory* must be pursued as a season fit
to assert their *Antient Right* and *Sovereignty*
of the Sea, and then those People thinking
that the odds before was not enough to destroy the *British Fleet*, they equipt out a Fleet
greater and far more numerous than the *Eng-*
lish, under the *Admirals*, *Van Trump*, *De Wit*,
the two *Evertsons* and *Kuyter*; but they suffered the same Fate as their former, about
some thirty four of their *Ships* on the coast of
Flanders, burnt and taken, and the rest chased home to their Ports, and not long after
followed the total defeat of their *Naval*
Forces, accompanied with the death of *Van*
Trump by the *English*, under the *Admirals*,
Blake and *Monk*, who had sunk and fired
about thirty more of their *Ships of War* (no

Hisp. Advo-
cat lib. 1.
cap. 14.

Anno Domini
1552.

June 2 and 3.

About the 8th
of *Aug* 1653.

quarter

quarter being given till the end of the Battle) six *Captains* and about a thousand *Men* were taken Prisoners, and about six thousand slain.   Of their *Presumptions* since (amongst other things) in denying the Duty of the *Flag*, and what punishment and check they have had for the same, to what condition they have been reduced, and made to acknowledge *that Dominion and Superiority* to that Crown (under which their *Ancestors* humbly * besought the acceptance of the *Sovereignty* of the *Netherlands*, might be annexed and protected) is now fresh in our memories ; so high and of so great Importance is this *Dominion* and *Sovereignty* signified by the *Duty of the Flag in the British circumjacent Seas.*

* Offered to Queen *Eliz. Cette cy entre autres merite bien une consideration speciale, Que la conjunction desdits Pays de Hollande, Zelande, Frieze, & des Villes de l'Escluz, & Ostende en Flanders, avec les Royaumes de vostre* Majesté, *emporte & soit l'Empire de la Grande Mer Oceane; & par consequent une assurance & Felicité perpetuelle pour les Subjects de vostre* Serenissime Majesté *John Stowe's* Supplement to Hollinshed, An. Dom 1585. *Vide* Sir *Walter Ralegh, lib.* 5 *cap.* 2. § 2 & 3.

CHAP.

CHAP. VI.

Of the Right of Pressing or Seizing of Ships or Mariners for Publick Service.

I. *That such Right is excepted in the Law of Dominion.*

II. *Whether the Ships of Nations who are in War at the same time, may be pressed, the danger being equal*

III. *Whether this Right extends to Ships to fight, and no more, or gives a Power to trade*

IV. *By the Laws of England the King may seize.*

V. *The reason why such a power was vested in the Admiral*

VI. *That such a Right of compelling Men to serve in Naval Expeditions may be.*

VII. *Objections legal refuted*

VIII. *Of the antient punishment of deserters of the King's service.*

IX. *Concerning the several Statutes now in force touching Mariners and Soldiers*

X. *Whether it be lawful for a private Man to execute Justice on such as fly and desert the service.*

XI. *Where a general Commission is given to Men to execute Justice*

XII. *Several Cases touching the Admiralty and their Jurisdiction. Ships or Boats found at Sea, Royal Fish and Deodands belong to the Admiralty.*

I. THE *Civil Law*, though it can command nothing which the *Law of Nature* forbids, nor forbid what it commands; nevertheless it may circumscribe natural Liberty, and prohibit what was naturally lawful, and also by its force *antevert* that very Dominion, which is naturally to be acquired. Hence it is that Princes, by the Law of Nations, may acquire a Right of use of things

K 2   that

that do belong to private Perfons, for property hath not (as hath been faid) fwallowed up all that *Right,* which rofe from the common ftate of things; becaufe as all Laws are to be conftrued as near as poffible to the intention of the Makers, fo we muft confider what was the mind of thofe that firft introduced fingular Dominions   Now the Rules to conftrue that muft be near as poffible to natural equity, and that in extrême neceffity that old right of ufing things fhould revive, as if the things had remained common, the fame ftanding with the Intereft of all human Conftitutions, and therefore in the Law of Dominion extreme Neceffity feems excepted. Hence it is, that the Veffels and Ships of what nature and nation foever † that fhould be found riding in the Ports or Havens of any Prince or State, may be feized on, and employed upon any fervice of that Sovereign that fhall feize the fame, being but a harmlefs utility, not divefting the Owners of their Intereft or Property.

II. If a Ship of the King of *Denmark* be in the Port of *London,* and the *Swede* is in War with that Prince; and it happens at that time the King of *Britain* is in War with the *Spaniard,* now the Poffeffor is here preffed with an equal neceffity, and by the fame argument is rather obliged to the defence of his own Country than another, whether by the Law of Nations the Ship ought to be detained, hath been doubted, moft certain it may. Who would not pluck a fhipwrackt Man from his plank, or a wounded Man from his Horfe, rather than fuffer himfelf to perifh? To flight which is a fin, and to preferve the higheft of Wifdom, befides, in the taking of of the Veffel the right is not taken from the Owner, but only the ufe, which when the neceffity is over, there is a condition of reftoring annexed tacitly to fuch a feizure.

And doubtlefs the fame Right remains to feize the *Ships of War* of any Nations, as well as thofe of private intereft, the which may be employed as occafion fhall prefent: So the *Grecians* feized * on Ships of all Nations that * *De Expedi-* were in Ports, by the advice of *Xenophon*, but *tione Cyri* in the time provided food and wages to the Mariners.

III Whether this Right extends fo far as to give Princes a Power to feize in order to traffick may be fome queftion; certainly if the Traffick may be for fuch Commodities, as Mafts, Timber, Tar, Powder, Shot, or 10 *Ed* 3 *m.* other Commodities or Accoutrements of 16 12. Arms, or Naval Provifions of offence neceffary for the defence of the Realm, it may be done (but then it is juft *freight* fhould be paid) 23 *Ed* 1. for what hurt can it do me to let another have *Rott* 77 in my Boat to pafs over the Ford, if he rewards the Exchequer. me? And if that be anfwered, the Owners are at no prejudice, for this is but a harmlefs utility

IV By the Laws of *England* there is no 12 *E* 3. in queftion, but the King may feize, and it appears by very many antient Records, that he Book of the might do it, and it was one of the Articles of Admiralty. Enquiry amongft others, " Item, foit enquis P 26 and 27 de Nefs, que font arreftees pour le fervice du 6 *Joh* m 11. Roy, ou pour autre raifonable caufe per les 9 *Joh* m 3 Officers du Roy, ou de l'Admiral, et debri- 24 *E* 2 *m.* 17. fent l'Arreft, et par les quelles avandictes *Rott Franc.* Nefs font emmenez, et retamer les Mariners qui font ordonnez pour le fervice du Roy, et fi retracent, et en cas que homme foit endite

qui la debrufe l'Arreft en fa Nef arreftee pour
le fervice du Roy, et de ce foit convicte par
xi il perdra fa Nef fi'l na grace du Roy ou
du hault Admiral, et pour ce quil a efte plufieurs fois debatu en Angleterre pour les ar-
reftes des Nefs, quant le Roy amande Sergeants
d'Arms, ou autre Miniftres pour arrefter Nefs
al oeps du Roy, et les Se gneurs des Nefs font
venus devant l'Admiral, et alleguent que
leurs Nefs neftoient mye arreftees, ordonne
eftoit au temps du Roy *Richard le Premier a
Grimfby* per advis de plufieurs Seigneurs du
Royalme, que quant Nefs feront arreftees pour
fervice du Roy, que le Roy efcripta par fes
Lettres Patentes a l'Admiral d'arrefter les
Nefs plus ou moins a la voulonte du Roy, et
felon ce quil a befoin, et l'Admiral efcripta
au Roy ou au Chanceler d'Angleterre les
Noms des Nefs ainfi arreftees affemblement
avec les noms des Seigneurs et Maiftres
d'icelles, et en tel cas le seigneur de la Nef
ne la Maiftre ne viendrout pas a dire que la
Nef neftoit mye arreftee ne a ce ne feront oyz,"
and that upon fuch Arrefts broken, the Parties might be punifhed and fined

De Offc. Ad-
miral. Angliæ
per Roughier,
Artic 10.
Again, *Inquiratur fi arreftatus, ad fer viendum
Regi fregit arreftum, hujufmodi tranfgreffor ftat
in gratia Regia five Admiralli fui utrum voluerint committere Carceribus mancipandum vel
finem facere, in hac parte fi arreftum hujufmodi
fatium manifeftum fuerit cognitum*

The Black-
Book of the
Admiralty,
fol. 28, 29. &
157, 158
15 R 2 c 3
If the *Admiral* by the King's Command
arrefts any Ships for the King's Service, and
he or his Lieutenant return and certify the
Arreft, or a Lift of the Ships arrefted into
Chancery, no Mafter or Owner of the Ships fo
arrefted fhall be received to plead againft the
Return, " pur ceo que l'Admiral et fon Lieutenant font de Record."   Item,

Item, *Inquirendum de omnibus Navibus quæ ad serviendum Domino Regi super mari arrestatæ fuerint, & postea Domini, possessores, sive Magistri dolo & fraude à servitio hujusmodi se subtraxerunt in deceptionem Domini Regis, qui si inde postea indictati fuerint, & convicti super hoc, naves suæ Domino Regi forisfactæ per ordinationem Domini Regis* Richard Primi; *& si Domini, Possessores, vel Magistri hujusmodi inde coram Domino Rege & Cancellario suo per aliquas allegationes se aut naves hujusmodi excusare voluerint, si Admirallus vel locum tenentes sui per Literas suas Patentes de arresto hujusmodi facto fidem fecerint pleniorem, Domini, Possessores, aut Magistri prædicti nullo modo audiri debeant, seu eis fides quovis modo adhiberi, eo quod Admirallus & locum tenentes sui sunt de recordo.*

And if the Ship so arrested break the Arrest, and the Master or Owner thereof be indicted and convicted, *devant l'Admiral,* by the Oath of twelve men, the Ship shall be confiscate to the King, which power the *General* maintains in all places where he has power, and the same seems to be provided for in the latter *Clause of* 15 R. 2. *Ca* 3 *Croke's Arg. in Hampden's Case, fol* 79, *to* 100. *Vide* State Trials, Vol. I.

IV. By King *Ethelred,* his *Bishops* and *Nobles* in the General Council of *Enham, Anno* 1009, for the setting out a Fleet every Year, and the punishment of those who hurt or spoiled any Ship, or deserted the Service, especially if the King was present in the Expedition, amongst others it was enacted, *Si quis Navem in Reipub Expeditionem designatam vitiaverit, damnum integre restituito & Pacem Regis violatam compensato, si verò ita prorsus corruperit, ut deinceps nihili habeatur, plenam luito injuriam & læsam præterea Majestatem* So Sir *Henry Spelman's* Version out of the *Saxon* *Spelmanni Concil.* 520, 521.

K 4   Copy

Copy renders it, but the antient Copy hath it more largely

Spelman 528.
expeditio Na-
valis.

Naves per singulos annos ob patriæ defensionem & munitionem præparentur, postque Sacrosanctum Pascha cum cunctis utensilibus competentibus simul congregentur, qua igitur etiam pæna digni sunt, qui Navium detrimentum in aliquibus perficiunt? Notum esse cupimus, quicunque aliquam ex Navibus per quampiam inertiam vel incuriam, vel negligentiam corruperit, & tamen recuperabilis sit; is Navis corruptelam vel fracturam ejusdem per solidam prius recuperit, Regique deinde, ea quæ pro ejusdem munitionis fractu a sibimet pertinent, rite persolvat.

Most certain it is, that the Kings of *England* have in all Ages, by their *Writs* and *Patents*, commanded not only the *Admiral*, but the *Wardens* of the *Cinque-Ports* and others, to arrest and provide Ships of War, and other Vessels, and impress and provide Masters of Ships, Seamen, Mariners, and all other ne-

Ro: Scotiæ
10 E 3 m
2. to 17. and
then to 34
intus & dorf.
to 28

cessary Tackle, Arms, and Provisions for Ships, for the defence of the Sea and the Realm against foreign Enemies, or for transporting of Armies paying their Freight (if not bound thereto by tenure) as well as to elect and provide all sorts of Soldiers, Carpenters, and other Officers, to be assistants in their several Expeditions

1 Eliz cap.
13 Vide 16
17 Car 1.
c 5

But Fishermen or Mariners pressed for the Service, are not to be employed as Soldiers, but only as Mariners; unless it be in cases of great necessity, or bound thereunto by Tenure, Custom, or Covenant.

Court of Ad-
m alty erect-
ed by Ed 3

V. The reason why the *Admirals* had such power given them, was because they being sometimes called *Capitanei*, and *Gubernatores Flotarum*, they had the ordering and governing

ing of the Ships of War, and the raifing and fitting up fuch Ships for the Navies, as they thought fit, other times called *Cuftodes Maritimarum partium*, their dúty being to provide all Naval Provifions, as well to fupply the King's Navies occafions, as to gratify any other of the King's Friends, when diftrefs fhould conftrain them to touch in his Ports, that his Subjects might receive the like retaliation again, they were called *Capitanei Nautarum & Marinellorum*, as in reference to the deciding all differences amongft thofe in the King's Service, and punifhing of fuch as tranfgreffed, and as the place was great, fo the power was large, efpecially in all things belonging to the *Navy-Royal*, in which they had the fupreme rule and government in all things belonging to it He fate formerly in the King's Houfe, and there kept his Court, as the *French Admirals* do at this day at the *Marble-Table*, in the King's Houfe at *Paris*.

Spelman's Gloff. *in tit. Admir* Lambert *Archeion tit. Admiral.*

VI And altho' there feems no queftion but the King may prefs Ships, yet there have been thofe who feem to doubt, if not to queftion, whether he may prefs Men to ferve, for my own part I think he may, my Reafons are thefe It is lawful for every Man to addict and yield up himfelf to whom he pleafeth, as appears both out of the *Hebrew* Law and *Roman* Law, why then may not any People, being at their own difpofe, give up themfelves to their Prince or Sovereign, fo as to transfer the right of commanding their aid and help, as often as need fhall require (it is not here enquired what may be prefumed in a doubtful cafe, but what may be done in point of right) moft certain fuch a power may well be, and that grounded on great Reafon, as

Exodus xxi. 6 *Inft de Jure perfon §Servi autem* Gell l. 2. c. 7.

if

if the Commonwealth fhould happen to be invaded by fuch a one as feeks not only the fubverfion of the Government, but the deftruction of the People, and they can find no other way to preferve themfelves, but that the fupreme Power fhould be vefted with fuch a Prerogative, as to enforce or prefs the Inhabitants to ferve in Arms in the Defence of the fame, and the contempt of which to punifh; or if they fhould be opprefled with want, and that fupplies of Provifions can no ways be had, but by compelling another by force, to exhibit the common Offices of humanity to a Nation in whofe Territories a Famine rages, that the Inhabitants fhould on fuch extraordinary Occafions be compelled by force to ferve in Arms

And this Dominion may be obtained feveral ways, either by a voluntary Refignation to a Conqueror, as they of *Capua* to the *Romans, Our Land, the Temples of our Gods, all Divine and Humane things we yield up unto your hands, O ye confcript Fathers* Again, Freedom may be granted to all by a Conqueror, except Mariners, which fhould in Cafes of neceffity be excepted; or that fome Prince, who will not fuffer any Mariner to go out of his Dominions, without fubjecting themfelves to fuch a reafonable command, befides the Majority of Nations on fuch grounds may abdicate from a part of them the entire Freedom of that Member.

Tacitus. Nor are there examples of this kind wanting, the *Germans* are every one Mafter of his own Houfe, but are almoft on every occafion fubject to their *Lords*, efpecially in their

2 *Inf*. 358 Goods. The *Irifh Cofherers*, which were reprendinations, when the *Chief Lord* and his

Retinue

Retinue came to his Tenant's Houfe, they fed upon his Provifions till they were fpent, all being folely at their Devotion, And as to the Sea, the King of *Britain* may at this day reftrain Merchants or Mariners to pafs out of the Realm, without Licence; and the various tenures that are introduced, which is prefumed were fince the *Conqueft*, were no other but the Will of the *Conqueror*; for the right is not meafured by the excellency of this or that form, but by the Will

As to the impreffing of Seamen, it is ftrange that its Lawfulnefs fhould ever be called in Queftion, by any Perfon who has read our Hiftory or our Statute-Book. The Crown has been in poffeffion of it from Time immemorial And if a new Race of People were this Day to fpring out of the Earth to poffefs this Ifland, if we may at the fame Time fuppofe them to unite under one Civil Polity, and to be conufant of the Neceffity of naval Strength for their Defence, the Power of impreffing them for the Sea-Service would be implied in the executive Part of their Government, let it's Conftitution be what it might, *viz* limited Monaichy, Ariftocracy, or Democracy, or any compound of them, or fome of them But, as was hinted above, our Legiflature has frequently maintained this Power as undoubted Law See 2 *Ann ch.* 6 concerning Protections to be granted to Apprentices to be bound to the Sea-Service. But more explicit is a former Statute, *viz* 2 and 3 *P. & M. ch* 16 by which Watermen on the *Thames*, who abfcond in Preffing-Time, and then return to row, are made liable to Imprifonment for two Weeks, and to be banifhed to row upon the River by the Space of

2 *E.* 1 *Memb.*
18 *Rott Patt.*
2 *E* 1 *m* 17
Rot. fin. 31.
E 1 *num*
44 *Ro Pat.*
17 *H* 6 *Ro.*
Cla in dorf
Vide the Cafe of *Bates,* in *Lane Rep* 4.
Vide fupra Sec. 4 *ad finem.*

See *Foft* Cr. Law 154.
Clar. Hift Rebel Vol I. B 4 p 257. 325. Fol Edit Obferv. on Stat 271. 2d. Edit. *Clarend.* Contin. P. 341.

of a Year and a Day. See also 2 *R* 2. *ch* 4. and 5 *Eliz ch.* 5. *fect.* 41, 43.

VII And though it hath been conceived by fome, that the King cannot prefs Men to ferve in his Wars, giving their Reafon, that of old he was to be ferved either by thofe that held by tenure, thofe that covenanted by Indenture to provide Men, or thofe who contracted with the King's Officers for Wages and entered into Pay, or thofe that were in Prifon for the King's Debts; but that only extended to thofe Wars that were by Land, not one word in all thofe Acts, or Mufter *Rolls*, relating in the leaft to Mariners, and yet what vaft Fleets were in thofe Days? But on the other Hand it hath been always accuftomed to prefs fuch fort of Men for the Naval Expeditions. The ancient Records that mention fuch Perfons fubject to be preffed by Law is that of 29 *E* 3. commonly called * *The Inquifition of Queenborough*, wherein it was exprefsly in charge amongft others, to enquire of thofe Mariners that were preffed for the King's Service, and deferted the fame So likewife by thofe other Articles tranflated by *Roughton*, it is in exprefs charge to the *Jury*, to prefent thofe that being preft to ferve brake the King's Arreft, in order to their Punifhment, and in thofe days it was efteemed an high offence, and the Oath which the *Jury* then took being impanelled, was this.

" This here fee my Lord the Admiral, that I *Jonathan Nafh* fhall well and truly enquire for our Lord the King, and well and truly at this time then ferve at this Court of the Admiralty, prefent as moch, as I have acknowlech, or may have by Information of eny of my Fellows, of all maner Articles or Circumftances

margin notes:

1 *Inft.* 71 *a*

* 2. *Apr.* 49 *E.* 3 in the Black-Book of the *Admiralty,* 32, 33, 34 *Art* and *fel* 62 *Art* 10

ftances that touchen the Court of the Admirate and Law of the Sea, the which fhall be grate to me at this time, and thereupon fworn or charged, and of all other that may renew in my mind, and in fhall for nothing lette, that is for to fay, for Franchife, Lordfhip, Kinreden, Allience, Friendfhip, Love, Hatred, Envy, Enemitee, for dred of loft of Goodnee, for non other cafe that I fhall foe doe, the King's Counfeils, my fellows, mine own, will and truly hele without fraud or malengyn, fo God me help at the holy dome, *fol* 17 and by this Book "

The Black Book of the Admiralty,

VIII And as the enquiry was ftrict, fo was the punifhment very great *Item, qui fugiet à Demino vel, focio fuo pro timiditate belli vel mortis in conductione Heretochii fui in expeditione navali vel terreftri, perdat omne quod fuum eft, & fuam ipfius vitam, manus mittat Dominus ad terram quam ei antea dederat.*

Lamb. inter Leg Edovardi 139. 13 *Car* 2 *cap.* 9 Ar. 17

IX. In the Service of the King two forts of perfons were always capacitated to attend the *Naval Royal* in their Expeditions, the one a Salt-water Land-Soldier, the other a compleat Mariner or Sailor · It was a doubt, whether fuch a Soldier, departing from the Service, were fubject to any other punifhment than that of *Martial Law*, which can at no time be executed in *England*, but when the King's Standard is in the Field, thereupon it was provided, *That if any Soldier being no Captain immediately retained with the King, which fhall be in wages and retained, or take any preft to ferve the King upon the Sea, or upon the Land beyond the Sea, depart out of the King's fervice without licence of his Captain, that fuch departing be taken, deemed, and adjudged Felony. And that all the Juftices in every Shire of England,*

7 H 7 *cap* 1 § 2. *Cro Car.* 71.

3 H 8 *cap.* 5 § 2.

where

*where any fuch Offender be taken, have power
to enquire of the faid offences, and the fame to
hear and determine as they do and may do of Felony, &c. expreffed in the King's Commiffion to
them made, as though the fame offences were done
in the fame Shire. And alfo that the departing
of fuch Soldiers, and alfo their Retainers, if it
be traverfed, be tried in the fame Shire where
they are for fuch a Caufe arrefted and arraigned.*
The Juftices have here a concurrent power to
enquire and try, but it does not fhut out the
Sovereign Courts, or hinder but the King
may try them upon a Commiffion of Oyer and
Terminer, or Goal delivery   It was a doubt
conceived by fome of the late Judges, if a
Man had run from his Colours at *Plymouth*,
and afterwards was taken in *Midalefex*, and
committed to *Newgate*, whether after a Bill
is found in *Middlefex*, the Juftices of Goal-de-
livery for *Newgate* could try him ; but it was
ruled more than once by the greater number
of the Judges, they might; and fo have the
Precedents been always fince the making of
this Statute, and upon the like Reafon, that
a Man that takes a fecond Wife, hath by the
Statute the fame directions to be tried in the
fame Shire where he is taken ; yet if taken
in *Middlefex*, was always tried at the *Old-Baily*
in *London*

Thefe Statutes were made, becaufe the Statute of 18 *H.* 6 *cap.* 19. was looked upon not
to be fufficient, for that Act had reference only
to the ancient Tenures, and thofe that covenanted with the King to provide Soldiers ;
whereupon a queftion afterwards arifing,
whether feveral who having then taken preft ·
43 *Eliz.*   Money to ferve the *Queen* againft the Rebels
in *Ireland*, and had departed and withdrawn
themfelves

themselves from the Service, should be within those Statutes, in regard some doubt seemed to arise on the same; but it was resolved by all the Judges of *England*, that those two Statutes of 7 *H. 7. Cap.* 1. and 3 *H. 8. Cap* 5. are all one in effect, and were perpetual Acts The great doubt and question, whether the Statute of 18 *H 6. Cap.* 19. did extend to Mariners and Gunners serving on the Seas, and taking Wages of the King, was in Parliament not long before cleared in these Words : *That the said Statute made in the eighteenth Year of the Reign of* H. 6 *in all pains, forfeitures, and other things, did, doth, and hereafter shall extend as well to all and every Mariner and Gunner, having taken, or who hereafter shall take prest or wages to serve the Queen's Majesty, her Heirs and Successors, to all intents and purposes, as the same did, or doth unto Soldiers, any diversities of opinion, doubt, matter, or thing to the contrary thereof notwithstanding.* But now Mariners deserting the Sea-service are particularly within the Provision of 13 *Car 2 Cap.* 9 which hath made the Offence Death, but the Trial is by a *Court Martial.*

6 Coke, 27.

Rastal doubted in his Abridgment.

Article 17.

And Land-Soldiers, though in Time of Peace, are likewise within the Statute of 7 *Hen. 7. Cap* 1. and 3 *Hen. 8. Cap.* 5. if they take any prest Money to serve the King upon the Sea, or upon the Land, or beyond the Sea, and shall desert the Service; but that is inquirable according to the Course of the *Common-Law*, where if the party shall depart without Licence, he shall suffer Death, without benefit of the Clergy

X. If such Persons shall so desert the Service, it hath been a Question, whether a private Person,

Non solis ducibus alisque potentibus Inna-

Perfon, under the fame obedience meeting with fuch a Deferter, might not put him to death, it hath been conceived that he might, and the act is lawful, and the party that flays him hath a true Right before God, as impunity before Men. But that is to be underftood partly by the Words, and partly by the Letter of the Law: For if the Law gives indulgence to Paffion, it takes away human Punifhment, and not the Fault, as in cafe an Hufband kills an Adulterous Wife or the Adulterer * in the Act, moft certain it is a Provocation in the higheft nature, and will juftify the Slayer: But if the Law refpect the Danger of future Evil, by delay of Punifhment, it is conceived to grant right and publick power to a private Man; fo that he is not then in the capacity of a private Man.

of one *Manning*, found fpecially at *Surrey* Affizes before Mr Juftice *Twifden*, who flew the Adulterer in the very Act   *Ventr* 158, 159 *Kel* 137 *pl* 4 *T. Raym* 212. *2 Keb. Rep.* 829 *pl* 49 *Foft* Cr. Law, 296 *Hawk* Pl Cr 82. *pl* 36. *Vide* Auguft *de Civit Dei eatat.m.* C *quæ.unque caufa* 23 *qu* 8.

Ar. 25 Eliz.
Co Litt. 74. b. And upon that very Reafon Queen *Eliza-beth* denied the conftituting of a *Conftable*, for the Trial of Sir *Francis Drake*, who ftruck off the Head of *Doughty, in partibus tranf-ma,inis*

XI Hence it is, that every Man hath a Licence given him to oppofe force againft plundering, and pillaging Soldiers. And the next the fubfequent Law about Deferters faith,

Cod. Juftin
tit quando li-
ceat unicuique. *Let all men know they have a power given them againft publick Robbers and Deferters that run from their Colours, and all are Minifters of Revenge, for the quiet of all,* to this purpofe is that of *Tertullian, againft Traytors or publick Enemies every Man is a Soldier:* And herein differs

fers the right of killing of Exiles and Out-
laws, or thofe whom they call *Banditoes*, from It was in force
thofe kind of Laws, becaufe there proceeds in *England* till
a fpecial Sentence, the Judgment of Banifh- thebeginning
ment or Outlawly being promulgated, but of the Reign
here a general Edict, the Fact being evident, *Co Litt* 128
obtains the force of a Judgment or Sentence *b* 12 *H* 4 *f*
pronounced, the Judgment of the latter muft 4, 5 37 *H* 6.
be according to the *Civil Law*, which yet re- *fol* 3 *Mii c,*
mains ftill in force, as to the Trial of fuch 4 § 4.
Deferters, which Impunity for fuch killing
feems allowed of at this day by that Law.

XII Cafes relating to the Jurifdiction of
the Admiralty as to Matters fueable there, or
at the Common Law

The Trial fhall be where the Original Con- *Trial where*
tract is made, which if in *England*, tho' the *the Original*
fubfequent Matter to be done be upon the *Contract a-*
Sea, the Trial fhall be at the *Common Law. rifes.*
But if the Contract, and what is to be done all
of it is beyond Sea, it cannot be tried at Law
here, but in the *Admiralty*; but if part be to
be done here and part beyond Sea, fo as it is
mixed, then it fhall be tried at Law. As an
Action upon the Cafe upon a Policy of Affurance made at *London*, that a Ship fhall fail
from *Melcomb Regis* in the County of *Dorfet*
to *Abville*, in *France*, fafely, &c. And the
Plaintiff declared, that the Ship in failing towards *Abville*, viz in the River of *Soame* in
France, was arrefted by the King of *France*,
&c and the Iffue was, whether the Ship was fo
arrefted or not, the Trial was by *Nifi Prius*
in *London*, and refolved to be well brought,
tho' 'twas objected, that this Iffue arifing merely
from a Place out of the Realm, could not be
tried at Law, for the Affumpfit being at *Lon-*
don was the ground and foundation of the

Action, and therefore shall be tried here, for otherwise it could not he tried at all   Cited in *Dowdale*'s *Case*, 6 *Rep.* 47. *b. Godbolt* 76. and 204.

And so if the Contract be made at Land, tho' beyond Sea, the Trial shall be at Law, tho' what is to be done, be all of it beyond Sea, by laying the Contract made at a Place in *England*, as in *Bourdeaux apud Islington in Com. Middlesex*   So is the Case of *Slaney* and *Clobery* against *Cotton*, where the Plantiff sued the Defendant in the *Admiralty* Court upon a Promise made in *Barbary*, to sail from *Sirborona* in *Barbary* to *Ricumpta* in *Brazil*, &c. upon suggestion that the Contract was made in *London*, Prohibition was granted: For, by *Jones*, the performance of the consideration does not give the Action without the Contract, and this was made at Land, tho' beyond the Seas, which may be supposed to be done in a place in *England* 2 *Rolls Rep.* 486.   See *Tucker* and *Caff*'s Case in the same Book 492, and 497, and 2 *Brow.* 10, 11.

Matters beyond Sea not triable in an inferior Court A Contract was made at *Newcastle*, that a Ship should sail from *Yarmouth* to *Amsterdam*, Debt was brought upon this Contract, in the Court of *Newcastle*, adjudged, that the Action would not lie there, being a limitted Jurisdiction, which shall not have conusance of any matters done in *partibus transmarinis*, but only the Courts at *Westminster*, *March*'s *Rep* 3.

Praemunire for suing in the Admiralty. If one Libel in the Court of Admiralty for a thing done upon the Land, and it appeareth upon the Libel, that the thing was done upon the Land, and they notwithstanding that hold Plea of it, a *Praemunire* lyeth upon it, but if the same do not appear within the Libel, then it is not within the 13 of *R.* 2. *c.* 5 and

15 of *R. 2. c. 3.* but a Prohibition shall only issue, 2 *Leon* 183.

The Admiralty hath Jurisdiction of *Flot-zam Tresilian* against *Jones,* 2 *Keble* 361.

A *Dutch* Ship was broken by a great Tempest in a Creek of the Sea, *Infra Corpus Comitatus de Dorset*, the Sailors upon pretence that the Goods in the Ship were *bona peritura*, procured a Commission of Sale out of the Admiralty-Court to sell them, and the true Owners to prevent such Sale, brought a *Supersedeas*, and upon shewing the Libel to the Court, a Prohibition was granted (1) Because the Cause of Action accrued *infra Corpus Comitatus* (2) Because the Sale of the Goods was good, as *bona peritura*. *Culmer* against *Brand.* 2 *Sid* 81

One having taken a Ship as Prize, which had *bona peritura,* entered into a Recognizance with sureties before the Judges delegate, to bring the Money raised by Sale of the Goods in the Admiralty-Court before such a day, if they upon a Plaint there depending did not adjudge the Ship and Goods to be lawful Prize, which they adjudged lawful Prize, and after at another time cited the Owner before the Judges of the Admiralty, and for his not coming and bringing the Money at the day, they threatned to sue Execution against the Bail or Sureties who were Merchants of *London,* Prohibition was prayed, for by their first Judgment or Sentence, their Recognizance was discharged, and they ought not by Colour of this to endanger the Credit of Men of Reputation, but the Court would not grant a Prohibition, for they said, an unjust Sentence of the Admiralty, in a cause of which they have original Conusance, is not

Admiralty hath Jurisdiction of Flotzam Supersedeas to the Admiralty

Unjust Sentence in the Admiralty where they have original Conusance is no Cause for a Prohibition,

2 Sid 152 Becks, v Ghelycoke

L 2   a Cause

a Cause of Prohibition. As if Tithes which in verity are paid, are found not paid in the Spiritual Court, yet a Prohibition lies not, and here the Judges Delegate have sole Power upon this Recognizance, to make Execution or defeat it.

Suit there for not ballasting a Ship. The Corporation of *Trinity-House*, under pretence of Letters Patents from Queen *Elizabeth*, for the ballasting of all Ships within the Bridge of *London* and the Sea, and that no Ship should take Ballast of any other but of them, sued one *Boreman* (a *Dutch* Man) in the Admiralty for taking Ballast of another, within the Place aforesaid *Per Curiam* the Place being alledged to be at *Ratcliffe*, a Prohibition was granted; resolved that the Letters Patents were void, for that thereby a Charge is raised upon the subject for the private gain of the House, for they would not ballast a Ship under 2 d. *per* Ton

2 Brownl 13

13 Co 51. In the Case of Sir *Richard Hawkins*, Vice-Admiral of the County of *Devon*, who was prosecuted in the *Star-Chamber*, for abetting and comforting *Hull*, and other notorious Pirates. It was there resolved, that by the Common Law the Admirals ought not to meddle with any thing done within the Realm, but only with things done upon the Sea, and also by the Statute of 13 *R* 2. *St.* 1 *c.*5 2 *H* 4. *c.* 11

It was likewise resolved, that the said Statutes are to be intended to hold Plea, and not of a power to award Execution, for the Judge of the Admiralty, notwithstanding these Statutes, may do execution within the Body of the County.

13 Co 53. The Court of Admiralty is not a Court of Record, because they proceed there according to the *Civil Law.*   Where

Where one admits the Jurisdiction of the *Admiralty* by pleading there, no Prohibition shall be granted *Jennings* against *Audley*, 2 *Brow.* 30 12 *Rep.* 77. Therefore on Mo- Lord *Ray-* tion for a Prohibition in a Suit for Seamen's *mond,* 247 Wages, there the Suggestion was, that the Court below refused to allow the Defendant's Allegation, that the Place where the Plaintiffs entitled themselves, was not a Port of Delivery This is no Foundation for a Prohibition, if any thing it must be an Appeal.

Cradock bought divers Things within the Suit there for Body of the County, which concerned the Contract furnishing a Ship, as Cordage, &c. the Ven- upon Land der sued him in the *Admiralty* Court; a Pro- Prohibition hibition was granted, 2 *Brow.* 37 *Cradock*'s Case, *Owen* 122. 3 *Keble* 552. *Merryweather* against *Mountford.*

Note, No Appeal from the Admiralty before a Definitive Sentence. Lord *Raymond,* 1248.

The Defendant being Master of a Ship of 1 *Lev* 243 which the Plaintiff was Owner, the Ship was *Yelv* 135 173. taken by Pirates upon the Sea, and to redeem 1 *Sid.* 320. himself and the Ship, he contracted with the 2 *Sam* 260. Pirate to pay him 50 *l* and pawned his Per- 2 *Lev* 25 son for it, the Pirate carried him to the Isle 1 *Ven* 173. of *Scilly*, and there he paid it with Money 308 borrowed, and gave Bond for the Money 1 *Sid* 367 at his Return; after the Redemption both *Cro Eliz* of the Ship and himself, he sued in the *Admi-* 685 *ralty* for the 50 *l.* and had a Sentence for it, and thereupon a Prohibition to the *Admiralty* was prayed but denied, because the Original Cause began upon the Sea, and whatever followed was but accessory and consequential. *Hard* 183 Prohibition was granted to the *Admiralty* Court on the 22d and 23d *Ca.* 2.

cap. 26

cap 26 *Sect* 11. in Suit there for the Forfeit of a Ship on selling Wares in *Ireland* without breaking Bulk, being put into *Ireland* from *America*, by contrary Winds, this being triable in the Plantations or any Court of Record in *Westminster* *Pidgeon con Trent*, 3 *Keble* 640, 647, 651. (*Vide Librum*)

A Master of a Ship agreed with certain Merchants concerning a Voyage, and received Orders from them to lay in Provisions of Meat and Drink, and to provide Mariners, &c and after the Voyage was finished, the Merchants refused to pay the Master of the Ship what they had agreed for, upon which he libelled against them in the *Admiralty*; Prohibition was granted upon the Statute of 2 *R*. 2 *cap*. 3. the Contract being upon Land, and denied the Case, *Hill* 8. *Ca* 1. *Cra.* 296. which saith, that when a Thing is in its Nature Maritime, as in the Cases of Mariners Wages, the Admiralty shall have the Conusance of it. *Woodward* against *Bomthan*, *T Raymond* 3 and 3 *Leviaz* 60 *Coke* against *Cretcher*, &c 2 *Vent* 181.

Prohibition does not lie for Mariners Wages.

Contract not Marine made at Sea. If a Contract or Obligation be made upon the Sea, yet if it be not for a Cause Marine, the Suit upon this shall be at *Common Law*, not in the *Admiralty*, *Hob.* 11

Contract at Sea settled at Land. If the Original Contract be made at Sea, on a Marine Cause, and after reduced into Writing at Land, the *Common-Law* not *Admiralty*, shall have the Conusance. *Hob.* 79. 212 *Palmer* against *Pope*

If a Charter-Party be made in *England* to do certain things in divers Places upon the Sea, tho' that no Act is to be done in *England*, but all upon the Sea, yet no Suit shall be in the *Admiralty* for Non-performance of the

the Agreement; for the Contract is the Origi- *Common* nal and is out of their Jurisdiction, and where *Law pre-* part is triable at *Common-Law,* and part in *ferred* the *Admiralty,* the *Common-Law* shall be preferred. *Maldonado* and *Slaney,* 1 *Roll. Abr.* 532, 533.

A Contract laid to be made *infra fluxum &* 2 *Lord Ray-* *refluxum Maris, &c.* is well enough laid to *mond* 1453 give the Admiralty a Jurisdiction: It was upon the high Seas, when the Water was at High-Water-Mark; and it might be at Land when the Water was at Low-Water-Mark. In that Case, there is *Divisum Imperium* between the *Common-Law* and *Admiralty* Jurisdiction.

It was moved for a Prohibition to the *Ad-* *Prohibition* *miralty,* because the Libel was to execute a *to the Admi-* Sentence of the Alcade, which is the *Admiralty ralty for pro-* at *Malaga* in *Spain,* upon a thing done within *ceeding to* a Port there; and after a Rule for a Prohibi- *execute an* tion *nisi,* 'twas moved that no Prohibition *Sentence of a* should be, for tho' this Court will not exe- *Foreign Ad-* cute the Sentences of any Foreign Court, in *miralty.* as much that it is governed by a distinct Law, yet these of the *Admiralty* may, and this in their use to do so, for this that all the *Admi-* *ralty* Courts in *Europe* proceed by the same Law, *viz.* the *Civil-Law,* and *Wibrel* and *Ro Ab* 530. *Wint*'s Case 5 *Ja* was cited, to be adjudged *pl* 12. *T.* accordingly. But upon Reading the Libel *Raym* 473. in the Principal Case, it appears, that the Sentence was not Definitive, but Interlocutory, concerning a Matter that sounds as an Action upon the Case, and no Sum set; and also the Alcade is not as an *Admiralty* there, and for this a Prohibition was granted *Ju-* *rado* and *Gregory,* 1. *Sid.* 418. 1 *Levinz.* 267. 1 *Vent* 32. and 2 *Keble* 511. 610.

Refcous and Contempt triable there.

Motion for a Prohibition to the *Admiralty*, for that they libelled againſt one for reſcuing a Ship, and taking away the Sails from one that was executing the Proceſs of the Court, againſt the ſaid Ship, and for that in the preſence of the Judge and Face of the Court, he aſſaulted and beat one, and ſpake many opprobrious Words againſt him Now ſeeing that theſe Matters were determinable at Law, the Ship being *infra Corpus Comitātus*, and they could not adjudge damages to the Party, or Fine or Impriſon, a Prohibition was prayed, but denied, for they may puniſh one that reſiſts the proceſs of their Court, and may fine and impriſon for a contempt tho' they are no Court of Record, but if they ſhould proceed to give Damages, they would grant a Prohibition *quoad* that. *Sparkes, &c.* againſt *Martyn* 1 *Vent* 1. The ſame Doctrine Lord *Raymond*'s Reports, 446 and 1 *Vent.* is there cited.

Goods taken by Piracy, triable there tho' ſold at Land.
Yelv. 135, 173 *Hard.* 183. 1. *Sid* 320, 367. 2 *Saun* 260 2 *Lev* 25 1 *Ven* 173 See Chap. X S XIV

A Prohibition prayed to the *Admiralty*, where there was a Libel for a Ship taken by Pirates, and carried to *Tunis* and there ſold, for that it did not appertain to the Court to try the Property of the Ship being ſold upon Land. *Curia* in regard it was taken by Pirates, it is originally within the *Admiral* Juriſdiction, and ſo continues notwithſtanding the Sale afterwards upon the Land. Otherwiſe where the Ship is taken by Enemies, for that alters the Property. Contrary to my Lord *Hobart* in the *Spaniſh* Ambaſſador's Caſe 78. 1 *Vent* 308. *Cro. Eliz.* 685.

Ships found at Sea belong to the Admiral

If Ships or Boats are found on the Sea or upon the Coaſt, without any Living Creature therein, and no Man claiming the ſame within a Year and Day, the finder formerly uſed

to

to have one Moiety, and the Prince the other Moiety, but now 'tis left to the discretion of the Admiral what the finder shall have for his Travail, Charges, Danger. And if the finder conceal such Goods, whether belonging to the Ship, as Anchors, Timber or other Goods, he shall not only lose his Part, but be fined at the Will and Pleasure of the Admiral.

If Whales or other regal Fish, Ships, or Boats, without any living Thing in them, be driven by force of Wind or Waves only, to any Coast or Land, then all doth belong to the Admiral, *Lex. Mercat* 120 *Royal Fish Deodands.*

See more of this Matter, 4 *Inst.* 134, &c. of the Court of *Admiralty.* 1 *Roll Abr* 528, &c. Title Admiralty.

After Sentence in the *Admiralty* Court for the seizing of a Ship, Trover and Conversion at Law will not lie, *Beake contra Tyrrell,* 3 *Mod* 194 *Carth* 31. *Trover after Sentence will not lie.*

Hutchinson killed one *Colson* in *Portugal,* and was acquitted there of the Murder, the Exemplification of which Acquittal he produced under the Great Seal of that Kingdom, which by the Opinion of all the Judges was such an Acquittal by their Law, that he could not be tried here again *Acquittal of Murder in the Admiralty in a Foreign Kingdom, he shall not be tried again here.*

The *Admiralty* hath not Jurisdiction of *Wiecke.* 5 *Rep.* 106 2 *Inst* 167 4 *Inst.* 154. 15 *R* 2. *c* 3

Case upon the Statutes, 13 *R* 2 *c* 5 15 *R* 2 *c.* 3 and 2 *H* 4 *c* 11. for sueing in the *Admiralty* for matters done upon the Land, and declared that the Plaintiff was going from the Port of *London,* with his Ship laden with Merchandizes, and that the Defendant brought a Suit in the *Admiralty* to stay the Ship, till caution should be given, that she should *Case for sueing in the Admiralty for matters at Land See Andr 231 2 Stra. 1097.*

should not traffick with Infidels, within the
Limits of the Charter of the *Eaſt-India* Company; and that they procured the Ship to be
arreſted by Proceſs of the *Admiralty*, and to
be detained, by which the Plaintiff loſt the
Profit of his Voyage; upon not guilty pleaded, a Special Verdict was found, *viz.* they
found the Charter of the *Eaſt-India* Company
of 13 *Car.* 2. by which they are incorporated,
and had the ſole Trade to the *Eaſt-Indies*,
granted to them, with a Prohibition to all
others to traffick with *Infidels* there upon pain
of Forfeiture of Ship and Goods, and that
the Plaintiff had prepared a Ship and Goods
to go to the *Eaſt-Indies* to traffick with Infidels
within the Limits of the *Eaſt-India* Company;
upon this they petitioned the King in Council
to ſtay the Ship, where an Order was made to
the *Admiralty* to ſtay the Ship by their Proceſs,
which iſſued accordingly, and the Ship was
ſtaid, *prout*, &c. all which was done by the
Defendants as Agents of the Company, and
they as Agents paid the Fees of the Proſecu-
tion, and if guilty, Damages for the Plaintiff *in*
duplo 1500 *l* ſo upon Arraignment judgment
for the Plaintiff, and on Error affirmed.
Sands againſt Sir *Joſiah Child* and others. 3
Levinz 351. 4 *Mod.* 176. *Carth* 294. A like
Caſe, 1 *Vent* 47. 1 *Mod.* 18. 2 *Keb.* 604.
Horne againſt *Ivie*,

4 *Inſt* 138.

CHAP. VII.

Of Dominion established by Treaties of Alliance in general.

ficulties used to delay, by which designs may secretly
be carried on

XXI. Consideration had on Leagues made for carrying on some particular Enterprize.

XXII. Of the Causes that generally occasion a Rupture.

XXIII. Of the Obligation on Confederates in reference
to mutual Succours.

XXIV. Of Aid granted to particular and common
Allies when invaded by one another, and of Protection granted a People when oppressed, whether Aid
to such may be consistent with a League.

XXV Whether the Oath taken for the Performance
of the League be personal, or binds the Successor,
and of the Interpretation of the same.

XXVI. Of Leagues made with Princes when driven
out of their Countries, whether they remain valid
and firm.

XXVII. Whether Leagues may be entred into by
Christian Princes with Infidels.

I. TREATIES are occasioned by a wise
and prudent Care of inspecting the
Motions of Neighbours and of their Affairs,
the which are generally reduced to these three.
Heads, upon the Considerations,

    1. How a Prince should govern himself
       with his Neighbours.

    2. In gaining a Credit among them, and
       to have a part in their Deliberations.

    3. Is the main, which is to pierce into
       his Neighbours Designs, for those
       Centers being discovered, a Prince
       easily knows how to draw his Lines.

II. In Treaties, the first thing to be considered is the manner of making the Overture,
and therefore it may so happen, that of two
Princes who are Enemies, the one will not seek
unto the other for an Accord; therefore the
general *Medium* is, that the motion be propounded by some greater Prince, or by some
                       Neighbour

Neighbour that is a Friend to both, and sometimes the Ministers of two Princes meeting * accidentally, if they be employed, yet propound an Accommodation. When a Prince or State is exafperated with another, and having gotten an Advantage, will often refuse to treat any where but in his own Country, nor that unless first sought to by a submissive Request, as by Letter, &c So they of † Holland and West-Friezeland, considering the miserable Diftrefs and incorrigible Diforders of their People, did submit thus to confefs their Errors.

* Argenton and a Steward of the Duke of Mantua meeting at Creal Carragio, to condole in their Mafters names for the Death of the Marquefs of Forcat, made an Overture for the Treaty of Peace betwixt Charles the Eighth and Lewis Sforfe

† March 8, 1653, by order of thofe States, fubfcribed Herbert Van Beaumont, and afterwards by a Letter from the States General, praying a Neuter Place, April 30, 1653, then by a Petition $\frac{20}{30}$ June after. Leo ab Aitzma, fol. 817, 818, 825

III Treaties are acted either by the interview of Princes, or by perfons fufficiently commiffionated for that purpofe.

Thofe that are by interview, have been often difapproved, though often practifed; but that depends rather on the Eftate of Affairs, and the conformity and diverfity of Honours, and manner of living of the Princes and their People, than of the interview, that of Lewis the Eleventh with Duke Charles of Burgundy, and of the fame King with Eward the Fourth of England paft fairly And in all fuch Treaties they govern themfelves in reference to their fupplies, according to the Confidence which they repofe in each other ‖ But thofe interviews of Princes have ever been obferved dangerous, for Princes meafure their quality not by the extent of their Dominions, but by the abfolutenefs of their Power So that he that is fupreme and independant in his own Country, counteth himfelf equal to

‖ Jugurtha taken by his Father-in-Law Bocchus, and delivered to the Romans, Charles the Seventh of France, at

any

a perfonal
Treaty with
the Duke of
Orleans, flew
the Duke
though a
Sovereign
Prince.
Mayer lib. 15
Phi. Comines,
lib. 4. cap. 10.
any other Prince, how great foever. Perchance fome youthful-Kings may difport and
folace themfelves in one another's Company,
whilft yet Pleafure is all the elevation of their
Souls, but when once they grow fenfible of
their own Greatnefs, (a Leffon they will quick-
ly learn, and fhall never want Teachers) then
emulation will be betwixt them; becaufe at
their interview they cannot fo go in Equipage, but one will ftill be the foremoft, either
his Perfon will be more proper, or Carriage
more Court-like, or Attendance more Accomplifhed, or Attire more Fafhionable, or
fomething will either be or be conceived to
be more Majeftical in one than the other
And Corrivals in Honour count themfelves
eclipfed by every beam of State which fhineth
from their Competitor; therefore fome hold
the beft way to keep great Princes together is
to keep them afunder, accommodating their
Bufinefs by their Ambaffadors, left the meeting of their own Perfons part their Affections,
RichardHove-
den in Rich 1.
fol. 666 as it fell out between King *Richard* of *England*
and *Philip* of *France,* and *Maximilian* the Firft
and *Lewis* the Twelfth.

IV It is prefumed, that the Perfonal Treaties of Princes are not for matters fmall and
trivial, therefore it is an undoubted Maxim,
That as Jealoufies may be increafed amongft
Neighbours, by reafon of fuch perfonal inter-
views, fo they muft find out fome apparent and
important pretext, which being made known and
publifhed to remove the Jealoufies of their Neigh-
bours, they may then under fuch colour and
fhadow, treat the moft fecret of their Affairs.
So Pope *Clement* the Seventh, under the borrowed Pretext of a general Peace and League
againft the *Turks,* (which founded pleafingly

in the Ears of all Princes) at *Marfeilles* concluded the Marriage of his Niece with *Henry* the Second of *France*

V. But if of two Princes, the one goes home unto the other, he is bound to do him the Honour of his Houfe, and if the Prince be inferior to him, he commonly fends forth fome of the principal Officers of his Court to receive him; but if he be his equal in Quality, as being both Kings, although there be fome debate betwixt them for Precedence, if he come firft to the place where the Treaty is to be made, he muft go in Perfon and not by Proxy.

In the Interview that was between *Lewis* the Twelfth and *Ferdinand of Arragon* at *Savona* (which then belonged unto the *French* King) *Lewis* the Twelfth at the approach of *Ferdinand's* Galley (before he could land) entered into it, accompanied only with his *Guard*, to teftify his confidence, and thereby to affure King *Ferdinand* of that which he had promifed he fhould find in him, and at their going to Land, King *Lewis* left the Right-hand to *Ferdinand*, who lodged in the Caftle, as the moft honourable Place, and himfelf went to the *Bifhoprick*.

Vide Æmilius Paulus's Hiftory of France, and Ferron his fupply of the fame, of the like of the Duke of Orleans, afterwards Lewis XII upon the failure of iffue male of Charles the 8th.

VI. By the Laws of *Treaties*, when two Princes unequal in Quality parley, the inferior is to come firft to the place of Congrefs there to attend the Greater, yet the contrary hath been moft commonly obferved upon this very reafon, that he that is lefs ought firft to wait on the Greater, and from thence go to the place appointed for the Parley, and this was particularly done at the interview of Pope *Clement* the Seventh and King *Francis* the Firft,

First, although that *Marseilles* were in the King's Subjection.

VII Again, Treaties by those that are sufficiently commissionated for that purpose, are to act either secretly or openly Treaties close or secret are usually made, in order to the compleating or settling of Leagues between two Princes or States, sometimes by entertaining him with whom they treat under such a Pretext, to deceive him in the end ; at other times to surprize an Enemy, or to assure a Prince of two Enemies, treating with one secretly, the other openly, and the like. These are the ordinary Policies among Princes, and wherewith the wisest of Kings †, and the most knowing Councils have been deceived and abused even to accept of a Treaty, when at the same time the Proposer hath no other thoughts than to betray them , the *Spaniards* have been famous at these Projects Memorable was that design of theirs to interrupt the League, which was ready to be made between the Princes of *Italy* and Pope *Clement* the Seventh, after the Battle of *Pavia*, propounding unto the Pope to treat and accord, the which not only hindred the League, and staid the preparations of War which he might make, but also caused him to discharge the Troops which he had drawn unto him for his safety So *Bourbon*, General of the Imperial Army, entertained the Pope with an accord, whilst his Army marched to the Walls of Rome

† So *Maximilian* and *Ferdinand* having twice abused H 8 proposed a third, which was, that he would resign up the Imperial Crown to him ; the Resignation is sent to *England* and approved, H 8. is to come to *Aquisgrave* to receive the Crown, and *Maximilan* is to accompany him to *Rome* to receive the last Right of the Imperial Dignity, and having given him the Investiture of *Milan*, *in feodo more Imperiali*, then in possession of the *French*, and in enmity with the House of *Austria*. All things being thus concluded, and H 8. having paid the Monies agreed on, and made ready his preparations *Charles* the Fifth, and Grandson of *Maximilian*, is a

VIII. Hence

rub

rub in this League, who muft be firft removed; thereupon the old Fox the Emperor fends a Propofal, that he would come firft into the *Netherlands* to take off his Grandfon, which while agitating, he ftrikes up a fecret Peace with the *French* King, and fo *H* 8 is betrayed a third time, and the Agreement refufed to be complied with, *Cotton Treaty of Amity, fol* 99

VIII Hence it is, that during Treaties, be they open or fecret, the Princes or States concerned in them muft watch the more carefully, have the diligenter Eye, and by all the ways imaginable reinforce their ftrength, not only to fruftrate their Enemies of all hopes to furprize them, but to the end the Confideration of their Force and Opulency may put them in a pofture to obtain Conditions of more Advantage   Befides, it is an undeniable Maxim, that no treaty muft be held firm, valid, and concluded, unlefs it be ratified by that Prince or State with whom the fame is made, efpecially if it be with a Prince whom they detain Prifoner, for by † Law the force by the which he hath been conftrained to promife, will at leaft difpenfe with him fo far as to re-advife, if not to break

† *Sacramento quidem vos te-norequi potuit, quum projectis fascibus & de-pofito Imperio privatus & captus ipfe in alienam veniffet poteftatem?* Curio *in* Cæfar, to thofe that had been the Soldiers of *Domitius,* fo fpake, *lib.* 11. *de Bello Civili   Vide Grot lib* 2 *cap* 13 § 18   Pope *Clement* the Seventh refufed to ratify the Treaty with Duke *Ferrara* which he made when a Prifoner, faying, That it was a difhonourable thing for a Man in Life to ratify a matter done in his Name when dead, not confiftent with his Honour nor Intereft   So *Francis* the Firft excufed himfelf to ratify the Treaty of *Madrid,* upon the inhumanity done to him by the permiffion of *Charles* the Fifth, they being extorted from him, nor did they take place, though the King left his Children as Hoftages

IX. Again, as in the Parlies of Princes, the place where the Interview is to be made is very confiderable, fo is it in Treaties which are tranfacted by Embaffadors, Agents, Envoys, *&c.* if it be to compleat a Peace, or fettle a League, it muft not be too far from the Confederates, but at some convenient place, to the end they may have the more speedy Answers from their Principals ; but then the first is always to be in some place Neuter, or sometimes upon the confines of Kingdoms , for that it is neither reasonable or honourable to treat a Peace in the Territory of one's Enemy ; but the latter touching Leagues may be any where. That of *Edward* the Fourth with *Lewis* the Eleventh, was in the Territories of the Duke of *Burgundy*, but that was personal . And that between *France* and *Spain*, concluded by Cardinal *Mazarine*, and *Don Lewis Mendez de Haro*, Plenipotentiaries of both Crowns, was in the Isle of *Pheasants* in the River *Bidassoa*,

November 7, 1659 upon the Confines of the *Pyrenean* Mountains. And the last great Treaty which begun at *Cologne* in the year 1673, under the Mediation of *Swedeland*, in order to put an end to that War, wherein most of the Crown'd Heads of *Europe* were involved, was looked upon as a place proper; but the seizing of Prince *William* of *Furstemburg*, and the taking of forty thousand Crowns out of the Waggons of the *French* Embassador in a Neutral City, broke off that Negotiation , and though the violence committed on this Prince, by the Emperor's Ministers, and the Injury done to the *French* King, gave ground to fear, that there was no Peace to be expected, and that the Most Christian King would never consent to the renewing of the Treaty, unless reparations were first made for those two injuries Nevertheless, at the instance of the King of *England* (whose Mediation was generally embraced by all the Princes concerned in that War) and at the solicitation of the Bishop of

Strasberg,

Strasberg, who publickly declared he preferred the Advantages of Peace before the Liberty of his own Brother, *Nimeguen* was pitched upon as a place neuter and proper for a Treaty, and thereupon the *French* King, 17 *February,* 1675, named for that Effect the Duke of *Vitry,* Monsieur *Colbert,* and the Count *D'Avaux,* his Embassadors.

X *Embassadors* having received Orders to treat, the Prince, to whom such are sent, is not by the Law of Treaties bound to treat personally, but only to depute some of his Council for that Effect, the Reason is, for that the Dignity of a Prince may receive some detriment, which cannot be maintained amidst the Contestations which happen in Conferences

But if an Embassador be deputed as Lieutenant to a Prince, there, indeed such Commissioner is not bound to treat but only with the Prince himself, and so it was where the Bishop of *Gurgia* was deputed by the *Emperor* to Pope *Julius* the Second, the Pope commissionated three *Cardinals* to treat with him, but the Bishop having notice in what quality he was like to be received, commissionated three Gentlemen to confer with them, excusing himself upon other Affairs, which afterwards was explained, that he came not as a single Embassador, but as a Lieutenant to the *Emperor,* in the which Quality he had been received at *Rome* by the *Pope* Yet it hath so happened, that Embassadors, if not admitted to a personal Treaty, have refused the Discharge of their Commission, and so did Chancellor *Menzel,* Embassador from the *French* King, who delivered his Message to *Philip* Duke of *Burgundy,* was interrupted

Julius Ferretus de Legatis Principum, & de eorum fide & officio.

There is commonly in the instructions provided for the Embassador in that point if the matter should come into debate

M 2   by

Phil. Comines
lib. 1

by *Charles* the Duke's Son, *I am sent*, said he, *not to treat with you, but with your Father*, and Mr. *Wade*, who being commissionated by Queen *Elizabeth* to *Philip* King of *Spain*, would by no means admit himself to be turned over to the *Spanish* Privy-Council, but would either have Audience from the King himself, or would return without it.

XI The *Deputies* being assembled, their Seats are considerable; they having no power to quit any thing of the rank which their *Masters* ought to hold; and by the Law of Treaties the first place is at the head or end of the *Table*, (if there be one) the second is the first on the right hand, and the third is the first on the left hand of him that is at the end, and if there be many *Deputies* to one Prince, they usually sit at one side, to have the more facility to confer together, if it be needful.

So *Julius* the Second did, who finding himself prest to make Peace with *Lewis* XI'. sent Cardinal *Final*, and Bishop of *Trevli* to *Paris*, but never armed them with Power to conclude the Consistory

XII The Embassadors having concluded and settled their Places, their Commissions of each side are to be inspected and considered, and therefore it is an undoubted Maxim, That when they are general or ambiguous, the Principals have no will to conclude, or if they are fair and plain, yet there may be wanting power to conclude, or having power to conclude, it may be with a Salvo till they are ratified.

this was to frustrate the important instance of

The principal Clauses generally are,

1 Either for Peace or Truce
2 For Restitution of that which they pretend hath been unjustly taken away
3. For the Cession of Rights.

4. For

4 For Limits and Bounds, the which if they cannot regulate, they put them in fufpence, or elfe they make fome Act, which may interrupt the prefcription of him which holds them.

5. For paffage, with confignation of Hoftage

6. For Forts or Caftles for Affurances.

7 For an Offenfive and Defenfive League

8 For Neutrality.

In the managing of all which, and of all other matters proper for fuch Treaties, a fpecial regard muft be had not to move for a Perfon odious to him with whom the Treaty is made, nor to yield to the firft demands though never fo juft, but refift them ftoutly, but if danger is imminent, then it is a certain Maxim, *Not to ftudy fo much to negotiate with advantage, as to provide for fafety*

XIII Treaties which are made with our Neighbours as Friends, are called *Treaties of Alliances, equal* or *unequal* The *equal* is either of fingle Friendfhip only, for the entertainment of Traffick, or for aid and fuccour, that of fuccour is for the *Defenfive* or *Offenfive*, and fometimes for both, with or againft all Men, or againft fome certain Princes and Republicks, and then Alliances are contracted, either from *Eftate* to *Eftate*, and for the Prefervation of the *Eftates* of each other (in which cafe by the death of the Prince they may not be interrupted) or elfe they are contracted betwixt *Prince* and *Prince*, and then the death of one fufpends till a new Treaty hath confirmed it, unlefs there is a time certain prefcribed by the *Treaty*, to the which the Alliance muft continue after the death of the

The Leagues between the Crown of France and Spain, are commonly between Kings and Kings, Realm and Realm, and Man and Man of their Subjects, and have in time paft been look'd upon to be the firmeft of Alliances *Phil Comines lib 2.*

Prince,

cap 8 And
in the very
Alliance with
France con-
cluded July
21/31 The first
Article is in
these words

Prince; or else they are made from an *Estate* to a *Prince*, where the death of the Prince does likewise, if not dissolve, yet at least suspend till a new Treaty of Confirmation of the precedents, although by the Laws of *England*, *Rex non moritur*

That there be an universal and perpetual, true, and sincere Peace and Amity between the Most Christian King and the King of Great-Britain, their Heirs and Successors, and between the Kingdoms, States, and Subjects of both, &c Vide 9 E 4 2 a The League then made with the Scots, and likewise between Edward the Fourth, and the Duke of Burgundy. Phil Comin l 3 c 6

XIV Sometimes *Alliances* are contracted for an Enterprize and for one effect only, in the part in which the Allies are interested, and such are generally called *Leagues*, which in *England* have been sometimes confirmed by *Act of Parliament* *

* Rot Par 2
H 5. and 4.
Coke 4 Inst.
156
Grot de jure
belli & pacis
L 2. c 15.
§ 5.

Leagues are such Agreements that are made by the Command of the supreme Power, and whereby the whole Nation is made liable to the Wrath of God, if they infringe it.

All leagues or Safeconducts are, or ought to be of Record, that is, they ought to be inrolled in the Chancery, to the end the Subject may know, who are in Amity with the King, and who not, who are Enemies and can have no Action here, and who are in League and may have Actions Personal here, 4 *Inst* 152.

Leagues commonly are *Offensive*, but in effect they tend to attempt against some one, and in the bottom are lodged *Articles of Secrecy for the Enterprize* And such was that of *Cambray* against the *Venetians*, in which they borrowed the *pretext of Religion and the Peace of Christendom*

Treaty of
Cambray, the
Confederates
of which were

XV The Pope *Julius the Second*, the *Emperor*, Kings of *France*, *Spain*, and *Arragon*, Anno 1558 *Vide* History of the Republick of *Venice*, fol 87

XV The ordinary causes for which *Prin-* *ces* and *Republicks* make Leagues, are either to facilitate a Conquest, as that that was made between *Lewis* the Twelfth and *Ferdinand* of *Arragon*, for the Realm of *Naples*, or to balance the Forces of one that is more mighty, in hindering him that he grow not greater; but Aims ought not to be taken to diminish such a Neighbour's power, for that fear is uncertain, but prudent Leagues may be made for diminishing their Power

The *English* made a League to succour the *Hollanders*, not only to balance the growing opulency of the *Spanish* Monarchy, but likewise to increase her own by the Alliance of the *Dutch*. *Quid sequitur?*

XVI. Again, Leagues may be made for the procuring of a general peace by way of *Mediation* of their Neighbours in War, and such was the Treaty of *Nimeguen* mediated by the King of *England*, and concluded *Aug* 10, 1678, between the Embassadors and Plenipotentiaries of his most Christian Majesty on the one part, and the Embassadors and Plenipotentiaries of the Lords *States General* of the *United Provinces* on the other part, such was also the League of Union propounded by his late sacred Majesty King *Charles* II. and afterwards concluded betwixt him and the *States General* of the *United Provinces*, for an efficacious Mediation of Peace between *France* and *Spain*, his sacred Majesty of *Britain* having a Prospect of what afterwards happened, and of a War, wherein most inevitably would be involved most of the Princes in *Christendom*, to the effecting of which Peace, his Majesty and the *States General* did obtain a promise from the *French* King to the *Dutch*, to lay

Sed ut vim pa-
ti posse ad vim
inferendam jus
tribuat, ab
omni æquitate
abhorret
Grotius *de*
jure belli &
pacis, l 2. c.
15. § 17

M 4   down

down Arms, on condition the *Spaniards* would formally and solemnly by a Treaty of Peace, quit to him all those Places and Forts, together with the Chaftellenies, and their Appurtenances, which they by force of Arms had taken in, or fortified in the then laft year's Expedition; or, otherwife that the *Spaniard* be brought to transfer to the *French* all their remainder in the Dutchy of *Luxemberg* (or to the County of *Burgundy*) together with *Cambray* and *Cambresis*, *Douay*, *Ayre*, *St Omers*, *Bergue*, St. *Winox*, *Furnes*, and *Lynk*, with the Baliwicks, Chaftellenies, and all other their dependencies; and the *French* King to

League of U-n on between his Majefty of Great Britain and the States General of the United Netherlands, concluded at the Hague, Jan 1/13. Anno 1668.

reftore to the *Spaniard* all Places, Territories, which they have by Arms taken fince their entrance into *Flanders*, on condition that the *States General* do reciprocally undertake and fecure to the *French*, to prevail with the *Spaniard* to confent to the fame Conditions, which once effected would (as was hoped) initiate the tranquillity, and be the intereft not only of the two Warring Crowns, but of all other the Princes of *Chriftendom*. To the effecting of which there were feveral Articles agreed, and likewife it was agreed, that if a peace fhould happen to be made, his Majefty and the *States General* fhould become Warrantees, and a place left for any other Prince or State to come into the fame, who fhould think it their Intereft to keep the Peace of *Chriftendom* undifturbed, and to reftore the *Low-Countries* to their tranquillity · There was provifion made likewife by the fame, for the Forces of each of the Warrantees to be ufed againft thofe that fhould break and violate the fame, obliging them to ceafe the violence, and repair the Party injured

XVIII. A

XVII. A *Defenſive League*, which hath no other benefit but a neceſſary defence, and in the which mean Eſtates are in a manner equally inteieſted, laſt uſually longer than an *Offenſive League*, which is voluntary, and from the which either of the *Confederates* will eaſily pait when he hath more intereſt So as in *balencing* the intereſt of the one and the other, he that ſhall find himſelf accompanied with diſtruſt, and an opinion to be irreconcilable to the common Enemy, generally proves the moſt firm in the League.

The *Wiſdom*, *Courage*, *Means*, and *Conſtancy* of the Prince or State is to be conſidered , ſo likewiſe the *diſtance* of the *Places*, as well in regard of thoſe with whom they unite, as of thoſe againſt whom they make the Leagues

XVIII. *Leagues* having no other limitation, *but the end of the Enterprize* foi which they are made, have admitted many large debates in caſes of accident : For inſtance, If an Enemy ſhould take the Country, for the defence whereof the Leagues was made, the Queſtion has been, whethei the *Confederates* be bound to aſſiſt him who hath loſt it in the Recovery , ſome have held, that the *Defenſive* did not extend ſo far, notwithſtanding if there were no Treaty, which had concerned this Conqueſt, yet it would ſeem more reaſonable to comprehend the Recovery in the defenſive, if it be general. For as its end is to preſerve the *Ally in his State*, and to attain it, the Forces muſt not only remain in the Country of the *Ally* to attend the Enemy, but aftei denunciation and other acts of Hoſtility done by the Enemy, they muſt enter into his Country, to the end to prevent him, or

The Anſwer of the Embaſſador from *Privernum* to the Senate .
Si bonam dederitis & fidam & perpetuam, ſi malam haud diuturnam,
Liv lib 8 21.

Pontius Samnis after reſtitution made to the *Romans,* and the Author of the breach yielded up, *expiatum* (ſaith he) *eſt quicquid ex fœdere rupto trarum in nos cœleſtium fuit. Satis ſcio quibuſcunque Dis cordi fuit ſubigi nos ad neceſſitatem cedendi res, iis non fuiſſe cordi tam ſuperbè à Romanis fœderis expiationem ſpretam* And a little after,

What more do I owe to thee, O Roman? What to the League? What to the Gods, the Judges of the League? Whom shall I bring unto thee to be the or divert him from attempting any thing against the *Ally*, the *Offensive* being judged by the *aggression*, and not by *that which follows*; by a strong reason they ought to enter into the Country conquered from the *Ally*, for the Recovery thereof, but Excuses in this kind proceed from those who fail in their faith, courage, or means to recover.

Judge of thy anger and of my punishment? I refuse no People, nor private Men.

Ar 1515 Vid Sir Robert Cotton Remonst of the Treaties of Amity and Marriage. XIX. *Contribution* is one of the main ingredients in a *League*, and is of great difficulty to regulate. It is made either in Men or Money, the Men are entertained *by all Parties*, or *by him only that hath need*, or otherwise as the League is   *Henry* Eighth made a League with *Francis* the *French* King against the Emperor *Maximilian* and *Ferdinand*, for the Recovery of *Milan*, which he did, for the protection of his Neighbour, and Reduction of the *Swisse* from the *Imperial* side, for which he employed the *Bastard of Savoy*; the agreement was of reciprocal Succour of 10000 Men, if the War were by Land, and of 6000 if it were made by Sea, and in all other occasions, the *French* King was bound to assist the King of *England* with 12000 *Lances*, and he the King of *France* with 10000 Foot at his charge that had need

So where *Contribution* is concluded for Money, there are difficulties that do arise from the *Person* or *Place* where it must be kept; to deliver it unto the hand of the strongest, is not safe, *for fear they shall not be able to call him to account*, to lay it in a weak place, were to expose it *to the attempt and force of the strongest*, or to him that shall first *take Arms*; but it has been usual for the sum

not

not to be advanced till after the War begun.

XX. Leagues concluded by the *Deputies* of the *Confederates*, there sometimes falls out a difficulty who shall ratify and declare himself first In the League which was made betwen *Francis* the First, the *Pope* and the *Princes* of *Italy*, the King refused to ratify until the *Pope* and *Venetians* had ratified before him, and in that he so cunningly wrought, that he procured the *Collegues* to declare and begin the War, whilst that he treated secretly for himself, to the end he might make his Conditions with more advantage, this he declared was for fear those *Italian Foxes should shew him the like*

Andreæ Maurocem Hist Ven.

XXI Leagues made for an Enterprize succeed seldom according to the hope of the *Allies, if the Enterprize be long*; for besides that the preparations be long, the opinions divers in the pursuit, the resolutions inconstant, the interests of Princes or States in a League may change with time, or with the practice of him against whom they are in League in withdrawing some one of them, or making him to suffer more loss than the rest, for seeing himself *ill defended or succoured* by his *Confederate*, and that he was in a greater danger to lose than his Companions, he then studies to retire *, and to make his *accord apart*, as did the *Venetians* with the *Turks*, after the loss of *Cyprus*

* If one part hath violated the League, the other may depart from it, for the several Heads of the League have every one the force of a Condition, so *Grotius* conceives, *l. 2. c* 13 §. 15

XXII The ordinary causes of the rupture of *Leagues* are *distrust* and *jealousy*, as if one hath had conference with the Enemy, without the consent of the rest, if that which serveth

Soluti fæderis culpam sustinent, non qui deserit ad alios se conferunt, sed qui quam

juravi promise-
rart opem re
rum præstant
alibi apud
eardem, si vel
tantillum ex
actis pars al-
terutra tranf-
grederetur,
rupta fore
pacta Thu-
cyd lib 1
19 E 4. V de
S.at 2 H. 5.
c. 6.
H l 14
E'z in the
Duke of For-
folk's Cafe 4
Inf fol 152

serveth for the *safety of one*, diminish the *safety of the other*, *inconstancy*, *variety*, cow-ardice, *division*, *usurpation* without the consent of the others

So if he treats with the Enemy, not comprehending the other *Allies*, but as *Adherents*, as *Lewis* the Twelfth left the League of the *Venetians*, for that they had made a Truce with him, and had presumed to name him only as an *Adherent* It was the opinion of *Bryan*, that if all the Subjects of *England* would make War with a *Confederate Prince* or *Republick* in League with the King of *England*, without the assent of the King of *England*, such a War was no breach of the League, and upon the same reason were the resolutions of the Judges in the Duke of *Norfolk's* Case, where the Question was, Whether the Lord *Herise* and other Subjects of the King of *Scots*, that without his assent had wasted and burnt divers Towns in *England*, and proclaimed Enemies, were Enemies in Law, within the *Statute* of 25 E. 3 the League being between the *English* and *Scots*, and resolved they were, and that the League remained.

In fidelitate
feruch datur,
tur, & si ser-
vero velle te a-
l quem jaste of-
fendere & ge-
n raliter vel
specialiter fue-
ro requisitus,
meum tibi, si-
cut potero,
præstabo aux-
ilium. Orat.
Demosthen
at Megalopol.

XXIII The Succours that one *Confederate* must afford another *Confederate* (according to the *Law of Leagues*) against a *Confederate*, is of great Consequence · Three Princes allied, the one makes War against the other, and demands succours from the third; in this Case, if the Treaties of Alliance be only for *Friendship* it is certain he is not bound to give any succours But if the Treaty carries an *offensive League*, he must succour the most *ancient allied by a precedent Alliance*, If the precedent Alliances have been made both

both at one time, he muſt ſuccour him that is allied in an *offenſive* and *defenſive League* But if the League be *offenſive* and *defenſive* of either ſide, *he ought not to ſuccour either*; but he may meditate a * Peace, and cauſe the difference to be judged by the *Common Allies*, which being propounded with a Declaration, that if one refuſe, or having once ſubmitted, will not yield to Judgment, he will ſuccour the other, as the *Sweds* and *Swiſs*, upon ſeveral occaſions have done, notwithſtanding in point of State on ſuch occaſions they uſually balance their Eſtate, and looking *more to ſafety than Juſtice*, they ſuccour him who being enforc'd, may weaken the powerful, who is more to be feared, yet to unjuſt Wars there is no obligation, then certainly he ought to be preferred, who hath a juſt cauſe of War.

Nihil intercedi, quo minus Samnitt populo pacis bellique liberum arbitrium ſit Liv l 8 Grotius de Jure belli ac Pacis lib. 2 cap 15 § 13. Vide Monmouth Hiſtory of France, fol. 31

XXIV By the *Laws of Alliances* Princes may aid *particular and common Allies*, if they be wronged by one of the *Allies*

But he which is not comprehended in the Treaty of Alliance, cannot be *defended* againſt him that is *allied* without breach of the *Alliance*, therefore *Mediation* in ſuch caſes is the only hopes of the *oppreſſed*, which not having its effect, if the *oppreſſed* put themſelves into the protection of the *Mediator*, they then become in the nature of his Subjects, and then their *Prince* is obliged to their *ſuccour and defence*, even againſt his *Allies*, and this is by natural Right

Equals cannot directly refuſe War, nor demand Peace.

Liv 3 Polybius in excerptis Legationum 35

XXV By the Laws of Leagues, though the Oath binds only the *Perſon*, yet the *Promiſe binds the Succeſſor*, for though ſome do hold, that Leagues do depend upon the Oath as their Firmament, though that is not ſo

When *Edward* the Fourth was chaſed out of the Kingdom, and *Henry* the Sixth was ſet up again; yet by Reafon there was inferted into the fame thefe words, *With the King and Realm,* that the League did remain perpetual. *Phil. Comines lib 3 cap 6* Ulpian. *Leg JureGentium, fect pactum D pactis Addeque Helvetiis caufantur poft mortem* Hen 3 *apud* Thuanum, *lib* 97 *in An* 1589 *ubi de Fœdere antiquo Gall & Scot*

for the moft part, yet the *efficacy* of fuch Leagues refts in the *promife itfelf,* to which for *Religion* fake the Oath is added Hence it is, that *Promifes* made to a *Free People* are in their nature *real,* becaufe the Subject is a *permanent matter*; although the State or Republick be changed into a *Monarchy,* yet the League remains, for that the body, *i. e* the *power* is ftill the fame, though the Head be changed And the Perfon is inferted into the agreement, not that the agreement may be perfonal, but to fhew *with whom it is made,* for if it be inferted into the League that it fhall be *perpetual,* or that it is made for the *good of the Kingdom,* or with the Perfon and his Succeffors, or for a time limited, the fame does moft apparently demonftrate the thing to be real

Vide & infigrem locum apud Cambden, *in Anno* 1572

However, in all Leagues which tend to *Peace,* though there may remain fomewhat, whereby words of ambiguity may arife, yet the moft pious way of interpreting, hath been to account the fame rather *real,* than *perfonal*; for all Leagues made for Peace or Commerce, admit of a favourable conftruction *Leagues defenfive have more of favour, offenfive of burthen.*

Quintus faid to *Nabis,* We have made no Friendfhip nor Society with thee, but with *Pelop.* the juft and lawful King of the *Lacedæmonians*

XXVI. Leagues made with *Princes,* although they happen afterwards to be driven out of their Kingdoms by their Subjects, yet the League remains firm and good, for the *Right* of the Kingdom remains with fuch an unfortunate Prince, notwithftanding he hath loft his Kingdom: The Prefident, Canon, and Plenipotentiary for the Duke of *Lorraine*

at the Treaty of *Nimeguen*, renewed his inftances with the *French* Embaffadors, that he
might obtain fome moderation of the Conditions that had been ftipulated for his Mafter;
the Emperor did the like, but without fuccefs;
however, the Duke would not neglect any
thing that might give the *French* King fiefh
Evidences of his defire to merit the Favour of
his Majefty, he got Sii *Leoline Jenkins*, and
the reft of the Mediators, to delare to Mon-
fieur *Colbeit*, that the Emperor had taken
into his Service all the *Lorraine* Forces, and
in the publick Declaration which the Duke
made at *Nimeguen*, he faid, *That he had delivered all his Forces to a Piince at Peace with*
France, *that he might make it appear to the
King, that though he was expelled his own Dominion, yet he would do nothing that might give
his Majefty ground to deprive him of the honour
of his favour* And notwithftanding all thefe
moft fubmiffive offers, this unfortunate but
gallant Prince was fhut out of that famous
Treaty, which put an end to a War, wherein
almoft all the Princes of *Europe* were engaged
On the other hand, Leagues made with the
Invader cannot be good, for his caufe being
unjuft, is odious, but if * the People will
make him King *de facto*, and inveft him, the
queftion is then out of all controverfy, for
then he is become a King *regnant*, and by the
Laws of *England*, if Treafon be committed
againft his Perfon, and † aftei he is beaten
out, and the King *de Jure* comes to his
Crown, the King *de Jvre* may punifh thofe
Traytors with death

  The Earl of *Warwick* having iaifed an
Army in *France* and *Flandeis*, invaded *England*, and within five oi fix days after his

       landing,

*11 H 7 c 1

† 4 E 4 1
9 *h* 4 12
3 *Inft fol* 7.

Ed 4 in ân.
1470.

landing, King *Edward*'s Forces betraying
him, the Earl became Master of the Realm,
the King flying for protection to his Kinsman
the Duke of *Burgundy*, he kindly in his misfortunes entertained him, yet while he was
in this banished estate, the Duke of *Burgundy*
renewed the League with the *English*, it being
agreed, that notwithstanding King *Edward*'s
misfortune, the League remained firm and

Phil Comines
l 3 c 6. inviolable between the Duke *Charles of Bur-*
gundy, and the King and Realm of *England*.
So that for *Edward* they should name *Henry*
(who was newly taken out of the *Tower* by
the Earl of *Warwick*, at his chasing out of

Reges qui reg-
nis exuti sunt
cum aliis regni
bonis etiam jus
legandi perai-
derunt King *Edward*)   Now the true reason that
Leagues remain, and are firm, notwithstanding such a change, is, because there goes
along with them a tacit condition, *viz* of
holding their possessions, and therefore the
World wondered not, that *Charles* II having
sworn a League with the King of *Spain*, expresly as he was King of *Portugal*, did notwithstanding receive two *Embassadors* from
the then new King of *Portugal*, and that
without being judged either in *England* or
Spain to have broken his former Oath and
League

The Duke of *Guise* having formed the
League against *Henry* the Third, which was,
in regard the King was so cold in the Profes-
sion of the *Romish Faith*, that it was in danger to be extinguished by the increase which
he permitted of the *Reformed* Religion, especially seeing *Henry* the Fourth then King
of *Navarre* was of that Religion, and was to
succeed to the Crown; wherefore, by the Mediation of *Philip* the Second of *Spain*, the
Pope qualified the Duke of *Guise*, Head of
that

that *Catholick League*, and (which in point of
Government was to set him above the King)
avowed him *Protector* of the *Catholick Faith*
in the Kingdom of *France* When *Henry* the
Fourth succeeded to the Crown, then this
League for security of Religion was most
violent, and the *Spaniard* without, hoped,
by nourishing thus the *division* within, to carry
all for himself at last To avoid which gin,
and to answer all, the King changed his Religion, and negotiated by *d'Ossat*, to be received by the *Pope* as a dutiful Son of the
Church of Rome, demanding absolution for
what was past, and making large promises of
due obedience for the time to come The
King of *Spain*'s interest was, that he should
not be received, and thereupon he endeavoured to persuade the *Pope*, that King *Henry* did
but dissemble with him, and that under this
Disguise he would easiliest ruin the *Romish* Religion Notwithstanding this, the Cardinal obtained his Reception, Absolution, and Bene-
diction, through the many Promises and Presents which he made to *His Holiness*, whereupon the *Spaniard*'s Designs were in a Moment all blown over from *France*, but fell
heavily upon the *United Provinces*, which
were sorely oppressed, for that they apprehended the Loss and Ruin of their Country ;
and thereupon they implored Assistance from
King *Henry*, who received their Embassadors
very graciously, and gave them Assurance of
Relief The King of *Spain*, who wanted no
good Intelligence in the Court of *France*, immediately remonstrated to the *Pope*, That his
former Intimations concerning *Henry*'s Dissi-
mulations, did now appear in the Face of all
the World, and that seeing *His Holiness* had

Peter Mat-
thew's His-
tory of *France*
in the Life of
Henry III.

been

been so credulous, he knew not now whether they
should be able to save the *Catholick Faith* from
being subjected to the *Reformed* Religion or
no; for whereas the *Hollanders* had revolted
from him, only because he resolved to use the
true Means for the Establishment of the *Romish
Faith* among them, and that now he was in
a fair way of reducing them (which conduced
so much (by *His Holiness* his Opinion) to the
Establishment of the *Romish Faith*) *Henry* had
taken their Party against him in that Work,
and that at *Paris* he had received their Embassadors to that Purpose, although he knew
they were his lawful Subjects, &c.

This startled the *Pope* not a little, who
charged *d'Ossat* for having betrayed him, and
put the Church in Danger. This Argument
was as subtile on the *Spaniard*'s side, as changing Religion was on King *Henry*'s, and therefore the *Cardinal* was not a little perplexed
how to answer it to the advantage of his Master; as also coherently to the Considerations
of his former Reception into the Church;
but at last he replied, That *His Holiness* need-
ed not wonder how in reason of State, those
different Religions might join together for
political Ends, without Hazard of altering
Religion Thus *David* sought Protection of
the *Philistines*, and *Abraham* redeemed the sin-
ful *Sodomites*; that he took it to be upon the
same Ground, that *His Holiness* himself, not
long before, received a *Persian Embassador*,
who was so far from being a Heretick, that
he never pretended to the Name of Christian ·
That it was a plausible Argument which the
King of *Spain* used in complaining of *Henry*'s
receiving and avowing their Embassador, especially knowing at the same time that they
were

were Rebels, and could pretend no Right or *Vide Peter*
Title separate from his Crown: " For Princes *Matthew's*
" (quoth he) when Embassadors are addres- History of
" sed to them, never inform themselves of the *France in Vita*
" Rights and Title of those Princes from *In Regno di-*
" whom they are sent, but whether they have *viso gens una,*
" Possession of the Force and Power of those *pro tempore*
" Places from whence the Embassadors are *quasi duæ gen-*
" employed, for it would be an endless And Princes
" Task, and require an infallible true History are to have
" of the World (which is not to be made by an Eye to the
" Man) if all the Embassadors, before their each King-
" Reception, should be obliged first to prove dom hath to
" clearly to the World, the just Right by afford Benefit
" which their Masters derive those Titles and one to the
" Jurisdictions which they assume to them- not to exa-
" selves." mine their

XXVII. And as Leagues are Covenants or *Titles.*
Agreements made by command of the highest
Powers, wherein the Parties are bound over
to the Divine Wrath, in case they break their
Faith, it hath been a famous question, Whether they may be entered into with those that
are Aliens from the true Religion, whereof *Coke 3 Instit.*
by the Law of Nature there is no doubt nor *fol* 155
difficulty, for that Law is so common to all
Men, that it admits not any difference of
Religion; but the question is about the Law
Divine, out of which it hath been discussed,
not only by Divines, but famous Lawyers, as
Oldradus, Decianus, Grotius, upon the whole *Grot Lib 2.*
they have agreed, that they may be entered *cap.* 15 §. 8.
into as well with Princes Infidels as Christians, 9, 10.
and that is evidently proved, for that before
the Law of *Moses* it was lawful to contract
Leagues with Aliens from Religion for an in-
offensive and harmless behaviour, as that of
Jacob with *Laban*; nor did the Law of *Moses*

make

make any change, the example of the *Egyptians* being exprefs in the point. 'Tis true, thofe feven Nations and other Kingdoms, as the *Amalekites*, that were deftinated by Divine Sentence to be extirpated, were excepted; but Leagues of Commerce, and fuch as pertain to the utility of both Nations, or of either Party, are by the Law permitted with the profane : So *David* and *Solomon* made League with *Hiram* King of the *Tyrians*, and that which is very obfervable in the Sacred Hiftory, of that Action it is faid, That the Alliance was made by *Solomon* according to the Wifdom which God had given him 'Tis very true, the *Jews* were generally very cautious of contracting with Idolatrous Princes, and the Reafon was, for that they had exprefs Promifes of Victory, but that was conditionally, *i. e* if they kept the Law, which if performed, they had the lefs need of human Aid　But now under the Gofpel fuch

contracts have a more favourable Admittance, according to that of *Tertullian*. *So long as* Ifrael *only was his people, God did juftly command mercy towards their Brethren alone, but after that he gave unto Chrift the Nations for his Inheritance, and the Ends of the Earth for his poffeffion, and that began to be paid which was promifed in* Hofea, *They that were not my people fhall be my people, and the Nations that had not obtained mercy fhall obtain mercy, from that time Chrift hath extended unto all the Law of Fraternal Benignity, excluding none from our compaffion, no more than from his Vocation.* and therefore as it is no evil to do good to the profane, fo neither is it unlawful to implore their help, as *Paul* invoked the Aid of *Cæfar* and the Chief Captain, fo that at this day

there

Lib 7 cap 3 Horum exemplum fecut Imperatore, & Rege, Chriftiani Fædera, aut cum non Chriftianis, aut cum non fane Chriftianis fecere, Conftantius cum Gothis & Vandalis, Juftinianus cum Longobardis, cum Saracenis Theodofius, Honorius & cum Maur s Reges Hifpania, cum Tar-

taris Rodolphus Habfpurgenfis, Adi Johannem de Carthagena, l 3 de Jure Belli Romani Pontificis c. 1. Julius fecundus Pontifex Turcis ufus, Vide Bulftrod part 3 fol. 28 cited in *Marfhe's* Cafe, the Cafe of *Samuel Pellagy*, that had been Embaflador to the *States* of *Holland* to treat with them from the Emperor of *Morrocco*

* Famous was the Piety of *Emanuel* Duke of *Savoy*, who, when he was able to take *Cyprus* by the aid of the Great *Turk*, refufed it

there is no intrinfical or univerfal Pravity; neverthelefs. thofe Alliances have their Circumftances or Rules of Government, as not to join with them but in extreme neceffity, according to that of * *Thucydides* · *They that are treacheroufly affaulted, as we are by the A-thenians, are not to be blamed, if they feek for fafety, and fecure themfelves by the aid not of* Greeks *only,* but Barbarians

CHAP.

C H A P. VIII.

Of Alliances unequal, and of Protection.

I. **U**NEQUAL Alliance is that, which is contracted betwixt Princes or States unequal in *Honour*, or in *Power*, with unequal Conditions,

Conditions, the acknowledging the other, *partes hoc ait*
not for Master or Lord, but by Honour as the *proprium, ut*
more powerful, and the better qualified, and *potentiori plus*
honoris, infir-
some for *Protector*; and these Treaties are *miori plus*
made with those States which take or give *auxilii defera-*
Penfion, or which put themselves into *Protec-* *tur* Grot
tion. And such was the League of * Protec- *lib 1 c 2 §*
21 n 2 It is
tion propounded to Queen *Elizabeth* by the the property
States-General of the *United Provinces*, who by of Friendship
Joos Van Menin most humbly besought Her 'twixt une-
quals, that
to accept of the Sovereignty and Supreme the stronger
Dominion over the said *United Provinces*, upon have more
certain and reasonable Conditions and Arti- Honour, and
cles, &c. the weaker
have more

Help *Procullus* adds, that such a Clause is inserted in the League,
to signify the one is superior in Authority and Dignity, for both are
free, but are *sub patricinio, non sub dictione. Liv. lib. 37 Cicero*
Offic 2

* *Non sine metu in posterum, quem tunc præsens neceffitas averterat*
Grotius *Annal lib 5 A E Mitoran lib 13 ad An* 1585. *Grim-*
ston, lib 12 ad An 1585

Tribute is paid by the *Subject*, or by him,
who, to enjoy his liberty, pays that which is
agreed upon to him that hath forced him to
do it But a *Penfion* is held voluntary from
him that is in *Protection*, or from him that is
in all other things *equal* to the *Treaty* of *Al-*
liance, to hinder the *Penfioners* that he join
not with the Enemy, as the *Swifs* to the
French, or to have Aid and Succours from
him.

II But that *Protection* is most true and *Leg. non dubi-*
honourable, when a Prince or *Republick* takes *D de Cap.*
upon him the defence of another, *freely with-*
out Reward, though some, if not all, find it
most neceffary to balance Honour with Profit,
from this Maxim, that *A pecuniary interest*
obliges more to succour, than when barely obliged
by Oath.

III. Again

III. Again, there feems to be a kind of
Protection or an Alliance, which indeed is no
more than a bare pecuniary retaining   Politicians have confidered the Subject diverfly,
either Abfolute or Conditional; Abfolute is
that which is meafured by the concurrence of
the greatnefs of Forces, Treafure, Munitions,
and other Military Preparations Conditional
is that, the which although it be lefs than an
abfolute, yet is more fit to fuccour us or do
us Harm · In this the Neighbourhood is of
very great confideration, for that a Neighbour
Prince of mean Forces may more eafily hurt
or fuccour us, than a great Prince that lies
far off, near Succours are always fooner ready
and with lefs Charge.   And this makes the
Bifhop of *Munfter* to be in that efteem with
the *States of Holland*, and the other Sovereign
Princes bordering on his Territory; and the
Reafon why he is fo much the more courted
into Affiftance and Friendfhip is, for that his
Forces being at hand, if Peace be concluded,
he is the more eafily difpatched, whereas remote and abfolute Princes, their Succours come
often too late after the Occafions to defend
us, and too foon to opprefs us

IV. By the Law of *Protection*, he that is
protected owes all *Respect* and *Honour* to his
Protector, againft whom, if he confpire or attempt, or ftrays from his duty, it is lawful
for the Protector to make *better affurance*;
nay, if he pleafes, to make himfelf *Mafter*.
But then on the other fide, the Protector
ought to defend and fuccour the protected,
and ufe him well, for otherwife he may withdraw himfelf from the Protection, and feek
another.

The *Genoefe*,
having put
themfelves in
the protection
of the *French*
King, re olt-
ed, he there-
upon changed
their Condi-
tions into
Privileges, to
the end, it
might be his
Will to de-
prive them
when he fhould think fit. *Vide Cardinal. Thufc. P. P. Concl* 935.

V. In

V. In Alliances that are unequal, there are four kinds of controversies may happen.

First, If the Subjects of a Prince or Republick, that is under the Protection of another, have committed any thing *against the League*.

Secondly, If the Prince or Republick be accused

Thirdly, If the Fellows, which are under the protection of the same *Prince* or *Republick*, contend with one another

Fourthly, If the Subjects complain of their own Ruler.

To the *first*, if a Fault appears, the Prince or Republick is bound either to punish the Offender, or to render him unto the Party injured, and see or endeavour that Damages may be recovered.

But one of the *Associates* in the League hath no Right to apprehend or punish the Subjects of his Confederate

To the *second*, the *Confederate* hath a Right to compel his Confederate to stand to the League, and if he will not, to punish him, for that one may take satisfaction or revenge of him that hath offended, and this happens as well amongst those that have no Confederation at all

To the *Third*, as in Confederacies equal, the Controversies are wont generally to be brought before an *Assembly* of the Confederates, that is to say, such as are *not concerned* in the Question, or else before *Arbitrators*, or else before the *Prince* of the *Association*, as a Common Arbitrator

So on the other hand in a *League unequal*, it is agreed for the most part, that the Controversies

---

This holds as well between Leagues equal as unequal.

Grotius *de Jure Belli ac Pacis, l* 1. *c.* 3 § 21

This hath the same Right in Leagues that are equal: *Nam ut quis ultionem sumat ab eo qui peccavit, satis est ut ipse ei qui peccavit subditus non sit.* Gro' *de Jure Belli, l.* 1. *c* 3. § 21 *n* 5.

But that proves not any power of commanding, for Princes do usually try their causes before Judges of their own chusing, *Eod. l.* 1. *c* 3. §. 21. *n* 6. *Decet eos qui Fæderis Principes sunt, circa suas quidem utilitates nihil præcipuum sumere; at in communibus rebus curandis eminere supra cæteros.*

In Orat Co-
rinthiorum
troverfies be debated before him who is *Superior in the League.*

To the laft, the *Confederates* have no *Cognizance.* In common Affairs out of time of Affembly, even where the *League* is equal, the Cuftom is for him who is chofe *Chief of the League,* to have Command over the Confederates, according to the Speech of the *Corinthians* in *Thucydides, It becomes them that are Princes of the League, not to feek their own particular advantage, but to content themfelves with an Eminency above the reft, in taking care of the common Intereft*

VI. Tho' that the Breach of Faith be much practifed in fuch Affairs, yet there are few Princes found which have not found a *pretext*, fome have pretended to be circumvented by error, others by Change of Affairs have pleaded an excufe, as great Wrongs or inevitable Lofs, and apparent danger of the ruin of their *States,* which are the Caufes, wherein fome fay, that *an Oath is not obligatory*; the Condition, by reafon of the Oath, being impoffible or unjuft; to thefe Limitations, fome hold they muft not keep faith Oldrad Conf
1. with an *Enemy of the Faith,* nor with him that hath broken his, nor with a Subject, nor with a *Thief* or *Pirate*, certainly, if it be not lawful for a Man in thefe cafes to keep *Faith,* Gregorius,
Perjurium Deo
culpam impingit negligen-
tie. it is not lawful to give it : If it be lawful to capitulate with fuch Men, it is neceffary to hold what we promife, that is, (we prefume) when the word is given by him that may give it, and that they rely upon it

VII. If *Hoftages* are taken, he that gives them is *freed from his Faith*; for that in receiving *Hoftages,* he that receives them hath relinquifhed the affurance which he hath in
the

the Faith of him that gave them, fo where a *Captain* for his *Prince* gives his Word without *Commiſſion* it binds not the *Prince*.

VIII. Some Lawyers would judge of *Treaties* as particular *Contracts*, by which means they would ſtretch the Conſciences of *Princes*; for, ſay they, that as a private Man is not bound by that which he hath promiſed by *force* or *fear*, ſo it ought to take place amongſt *Princes*, and in Treaties which are made betwixt Sovereigns, but that is ridiculous, for that were in effect to baniſh *Faith* from all publick Negotiations, for there is no Treaty but what is uſually made in *Arms* by *force*, or through *fear* to loſe either Life or Goods, or Liberty, or the *State*, which are cauſes of *juſt fear*, and may ſhake the moſt conſtant

IX Some Princes deſirous to ſhew themſelves more *irreligious* in theſe Ruptures, have taken ſubject and occaſion upon the *Ambiguity* of ſome Clauſes in the *Treaty*, or upon *Equivocation*, as *Charles the Fifth* did, or elſe they ſeek other Occaſions, as attempting againſt thoſe whom their Ally is bound to defend, to the end that drawing him into the field, *he may lay the cauſe of the Rupture on him.*

Upon the words *Evuing* and *Euig*, to retain the *Landgrave of Heſſe*

But Princes, who reſpect ſuch Treaties with a pious Intention of preſerving them, always remain conſtant and firm; and though occaſion may offer itſelf, by which they might get *advantage* by the Breach, yet when they remain durable, ſuch reſpect is afterwards had to their Word and Honour, that fewer and leſſer Securities will be demanded of them, than one *whoſe Faith is doubted.*

X. But

X. But Affurances in cafes of this Nature have been found more in *Republicks* than in *Princes*; for though Republicks have the fame Mind, and the fame *intentions* as Princes, yet for that they move but flowly, it will cause them to ftay longer in refolving. Famous is that of the *Athenians*, when *Themiftocles* in his Oration told them, That he could difcover a Matter in which the *Athenians* would reap great Advantages, but he could not tell it, for fear the difcovery would take away the Opportunity of atchieving it: Whereupon the *Athenians* deputed *Ariftides*, to whom he fhould communicate the Secret, and with him fhould confult about the obtaining it: They meeting, *Themiftocles* demonftrated, that it was in the Power of the *Athenians* to make themfelves Mafters of all *Greece*, for the *Grecian* Naval Army was then in their Ports and Protection; whereupon *Ariftides* replied, *The fame was a Breach of Faith*: But it was anfwered, *It being for the Publick, all confiderations of that kind ought to be laid afide*, whereupon *Ariftides* being called by the People to give Report, told them, *Themiftocles's advice was exceeding profitable, but difhoneft*, for which caufe the People wholly refufed it

Famous was the Anfwer of the Carthaginian Senate to the Romans upon the affaulting of Saguntum: Whether Saguntum was affaulted by private or publick Council, we conceive it not to be made the Queftion, but this, whether it was affaulted juftly or unjuftly; for to ourfelves an Account is to be given by our Citizens, whether it did it of itfelf, or by Commiffion; with you this alone is difputable, whether it were a violation of the League, or no   Livy B 31.

XI If one party has violated the League, the other may moft certainly depart from it; for the Tranfgreffion of the Articles, be it never fo little, makes a *Breach* of the *Agreement*, unlefs it be *otherwife* prevented by *Condition*, which may be, by inferting into the fame, * *that for every Offence it may not be lawful to depart from the League.*

* *Grot. l. 2. c 15. §. 15.*

XII. In

XII. In all *Leagues*, the Thoughts of Prin- *In fide quid* ces and States are to be confidered, not what *senseris, non* they faid; yet becaufe internal Acts are not *quid dixeris* vifible by themfelves, it is necessary that fome- *cogitandum.* what certain fhould be determined, *i. e.* re- *Cic. de Offic* duced to *Heads* or *Writings*, otherwife there *1.* would be no Obligation at all, for then every one might free himfelf, by affixing on his own Words what Senfe he pleafes. Hence it is, that by the Dictates of *Natural Reafon*, he to whom any thing is promifed, hath a Right to compel the Promifer to that which right *Interpretation* fuggefteth, for otherwife the matter would have no End. And as the reducing of the Treaties into Writing makes the Agreements plain and obvious, fo the mutual Advance of the Minifters proportionably haftens the Accomplifhment. The Counts *Avaux* and *Servient*, being appointed for the Treaty at *Munfter*, as they paffed through *Holland*, they entered into a Confederacy with thofe States, wherein each Party reciprocally did bind themfelves by Articles, not only not to treat of any thing without the Affent and Participation of the other Col- *Monmouth's* league, but that the Treaty fhould be carried *Hiftory of* on fo equally, as if one of the Parties fhould *France, fol* fee the other's Bufinefs advance further than *28* his, it fhould be lawful for the one to defire the other to proceed no further, till his Affairs were equally advanced, which Articles bounding the Approaches of each other, foon haftened the end of that tedious Treaty.

XIII. Again, in all Leagues and Treaties *Qui promittit* for Peace, there is this Exception to be fup- *non offendere,* pofed in the Contractors, unlefs fome new *is fubintelligit* Caufe intervene, or unlefs it be by the default *exceptionem—* of him with whom the League and Compact *Nifi caufa fu- pervemat, nifi is culpa accefferit* is made, or Affairs continuing in the same posture and state in which they were at the Time of the Contract. And that Saying of *Ulpianus* and *Pomponius* concerning private Compacts, viz. *That an Agreement is not violated, from which a Man recedes upon a just reason and motive*, is by Interpreters extended to National Leagues betwixt Princes and States.

XIV. In the *Interpretation* of Leagues and Truces, there ought to be a very great Care had, in regard of the *Sacredness* of them; therefore in things promised or secured by such Leagues, some are favourable, some odious, some mixt, or of a middle Nature. Those that are most favourable, are those whose Words tend to Peace, not to War, whose Footsteps leave ever behind the deep Impressions of Misery, Devastation, and Poverty, but more especially when such Leagues are made for *War Defensive* than otherwise; but those are called *odious*, which *burden* or *oppress* one part only, or one more than the other, and likewise such as tend to matter of *Revenge* or *Punishment*, or to violate some former acts or obligations, *or the bringing in a change or innovation of what hath been constantly settled, and used before*. Mixt, as where a Change is propounded, but that is with the Sisters of *Moderation* and *Peace*, which are proportionably good, according, as the Change may be esteemed ——Therefore the Standard Rule is, *That in Leagues and Treaties* not odious, *the Words are to be taken according to the full extent and propriety of popular use; and if there be more Significations, the largest is best*. On the other hand, we are not to recur to Significations plainly improper,

improper, unless otherwise some absurdity or inutility of the Agreement would follow Again, Words are to be taken ever more strictly than Propriety suffers, if it be necessary for the avoiding of *inequity* or *absurdity*. But if there be not such necessity, *manifest equity* or *utility* in the Restriction, we are to stay them within the narrowest Bounds of Propriety, unless the Circumstances dissuade. On the other hand, in *Leagues* or *Promises odious*, even a figurative Speech is admitted to avoid the *Odium*, or burden; therefore in *Donation, Remission* of one's *Right, Dominion or Property*, they are always to be construed to those things which were probably thought on, and really intended. So Aids and Succours promised from one part only, is to be understood to be due at the *Charges of him who shall acquire them*

Vide exemplum in L cum virum C de fidei commissis.

Grotius *lib.* 1. *cap.* 16 § 12.

CHAP

CHAP. IX.

Of Treaties of Truce, Neutrality, and Peace.

I. T*Reaties* are either with *Enemies* or *Friends,* or with Perfons which defire to continue *Neuters* with us, or we with them.

The Treaties which are made with our *Enemies* are either for *a time,* or *perpetual*

Perpetual, as the Peace that is made to compofe all differences, and the War that is undertaken for *Conqueft,* or for *Reparation* of Injuries, or to *reftore* the *Commerce.*

Treaties, which are made for a time with our Enemies, are called *Truces,* the which are either *general,* for all the States of the one or the other Prince, for all Perfons, and for all forts of *Commerce.* Or elfe they are *particular,* for certain *Places,* for certain *Perfons,* and for the *Commerce,* and fometimes no further than a bare fufpenfion of Arms

A Truce

A Truce is an Agreement, whereby, tho' Truce, what it is. the War continue, yet all Acts of Hostility do for a while cease, for between War and Peace there is no Medium, it is, and may be called a War, tho' at present its Operations are intermitted An Habit may be, tho' at present it doth not operate A Man may be said to be wise or prudent, tho' he be asleep, and virtuous, tho' for a while he be void of Action So that a Truce cannot be called a Peace, for tho' the Fight cease, the *Grot de Jure Belli & pacis, lib 3 c 21. § 1.* War continues, 'tis but a bare Suspension of the Acts of War

II. When any one is bound by *Alliance* not to make *Peace* or *Truce*, without the Consent of his *Ally*, and whose Agreement seems doubtful, they add in the Treaty, that it shall take place for all those the Contractors shall Name, and they set down no prefixed time, but that *it shall continue till he refuse*, and some *reasonable time ascertained after*, as that which was made betwixt *Charles* the Eighth and the King of *Spain*.

In the Truce that was made between Edw the Fourth and Lewis the Eleventh, there was like provision

made for *Charles* Duke of *Burgundy*, but he refused, and concluded a Peace for himself apart, being angry with *Edward* the Fourth for making the same *Phil Comin lib 4 cap 40* So *Lewis* the Eleventh concluded a Truce for nine Years with *Edward* the Fourth when he had invaded *France* *Phil Comin lib 4 cap. 8.*

III. Sometimes a *general Truce* holds the place of *Peace*, as that of a hundred years. Such Truces are commonly made betwixt Princes that are *equal in Power*, as that betwixt *Spain* and *Portugal*, and will not *quit* any thing of their *Rights* by Peace , and yet desire to live quietly in the State wherein they are, *satisfying by this Medium the point of Honour.*

IV. *Treaties of Truce* are many times lefs fubject to *Rupture* than a *Peace*, which is made *perpetual*; for Princes or States that find themfelves aggrieved with a Treaty that is perpetual, feek out plaufible Reafons to forfake it, feeing the Grievances cannot be otherwife repaired, but if the time be limited and expired, they may purfue that which they think *ought to be granted*, and the other may oppofe, and if they have a defire to continue the *Truce*, there is nothing fo eafy as to renew it. Hence it is become a *Maxim* in State, That feeing Treaties are grounded on the *Interefts of Princes which change with the time, it is neceffary to change and fettle them at the end of the time, or to break them off*; for it is in vain to truft to a bare Friendfhip.

'Tis true, the *Swedes* and the other Confederates with *France* were for a Peace, and the Marquis *Caftel Rodrigo* then offered a Blank unto the *Hollanders* which they might treat of at home.
* *Monmouth's* Hiftory of *France, fol* 28.

V. A *Truce* is likewife made to advance a Peace, and to treat of it; and fuch was the Truce of the *Hollanders* propounded at the Treaty of *Munfter*, who refufed abfolutely to liften to any more than a Truce; and the Reafon that they then gave was, that their Commonwealth was to be maintained by Arms, and that by admitting a Peace, the fame might be a means to reduce it to weaknefs, which would in the end tend to the deftruction of that State, nay, they offered the Truce on Terms, that if * *France* fhould enter thereunto, fhe fhould oblige herfelf upon any Breach to reaffume War, and that Treaty of Truce was continued, which not long after was converted into a perpetual Peace.

Again, *Truces* are fometimes promoted for the more honeft difcharge of a *League*, which is made with fome other Prince, whom they

they have accuftomed to comprehend therein · So as a Peace following it; or a Truce
not being accepted by him, they take occafion to leave the League, *it being not his
fault* that leaves it, that the War was not
ended.

VI. And although it feems that a *Truce*
cannot by its condition prejudice the *preten-
fion* in the *Principal*, yet it is moft certain,
that if he which is chafed out of a contentious
State, confents, that during the *Truce the
Commerce fhall be forbidden to his Subjects, he
doth wholly ftop the gate*, as * *Lewis* the
Twelfth did in the *Truce* which he made with
Gonfalve after the Conqueft of the Realm of
Naples.

VII. In *England* by the *Statute* of 2 *H* 5
cap. 6. Robbery, Spoiling, breaking of *Truces*
and *Safe-Conducts*, by any of the King's Liege
People and Subjects within *England, Ireland,*
and *Wales*, or upon the main Sea, was adjudged and determined to be High-Treafon,
but this branch concerning High-Treafon,
is repealed by the *Statute* of 20 *H.* 6. *cap.*
11. 1 *E* 6. *c.* 12. 1 *M. Seff.* 1. *c* 1. But
by the faid *Act* of 2 *H.* 5. for the better obfervation of Truces and Safe-Conducts, *Con-
fervator Induciarum & falvorum Regis conduc-
tuum*, was raifed and appointed in every Port
of the Sea by Letters Patents: His Office
was to inquire of all Offences done againft
the King's Truces and Safe-Conducts upon
the main Sea (out of the Counties and out
of the Leagues of *Cinque Ports)* as *Admirals*
of Cuftom were ufed to do Sir *John Trebiel*
was committed to the *Tower* for taking a
French Ship, and being brought into *Parliament*, did there juftify the fame, but at laft

* For the
Right re-
mains with
him, however
he hath loft
the poffeffion.
Grot. lib. 2
cap. 16 §. 18.

11 *H* 4.

O 2 confeffed

confessed his fault, and begged the King's Pardon And at the request of the Lords and Commons was pardoned, he making satisfaction for the loss †. Generally all Leagues and Safe-Conducts are, or ought to be of *Record*, that is, they ought to be *Inrolled in the Chancery*, to the end the Subject may know who are in Amity with the King, and who not, who be Enemies, and can have no Action here, and who in League, and may have Actions personal here.

† *Ad Parliam. tent. quinsen Hill Vide* Cotton Abridgment .
19 *E.* 4 *6 B*
15 *H* 6. *c.* 3
18 *H* 6 *c.* 8.
20 *H* 6. *c* 1.
14 *E* 4 *c.* 4.
19 *E* 4. 6. *B.*

Sometimes they have been inrolled in the *Wardrobe*, as being matters of State

Maxim.

Note, *In all Treaties, the power of the one party, and the other, ought to be equal, nor are they to be held firm till ratified.*

Rott. Scotiæ de Anno 10 *E.* 3. *in* 36 *intus, ae puniendo ille. qui contra formam Treugæ hominibus de Scotia concessa deliquerint.*

Before the Statute, when any breach of Truces or Leagues happened, or was occasioned by the misdemeanors of any of the King of *England*'s Subjects, there did usually issue forth Commissions under the *Great Seal* of *England*, to inquire of the Infringers of the same, and to punish and award Satisfaction to the injured

VIII. *Princes*, who neither love nor hate any thing absolutely, seem generally inclined to *Neutrality*, and in that govern themselves in their Friendships according to their Interests ; and *Reason of State*, in effect, is no other but *Reason of Interest*.

Neutrality may be of two sorts; the one with *Alliance with either part*, the other *without Alliance*, or so much as the least Tye to the one or other, which is that which properly may be called *Neutrality*

The first is governed by the *Treaty of Neutrality*, the latter by the *Discretion of the Neuter Prince*, whose Carriage ought always

to

to be such, as that he may not give the least glimpse of inclining more to one than to another

IX. The Advantages of Neutrality are, that the Neuter Prince or Republick is honoured and respected of both Parties, and by the fear of his declaring against one of them, he remains Arbitrator of others, and Master of himself.

And as a Neuter neither purchases Friends, nor *frees himself from Enemies*, so commonly he proves a Prey to the Victor, hence it is held more advantage *to hazard in a Conquest with a Companion, than to remain in a State, wherein he is in all probability of being ruined by the one or the other.*

But Princes that are *powerful*, have used generally to preserve a *Neutrality*; for whilst Petty Princes and States ruin themselves by War, he fortifies himself with *means*, and, in the end, may make himself Judge of their Differences

On the other hand it hath been conceived, that Republicks that are weak, what part soever they take, it will be dangerous to them, especially if they are in the midst of two more powerful States than themselves; but Experience hath made it appear to the contrary, that *Neutrality* is more beneficial to a *weak Prince* or *Republick*, so that they that are at War be not barbarous or inhuman. For although a Neutrality does not please either Party, yet in effect it wrongs no Man, and as he doth not serve, so he does not hurt · Besides, his Declaration is reserved till the Issue of the War, by which means he is not obliged, by siding with either party, to gain or lose by the War

Much practised by the Princes of the Empire and petty States

O 3   X. But

X. But if the Neuter be preſt by Neceſſity. to declare himſelf, he muſt do it *for the moſt powerful* of the two Parties, following that *Roman* Maxim, *That either they muſt make themſelves the ſtrongeſt, or be a Friend to the ſtrongeſt* · So they of *Straſbourg* * declared for the Empire againſt the *French* On the other hand, if the Neuter ſees, that joining to the weaker, will balance the Power of the ſtronger, and by this Counterpoiſe reduce them to Reaſon ; the ſame hath been generally followed, upon the Maxim, *That the ſafety of States conſiſts in an equal counterpoiſe of the one, and the other* ; *for as the greatneſs and opulency of a Prince draws after it the Ruin of their Neighbours, it is wiſdom to prevent it.*

* *Anno* 1674. *Conſul Quintus ad Achæos, quod optimum eſſe dicant non interponi vos bello. immobil tam alienum rebus veſtris eſt : Quippe ſine gratia vel dignitate præmium victoris eritis Luctus, lib.* 35. *Scripta Ammirat. diſc polit. l.* 18.

CHAP.

C H A P. X.

Of the Immunities and Privileges of Ambaſſadors, and other publick Miniſters of State.

I. *Of the Function of Ambaſſadors and Agents generally conſidered.*

II. *Of the Difference between Ordinary and Extraordinary*

III. *Of the Qualifications and Matters requiſite to be in ſuch.*

IV. *Whether any but Sovereign Princes and States may qualify ſuch, and who may not.*

V *Of the Right of Ambaſſadors, how ſecured by the Laws Divine, and of Nations.*

VI. *Of Precaution, whether the ſame may be given to ſuch not to come, and attempting againſt ſuch interdiction, how to be dealt with; and of the puniſhment of thoſe that ſhall violate them, by the Laws of* England

VII. *How Princes and States may govern themſelves in reference to their Reception or Refuſal.*

VIII. *Whether Ambaſſadors may be ſubjected to Puniſhment when they offend againſt the Laws of Nations*

IX *Of proceeding againſt them by Princes and Republicks at this day according to the Laws of Nations.*

X. *Whether privileged in that State or Country thro' which they paſs without leave, and of the various Proceedings againſt them by ſeveral Princes and States, illuſtrated in Precedents and Examples.*

XI. *Of proceeding againſt them according to the Laws of* England.

XII *Where they forfeit their Privilege, according to the Laws of* England, *in things Capital.*

XIII. *Where preſerved in Matters ordinary not* malum in ſe.

XIV *The Office of a publick Miniſter, what it in-*

cludes

cludes in Matters Civil for the King and Nation whom they represent.

XV. *Whether the House of an Ambassador can be a
Sanctuary to offenders, or that he may exercise
Royal Jurisdiction over his own Domesticks and
Vassals.*

XVI. *Whether the Goods of an Ambassador are subject to seizure for Debts contracted by himself*

XVII *Outrages committed by Ambassadors, where
a Forfeiture of their Privilege*

XVIII *Of Punishment on those that shall offer Violence to their persons.*

XIX *Observations touching the Immunities and Governments of the publick Ministers of* Venice.

XX *How introduced by the Laws of Nations.*

XXI *Wars whether just for Violation done to publick Ministers.*

XXII. *The Privileges of Ambassadors and their Servants, as to civil Suits, by the Law of* England.

Coke 4. Instit
fol 153
Agents are
generally
used when
there is some
Suspicion
that the Am-
bassador will

I. AN *Ambassador* and *Agent* is the same
thing, if we consider only the Function of their Charges . Only in this they dif-
fer , an *Agent* hath charge to represent the
Affairs only ; but an *Ambassador* ought to represent the *Greatness of his Master, and his
Affairs.*

not be honoured as he should be ; therefore the *French* Kings of late
Years have no Ambassadors in the *Emperor*'s Court, but Agents, because of the Competition for Precedence betwixt him and *Spain.*

II Ambassadors are in two Capacities,
either Ordinary or Extraordinary . The Ordinary or Lieger Ambassadors, are those who
are commanded to reside in the Place whither sent, unless they receive Letters of Revocation , and as the time of their Return is
indefinite, so their Business is uncertain, arising
out of emergent Occasions, and commonly
the Protection and Affairs of the Merchants,
is their greatest Care. The Extraordinary or

pro

pro tempore, are thofe that are employed upon fome particular great Affairs, or Condolements, or Congratulations, or for Overtures of Marriage, &c. Their Equipage is generally very magnificent and illuftrious, and they may return without requefting of Leave, unlefs there be a reftraining Claufe in their Commiffion

III. An Ambaffador or Agent ought to be converfant in all forts of Hiftory, reading with Judgment, and weighing all the Circumftances of Action which are there reprefented, by which he will be qualified to know (but efpecially of that Country whither he his fent)

    1. The Eftablifhment of Eftates.
    2. The Rights of Limits.
    3. The Genealogies of Princes.
    4. The Pretenfions of Kings upon the Eftates of others
    5. Their Forces, Means, Alliances, and manner of living Perfonally he muft be

1. Refolute and Couragious in that which he hath wifely deliberated
2. Secret in Affairs of Importance.
3. Difcreet in his Speech.
4. No Detractor or Evil Speaker of any King or State, but more efpecially of him or them with whom he remains.
5. One that will fpeak freely of his Mafter's Pretenfions, if there be a Queftion to maintain them.

IV. By the Laws of Nations, none under the Degree of a Sovereign Prince can nominate or fend any in that Quality, nor can any Subject fend or receive any Ambaffador, be he never fo Great; if a Viceroy doth it, it is no lefs

The Trumpeter that brought the Letters from the Maid of *Orleans* to the Earl of *Suf-*

folk was burnt; and the Reason of that was, because he came from no lawful Prince, nor one commissionated, or capable of sending a Trumpeter. Grimston's History of France, fol 326

less than High-Treason; and so it was declared when the *Scots, inconsulto Principe,* sent *Lowden* and others in Quality of private clancular Commissioners, to treat with the *French* King *Lewis* the Thirteenth, in the Name of the whole Nation for Assistance, the King would not admit or hear them. So did Queen *Elizabeth,* when *Christopher Assonville* came into *England* in Quality of a Minister of State, sent from the Duke of *Alva,* then Governor of *Flanders,* she refused to admit him, he not having any Commission or Credentials from the King of *Spain* 'Tis true, the Electors and Princes of *Germany* have obtained the Privilege of sending, and the Reception of Ambassadors, * but that is limited only to Matters touching their own Territories, and not the State of the Empire. And so likewise the *Hans* Towns may do the same; for they claim the like Privilege, they being free Imperial Cities, and partake of the same Regalias, either by Prescription or by Grants from former Emperors, whose Necessities enforced them to part with such Royal Flowers of the Empire; and generally they † send for their Ambassadors always two Persons, one of great Birth, and that hath been a Soldier, to maintain Decency, and the other a Doctor or Lawyer to regulate Affairs with Learning, and by the Pen.

* That the German Princes may have such a Prerogative, but it is secundario tantum jure Et qui jus mittendorum Legatorum secundario tantum jure habent, mittantur Legati non de Rebus universum concernentibus Imperium, sed tantum sui Territorii ratione; eo enim ipsis intuitu tantum datum, ultra igitur terminos non est procedendum, fieret enim alias præjudicium Imperato ., &c. Kirknerus, §. 25 Memorable was that of the Switzers, who sent a Message to the French King, that he should not send them an Ambassador with store of Words, but a Treasurer with Plenty of Money.

† Monmouth's History of France, fol 27, 28.

V. The Right of Ambassadors is secured both by the Safeguard of Men, and also by the Protection of the *Law Divine;* therefore

to

to violate this, is not only *unjust*, but *impious* Pompon. Leg.
too: And as *Protection* is given to the *Legates* si quis D de
of Supreme *Rulers* by the *Laws of Nations*, Legationibus.
so by the *Civil Law* there is a Protection likewise for *Provincial Legates, Heralds*, and *Con-
suls*. This Right of Legation was originally
provided, saith *Livy*, for a *Foreigner*, not a Liv. lib. 16.
Citizen; yet in Civil Wars, Necessity some-
times makes Place for this Right besides the
Rule, as when the People are so divided into
equal Parts, that it is doubtful on which Side
the Right of Empire lieth, as that unhappy
Spot of *Flanders*; or when the Right being
much controverted, two contend for the Succession to the *Throne*, for in this Case one
Nation is reckoned as two; and so was the
State of *England*, when the *Houses* of *York* and
Lancaster contended for the *Crown*, properly Kings con-
then called Commissioners Nay, this Right quered in a
of *Legation* hath been so preserved, that the solemn War,
very Messengers of Rebels have been protected, of their King-
as were those of *Holland* by *Philip* of *Spain*. dom, with
So great a Respect have Nations had in all other Royal-
times to such Men, that even * *Traitors*, nay Right of Le-
Pirates and *Robbers*, who make not a Society, gation P.
nor have any Protection by the *Law of Na-* Æmilius de-
tions, and with whom neither Faith nor Oath tained the
(as some conceive) may be kept, Faith being Perseus,
given them, obtain the Right of *Legation*, whom he
as once the Fugitives in the *Pyrenean Forest* conquered.
did. * *C Poole* a
Traitor fled
to *Rome*, the *Pope* sent him Ambassador to the *French* King, of whom
the King of *England* demands his Subject, *sed non prævaluit*. *Coke
Inst* 4 *fol* 153

VI. *Ambassadors* may by a *Precaution* be
warned not to come; if they dare they shall Lucas's Rep.
be taken for Enemies; but once admitted 4· 5·
even with Enemies in Arms, much more with

Enemies

Enemies not in actual Hostility, have the Protection and Safe-guard of the Laws of Nations; and therefore their Quality being admitted by Safe-conduct, they are to be preserved as Princes; and so it was declared in *Parliament*, where the killing of *John Imperial*, Ambassador from the States of *Genoa*, was High-Treason, *Crimen læsæ Majestatis*

Rot Pat 3.
R 3. num 18

† So likewise of *A de Walton*, the King's Ambassador, *Nuncium Domini Regis missum ad mandatum Regis exequendum*, who was murdered by one *John Hill*, which Offence was adjudged High-Treason, and accordingly he was drawn, hanged, and beheaded.

† Legatus ejus vice fungitur à quo destinatur, & honorandus est sicut ille cujus vicem gerit, & Legatos violare

centra jus Gentium est, 22 *Assize*, *pl* 49. *Note*, This was three Years before the making of the Statute of 25 E 3 *quære*, if such a *Prorex* is within the Statute at this Day

And by the *Julian* Law, he that violates Ambassadors is guilty of publick Violence; that is, of prostituted Faith of publick Authority, and of a Breach of the Laws of Nations; and by the *Pontifical* Law it is no less than a Piacle, and to be interdicted from the Benefit of holy things. *Philomela* sung a fatal *Requiem* for the bloody Entertainment which she gave the Ambassadors of *Frederick Barbarossa*, the Emperor having sent them to treat in order to Peace; but they instead of that, avowed the Action of those that murdered his Ambassadors · The offended Emperor having taken the City, razed it to the Ground, and executed all the People therein, as Rebels and Traitors against the Laws of Nations

Qui violarit Legatum, Lege Julia de vi publica tenetur.

Fuller's Holy War, l 3 c 4

VII On the other hand, Ambassadors may not always be received, though they ought never to be rejected without Cause, for there may be Cause from him from whom they come,

come, as the *Roman Senate* would not admit of the Embaſſage of the *Carthaginian,* whoſe Army was then in *Italy,* the King of *Spain,* thoſe of *Holland,* and the then *Pope,* the Ambaſſador of *Henry* the Second, after the Murder of *Becket* Archbiſhop of *Canterbury.* So likewiſe from the very Perſons that are ſent, as *Theodorus* the *Atheiſt,* whom *Lyſima-chus* would not give Audience to, and Mr *Oliver, Lewis* the Eleventh's Barber, whom they of *Gaunt* refuſed Yet *Matthæus Palme-rius,* an Apothecary of *Florence,* had better Fortune than the *French* Barber; for he being ſent in Quality of Ambaſſador to *Alphonſo* King of *Naples,* and having acquitted him-ſelf elegantly, and with much Generoſity at his firſt Audience, the King having Informa-tion that he was an Apothecary, ſaid, *Se tali ſono gli ſpeciali di Fierenze, quali debbono eſſere gli Medici?* If the Apothecaries of Florence are ſuch, what ſhall we think of their Phy-ſicians?

Camden 1571 Daniel's Hiſtory of Henry 2 Carolus quintus Imper Galliæ, Venetorum, & Florentinorum ad bellum ſibi indicendum miſſos deduci juſſit in locum qui à comitatu ſuo abeſſet, triginta millia-ria Guic l. 18 Bellaius, l 3.

So likewiſe where the Cauſe of ſending is ſuſpected, in reference to diſturb the People, or with Intentions rather to ſow Sedition, than to conclude a Peace (if ſuch be their Errand) or not honourable or unſeaſonable As for thoſe aſſiduous Legations which are now in uſe, they may with very good Right be re-jected, for the Neceſſity of them appears by the antient Cuſtom whereto they are un-known, which made *Henry* the Seventh admit of none.

Bacon's H. VII

The *Venetian* having admitted *Henry* the Fourth of *France* his Ambaſſador, yet they interdicted him * to come with the other Ambaſſador to the *Chapel,* till the King was reconciled to the *Church of* Rome.

* Card Ar-nold Oſſat in his 353 Epiſ-tle Coke Inſtit fol 153.

VIII. By

*Menander Protector Justino Imper. Avarorum Legatos contra jus Legationum in vinculis habuit, Gothmann. Resp. 32. n. 29 Coke Instit 4. 153. 2 H. 5. cap 6. 1 M. Seff 1 c. 1.
* Quanquam visi sunt commisisse ut hostium loco essent, jus tamen Gentium valuit
† Et reus magis ex equo bonoque quam ex jure Gent. Bomilcar comes ei qui Romam fide publica venerat
An Enemy is bound to whom they are sent; but their Privilege obliges not those

VIII. By the Laws of Nations, only unjust Force is kept from the Bodies of Ambassadors; for if the Laws of Nations be broken by him, he is subject to Punishment. Yet the Opinions of Nations, and Men eminent for Wisdom, have been doubtful in this Point, and Precedents on both Sides have been avouched; one which seems to refute that Position of punishing such Ministers of State: The Ambassadors of *Tarquin*, who had committed Treason at *Rome*, and as * *Livy* observes, were in the State of Enemies, yet the *Right of Nations* (as he calls it) *prevailed so far as to preserve them, though in a Case of Hostility.* On the other hand, † *Salust* observes, that *Bomilcar*, one of the *Carthaginian* Ambassadors, who came to *Rome* on the publick Faith, *was adjudged Guilty, rather* (saith he) *by the Rules of Equity, than by the Laws of Nations*: Equity, that is the mere *Law of Nature*, suffers Punishment to be exacted where there is found a Delinquent, but the *Laws of Nations* except the Persons of *Ambassadors*; for certainly their Security outweighs *the Profit arising from Punishment*, which may be inflicted by him that hath sent him (if he be willing) if unwilling, it may be exacted of him as an Approver of the Crime.

through whose Rounds they pass without Leave, for if they go to, or come from their Enemies, or make any hostile Attempt, they may be slain *Liv lib.* 26.

Grotius, l. 2 c 18. §. 4. 4, & 5 Senatus faciem secum attulerat auctoritatem Resp M Tull 8.

IX. Again, as *Ambassadors* are not to render a *Reason of their Actions to any other*, but to *him* by whom they are sent, so it is impossible, by reason of various *Interests* and other *Secrets* of State, which pass through their Hands, but somewhat may be said, which

which bears a Show or Face of Crime, (which perhaps may prove otherwise) yet the examining and tracing of the Truth, may be of a dangerous consequence; and therefore if the Offence be such as may be contemned, it is usually to be dissembled or connived at, or else the Ambassador be commanded to depart the *Realm*; and if the Crime be cruel, and publickly mischievous, the Ambassador *Coke Instit 4* may be sent home with *Letters of Request* to *fol 152.* his Master, to inflict Punishment according to the Offence • So likewise in the Precaution of a great Mischief, especially publick, (if there be no other Remedy) Embassadors may be *Sic Carolus* apprehended and executed; and if they op- *quintus Legato* pose by force of Arms they may be slain. *Ducis Medio-lanensis ut sub-* *diti sui imperavit, ne à Comitatu suo abcederet, Guicciard. in dict. jam loc* Vide Camden's *Eliz. Anno* 1571 1584.

In the Bishop of *Ross*'s Case, *An* 13 *Eliz.* *Co 4 Inst fol.* the Question was, *An Legatus qui rebellionem* 152. *contra Principem ad quem legatus concitat, Legati privilegiis gaudeat, & non ut hostis pœnis subjaceat*, and it was resolved, That he had lost the Privilege of an Ambassador, and was subject to Punishment, nor can Ambassadors be defended by the Law of Nations, when they commit any thing against the State or Person of the Prince with whom they reside.

X. And why Ambassadors are in Safety in Case of the their Enemy's Countries, and are to be spared Ambassador when they commit Offences, is not so much of *Muscovy.* for their own or *Master*'s sake, *but because* Lucas's Re- *without them there will never be an End of* ports, 4. 5 *Hostility, nor Peace after War* Neither is the *Name* or *Person* of an *Ambassador* so inviolable, either in Peace or in time of War, but there may be both a convenient time and a good
Occasion

Occasion to punish them, and this standing with the Laws of Nations, as may appear by these following Examples.

Thucyd. lib. 2. Appian de Bello Illirica Sicu- li Athenienfium Socii Legatos Syracusanorum missos ad Civi- tates alias ce- pere.

1 The Law does not pertain to them through whose Bounds Ambassadors pass without Leave; for if they go to their Enemies, or come from their Enemies, or make any hostile Attempt, they may be slain. So the *Athenians* did to the Ambassadors between the *Persians* and *Spartans*, the *Illyrians* to the Ambassadors between the *Esseans* and *Romans*

2. The Emperor *Charles* the Fifth, adver- tised of the League made against him, would not dismiss the Ambassadors of *France*, *Eng- land*, and *Venice*, till his own were in Safety, but he sets Guards upon those of *France*, *Ve- nice*, and *Florence*, causing them to be con- ducted thirty Miles from his Court, with a Prohibition not to speak to them, nor for them to write. As to him of *Milan*, as his Subject, he was enjoined not to part from Court, but as for him of *England*, there was no Alteration

De Gallorum ac Turcam le- gatis, quos in Pado Hispani cepere occide- runt, vide Ju- dicia Peruta, lib. 11 Camden, Eliz. Anno 1571 Hiftory of the Repub- lick of Venice, fol 450, 451

3. The *Venetians*, having destroyed some of the *Corsairs*, *Amurath* commanded *Luigi Con- tarini*, then *Bailio of Venice*, to be imprisoned

4. The *Seignory of Venice* understanding that certain Traitors, who had revealed their *Secrets* to the *Turk*, were fled for Protection into the House of the *French* Ambassador at *Venice*, sent Officers to search the Embassa- dor's House; but the Ambassador's refusing them Entrance, the *Senate* commanded cer- tain Cannon to be brought out of the *Arsenal* to beat down his House, which, when he saw planted, he surrendered up the Traitors

5 The

5. The Ambassadors of *Tarquin*, *Morte affligendos Romani non judicarunt, & quanquam visi sunt ut hostium loco essent, jus Gentium tamen valuit*

6. The *State of Rome*, though in Cafe of moft Capital Crimes, exempted the *Tribunes* of the People from Queftion during the Year of Office. | *Goodwin de Leg. Antiq. Rom.*

7. The Ambaffadors of the *Proteftants* at the *Council of Trent*, divulging there the *Doctrine* of the Church, contrary to a *Decree* there, whereby it was enacted a Crime equivalent to Treafon, yet ftood they protected from any Punifhment. | *Acta Tridenti Concilii.*

It is generally confented by all the *Civilians*, That *Legatis de jure Gentium indictum eft, & eorum corpora falva fint, propter neceffitatem Legationis, ac ne confundantur Jura commercii inter Principes.* | *Pompon Leg. ult D de Legatis.*

8. *Viva*, the *Pope's Legate*, was reftrained by *Henry* the Second for exercifing a Power within his Realm, not allowed or admitted of by the King, in difquiet of the State, and forced to fwear not to act any thing *in praejudicium Regis vel Regni* | *Benedict in Vita Hen. 2.*

On the other hand, it hath been anfwered, That they are by the Laws of Nations exempted from Regal Trial, all Actions of one fo qualified, being made the Acts of his Mafter, or of thofe whom he reprefents until he or they difavow; and *Injuries* of one *Abfolute Prince* or *State* to another, is *factum hoftilitatis*, and not *Treafon*, the Immunity of whom *Civilians* collect, as they do the reft of their Grounds from the Practice of the *Roman State*, deducing their Arguments from thefe Examples.

VOL. I. P 9. The

9. The *Fabii* Ambassadors from *Rome*, were returned safe from the *Chades*, with demand of Justice against them only, although they had been taken bearing Arms with the *Etrurians*, their Enemies.

10. King *Edward* the Second of *England*, sent amongst others a *French* Gentleman Ambassador into *France*; the King upon this arraigned him as a Traitor, for serving the King of *England* as Ambassador, who was his Enemy (but the Queen procured his Pardon).

11. *Henry* the Third did the like to one of the *Pope*'s Ambassadors, his *Collegue* flying the Realm secretly, fearing, *timens pelli suæ*, as the Records have it. *Edward* the First restrained another of the *Pope*'s turbulent Ambassadors, till he had (as his Progenitors had) informed the *Pope* of the Fault of his *Minister*, and received Satisfaction for the Wrongs.

12. *Henry* the Eighth commanded a *French* Ambassador to depart presently out of the Realm, because he was the professed Enemy of the See of *Rome*

13 *Lewis de Prat*, Ambassador for *Charles* the Fifth, was commanded to his House, for accusing falsly Cardinal *Wolsey* to have practised a Breach between *Henry* the Eighth and his Master, to make up the Amity with the *French King*.

14. Sir *Michael Throgmorton*, by *Charles* the Ninth of *France*, was so served, for being too busy with the Prince of *Condé*'s Faction.

15. The *Pope*'s Ambassador at *Paris* was arraigned, for practising certain Treasons in *France* against the King, in the Parliament

of

of *Paris*, and was found there guilty and committed to Prison.

16. Doctor *Man*, then Ambassador, was taken from his House at *Madrid* in *Spain*, and put under a Guard to a straiter Lodging, for breeding a Scandal (as the *Conde Teri* said) in using by Warrant of his Place, the Religion of his Country, although he alledged the like permitted to *Guzman de Silva*, their Ambassador in *England*, and to the *Turk* no less than in *Spain*.

Camden's Hist Q Eliz. A 1567

17. *Francis* the First, King of *France*, sent *Cæsar Fregosus* and *Anthony Rincome*, Ambassadors to the *Turk*, they were surprized by the Armies of *Charles* the Fifth on the River *Po* in *Italy*, and were put to Death, the *French* King complained that they were wrongfully murdered, but the *Emperor* justified their Death, for that the one was a *Genois*, and the other a *Milanois*, and his Subjects feared not to serve the King his Enemy.

Guicciard lib 18

18 *Henry* the Eighth, being in a League with the *French*, and at Enmity with the *Pope*, who was in League with the *French* King, and who had sent Cardinal *Pool* to the *French* King, of whom King *Henry* demanded the *Cardinal*, being his Subject, and attainted of Treason, *sed non prævaluit*.

Herbert's Hist H 8.

19. *Samuel Pelagii*, a Subject to the King of *Morocco*, pretended that he was an Ambassador sent unto the *States General* of the *United Provinces*; he came to them, and accordingly they treated with him, afterwards he departed, and being upon the Sea, he there took and spoiled a *Spanish* Ship, and then came into *England*, the *Spanish* Ambassador here having received Intelligence of the

spoliation,

spoliation, caused his Person to be seized upon, intending to proceed against him as a Pirate, and imprisoned him ; and upon Conference with the Lord *Coke*, *Doderidge*, and other Judges and *Civilians* ; they declared their Opinions, That the Caption of the *Spaniard*'s Goods by the *Morocco* Ambassador, is not in Judgment of Law a Piracy, in regard it was apparent, that the King of *Spain* and the King of *Morocco* are Enemies, and the same was done in *open* 'Hostility ; and therefore in Judgment of Law could not be called *Spoliatio, sed legalis Captio* ; and a Case out of 2 *R.* 3. *fol.* 2. was vouched, where a *Spanish* Merchant before the King and his *Council in Camerâ Scaccarii* brought a Bill against divers *Englishmen*, therein setting forth, *quod deprædatus & spoliatus fuit* upon the Sea, *juxta partes Brittaniæ, per quandam Virum bellicosum de Britannia de quadam Navi*, and so of divers Merchandizes therein, which were brought into *England*, and came into the Hands of divers Englishmen, naming them, and so had Process against them, who came in, and pleaded, That in regard this Depredation was done by a Stranger, and not by the Subjects of the King, therefore they ought not to be punished , in regard that the *Statute* of 31 *H.* 6 *Cap* 4 gives Restitution by the *Chancellor, in Cancellaria sibi vocato uno Judice, de uno Banco vel altero*; and by the *Statute* of 27 *Ed* 3 *cap* 13. that the Restitution may be made in such a Case upon Proof made, by the *Chancellor* himself without any Judge, and upon that Case it was resolved, *Quod quisquis extraneus, &c.* who brings his Bill upon this *Statute* to have Restitution, *debet probare quòd tempore captio-*

3 *Bulstrode* 28. 1 *R. Rep* 175

nis

nis fuit de amicitia Domini Regis, and also, *quod ipse qui eum ceperit & spoliavit, fuit etiam sub obedientia Regis, vel de amicitia Domini Regis, sive Principis querentis tempore spoliationis, & non inimicus Domini Regis sive Principis querentis, qui si fuerit inimicus, & sic ceperit bona, tunc non fuit spoliatio, nec deprædatio, sed legalis captio, prout quilibet inimicus capit super unum & alterum* · The Judgment of which Case was held to be Law, and thereupon the Judges delivered their Opinions, that the *Morocco* Ambassador could not be proceeded against as a Pirate.

20. In the time of *Philip* the Second of *Spain*, the *Venetian* Ambassador in *Madrid* protecting one *Bodovario*, a *Venetian*, an Offender, that fled into his House, and denying the *Corrigidor* or *Justice*, to enter his House, where the Ambassador stood armed to withstand them; upon Complaint made, the Ambassador was removed unto another House, till they had searched, and found the Offender; then conducting back the Ambassador with all due respect, a Guard was set upon his House to stay the fury of the enraged People, the Ambassador complaining to the King, he remitted it to the *Supreme Council*. They justified the Proceedings, condemning *Bodovario* to lose his Head, and other the Ambassador's Servants to the *Gallies*, all which the King turned to Banishment, and to satisfy the most *Serene Republick*, sent the whole Process to *Inego de Mendoza*, his Ambassador at *Venice*, declaring by a publick Ordinance unto that State, and all other Princes, *That in case his Ambassadors should commit any Offence unworthily, and disagreeing to their Qualities and Professions of Ambassa-*

P 3 *dors,*

dors, they should not enjoy the Privilege of those Officers, but he would refer them to be judged by the Laws of that Prince or State where they then resided, and where they had injured. It was a great and noble Saying.

Sir Hen Woot-ton · State of Christendom, fol 211
Vide S r Robert Cotton's posthum and the Proposition to King James.

21. In the Year 1568, *Don Gubernon d'Espes* was ordered to keep his House in *London*, for sending scandalous Letters to the Duke *d'Alva* unsealed; and in 1586, *Don Bernardino de Mendoza* was restrained first, and after commanded away.

XI The manner of proceeding against them, according to the practice in *England*, hath been conceived necessary to be, that some of the Chief Secretaries of State were sent to the Ambassadors, and by way of advice, that understanding that the common People having received notice of, &c " And " that they cannot but conceive a just fear " of uncivil carriage towards their *Excel-* " *lencies* or their Followers, if any the least " Incitement should arise, and therefore for " Quiet of the State, and securing of their " Persons, they were bound in Love and " Respect to their *Excellencies* to restrain as " well themselves as Followers, till a further " Course be taken by legal Examination, " where the Aspersion began, the same being " in their opinions the best and the only way " to prevent the danger, &c "

Sometimes, if the *Parliament* be sitting, the King acquaints the *Lords*, and then departs; who having had Conference with the *Commons*, conclude of a *Message* to be sent to the Ambassadors, (either by requiring an account of the matter or confining of them) the Persons to be sent, the two *Speakers* of both *Houses*, with some convenient number

of

of either, having their Maces, or Enfigns
of Offices born before them to the Ambaffador's Gates, and then forborn ; and then
requefting Speech with them, let them know,
that a Relation being made that Day, in
open *Parliament* of, *&c* they were deputed
from both *Houfes, the great Council of the
Kingdom*, to the which, by the Fundamental
Laws of this Nation, the chief Care of the
King's Safety, and the publick Peace and
Quiet of the Realm is committed , and that
they were no lefs the *High Court of Juftice,*
or *Superfedeas* to all others, for the examining and punifhing all Attempts of fo high a
nature, *&c* if it carry truth , and having
executed their Commiffion, conclude that
the Houfes, to fhew that reverence which
they bear unto the Dignity of his *Mafter* by
their *Meffage*, declare that they two, who are
never employed but to the King alone, were
at that time fent, *&c.* and if the Houfes
fhall upon return of their *Speakers* conceive
their Anfwers (if it be a Matter that requires
it) are fuch as may juftly deferve their being
confined, they then make an addrefs to his
Majefty to confine them to their Houfes, reftraining their departure till the Prince or
State, whom they reprefent, be acquainted
with their offence · And fo it was done in
44 *H.* 3. to the *Pope's Legates* in *England,*
and 28 *E* 1.

*The Parlia-
ment* nor fit-
ting, the Se-
cretaries of
State may fig-
nify the like,
if occafion,
&c.

  XII. If a Foreign Ambaffador, being a
Prorex, commits here any Crime which is
contra Jus Gentium, as Treafon, Felony,
Adultery, or any other Crime which is a-
gainft the Law of Nations, he lofeth the
privilege and dignity of an Ambaffador, as
unworthy of fo high a place, and may be
punifhed

*The opinion
of the Lord
Coke,* 4 *Inftit.
fol.* 153, *&c*

punished here as any other private Alien, and not to be remanded to his Sovereign but of courtesy.

XIII. But if any thing be *malum prohibitum* by any Act of *Parliament*, private Law, or Custom of this Realm, which is not *malum in se Jure Gentium*, nor *contra Jus Gentium*, an Ambassador residing here, shall not be bound by any of them ; but otherwise it is of the Subjects of either Kingdom ; for if a *French* Merchant or *Spanish* Merchant trades or imports any prohibited Goods, he must at his peril observe the Laws of *England* ; and so it was adjudged *Pasc.* 33 *Eliz.* in the *Exchequer*, *Tomlinson*, *quitam versus Henry de Vale & al.* upon the *Statute* of 19 *H.* 7 *Cap* 21 but if an Ambassador imports any prohibited Goods, *è contra*

The *Florentines*, having sent Ambassadors to *Charles* the Fifth and *Clement* the Seventh, being then at *Bolonia*, together with their Houshold-stuff, they brought covertly many rich Commodities to sell and traffick with, supposing that they might be free from paying the Gabel , but the Searchers of the Custom-house having discovered it, they became objects of laughter and mirth to the *Bolonians*, and for that, as unworthy of the Office of Ambassadors, were remanded home without Audience.

Jovius, fol. 125.

Sir *Thomas Challoner*, having been sent Ambassador to *Spain* by Queen *Elizabeth*, remitted a Complaint to the Queen, that his Chests had been searched . Upon which the Queen demanded the opinion of her Council in the point, who upon the whole matter resolved the Action into this, *Legato omnia æqui boníque ferenda dummodo Principis Honor non direttè directè violetur*, the very words of Mr *Camden*, An Ambaſſador muſt bear all things patiently, provided that the Honour of the Prince (whom he ſerves) be not directly violated.

XIV The Office of an Ambaſſador does not include a protection private but publick, for the King his Maſter, not for any ſeveral Subjects, otherwiſe than as it concerns the King and his publick Miniſters, to protect them, and procure their protection in foreign Kingdoms, in the nature of an *Office* and *Negotiation of State*, therefore their Quality is to mediate and proſecute for them or any one of them, at the *Council-Table*, which is as it were a *Court of State*; but when they come to ſettled Courts, which do and muſt obſerve eſſential forms of Proceeding, *ſcil. proceſſus legitimos*, they muſt be governed by them. And therefore in the Caſe of *Don Diego Serviento de Acuna, Ambaſſador Lieger* for the King of *Spain*, who libelled in the *Admiral Court* as *Procurator-General* for all his Maſter's Subjects, againſt one *Jolliff* and *Tucker*, and Sir *Richard Bingley*, for two Ships and their Lading of divers kinds, of the Goods of the Subjects of the King of *Spain* generally, and not naming of them *adduct ad Port de Munſter*, in the Preface of the Libel generally againſt them all, and then proceeds and charges them ſeverally thus, That *Jolliff* and *Tucker* Captain *Piratæ, in alto Mari bellicè dictas Naves aggreſſi ſunt, & per vim & violentiam* took them, and that they were *adductæ in partes Hiberniæ*, and that coming into the hands of Sir *Richard Bingley*, he converted them to his own uſe, (not ſaying where) and refuſing to render them

Leg. ſi F. de lega in aut. de ſanctiſſ. §. rerum, call. 9.

Lord *Hobart, fol. 78 Sed Vide Cro El. 685 Yelv. 135, 173. Hard. 183. 1 Sid 320, 367 2 Saund. 260 2 Lev. 25 1 Ven. 173, 208.*

them being required, it was there held that a *Prohibition* should go, for the matter is Triable merely at the *Common Law*, and that such a Procuration was not good, though to an Ambassador.

Don Alfonso de Valesco, Ambassador from the *Catholick* King, attached Tobaccoes at Land here, which one *Corvero*, a Subject of the King of *Spain*, brought hither, and the Ambassador by his Libel supposed to belong to his Master, as Goods confiscated, as all other his Goods were. Sir *John Watts*, the Plaintiff in the suggestion, prayed a *Prohibition*, which was granted accordingly, for the Property of Goods here at Land must be tried by the *Common Law*, however the Property be guided ; and it was likewise ruled, that if any Subject of a Foreign Prince bring Goods into this Kingdom, though they were confiscate before, the Property shall not be questioned but at the *Common Law*, *Don Alfonso verf. Corvero*, *Mich* 9. *Jac. Hob* 212. *Hill.* 9. *Jac.* upon the like Libel by *Don Pedro Surega* Ambassador for *Spain*.

XV. Whether an Ambassador hath Jurisdiction over his own Family, and whether his house be a *Sanctuary* * for all that fly into it, depends upon the concession of him with whom he resides, for this belongs not to the Law of Nations † ; and it hath been seen, that an Ambassador hath inflicted punishment on his own Servants and Vassals, as the *Muscovite* did here in *England* , but that must be purely by concession, as the *Turk* permits it to the *English* Ambassador at *Constantinople* : But Fugitives that fly into their Houses, nay, their own Servants if they have greatly offended, cannot be drawn out by force,

marginal notes:
* *Distingui ferme hac in re solent crimina Vide Parutam, lib* 10. *ubi Rex Galliæ hanc ob caufam iratus pacatur Vide eundem, lib.* 11
† *Gro. de Jure Belli ac Pacis, lib* 18. §. 4, 5, 6, 7

force, without a Demand and Refusal, which when done, it is then become as an offence in them.

XVI. Most certain by the *Civil Law*, the moveable Goods of an Ambassador, which are accounted an accession to his Person, cannot be seized on, neither as a pledge, nor for a payment of a Debt, nor by *Order* or *Execution of Judgment*; no nor by the King or *States* leave where he resides (as some conceive) for all coaction ought to be far from an Ambassador, as well that which toucheth his necessaries as his Person, that he may have full security, if therefore he hath contracted any Debt, he is to be called upon kindly, and if he refuses, then Letters of *Request* are to go to his Master*, so that at last that course may be taken with him as with Debtors in another Territory; to some this may seem hard, yet Kings, who cannot be compelled, want not Creditors, but the Lord *Coke* seems to be of another opinion †, for as to Contracts and Debts that be good *Jure Gentium*, he must answer here.

Rexfacitsne metu regium nuntium populi Romani Quiritum vasa comitesq; meos yet an Ejectment hath been brought and left at the House of the Ambassador, and it was allowed good, and conceived no breach of their privilege in the Case of *Monf. Colbert* for *York* House, *Mich* 28 *Car*. 2 *in Banc. Reg*

* *Grotius lib.* 2. *cap* 18

† *Coke* 4. *Instit fol* 153 Certain it is, that none dareth presume to meddle either with their Persons, Goods, or Servants, without leave had, the contempt of which hath been punished with Imprisonment. *Lucas* 4 *Vid Stat* 7. *A ch* 12. § 5.

XVII If an Ambassador commits any private *outrage* against one of the Prince's Subjects with whom he resides, unless it be to defend the Dignity of his Charge, or of his Master, it hath been conceived by some not to be justifiable before the Prince with whom he resides, (say they) there is a great difference between the *Dignity*, and *Authority* of the Prince in the Country of another Sovereign, for he may well retain his *Dignity*, but

but not his *Authority*. Usually Injuries of that nature being done, they have admitted debates at a *Council of State*, where the Sovereign, with whom the Minister of State hath resided, being satisfied, that Reparation ought to be made to the party injured, he hath been ordered, or at least requested, to comply with the same.

XVIII But, on the other hand, if any private *outrage* be committed by the Subjects of that Prince with whom he resides, upon his Person, the Offenders may be subjected to punishment   The Queen of *Sweden* having made the incomparable *Grotius* (after he had escaped by Providence out of Prison, and by a greater from his *Countrymen*) her *Barkseate in memor. Grotii.* Ambassador with *Lewis* the Thirteenth, with whom he resided at *Paris*, coming one day from *St Germains*, the *Secretary of Ceremonies* being in the Coach with him, it chanced that, in one place as they passed, a great number of People were in the way seeing of an Execution, his *Postilion* and *Coachman*, driving boldly through the Company, the *Archers* then attending the Execution with short Pieces, (concerned somewhat angerly that the Execution was disturbed) made after the Coach, shot his *Postilion* and *Coachman*, and through the Coach, even through his Hat . The matter coming to be examined, the King ordered three or four of them to be hanged, but that Good Man first pardoned them himself, and then obtained the King's

XIX. The Republick of *Venice* employeth generally more Ambassadors abroad than any other State, and they are as those of other Princes be, *Ordinary* and *Extraordinary*; the Commission of the Ordinary continueth

tinueth for three Years, but he who refides at *Conftantinople* is not called Ambaffador, but *Bailio*, refiding there perpetually; and that Republick allows him a greater Provifion to fupport his Grandeur, than to any other, and by the Laws of *Venice*, whatfoever he expends is allowed him upon his accounts without any examination; the which no other of their publick Minifters of State have like privilege.

By the Laws of *Venice* there can be no extraordinary Ambaffador employed, unlefs they have been Ambaffadors formerly, and upon their return are ftrictly examined of their Comportment in their Legation, and are to difcover what prefents they have received from the Prince or Sate to whom they were fent, the concealment of which is of a very dangerous confequence *Bodinus de Republ lib 3*

Nor may any of their Ambaffadors receive any Preferment from any other State during their Legation. The *Patriach of Aquielia* dying, *Hermolao Barbaro* being there Ambaffador for that *Republick*, the *Pope* conferred on him that *Ecclefiaftical Dignity*, and made him a *Cardinal*; which being known at *Venice*, notwithftanding he was a Perfon of great Merit, and had given notice to the *Senate*, rich, well allied, and had good Friends, they fent exprefs command that he fhould refign the *Patriarchfhip*, otherwife they would take from his *Father* the *Procuratorfhip* of St *Mark*, and confifcate all his Eftate. *Jac. Aug Thuanus, l 27 in Vita Auguftini Barbadico Duke of Venice, Anno 1486.*

But if fuch Ambaffadors, have received any Prefent, Gift, or Reward, from any Foreign Prince or Republick, and fuch Minifters of State are thought worthy of retaining the fame, fuch a Grace muft pafs by the Suffrage *Paulus Paruta in Hift Ven lib 7*

frage of the Senate, to oblige them more to the benevolence of the Republick, than to the bounty of any Foreign Prince. The confideration of which put the fame generous fcruple into the Breaft of Sir *Amias Paulet*, who returning from his Ambaffy in *France*, would not at his departure receive from the *French* King the Chain of Gold which is given of courfe, till he was half a League out of *Paris* But more famous was the action of Sir *Leoline Jenkins*, the *Englifh* Ambaffador at *Nimeguen*, who, tho' after the Treaty concluded, abfolutely refufed the *French* King's Prefent.

Francis Hottoman, fol 23, 24.

XX. By the Laws of Nations, in the Reception of Ambaffadors, thofe from a King are generally introduced by an Earl or Count, thofe from a Duke or Republick by a Baron, nor are they to be allowed that Honour but only at their firft and laft Audience.

XXI. Prophane Hiftories are full of Wars, becaufe of wrong done to Ambaffadors, and in the facred Story is extant the memory of the War which *David* upon that Ground waged againft the *Ammonites*; nor doth *Cicero* efteem any Caufe more juft againft *Mithridates*, and at this day not only *Lawyers* *, but *Divines* † are all of the fame opinion, That a War cannot be more juftly commenced than for the Violation done to their Publick Minifters.

* *Grot l 2 c.* 18 § 11
† *Montague's* Acts and Monuments, *fol* 450

XXII. The Privileges of Ambaffadors and their Servants, as to civil Suits, by the Law of *England*.

Blak Com 254, 255, &c

In refpect to civil Suits, all the foreign Jurifts agree, that neither an Ambaffador, nor any of his Train or *Comites*, can be profecuted

for

for any Debt or Contract in the Courts of
that Kingdom wherein he is fent to refide :
Yet Sir *Edward Coke* maintains, that, if an 4 *Inft* 153.
Ambaffador make a Contract which is good
jure Gentium, he fhall anfwer for it here. But
the Truth is, fo few Cafes (if any) had arifen,
wherein the Privilege was either claimed or
difputed, even with regard to civil Suits, that
our Law Books are filent upon it   Previous
to the Reign of Queen *Anne*, when an Am-
baffador from *Peter* the Great, Czar of *Muf-* 21 *July* 1708,
covy, was actually arrefted and taken out of *Roger's An-
his Coach in *London*, for a Debt of fifty nals of Queen
Pounds, which he had there contracted In- *Anne.*
ftead of applying to be difcharged upon his
Privilege, he gave Bail to the Action, and the
next Day complained to the Queen. The
Perfons who were concerned in the Arreft
were examined before the Privy Council (of
which the Lord Chief Juftice *Holt* was at the
fame Time fworn a Member) and feventeen 25 *July* 1708.
were committed to Prifon, moft of whom *ibid.*
were profecuted by Information in the Court
of *Queen's Bench*, at the Suit of the Attorney-
General; and at their Trial before the Lord
Chief Juftice were convicted of the Facts by
the Jury, referving the queftion of Law, how
far thofe Facts were criminal, to be afterwards argued before the Judges; which queftion was never determined In the mean
Time the Czar refented this Affront very
highly, and demanded that the Sheriff of
Middlefex, and all others concerned in the
Arreft, fhould be punifhed with inftant Death.
But the Queen (to the Amazement of that
defpotic Court) directed her Secretary to inform him, " that fhe could inflict no Punifhment upon any, the meaneft of her Subjects,
                                          unlefs

unlefs warranted by the Law of the Land, and therefore was perfuaded that he would not infift upon impoffibilities." To fatisfy however the Clamours of the foreign Minifters (who made it a common Caufe) as well to appeafe the Wrath of *Peter*, a Bill was brought into Parliament, and afterwards paffed into a Law, to prevent and to punifh fuch outrageous infolence for the future. And with a Copy of this Act, elegantly engroffed and illuminated, accompanied by a Letter from the Queen, an *Mr. Whit-worth.* Ambaffador Extraordinary was commiffioned to appear at *Mofcow*, who declared, " That though her Majefty could not inflict fuch a Punifhment as was required, becaufe of the Defect in that particular of the former eftablifhed Conftitutions of her Kingdom, yet, with the unanimous confent of the Parliament, fhe had caufed a new Act to be paffed, to ferve as a Law for the future." This humiliating Step was accepted as a full Satisfaction by the Czar, and the Offenders, at his Requeft, were difcharged from all farther Profecution.

This Statute recites the Arreft which had been made, " in Contempt of the Protection granted by her Majefty contrary to the Law of Nations, and in Prejudice of the Rights and Privileges, which Ambaffadors and other publick Minifters have at all Times been thereby poffeffed of, and ought to be kept facred and inviolable " Wherefore it Enacts, that for the future all Procefs, whereby the Perfon of any Ambaffador, or of his Domeftic or Domeftic Servant, may be arrefted, or his Goods diftrained or feized, fhall be utterly null and void, and the Perfons profecuting, foliciting, or executing fuch Procefs, fhall be

deemed

deemed Violaters of the Law of Nations, and Difturbers of the publick Repofe, and fhall fuffer fuch Penalties and corporal Punifhment, as the Lord Chancellor and the two Chief Juftices, or any two of them, fhall think fit. But it is exprefsly provided, that no Trader, within the Defcript on of the Bankrupt Laws, who fhall be in the Service of any Ambaffa-dor, fhall be privileged or protected by this Act, nor fhall any one be punifhed for arreft-ing an Ambaffador's Servant, unlefs his Name be regiftered with the Secretary of State, and by him tranfmitted to the Sheriffs of *London* and *Middlefex*. Exceptions that are ftrictly conformable to the Rights of Ambaffadors, as obferved in the moft civilized countries And, in confequence of this Statute thus declaring and enforcing the Law of Nations, thefe Pri-vileges are now held to be part of the Law of the Land, and are conftantly allowed in the Courts of Common Law

Lord Chan-cellor Talbot faid, the Ex-ception of Perfons trad-ing, relates only to the Servants of Ambaffadors the Parlia-ment never imagining the Minifters themfelves would trade. Cas. Temp. Talb 282.

The Courts of Common Law have come to the following Refolutions, upon Applica-tion, on the faid Act.

That it is not neceffary the Party fhould live in the Ambaffador's Houfe, 2 *Stra* 792. 2 *R Raym* 1524. *Fitzgib* 200 *pl.* 12

When Party comes for Benefit of the Act, it is not enough that he be regiftered in the Secretary's Office as a Servant, but muft fhew the Nature of his Service, that the Court may judge whether he be a Domeftic Servant with-in the meaning of the Act of Parliament, *Fitzgib* 200 *pl* 12 2 *Stra* 797.

A Trader, an Annuitant, a Juftice of Peace, a menial Servant, an hired Clerk, a Perfon who receives no Wages, a Courier, a Mef-fenger, a Landwaiter at the Cuftom-houfe, denied the Benefit of the Act. *Fitzgib.* 200. *pl.* 12. 2 *Stra.* 797. Pract. Reg. C. P. 14. *Barnes's* Notes, C P. 264, 271. Rep. and Cas of Pract. C. P. 65, 134, 272. *Barnard,* K. B. 401. *Bur.* Rep. 401.

The Party must serve in the Capacity he was hired, *Barnard,* K. B. 401. where a Person does not execute the Office which he has his Testimonial for, but only gets himself entered in the List to have the Benefit of a Protection, the Court will not suffer it. *Barnard,* K. B. 79

Abr. Eq. 350. pl. 4 Goodwin and Archer, Pasch 1729 2 Will. Rep. 452. And a like Order said to be made by my Lord Cowper, after One protected by the *Genoese* Ambassador brought a Bill in *Chancery,* and was ordered, though after (1) Answer put in, to give (2) Security to answer the Costs, in the same manner as if he were a Foreigner, because, by the above Statute, all Processes against Ambassadors and their Servants are made void; so that if the Bill should be dismissed, no Process could issue against him.

Answer put in, Trin 1709, between *Barret* and *Buck.* (1) But it has been denied in the *Exchequer, Bunb* Rep 183 *pl* 258 and so it has in that Court, even before Answer, where the Bill was for an Injunction to stay the Defendant's Proceedings at Law in Ejectment, because the Plaintiff was in a manner forced into this Court, (viz the Exchequer) and did not come in originally *Bunb.* Rep 272. *pl.* 349. If the Motion be before Answer, the Defendant will not be obliged to put one in, until the Plaintiff give Bond, with a Surety to the Senior Six-Clerk, not towards the Cause, in 40 *l.* Penalty for answering Costs. 2 *Will* .452 *pl.* 142 *Mosely* 7 175. *pl.* 89 (2) A Deposit in Money will not be permitted instead thereof. *Bunb.* Rep. 35, *pl* 53.

CHAP.

CHAP. XI.

Of the Right of delivering Persons fled for Protection.

I. *Where Superiors may become culpable for the Crimes of their Subjects.*

II *Offences by whom properly punished, whether by the injured State, or they into whose Territory the Offender is fled.*

III. *Whether Kingdoms and States ought to deliver up Fugitives, if required, or not*

IV. *Where Persons are fled, the places whither they come, ought to be Assylums.*

V. *How distinguished, and when to be punished or delivered.*

VI. *Whether an innocent Man may be deserted and delivered up to the enraged Power that demands him.*

VII *Whether an innocent Person may be deserted and yielded, if War be threatened.*

VIII *Whether an innocent Person refused to be delivered up, ought to yield himself*

IX *If Charity in an innocent to yield himself, whether Compulsion may be used if he refuses*

X *Whether this of delivering up does extend to Sovereign Princes driven out of their Country*

XI. *Persons running away with the Publick Revenue, where their Persons and Goods have been seized till reparation and satisfaction be made*

I. **F**ATHERS are not bound for the fault of their Children, nor Masters for those of their Servants, nor Princes for the Actions of their Subjects, unless they become partakers in the Crime; the which may be done in two respects, by sufferance and receipt, therefore if Princes shall suffer or countenance their Subjects, by Pictures or Libels, or otherwise, to abuse another Nation or Com-monwealth,

Zeno interceding for the Magnets to T. Quintus, and the Legates with him besought them with tears Ne urius amentiam civitati assignarent, suo quemque

Q 2

periculo facere,
Liv l. 40.
monwealth, it is the same as if they should authorize it. *Brutus* to *Cicero, How can you make me guilty? Yes, well enough, if it were in you to hinder it*, but receipt may admit of some further scrutiny.

II *Commonwealths* being instituted, it was agreed that Faults of Particulars, which do properly belong to their own Society, should be left to themselves and their Sovereigns, to be punished or connived at, as they judged most fit

Yet that *Right* is not so absolutely left to them, but Offences, which tend to the Destruction of Society or Government, whereof *Treason* is the chiefest, may seem to be excepted; for if a Subject shall commit an Act tending to the Subversion of his Sovereign's Government, the same is an Offence that's subject to an *universal Punishment*, i e it is to be punished every where, and the Governors into whose Territory such fly, seem to have a Right

Full Abridg-
ment fol
530 Boger's
Case
of prosecuting for the Offence In Civil Actions, which tend to Commerce that supports Society, the Subjects of foreign Nations, having justly contracted Debts in their own Country, may obtain Justice in another, by a stronger Reason it is thought, that Princes or Republicks, that have received publick Injuries, have Right to require Punishment for the Indignity that is offered them, at least for that which tended to the Subversion of their Government, and to have the Offenders delivered up.

For the
Knowledge
of the Cause
ought to pre-
cede the Red-
dition; nor
fct ésm.nr
III The Question is illustrious, Opinions grounded on several great Precedents have been both ways produced: It hath been generally held, That those Kingdoms where the Offenders are fled ought to do one of the two,

either

either *punish them according to their Deserts being called upon, or leave them to the Judgment of the offended State*, others on the contrary, most certain it is, by the *delivering up* is understood, to leave him to the legal Judgment of that Prince or State, whom he hath offended · And such was the Declaration of *Ferdinand* King of *Spain*, who had been often requested by *Henry* the Seventh, to deliver up *Edmond de la Pool* Earl of *Suffolk* his Subject, then fled for Protection to that Prince's Country, but was always refused, but being continually importuned by Promises that he should not be put to Death, caused the Earl to be delivered up to him, who kept him in Prison, and construing his promise *to be personal to himself*, commanded his Son *Henry* after his Decease to execute him, who in the fifth Year of his Reign in *cold Blood* performed the same   But the Malice of that politick Prince the Father, and the uncontroulable Will of the Son, are Precedents but of small Force, the Example of which, not long after, gave the *French King* occasion to beware of trusting the latter with a Subject of his on the like occasion, for *Cardinal Pool*, not many Years after, coming Ambassador from the *Pope* to the *French* King, they both being then in Amity, and *Henry* the Eighth in League with the latter, but in Enmity with the first, requested to have the *Cardinal* delivered up, but could not prevail, being doubly armed, as the Ambassador of a Sovereign Prince, (for such is the *Pope)* and in the Territory of a foreign State

The *Israelites* required of the *Benjamites* to deliver up the wicked Men, the *Philistines*, *Samson*. *Cato* gave his Vote that *Cæsar* should

dedere causa non cognita Plutarch in his Romulus.

Attainted by Act of Parliament 12 H 7. *Co Inst fol* 180.

Herbert's Hist H 8. *Pepin* received, and would not deliver up those that fled to him out of *Neustria*, opprest by Tyranny *Fredegar in reb Pep. An.* 1188.

Q 3   be

be delivered to the *Germans*, for spoiling them without just Cause. Nor are innocent Persons injured, if they are either delivered up, or punished; yet does it not thence follow that they must be delivered up or punished. The *Romans* delivered up those that had done Violence to the *Carthaginian* Ambassadors; yet the Ambassadors of the *Abassines* having been traiterously murdered by one of the Templars at *Jerusalem*, the Offender being demanded, that so Justice might be executed on him for the Act, the *Grand Master* answered, That he had already enjoined him Penance, and had directed him to be sent to the *Pope*, but absolutely refused to deliver him up.

Tyrus, lib 20. cap 23. Anno 1173

IV. But then, and as in this last, so in all other, the Offender must have committed some publick Offence *, as Treason, for most certainly it extends not to private Injuries, because there is no Precedent that ever a War was begun for such, though they may contribute much, but for those which tend to the Subversion or Ruin of a Country, they often have been delivered up, *Jugurtha* of *Bocchus* in *Sallust*, *So shall thou at once free us from the sad necessity of prosecuting thee for thy Error, and him for his Treason* And by most Writers it is agreed, that such Offenders must either be delivered up or punished, the Election is left to their Choice, into whose Territory they are fled. though some have held, that in case of Protection or Sanctuary for such unfortunate Persons, Princes do make their Countries Asylums †　　　*T. Quintus*

* Yet out of Churches beyond Seas for private Offences, which are universal Sanctuaries, the Offenders have been taken: In *Lucitania*, *Ferdinand* Lord Chamberlain was taken by Force out of the Church and burnt, for forcing a Noble Virgin *Mar.ana, lib 11*

† *Charles* Duke of *Burgandy* delivered up to *Lewis* the Eleventh, the Earl of St *Paul*, Constable of *France*, who flying to some of his own Cities obtained Letters of Safe-Conduct to come and commune with the Duke, in order to the making his Peace with the King, but the Duke,

Duke, after he had him in Cuſtody, delivered him to the King of *France*, who immediately after cut off his Head   *Phil Comines, l. 4 c 12*

† *Ludovicus Pius* the Emperor received thoſe that fled to him from the *Roman Church*, as appears by his Decree, *Anno* 817, and *Luther* himſelf did not want Princes to protect him from the Fury of St. *Peter*'s Chair   *Vide his Colloquiums*

T. Quintus Flaminius ſent Ambaſſador to *Pruſſias* King of *Bythinia*, for the procuring the delivering up the brave but unfortunate *Hannibal*, who accordingly being ſeized on, *I will now*, ſays he, *deliver the Romans of that Fear which hath ſo many Years poſſeſt them, that Fear which makes them impatient to attend the Death of an old Man · This Victory of Flaminius over me, who am diſarmed and betrayed into his Hands, ſhall never be numbered amongſt the reſt of his Heroical Deeds · No, it ſhall make it manifeſt to all the Nations of the World, how far the antient Roman Virtue is degenerate and corrupted, for ſuch was the Nobleneſs of their Forefathers, as when* Pyrrhus *invaded them · in* Italy, *and was ready to give them Battle at their own Doors, they gave him Knowledge of the Treaſon intended againſt him by Poiſon, whereas theſe of a latter Race have employed* Flaminius, *a Man who hath heretofore been one of their Conſuls, to practiſe with* Pruſias, *contrary to the Honour of a King, contrary to his Faith given, and contrary to the Laws of Hoſpitality, to ſlaughter or deliver up his own Gueſt. Then took a Draught of Poiſon, and died* *Sir Walter Ralegh's* Hiſt. Vol. 11 *p* 781. Edit. 1736

V. Though Kingdoms and States are looked upon as places of Refuge, yet that muſt be underſtood for thoſe that are perſecuted with cauſeleſs Hatred, not to ſuch as have committed that which is injurious to human Society, or to other Men   *Gilippus the Laco-*

nian in *Diodorus Siculus,* speaking of the Right of such miserable Fugitives, saith, *They that introduced these Rights at first, meant the Unfortunate should expect Mercy, the Injurious Punishment*—— After — *These Men, if by the unjust Desire of that which is another's they have fallen into these Evils, must not accuse Fortune, nor impose on themselves the Name of Supplicants, for that by Right belongs to them that have an innocent Mind and adverse Fortune.*

Carum occidisti, dum vis succurrere. nullum
Crimen habes, manus est ibi purior, ac fuit ante

But the Life of those Men full of wicked Acts, shut up against them all Places of Refuge, and leaves no room for Compassion Cicero hath a Saying out of *Demosthenes : We must shew Compassion to those whom Fortune, not their own evil Deeds, hath made Miserable.* And by the holy Law, when any one had been slain by an Axe slipping out of another's Hand, the Cities of Refuge were open : The most holy Altar itself was no Protection for those that had slain an innocent Man maliciously, or had troubled the Commonwealth ; which Law *Philo* explaining, saith, *Unholy Men have no Entertainment in the Holy Place.* *Lycurgus* the Orator relates that one *Callistratus,* having committed a Capital Fault, and advising with the Oracle, received Answer, *That if he went to* Athens *he should have Right :* And thereupon, in Hopes of Impunity, he fled to the most holy Altar there, notwithstanding which he was taken from thence, and put to Death by the City most observant of her Religion, and so the Oracle was fulfilled. *Princes indeed* (saith *Tacitus*) *are like Gods, but neither do the Gods hear the*
Prayers

Prayers of Supplicants unless they be just. Such then are either to be punished or delivered up at least, yet surely this hath been observed to extend only to those Crimes that touch the State, or at least are of a very heinous Nature, sometimes they are expresly stipulated by Leagues to be delivered up; however this is to be observed, that such sort of Fugitives and Supplicants, be they Foreigners or Subjects, are to be protected till they have been fairly tried, and if that whereof they are accused, be not forbidden by the Law of Nature or Nations, the Cause must be tried and adjudged by the Municipal Laws of that Kingdom or State from whence the Crime doth arise. From which it may be observed, that a Fault committed in *England*, and the Person flying, and Request made, yet, by Reason that none can by the Laws of that Nation be tried but *per Pares*, nor then but in Person, it will thence follow, that such may seem out of the general Rule · However, it may stand with the highest Reason, that the Fact and Proof being remitted over with the Request, there may appear a just Ground for the Demand.

They of Holland lately delivered up the famous poisoning Cook that had been in the wicked Conspiracy with the Countess of Soissons in France.

VI Whatever the Opinion of those Writers have been, the Practice of latter Ages hath seemed to incline otherwise Queen *Elizabeth* demanded *Morgan* and others of her Subjects fled into *France*, that had committed Treason against her, the Answer of the *French* King was, *Si quid in Gallia machinarentur, Regem ex jure in illos animadversurum, sin in Anglia quid machinati fuerint, Regem non posse de eisdem cognoscere, & ex jure agere, omnia Regna profugis esse libera, Regum interesse, ut sui quisque Regni libertates tueatur, imo Elizabe-*
- *tham*

tham non ita pridem, in suum Regnum Mount-

34 Eliz. Cam-
den, fol. 35
Vide Camb.
Anno 1585.
gumerium, Principem Condæum, & alios è Gente Gallica admisisse, &c. and they were never delivered up; but the like was not returned by the King of *Scotland,* for he promised that he would transmit *Ferniburst* and the *Chancellor* too, if they were convicted by a fair Trial.

Liv. lib. 22.
cap. 37.
Perseus King of *Macedon,* in his Defence to *Martius,* speaking of those that were said to have conspired against *Eumenes: So soon as I was admonished by you, and finding the Men in* Macedonia, *I commanded them away, and charged them never to return into my Dominions.*

Anno 1660.
In the Alli-
ance between
those Crowns
Feb 13, 1660,
provided for
in the fifth
Article.
The Cry of the *Royal Martyr*'s Blood, justly procured them of *Holland* to deliver up the *Regicides* to the injured Successor. And from the Crown of *Denmark* it was expresly stipulated they should be delivered in these Words: *Item quod si qui eorum qui rei sunt illius nefandi Parricidii in Regem* CAROLUM *Primum beatissimæ Memoriæ admissi, ac legitimè de eodem scelere attincti, condemnati, vel convicti, &c.*

" If any of them who are guilty of the horrid
" Murder committed upon King *CHARLES*
" the First of Blessed Memory, be either
" now in the Dominions of the King of *Den-*
" *mark* and *Norway,* or shall hereafter come
" thither, that as soon as it shall be known
" or told to the King of *Denmark,* or any of
" his Officers, they be forthwith apprehend-
" ed, put in safe Custody, and sent back into
" *England,* or be delivered into the Hands
" of those whom the King of *Great-Britain*
" shall order to take charge of them, and
" bring them home "

That politick
Princess
Queen Eliza-
beth, gave the
VII. Most certain it is, if War be threatned to a Nation or People, if they deliver not up the Offender, tho' perhaps he is innocent, and

and that such is the Malice of his Enemies, that they know they will put him to death, yet he may be deserted, especially if that Nation or Kingdom is inferior to others; but then the same ought not to be done rashly. The *Italian* Foot that forsook the unfortunate *Pompey* before all was lost, being assured of Quarter from the victorious *Cæsar*, were condemned by most that reported the Story of that day.

Scots a more equitable answer, when they demanded *Bothwell*; she answered, that she would either render him up, or send him out of *England*, *Camden, Anno* 1593.

Pope Alexander (in the mortal Feud between him and the Emperor *Frederick*, who favoured *Octavian* the *Antipope*) fled disguised to *Venice*, the Duke and Senate being jealous that the *Emperor* would demand him, sent an Embassy to the *Emperor* to endeavour a Mediation and Peace, which was no sooner offered, but the *Emperor* broke out into a Rage, bidding them go home, saying, "Tell your
" Prince and People, that *Frederick* the *Ro-*
" *man* Emperor demands his Enemy, who is
" come to them for Succour, whom if they
" send not presently bound hand and foot,
" with a sure Guard, he will proclaim them
" Enemies to him and the whole *Empire*, and
" that there is neither Alliance or Laws of
" Nation which shall be able to free them
" from revenge for such an Injury, to prose-
" cute which he is resolved to overturn all
" divine and human Laws, that he will sud-
" denly bring his Forces before their City,
" and contrary to their expectation plant his
" *Victorious Eagles* on the Market-place of
" St *Mark*" This Message being faithfully delivered, the *Senate* decreed *Arms, Arms*; and while they were preparing, News was brought that *Otho*, the Emperor's Son, and General of the *Cæsarean* Fleet, was entered

Hist Reip. Ven In Vita Sebastiani Cyani Duke of *Venice, Anno* 1164.

the

the *Gulph* with feventy-five Gallies; the moft valiant and religious *Sebaftiano Cyani* refolved to meet him, and having encountered them on the Coaft of *Iftria*, defeated *Otho* and all his Naval Forces, taking forty-eight Gallies, *Otho* their Admiral, and the reft either burnt or deftroyed; he returned in Triumph for *Venice*, and not long after *Frederick* became convinced, that *Heaven* fights the Battles of the Innocent, and on his Knees begged Pardon of *Alexander* the Fugitive *Pope*.

Lewis the Eleventh of *France* required by Ambaffadors of *Philip* Duke of *Burgundy*, the delivering up of Sir *Oliver de la Marche*, (who being a *Burgundian*, had wrote (as was conceived) fomewhat againft the Claim of the *French* to feveral Territories) upon a publick Audience at *Lifle*, they were anfwered by Duke *Philip*, *That* Oliver was *Steward of his Houfe*, *a* Burgundian *by Birth, and in no refpect fubject to the Crown of* France , notwithftanding if it could be proved, that he had faid or done any thing againft the King's *Honour*, he would fee him punifhed according as his Faults fhould deferve

VIII. But admitting that fuch an innocent Perfon ought not to be delivered up, whether he is bound to yield himfelf, by fome it is conceived he ought not, becaufe the nature of civil Societies, which every one hath entered into for his own Benefit, doth not require it; from which it follows, that though fuch Perfons are not bound to that by Right, properly fo called, yet it doth not follow, but in charity he feems bound to do it , for there may be many Offices not of proper Juftice, but of Love, which are not only performed with Praifes, but alfo cannot be omitted

ted without blame; and such indeed is the Act of such a Person's voluntary yielding up himself, preferring the Lives of an innocent Multitude before his own. *Cicero* for *P. Sextus, If this had happened to me sailing with my Friends in some Ship, that Pirates surrounding us should threaten to sink us, except they would deliver me, I would rather have cast myself into the Sea to preserve the rest, than to bring my Friends either to certain Death, or into great danger of their Life.* *Idem de finibus 3 Vir bonus & sapiens, & Legibus parens, & civilis officii non ignarus utilitati omnium plusquam unius alicujus, aut suæ consulit.* And in *Livy* there is a most excellent Saying of some *Molossians Equidem pro Patria qui lethum oppetissent sæpe fando audivi; qui patriam pro se perire æquum censerent, hi primi inventi sunt* LIV. lib. 45.

IX. But whether such an innocent Person may be compelled to do that which perhaps he is bound to do, may be a question; rich Men are bound by the precept of Mercy to give Alms to the Poor, yet cannot be compelled to give It is one thing when the parts are compared among themselves, another when Superiors are compared to their Subjects, for an Equal cannot compel his Equal, but unto that which is due by right strictly taken, yet may a Superior compel his Inferior to things which Virtue commands, in a Famine to bring out provisions they have stored up, to yield him * to Death that deserts his Colours, or turns Coward, to mulct those that wear excessive Apparel †, and the like. *Phocion,* pointing to his dear Friend *Nicocles,* said, *Things were come to that extremity, that if Alexander should demand him, he should think he were to be delivered up.* It hath seemed that such an innocent Person might be deserted and compelled to do that which Charity requires, but the late ROYAL MARTYR seemed

** Leg Desert
†Coke Instit 3 fol 199
Plutarch Phocion Fides agi visa deditos non prodi Liv l 7 Statius judicemus esse paucos aliquos mala ferre, quam immensam multituden*

The Son of seemed of another Opinion, when he came
Pompey was so to die, in the Case of the *British Protomartyr*
worthy a Son Strafford.
of so great a
Father, that he contended with *Anthony* and *Augustus* about the *Empire of the World*; this *Pompey* entertaining *Anthony* and *Augustus* in his
Galley, the Captain which commanded it, demanded leave of him
to weigh Anchor and to carry away his Guests, and to make his Ri-
vals Prisoners He answered him, that he ought to have done it without telling him of it, and should have made him great without having made him forsworn : Certainly an honest Person will never be of
the Mind of this Captain , therefore in such extremities, *Counsellors*,
either for high advantages, or in the great necessities of their *Prince*,
should serve their Masters with their Estates and Goods, but not with
their Honour and Conscience.

     X But this delivering up does in no re-
spect extend to Sovereign Princes, who are
by Divine Permission unfortunately driven
out of their own Country ; and therefore
memorable is the great Treaty, commonly
called by the *Flemings, Intercursus Magnus*,
where there was an express Article against
12 H. 7. the reception of the Rebels either of *Henry*
Bacon's Henry VII. or of the *Arch-Duke* of *Burgundy* by
the Seventh, others, purporting, that if any such Rebel
fol 162. should be required by the Prince, whose
Rebel he was, of the Prince Confederate,
that forthwith the Prince Confederate should
by Proclamation command him to avoid the
Country, which, if he did not within fifteen
days, the Rebel was to stand proscribed, and
put out of Protection But a Prince, or one
that hath a Sovereign Power, and had been
contending for his Right, but Success not
crowning his hopes, occasioned his flight,
hath always been excepted , to deliver up
such, is even against Nature and the Majesty
of Power , and therefore it is very remarkable, what attempts were made for *E* 4 *H.*
7. nay, in the very Treaty of *Intercursus
Magnus*, it is memorable, that at that time
                          Perkin

Perkin Warbeck was contending with *H. 7.* for the Crown of *England*, by the name of *Richard* Duke of *York*, younger Son and surviving Heir Male of *Edward* the Fourth. My Lord *Bacon* does take a particular notice, that *Perkin Warbeck* in that very Treaty was not named nor contained, becaufe he was no Rebel, but one that contended for the Title. Afterwards, when *Perkin* was fled into *Scotland*, and there received by the *Scottifh* King, *Henry* the Seventh fent to have *Perkin* delivered up, and it was one of the principal Inducements of the King to accept of a Peace upon that condition, giving for an Argument, that *Perkin* was a Reproach to all Kings, and a Perfon not protected by the Laws of Nations; but the *Scotch* King peremptorily denied fo to do, faying, *That he (for his part) was no competent Judge of* Perkin's *Title, but that he had received him as a Suppliant, protected him as a Perfon fled for refuge, efpoufed him with his Kinfwoman, and aided him with Arms, upon the belief he was a Prince, and therefore he could not now with his Honour fo unrip, and (in a fort) put a lye upon all that he had faid and done before, as to deliver him up to his Enemies.* This was fo peremptorily infifted on by the *Scotch* King, that *Henry* the Seventh was at length contented to wave the Demand, and conclude a Peace without that Article, notwithftanding the King of *Scotland* had often in private declared, that he fufpected *Perkin* for a Counterfeit.

Lord *Bacon*'s *Henry* the feventh, *fol.* 176.

XI. Perfons that have wronged or defrauded Kings of their Revenue, efpecially in *England*, upon Letters of Requeft to those thofe Princes whither they have fled, have been delivered up.

Some *Florentine* Merchants of the Society of the *Frifcobaldi*, being made Collectors and Receivers of the King's Cuftoms and Rents in *England*, *Wales*, *Ireland*, and *Gafcoigne*, running away with thofe Monies, together with all their Eftates and Goods, for *Rome*, the King fent his Letters of Requeft to the *Pope*, defiring that they might be arrefted, and their Perfons and Goods feized, and fent over to fatisfy him for the damages he and his Subjects had fuftained by them, promifing not to proceed againft them to the lofs of their Limbs or Lives. Upon which Letters, the *Pope* feized on their Goods, and not long after the King writ for the feizing of their Perfons, for anfwering of other Frauds and Injuries.

The like was done for one *Anthony Fazons*, who had received 500 *l.* of the King's Monies, and running away with it to *Lorraine*, the King writ to the fame *Duke*, defiring that fearch might be made, and his Perfon feized upon, and his Goods fecured in every place within his Territories, till he fhould fat sfy the faid 500 *l.*

Rott. Romæ An. 4. E 2. M. 17. Dorfo.

Rott Romæ 4. E 2. M 16 Dorfo.

Clauf. 8 E. 2. M. 31. Dorfo. pro Rege.

CHAP.

C H A P. XII.

Of Contribution paid by Places Neuter
to both Armies in War.

I *Of force ufed to Neuters whether lawful.*

II *Of Neuters, their duty confidered in reference to
either of the warring Parties*

III. *Confiderations general touching the fame, and the
chief matters that are objected by thofe that fcruple
thereat*

IV. *The Cafe ftated generally in the queftion propounded to our Saviour of paying tribute to Cæfar.*

V *In the payment of Contribution to an Enemy,
what is neceffary to be diftinguifhed in the beginning of a War*

VI *Of a fecond diftinguifhment drawn out of the
firft, of fuch payments, when a War is actually
formed*

VII *Where a man pays, but miftakes the caufe,
whether excufable, the War not yet actually formed
in place*

VIII. *Where a Country is fully poffeft, whether payment then is lawful.*

IX *Of the ftate of thofe that live on Frontiers,
their condition confidered in reference to procure
their Peace by Contribution*

X *Of interdiction by him to Places from whom
faith is owing, Contribution notwithftanding being
paid, whether the fame creates an offence in them*

XI. *Of the genuine Conftruction of fuch interdictions
according to the true intention of the fame*

XII *Of the impunity and punifhment that fuch innocent Offenders may be fubjected to, in cafe of being queftioned for the contempt by their right Governors.*

I. **I**T is manifeft there is no Right of War
over Neuters in War, yet becaufe by
occafion of the War many things are ufually done againft fuch (Borderers efpecially)

on pretence of neceffity, there can be no Excufe for the act, unlefs it be apparent Neceffity, and that the fame ought to be extreme, for then it may give a Right over what belongs to another Man, for in fuch cafe, if the neceffity be manifeft, there may be fuch a proportion exacted as the neceffity requires, that is, if the Cuftody fuffices, the Ufe of the thing is not to be taken; if the Ufe, not the Abufe, be neceffary, yet is the Price of the thing to be reftored *Mofes*, when the higheft neceffity urged him and the People to pafs through the Land of the *Idumeans*, firft he faith, *he would pafs along the highway, and not divert into their Corn-fields or Vineyards; if he had need but of their Water, he would pay a price for it* The worthy Captains, both *Greek* and *Roman*, have done the like In *Xenophon* the *Greeks* with *Clearchus*, promife the *Perfians* to march away without any damage to the Country, and if they might have neceffaries for Money, they would take nothing by force. This Virtue is often commended in * *Belifarius* by *Procopius* his Companion and Witnefs of his Actions

* See to this purpofe his excellent Speech to his Soldiers near *Sicily*, when he marched into *Africk*, and the Narration of his March through *Africk Vandal* 1.

II. And as the Law doth preferve the Eftates and Territories of fuch Neuters, or thofe that abftain from War, fo on the other hand, fuch ought to do nothing for either Party, but efpecially for him who maintains a bad Caufe, or whereby the Motions of him who wageth a juft War may be retarded, and in a doubtful Cafe they ought to fhew themfelves equal (as we have mentioned elfewhere) elſewhere) to both in permitting paſſage, in *Exempl m* affording Proviſion for the Legions or Navies, *nobile vide* and in not relieving the Beſieged   It is the *apud Paru-* *duty of the* Athenians, *if they would not ſide tam, lib 8.* *with any Party, either to prohibit the* Corin- *Thucydides, l.* thians *from raiſing Soldiers out of* Attica, *or* 1 *permit them to do the like.*   So the Emperor and Confederate Princes of the Empire, with the Cantons of *Switzerland* in the late *German* War, and ſo of the King of *Eng-* *land*, who was ſo careful to preſerve the Neutrality, that he iſſued forth his Proclamations to prohibit all Perſons, of what Condition ſoever, to become Soldiers in the Service of any of the warring Princes.   It was objected by the *Romans* againſt *Philip* King of the *Macedonians*, That the League was violated by him two ways, *both becauſe* *he did injuries to the Fellows of the Roman* *People, and becauſe he aſſiſted the Enemy with* *Aids and Money.* The ſame things are urged by *Titus Quintus* in his Conference with *Nabis*, Yet thou ſayeſt, *I have not violated* *you, nor your Friendſhip and Society*, how often ſhall I prove the contrary? In ſhort, wherein is Friendſhip violated? By theſe two things eſpecially   *If thou haſt my Friends for Procop Goth* *Enemies   if thou art a Friend to my Enemies* 1 *he is reckoned an Enemy, who ſupplieth them* *with what is uſeful for the War.*

III. But now there are many things that are uſeful for the War worthy of ſome conſideration, the which are not ſo accounted at this day by the Laws of Nations, underſtand me, That I call the *Laws of Nations*, which is at this day univerſally practiſed, as namely, the ſupplying either or both of the warring Parties with Monies, or that which is called *Contribution.* Now if the Minds of the Subjects cannot be satisfied by the declaration of the Cause, it will certainly be the Office of a good Prince or General, rather to impose upon them Contribution than Military Service, especially when that Prince or General hath an Army sufficient to prosecute his Designs, the which a just Commander may use as God doth the ready Service of the Devil.

Sil in Verb. bellum p 1. n 7 circa finem.

The most excellent *Grotius* having most incomparably treated on, and cleared all the important Objections against a just War, together with the Incidents of the same, yet this main one of *Contribution,* or paying to both Armies, whether lawful, he hath not touched in any other words but these, *Quod sub tributo utrique parti præstando factum diu in Belgrico, Germanico bello nuper vidimus, estque id consentaneum mori veteri Indorum* † : and so cites a saying in *Diodorus Siculus* *, of the Peace that those People maintained in their Possessions by reason of such Contributions   But to many Persons this Instance, without further scrutiny, proves insufficient ; for there are many, who not finding this Liberty in their Consciences, unnecessarily chuse rather to give up their Bodies to restraint, and to abandon their whole means of Subsistence in this World, both for themselves and their Children, (which ought not fondly to be done, *unless we would be worse than Infidels,* as St. *Paul* saith) they ground their Resolution on this Reason, that they know not whether the Monies they give may not furnish to the Destruction of many Innocents, and perhaps the just Magistrate, yea, and the total subversion and ruin of

† Gro: de Jure Bell 'ac Pacis, lib 3 cap. 12. § 4. n 2. * Lib 2.

                                              their

their Country, Liberty, and Religion · And therefore, though Men give and beſtow their own where they pleaſe, yet in ſuch Caſes they may not ; therefore it may not be impertinent to examine whether theſe be neceſſary Scruples in themſelves, and ſuch as admit of no exception of Liberty, or whether thoſe Scruples be reaſonable, or indeed meer ſcandal.

IV. The *Scribes* and *Phariſees* ſought two ways to entrap *Our Saviour*, one was, if he had blaſphemoiſly taught a new Religion, and a new God, (*viz* himſelf) they hoped the People would be provoked to ſtone him for this, according to the *Hebrew Law* : Deut. xiii. The other was, to bring him within the compaſs of *Treaſon*, as if he could not lead great Multitudes after him without traiterous Deſigns ; but this Gin failed too, becauſe the Multitudes which followed him were always ready to defend him. However, when he was at *Jeruſalem*, where the *Roman* Troops and *Prætor* were, they thought they had him ſure, by propounding this Subject to him .

Is it lawful to pay Tribute to Cæſar ? Which was as much as to ſay, We who are deſcended from *Abraham*, and are the peculiar People, to whom God hath given the large Privileges of the Earth at home, to bathe ourſelves in Rivers of Milk and Honey, to have full Barns and many Children , yea, that G O D himſelf would be adored in no other place of the World but at this our *Jeruſalem*, and that abroad we ſhould triumph over the *Barbarous* and uncircumciſed World by virtue of that *Militia*, which he never ordered for any but ourſelves , how are we then in Duty or Conſcience to ſubmit now to the Ordi-

R 3   nances

nances of the *Uncircumcised Romans?* Or
what Right can he have to exercise supreme
Jurisdiction over us, the privileged *Seed of*
Abraham, by levying of Taxes on our
Estates and Lands, which GOD himself
laid out for us, by which means the *Emperor*
and *Senate* hold this very Temple in slavery,
and insult over our very Consciences and Religion, by defiling our very Sacrifices with
the mixture of impure Blood, which as
they are the price of our Blood, and a Tribute far above *Cæsar's*, (payable in no other
Place but this Temple, which GOD himself built) so our Blood ought not to seem
too dear to be sacrificed for the Liberty of
these: And though the *Roman State* could
pretend, yet what can this *Cæsar* pretend
Every man's Conscience knows that it was
but the other day he usurpt over the *Senate,*
in which resides the true Jurisdiction of *Rome,*
and if that were otherwise, yet how can he
pretend to a Title unless Poison be a Pedi-
gree, or violent Usurpation a just Election,
by which he, who is but the greatest Thief in
the World, would now pass for the most Sovereign and Legitimate Prince? How then are
we in Conscience obliged to pay Tribute to
this *Cæsar?* Though those Lawyers thought
in there Consciences that they were not to
pay it, and that *Our Saviour* likewise, as a
Jew, thought so too; yet they supposed he
durst not say so much in the crowd, nor yet
deny it by shifting it off with Silence, lest
the *Roman* Officers should apprehend him:
But when *Our Saviour* shewed them *Cæsar's*
Face upon the Coin, and bade them *Render*
to Cæsar that which was Cæsar's, and to GOD
that which was GOD's, His Answer ran
quite

quite otherwife, not as fome would have it, that by a Subtilty he anfwered not to the Point propofed, for then the fenfe of the whole Text would found very ill in fuch Terms, *viz.* If there by any thing due to *Cæfar*, pay him it ; and if any thing is due from you to GOD, then pay it likewife : This had been a weakening of GOD's Right for *Cæfar*'s, and to have left a defperate doubting in a neceffity : 'Tis beyond all cavil, that *Our Saviour*'s Opinion was pofitive Matt. xxii. for paying of *Tribute* to that *Cæfar*, becaufe 20 *de facto* he did pay it, and the plain Reafon of it appears evidently in this his Anfwer : *Cæfar*'s Face was upon the Coin, that is to fay, *Cæfar* by Conqueft was in Poffeffion of that Coin, by poffeffing the place where he obliged them to take it ; coining of Money 3 *Inftit* 16, being one Prerogative of Sovereign Power. 17

V. But to come more clofe to the Queftion, whether Contribution may lawfully be paid : Firft, we are to make a Difference betwixt *perferre & inferre bellum*, the one is active, and properly at the beginning of a War, and in a place where yet no War is, and where its Caufe only, and not its Effects, can be confidered, in this cafe every thing ought to be very clear for Warrant of a Man's Confcience, becaufe of the Calamities which he helps to introduce, and is in fome manner the Author of, the other is paffive, and there where War, or the Power of War is actually formed, which is the Cafe of this Difcourfe

VI. Secondly, we are to diftinguifh betwixt that which cannot be had, nor the Value of it, unlefs we actually give it, and

that,

that which may be taken by the Law of War whether we contribute or no.

VII. Moſt certain it is, though a War be not yet actually formed in a place, yet a ſcrupling Conſcience, which likes not the Cauſe, may be excuſed in contributing to it in this one Caſe, *viz.* If ſome number of Men, able to take what they aſk, demand (with an armed power) the payment of a certain ſum to be employed in War, then in ſuch a caſe, the Man, whom we ſuppoſe, may pay it as a Ranſom for his Life, or give it as a Man doth his Purſe, when he is ſurpriſed in the Highway, becauſe to this Man it is as much as if the whole Country were poſſeſſed with an armed Power. So ſeveral *Dutchies* and *Seigniories* dependent on the *Empire*, did in the War between them and the Crown of *France*, pay Contribution.

4 H. 4. 2.

Procopius in the third of *Goth.* of *Tatilas* when he beſieged *Rome* ſaith, *Agricolis interim per omnem Italiam nihil mali intulit, ſed juſſit eos ita, ut ſoliti erant, terram perpetuo ſecuros colere, modo ut ipſi Tributa perferren.* This, ſaith *Caſſiodore*, is the greateſt Praiſe, 12, 15.

But if the Perſon or Country be not for the time in full Poſſeſſion of him whoſe Cauſe he ſcruples at, and that he or they have not a probable fear of extreme danger, nor as probable aſſurance, that without his help the thing demanded nor its value can be taken from him or them, then there is little Excuſe remains for the Act, becauſe the very Act (which his Conſcience diſlikes) participates more of Action than of Paſſion.

VIII. But where a Man or City is fully poſſeſſed by an invading Power (be the ſame juſt or unjuſt) from whom he or they cannot fly, nor remove their Subſtance, moſt certain the payment of Contribution is no gift, any

more

more than he (as above) who with his own
Hands being set upon by Pirates or Robbers,
puts his Purse into their Hands; for the
Laws calls not that a *Gift*, nor excuses the
Party from taking it: And altho' the Parties
may employ the same to the Destruction
perhaps of Innocents, and the like, yet that
is an Action out of their Power that give,
as far as Winds and Tempests are, to which 44 *E.* 3. 14.
two as we contribute nothing, so we cannot 4 *H* 5. 3.
be scrupulous in our Consciences concerning *Coke* 3 *Inst.*
their bad Effects, nor is the same repugnant *fol.* 68
to the *Canon Law*, (which teaches us huma-
nity, and the imitation of all their Virtues) *C* 2 *deTreug.*
and therefore Persons, whose Lives are inno- *& Pace Nic.*
cent and harmless, ought not to be subjected *Damasc.*
to Danger or Plunder, which hardly can be
avoided without Contribution or Tribute

IX. Again, those that live on Frontiers, The quiet of
whose condition is more ticklish and deplora- the World
ble, because they are not fully possest, nor cannot be had
taken into the Line of either Party, these live Arms, no
as it were in the Suburbs of a Kingdom, and Arms with-
enjoy not the Security or Privileges of others, out Soldiers
yet such Persons may lawfully contribute to Pay, nor Pay
both, for though they be but partly possest tribution.
by one, and partly by the other, in respect of *Tacit. Hist.* 4.
their sudden abandoning them, yet both Par-
ties have the Power of destroying them wholly;
wherefore those former Reasons which justify
those fully possest, do also acquit the Payments of these, for their condition here is
more calamitous, seeing they are really but
Tenants at Will, exposed to a perpetual
Alarm, and that both Parties wound one the
other only through their sides, as those this
day that are situate between *France* and *Germany*, for being perhaps Neuters in the War,
they

they are in that cafe by the Law of Arms to shew themselves equal to both, in permitting of Paffage, in affording Provifions for the Armies, and in not relieving the Befieged.

X. Nor can the Interdiction of him to whom fuch owe Faith and Obedience, any ways create the fame an Offence, fince the declared Wills of our Governors cannot make all thofe of our Acts Sins, when we obey or fubmit to that Power, which againft our Wills (as much as againft theirs, and it may be with more of our Mifery) hath diveffed them of the Power of their Rights, and deprived us of the Power of their Government; and by the Laws of

War, they who have overcome, fhould govern thofe whom they have overcome, and therefore whatfoever is exacted by the Conquerors, may juftly be paid by the Conquered

And fince Princes by their Commands cannot change the nature of human Condition, which is fubject naturally to thofe fore-mentioned Changes, it would feem exceeding hard to oblige us to almoft moral Impoffibi-

lities, and though thofe Political Commands were as Laws, yet doubtlefs they ought not to be obliging, but according to the Legiflative Rule, which is, *cum fenfu humanæ imbecillitatis,* this is that which is called the prefumed Will * of a Governor, or the Mind of a Law, for in extreme Neceffity it is to be prefumed, that both their Wills proceeding from the Rigour of what they have declared, rather than by holding to that which is their fuppofed Right, introduce certain Miferies and Confufion, without receiving any Benefit thereby to themfelves Nor could they of *Utrecht,* and others of the conquered Cities in *Holland,*

abandoned

abandoned afterwards by the *French*, and entirely preserved from Destruction, be condemned by their *Confederates*, for the Sums by them promised to the Enemy for the Preservation of the same.

Neither *are such Commands or Interdictions without their sense and profit, though they be not positively obeyed*, for thereby Governors shew to all the World, that they renounce no part of their Right, no, though it be there where they cannot exercise any part of their just Power.

And that is apparently evinced by the Laws of Leagues, for such being made, the same remains, altho' the same King or his Successor be driven out of his Kingdom, for the Right of the Kingdom remains, although he hath lost the Possession. *Grotius, lib 2 cap 17 § 19*

XI. Now the true Intention of such Commands or Interdictions is, that the Enemy should not by any means be assisted or strengthened, but if such Prohibitions should be obeyed, nay, at such a time, when they and all their substance are absolutely possest by the Enemy, most certain such Commands dash against themselves, and the one countermands the other, for if they refuse to submit in such a Case, then they do that which advantages their Enemies, because at that time they will take all, whereas in Case of Submission they ask but a part

XII In all Wars there are always some, by whose Disaffections Enemies gain more than by their Compliance, just as Physicians do by Distempers

And although by variety of Successes, the just Governor should after recover that Place, which so submitted to the Power of their Enemies, and for that reason should punish those that were pliable to extreme Necessity, yet it follows

follows not upon that, that they who so conformed, sinned, or did that which was absolutely unlawful, for we well know, that reason of State often calls for Sacrifices where there is no fault to expiate: *Ostracism* and *Jealousy* may make away those who are known to deserve most, but in strict Right (which is the Term of this Question) the just Governor ought to look upon them as more Unfortunate than Faulty.

In Republica idem est nimium, & nihil mereri.

CHAP.

CHAP. XIII.
Of the Naval Military Part.

I. *The Advantage that Princes have by a good Commander.*

II. *The Love that naturally proceeds from the Mariners to those that are valiant and generous.*

III. *Princes in Prudence ought not to listen too much to the Complaints against Commanders.*

IV *Of the Faults generally considered in Soldiers and Mariners.*

V *Of the Punishments that generally wait on such Offenders*

VI. *Of Drunkenness, Swearing, and other such sort of Impieties, not to be suffered in Fleets.*

VII. *Spies, 'tis lawful to use them by the Laws of Nations, but being deprehended, are to suffer Death; and how they are to be dealt withal by the Laws of England.*

VIII. *It is not lawful for a Friend or Neuter to relieve an Enemy, and Persons so offending, how punished.*

IX *Ships taken as Prize, the Ship, Papers, and other matters concerning the same, are to be preserved.*

X. *Of things taken and acquired in War, how the Right of them becomes vested in the Captors, and how that is to be understood by the Law of Arms.*

XI. *To steal the Cables or other Furniture of the King's Ships, how punishable at this day.*

XII. *Ships surrendered or voluntarily yielded, how to be dealt with, and to those that shall resist, if entered by force, whether quarter may be refused.*

XIII *Ships of War generally ought not to be yielded, but if entered or disabled, whether they may not accept of Quarter, standing with the Oath, called Sacramentum Militare*

XIV. *Of obeying Orders, the same ought punctually to be followed, and if broken, though the Act succeeds well, whether the same subjects not the Actor to Punishment*

XV. *Of the Obligation incumbent on Commanders and Soldiers, to behave themselves valiantly, and the right of slaying an Enemy, where lawful.*

XVI, *Ships*

I AN excellent *General* is an Evidence of
the Fortune of a *Prince*, and the In-
strument

ftrument that occafions the Happinefs of a Kingdom, and therefore when God makes choice of a Perfon to repair the Diforders of the World, or the Good of a particular State, then is his Care fhewed in the furnifhing him with neceffary Principles to undertake great Matters, the Thoughts are put in his Soul by that eternal Commander to execute, he troubles and confounds his Enemies, and leads him as by the Hand to Victories and Triumphs · And one of the greateft Expedients whereof he ferves himfelf for this Purpofe, is to raife unto him excellent Men, both in Courage and Conduct, to whom he communicates his Care, and who help him to bear the Weight of Affairs. *Alexander* had never conquered *Afia*, or made the *Indies* to tremble, but for *Epheftion*, *Parmenio*, and *Clitus*, *Cæfar* gained many a Battle by his Lieutenants, and the faireft *Empire* of the World, which Ambition and the Evil of the Times had divided into three Parts, was reduced under the Dominion of *Auguftus* by the Valour of *Agrippa*; *Juftinian* triumphed over *Perfia*, and deftroyed the *Vandals* in *Africa*, and the *Goths* in *Italy*, by the Aid of *Belifarius* and *Narfes* And it is moft certain, that *Noble Commanders* are the Glory of their *Princes*, and Happinefs of the *People*, on the other hand, Bafe, Cowardly and Treacherous Generals are the Shame of the one, and the Defpair of the other

II Hence it is, that Soldiers and Mariners draw their Lines of Love even to the Mouths of Cannons with a good General, but Mutiny and Hate to the main Yard end againft one that is Bad, for to obey them who are not their Sovereigns when they do them, hurt,

hurt, when they infult and are cruel in cold
Blood, and Bafe, Cowardly or Treacherous in
Battle, is a fad Neceffity for them, and a hard
Effay of Patience; yet muft they be obeyed,
and the Soldiers and Mariners muft not rebel
or repine, but fubmit till their Sovereign re-
dreffes their Misfortunes.

III Again, *Princes* ought not to liften too
much to the mutinous Demands of the *Crew*,
or any others, whofe Ambition watches their
Ruin, whereby to conceive Anger againft
their *Commanders*; for it is eafier to purge out
the Choler and Difcontent that is got under
the Hatches, than to provide *Commanders of
Conduct*, Courage, and Faithfulnefs to govern
their Expeditions. *Belifarius*, that moft excellent Commander, who had no other Crime
than his *Reputation*, and was not culpable, but
that he was Powerful, having conquered *Per-*
Procopius Hift. *fia*, fubdued *Africa*, humbled the *Goths* in
Vandal. in Vi- *Italy*, led Kings in Triumph, and made ap-
ta Belifarii pear to *Conftantinople* fomewhat of *Old Rome*;
an *Idea* of the antient Splendor of that proud
Republick; after all his eminent Services, this
Vide Sir Wal- great *Perfon* is abandoned to *Envy*. A Suf-
ter Ralegb'- picion, ill-grounded, deftroys the Value of
Hift. Vol II fo many Services, and a fimple *Jealoufy of*
p. 782. *State* wipes them out of the Memory of his
Edit. 1736 Prince; but he refts not there, for the De-
meanour had been too gentle, if Cruelty had
not been added to Ingratitude, they deprive
The Ingrati- him of all his Honours, they rob him of all
tude that hath his Fortune; they take from him the Ufe of
been fhewn the Day and Light, *they put out his* Eyes,
by Princes to and reduce him to the Company of Rogues,
many Brave
and Noble and the miferable *Belifarius* demands a Charity,
Generals and even that *Belifarius*, the chiefeft General of his
Age,

Age, and the *greateſt Ornament of the Empire*, Commanders who after ſo many Victories and Conqueſts, there particularly enumerated accompanied with ſo high and clear a Virtue, and in the midſt of *Chriſtendom*, was reduced to ſo abject and low a Miſery

Nor was this cruel and haſty reckoning of *Juſtinian* let ſlip without a cruel Payment, for *Narſes*, who was as well a Succeſſor in Merit as in Authority to *Beliſarius*, having notice of a Diſdain, conceived likewiſe againſt him upon a ſingle Complaint, reſolved not to expoſe himſelf as a Sacrifice to their Malice; and therefore thinking it better to ſhake off the Yoke, than ſtay to be oppreſſed, ſoon ſpoiled the Affairs of *Juſtinian*, for the *Goths* revolted, and Fortune would not forbear to be of the Party which *Narſes* followed, nor to find the *Barbarian* where ſo brave a Captain was engaged   Therefore not one or many Faults are to be liſtened to againſt Commanders, but patiently heard and redreſſed, not to diſgrace or loſe them; for ſuch having committed a Fault, yet being admoniſhed by love, may endeavour by future Services to make recompence by ſome noble Exploit; but diſgraced, become Inſtruments often of Danger and Ruin to their Superiors.

IV. Soldiers and Mariners Faults are either proper to themſelves, or common with others.

Thoſe are common with others which other Men fall into, and are corrected with like ordinary Proceedings as other Crimes of like Nature, as Manſlaughter, Theft, Adultery, and ſuch like.

Thoſe are proper which do purely appertain to the *Naval Military* part, and are puniſhed by ſome unuſual or extraordinary Pu-

§ *De re milit*
De castrensi
peculio, & C.
eodem tit l 12
C. de erogatio-
ne militaris
annonæ & C
de vest Mili-
tari.

nishment: As are these, Not to appear at the over-musters or calling over the Ship, to serve under him he ought not to serve, to vage or wander long from on Ship-board, although he returned of his own accord, to forsake his Fleet, Squadron, Ship, Captain, Commander, or Officer; to leave his standing to fly over to the Enemy, to betray the Fleet, Squadron, or Ship, to be disobedient to his superior Officers, to lose or sell his Arms, or to steal another Man's; to be negligent in his Officer's Command, or in his Watch; to make a Mutiny, to fly first out of the Battle, and the like, which are very frequently set forth in the Titles of the *Digest* and *Code* of Military Affairs, and other like Titles which accompany them.

Arrian, who wrote the Life of *Alexander the Great*, observes, *Every thing is counted an Offence in a Soldier, which is done contrary to the common Discipline*, as to be neglectful, stubborn, and slothful.

V. The Punishment wherewith Soldiers and Mariners are corrected, are those corporal Punishments, or a pecuniary Mulk or Injunction of some Service to be done, or a Motion and removing out of their Places, and sending them away with Shame.

By capital Punishment is understood for the most part Death, or at least beating with *Cat with Nine Tails*, as they commonly term it, *Ducking, Wooden-Horse, Gauntlet*, and such like, unless happily it be pardoned, either for the unskilfulness of the Mariner or Soldier, or the Mutiny of the Crew or Company, being thereto drawn by Wine, Wantonness, or for the Commiseration or Pity of the Wife and Children of the Party offending; all
which

which is left to the Difcretion of the *Lord Admiral*, and others the Supreme Commanders or Captains.

VI. It is neceffary that in Armies and Fleets, all manner of Impiety fhould be prohibited, efpecially that of Swearing and Curfing, for fuch Sins are fo foolifh, that they unawares trip Men into Damnation, rendering Men worfe than Beafts, by how much the more they court that Vanity of Sin, without any of the appendent Allurements, which other vitious Actions are accompanied with, the fame in the end teaching Men to difavow GOD in their difcourfe and actions, by their intemperate and inconfiderate invoking him in their Oaths *Againft fuch, as alfo againft thofe that fhall give themfelves up to Curfing, Execrations, Drunkennefs, Uncleannefs, or other fcandalous actions in Derogation of God's Honour, and corruption of Good Manners, Fines and Imprifonment, or fuch other Punifhment may be inflicted on them by a Court Martial.*

VII By the *Laws of Nations*, *Spies* may be fent to furvey the Enemy's Force, Fleet, Station, or Squadron, and make difcovery of whatfoever may give advantage to the Perfons fending. So *Mofes* and *Jofhua* did into the *Holy Land.* On the other hand being deprehended, they are to be put to death, as *Appian* faith But whether it be lawful to make Spies of the Subjects of that Prince with whom the War is begun, hath been fome doubt It is not lawful for a Subject to kill his King, nor to yield up his Ships of War without publick Council, nor to fpoil his fellow Citizens, to thefe things it is not lawful to tempt a Subject that remains fuch, nor may any reply,

Lib 2 c 3. § ult ad Leg. Corn de Sicarus pan

That to him who impelleth such a Man to a wicked Act, that Act, as namely the betraying of his Enemy, is lawful; no body doubts he may indeed do it, but not in that manner; but yet if a Subject will voluntarily desert his Prince and Country, *i. e.* so enter into a Correspondency with the Enemy of it, without any impulse but his own covetous or revengeful Mind, surely it cannot be unlawful for the other to receive him. *We receive a Fugitive by the Law of War,* saith *Celsus,* that is, it is not against the Law of War to admit such, even a Traitor, *who having deserted the Enemy's part, electeth ours*; however, such Persons ought not to be rendered, unless expressly stipulated *, but ought to be pardoned. *By the Laws of* England, *if any Officer, Mariner, Soldier, or other Person of the Fleet, shall give, hold, or entertain Intelligence to or with any Enemy or Rebel, without Leave from the King's Majesty, or the Lord High-Admiral, or Commissioners of the Admiralty, Commander in Chief, or his commanding Officer, such Person shall be punished with Death* Now the bare receipt of a Letter or Message from an Enemy, will not make a Man subject to the Penalty of this Article, and therefore the subsequent Article explains the precedent, in which it is provided, that *If any Letter or Message from any Enemy or Rebel, be conveyed to any Officer, Mariner, Soldier, or others in the Fleet, and he shall not within Twelve Hours, having Opportunity so to do, acquaint his Superior Officer or the Officer commanding in Chief with it, he shall be punished with Death*; so likewise *shall any superior Officer, being acquainted therewith, shall not in convenient Time reveal the same to the Commander in Chief of the Squadron.*

All

Leg transfug De de acq retrum Dom.

* As was in the Peace with *Philip,* the *Ætolians, Antiochus, Polyb iv excerpt legat.* 11 28. 38. *Mer and Protect idem, non decet.* Stat. 22 Geo. 2. cap 33 Artic 3

Artic 4

All Spies, and all Perfons in Nature of Spies, *Artic.* 5. *bringing or delivering any feducing Letters or Meffages from any Enemy or Rebel, or endeavouring to corrupt any Captain, Officer, Mariner, or other in the Fleet, to betray his Truft, fhall be punifhed with Death, or fuch other Punifhment as the Nature and Degree of the Offence fhall deferve, and the Court Martial fhall impofe.* Now *Spies* are put to Death fometimes juftly by thofe that manifeftly have a juft caufe of Warring by others, by that licence which the Law of War granteth, nor ought any Perfon to be moved with this, that fuch being taken, are punifhed with Death, for that proceeds not from their having offended againft the Law of Nations, but from this, that by the fame Law every thing is lawful againft an Enemy, and every one, *Ad Leg Corn.* as it is for his own Profit, determineth either *de Sicariis pun.* more rigoroufly or gently But that *Spies* are *Tacit. Hift* 5. both lawful and practicable, theie is no Queftion, for at this day, by the general Inftructions of Fleets, there are always out of each Squadron fome Frigates or Ships appointed to make difcovery of the Enemy, and upon fight to make Sail, and to ftand with them, in order to take cognizance of their Force, as well Ships of War as Fire-Ships, and in what Pofture they lay, which being done, *thofe detecting Frigates are to fpeak together, and to conclude on the Report they are to give, which done, they return to their refpective Squadrons,* fuch Ships in fuch Service are not obliged to fight, efpecially if the Enemies Force exceed them in number, or unlefs they fhall have an apparent Advantage.

VIII Again, it is not lawful for any, be *Bartol. Leg. nullus Leg* 2. he Friend or Neuter, to relieve an Enemy, *de Judæis Cæ-*

much *licolis*

much lefs for a Soldier or Mariner in pay, *to
supply him that conspires the destruction of my
Country, is a liberality not to be allowed of.*

*Procop.us
Goth.* 1. He is to be accounted an Enemy that supplies the Enemy with Neceffaries for the
War, and therefore by the Laws of War is
fo to be efteemed; and by the Laws of *England, No Perfon in the Fleet shall relieve an Enemy or Rebel with Money, Victuals, Powder,
Shot, Arms, Ammunition, or any other Supplies whatfoever, directly or indirectly, upon Pain
of Death*

Artic. 6.

Artic. 7. IX *All the Papers, Charter-Parties, Bills
of Lading, Pass-ports, and other Writings whatfoever, that shall be taken, seized, or found
aboard, are to be duly preferved, and the very
Originals are to be fent entirely, and without
Fraud, to the Court of Admiralty, or such other
Court of Commiffioners, as shall be authorized to
determine whether such Prize be lawful Capture,
there to be viewed, made ufe of, and proceeded
upon, according to Law, upon Pain that every
Perfon fo offending herein, shall lofe his Share of
the Capture, and shall fuffer such further Punishment, as the Nature and Degree of his Offence
shall be found to deferve, and the Court Martial shall impofe*

X. The Right of taking of Spoil was approved of God, within thofe natural Bounds
which have been already mentioned, as is further evinced by the Appointment of God in
his *Law,* concerning the Acquifition of Empire over the conquered, after refufal of Peace,
Deut xx 14 *All the spoil thereof shalt thou take unto thyself,
and thou shalt eat the spoil of thine Enemies,
which the* LORD *thy* GOD *hath given thee.*
Hence it is, that things taken from the Enemy, prefently become theirs that take them,
by

by the Law of Nations, and such Acquisition is called *Natural*, for not any cause, but the naked fact is considered And thence a Right ariseth; for as the Dominion of things began from Natural Possession, and some print of the same remains in the things taken in the Land, the Sea, and the Air, so likewise of things taken in War; all which instantly become theirs that first become Captors, and from the Enemy are judged to be taken away those things also which are taken away from the Subjects of the Enemy. But though this gives a Right to the Captors, yet that must be understood to the Sovereign, or to the State that imployed them, and not to themselves; but if they have any share of the Prize, the same proceeds by the condescension or grant of the Sovereign, which may be enlarged or abridged as occasion serves; and therefore by the Laws of *England, the full and entire Account of the whole Prize, without Embezzlement, shall be brought in, and Judgment past without Fraud*, but that is to be understood, where the Ship voluntarily yields But Ships whom they shall assault, and take in fight as Prize, the pillage of all manner of Goods and Merchandizes (other than Arms, Ammunition, Tackle, Furnitures or Stores of such Ships) as shall be found by the Captors, *upon or above the Gun-Deck of the Ship, become theirs*, but this is to be understood where such Prize may lawfully be possest, for there are times when such are not to be meddled with, and therefore it is against the Rules of War in Fight, if some of the Enemies Ships are there disabled, yet those Ships that did so disable them, if they are in a condition to pursue the Enemy, cannot during the Fight take, pos-

Leg Nat § ult de D acq rer, Dom ut de rerum Deo.

Quæ armis quæsita essent & parta belli jure non dimittenda.

Artic. 8.

By the donation of his Majesty

sess,

fefs, or burn fuch difabled Ships ; and the reafon is, *left by fo doing fome more important fer-*
vice be loft, but they are to wait for fuch Boo-
ty, till the *Flag*-Officers fhall give command
for the fame

Vluzzali, King of *Algier*, in the famous Battle of *Lepanto*, having behaved himfelf very
valiantly there againft the *Chriftians*, fo that
he deftroyed feveral of their Gallies, and
others, he took amongft the reft of the Gallies of *Pietro Bua* of *Corfa*, of the *Prior of*
Meffina, and *Ludovico Tipico* of *Trabu*, and
Benedeto Soranzo, the which he towed after
him before the Battle was compleated ; but
that getting proved the lofs both of the one
and of the other ; for the *Turks*, out of
Covetoufnefs of the Plunder, or otherwife
thronging into them, occafioned their taking
fire, in which the *Victors*, in thofe Flames
became *Victims*, and after followed the total
Rout of the *Ottoman* Power.

Hift. Re.publ
Venet fol
127, 128.

XI It is almoft impoffible, but that in
Ships of War, which in thefe days carry fo
confiderable a force of men, there will be
fome amongft them that have Heads of kna-
very, and Fingers of Lime-Twigs, not fearing to fteal that from their Prince, which is
applicable only for the Good of their Country ; fuch fort of *Night-wolves* when caught,
are to be feverely punifhed

Artic 9
Crafus per-
fuading C,-
rus not to give
up *Lydia* to be
pillaged by
his men, tells
him, *Nor me-*
am nouit, non
res meas diri-

XII. By the Ninth Article, *If any Ship or*
Veffel fhall be taken as Prize, none of the Offi-
cers, Mariners, or other Perfons on board her,
fhall be ftripped of their Cloaths, or in any fort
pillaged, beaten or evil intreated, upon Pain
that the Perfon or Perfons fo offending, fhall be
liable to fuch Punifhment as a Court Martial
fhall think fit to inflict This Law moft exprefsly
doth

doth not extend to thofe that obftinately shall maintain a Fight , for moft certain, by the Law of Arms, if the Ship be boarded and taken, there remains no reftriction but that of Charity , and if a Ship fhall perfift in the Engagement, even till the laft, and then yield to Mercy, there hath been fome doubt, * whether Quarter ought to be given to fuch (for they may ignorantly maintain with Courage a bad Caufe) but in Captives, and thofe that yield or defire to yield, there is no danger. Now that fuch may be juftly killed, there muft be fome antecedent Crime, and that fuch a one as an equal Judge would think worthy of Death ; and fo we fee great feverity fhewed to the Captives and thofe that have yielded, or their yielding on condition of Life not accepted, if after they were convinced of the Injuftice of the War, they had neverthelefs perfifted with Hatred or Cruelty , if they had blotted their Enemies Name with unfufferable difgraces ; if they had violated their Faith or any Right of Nations, as of Ambaffadors ; if they were Fugitives But the Law of Nature admits not Taliation, except againft the very individual Perfon that hath offended , nor doth it fuffice, that the Enemies are by a fiction conceived to be as it were one Body , tho' otherwife by the Laws of Nations, and by the Laws of Arms, and at this day practifed, in all Fights, the fmall Frigates, Ketches, and Smacks are to obferve and take notice of the Enemies Fire-fhips, and to watch their Motion, and to do their beft to cut off their Boats, and generally *the perfons found in them are to be put to death, if taken,*

pies, nihil enim ad me jam ifta pertinent tua funt, tua illi perdent. Herod. *lib.* 1. *Victor de Jure Belli, n* 49. *&* 60.

D & C. de Jutis & facti ignorantia

Princes indeed are *Gods*, but neither do the Gods hear the prayers of fupplicants, except they be juft.

The *Syracufians* were accufed for that they flew the Wives and Children of *Hycetas*, becaufe *Hycetas* had flain the Sifter and Son of *Dion*. Plutarch *Timon & Dion*.

taken, and the Veſſel, if not taken, deſtroyed; and the reaſon why the extremity of War is uſed to ſuch, is that by how much the Miſchief is the greater by the Act of ſuch Men, if executed, by ſo much the Puniſhment is aggravated, if taken, and Quarter denied them by the Law of War[']

Artic 10.

XIII. *Every Flag Officer, Captain and Commander, who upon ſignal or order of Fight, or ſight of any Ship which it may be his Duty to engage, or who upon likelihood of engagement, ſhall not make the neceſſary preparations for Fight, and ſhall not in his own Perſon, and according to his Place, encourage the Inferior Officers, and Men, to fight couragiouſly, ſhall ſuffer Death, or ſuch other Puniſhment as from the Nature and Degree of the Offence, a Court Martial ſhall deem him to deſerve, and if any Perſon in the Fleet ſhall treacherouſly or cowardly yield, or cry for quarter, ſhall ſuffer Death.* Now, though Soldiers, or Mariners, have obliged themſelves faithfully to ſerve in the Expedition or Navy; yet that is to be underſtood no further than his or their power to do their utmoſt in his or their Quality, for though the Obligation for the Service be taken in the ſtricteſt Terms of undergoing death and danger, yet it is to be underſtood always conditionally as moſt Promiſes are, *viz.* if the action or paſſion may be for that Fleet or Prince's Advantage, and therefore if the Fleet or Squadron is beaten and the Ships are diſabled, and left ſcarce without any to defend them, now the Soldiers or [*] Mariners remaining can do no more for their Prince than die, which indeed is to do nothing at all, but to ceaſe for ever from doing

[*] *Lipſus de Mil. Rem l 2. cral 6 & 4 And Polybius expreſſeth the*

doing any thing either for him or themselves , in those straits therefore it is not repugnant to their Oath, called *Sacramentum Militare,* to ask quarter or to strike, and having begged a new Life and taken it, they are bound in a new and just Obligation of Fidelity to those whom they were bound to kill few hours before , neither can the Prince or General expect by virtue of their former Obligation to him, they should kill any in the place where the Quarter was given. However, this Fidelity hath not its inception from the time of taking quarter , but when the Battle is over, and that time which is termed cold blood , for without all controversy, if a Ship be boarded, and Quarter is given, yet if while the Fight lasts, the Persons Captives can by any possibility recover their Liberty and Ship, they may, by the *Law of Arms,* justly acquire the same *.

Oath thus, *Obtemperaturus sum, & facturus quicquid mandabitur ab Imperatoribus, juxta vires* and such, says he, were termed *Milites per Sacramentum.*

* Sr *Thomas Chichley* did so aboard the *Katharine* in the War with *Holland.*

And since Impunity is granted to such unfortunate Deserters, yet it must be apparently evident and fully proved, that they were reduced into a Condition beyond all hope in the Battle , and therefore the Foot that forsook the *Unfortunate Pompey* before the Field was lost, were justly condemned for the breach of the *Roman* Discipline and Law of Arms . And therefore the Article hath not positively declared Death only, but added, *or such other Punishment as the Offence shall deserve,* which Provision leaves the Action to be judged and punished by a *Council of War,* who know best what's to be done in Cases of that nature , however, *a base or cowardly*

cowardly yielding, or crying quarter, is to be punished with Death, and that without Mercy.

XIV. The obeying of Orders hath in all Ages been in mighty esteem, *Chryfantus,* one of *Cyrus*'s Soldiers, being upon his Enemy, withdrew his Sword, hearing a Retreat founded, but this comes not from the external *Laws of Nations,* for as it is lawful to feize on the Enemy's Goods, fo likewife to kill the Enemy, for by that Law the Enemies are of no account; but fuch Obedience proceeds from the *Military Difcipline* of feveral Nations. By the *Romans* it was a Law noted by *Modeftinus,* That whofoever obeyed not his Orders, fhould be punifhed with Death, though the matter fucceeded well: Now he alfo was fuppofed not to have obeyed, who out of Order, without the Command of the *General,* entred into any Fight. For if fuch liberty were lawful, either Stations would be deferted, or (licence proceeding) the Army, Fleet, or Squadron would be engaged in unadvifed Battles, which by all means is to be avoided. *M. Capello,* a *Venetian* Gentleman of an antient Extraction, having the Charge of the *guarding the Venetian Gulph* *, met with the *Barbary Fleet,* whom he fo affaulted, that he burnt and took divers of them, amongft the reft the *Admiral Galley of Algier,* (a Veffel of vaft bignefs) which he brought with him away, and fhe remains at this day a *Trophy* in the *Arfenal of Venice,* the Service, although Noble and Honorable, and fuch as brought renown to the Republick, yet in regard it was an Action exceeding his Commiffion, he was adjudged to punifhment (but his great
Merit

Zenoph. Cyr. Plutarch Quæft. Rom. 39. & Marcello.

Vide in Tit. Ships of War.

Leg. defert D. de re Milit.

L. v. lib. 7 Marham Imperia.

The Order of Battle is to be preferved, and in all cafes they are to endeavour to keep in one line as much as may be; and though they have beaten fome of the Enemy, yet muft they not purfue a fmall number, before the main

Merit and Alliance preserved his Life . (such an exact Obedience that *Signory* expects to be paid to her Orders, be the Success never so glorious. And by the Eleventh Article, *Every Person who shall not duly observe the Orders of the Admiral, Flag Officer, Commander of any Squadron or Division, or other his Superior Officer, for assailing, joining Battle, or making Defence against any Fleet, Squadron or Ship, or shall not obey the Orders of his Superior Officer as aforesaid, in time of Action, to the best of his Power, or shall not use all possible Endeavours to put the same effectually in Execution, he shall suffer Death, or such other Punishment, as from the Nature and Degree of the Offence a Court Martial shall deem him to deserve.*

XV. Again, *Every person in the Fleet, who thro' Cowardice, Negligence, or Disaffection, shall in time of Action withdraw or keep back, or not come into the Fight or Engagement, or not do his utmost to take or destroy every Ship which it is his Duty to engage, and to assist all his Majesty's Ships, or those of his Allies, which it is his duty to assist, shall suffer Death.* By the word *Captain* the General or *Admiral* is not included, but all *Flag-Officers,* and others under them, are within the purview of the *Statute* by the denomination of the word *Captain,* &c and the Reason wherefore such Commanders in Chief are not within the *Law,* is, because the Weapon of a *General* is his Truncheon, but of all other Officers is the Sword , a *General* is only to command, and the rest to execute, for in the latter is the danger only or one Man's life, but in the first is the hazard of all , therefore by the Law of Arms no *General* or *Admiral* in Chief ought to expose their

of the Enemy be beaten or run *Nor* ought they in chasing, chase beyond sight of the Flag, and at night all chasing Ships are to return to the Flag *Instr.* 22, 23 in *May* 1, 1666. * History of the Republick of *Venice,* *fol* 170, 171.

Artic. 12. It was on this Article that Admiral *Byng* suffered the 14th of *March* 1757. See his Trial

In milite unius sois est, in Imperatore universorum periculum unus homo pluris fuit quam universa civitas. ClearchusCyro dedit consilium, ne ipse se in periculum offerret sed inspectorem se pugnæ gereret, pugnantem enim corpore nil magni effi-

ceret, si verò quid damni acceperit, omnes se perditurum quos secum haberet Polyb. Stra. lib. 2.
†*Guicciard l 3 Apbor* 28.

their Person to apparent Peril, but in case of a general Overthrow and manifest Defeat. *Peter Capponi,* the Famous *General* for the *Florentines* besieging *Soiana,* and encamping on the River *Casina* †; being in a Place of danger, extremely industrious about planting his Battery, was shot with a Harquebuss, immediately upon which the Siege was raised, yet, on the other hand, let it be examined where any famous battle hath been obtained, and the same was not got, not only by the Conduct, but likewise by the single and personal Courage of the *General*

There are some Offices to be done, even to them from whom you have received an Injury; for Revenge and Punishment must have a measure, and therefore the Issues Cicero Offic. 1. & 2. of the *Roman Wars* were either mild or necessary. Now, when killing is just in a just War, according to internal Justice, may be known by examining the Causes or End of the War, which may be for the Conservation of Life and Members, and the Grotius *de Jure Belli ac Pac s, l 1 c 2 §. 1.* keeping and acquiring of things useful unto Life, now in the assaulting of Ships, it happens that one is slain on purpose or without purpose, on purpose can no man be slain justly, unless either for just punishment, as if without it we cannot protect and defend our Life, Goods, and Country, &c. That such Punishment may be just, it is necessary that he who is slain have offended, and that so much as may be avenged with the punishment of Death in the Sentence of an equal Judge. Now we must note, between full In- *Misericordia infortuniis debetur. at qui del berata* jury and mere Misfortune often intercedes some mean, which is as it were composed of both,

both, so that it can neither be called the Act of one knowing and willing, nor merely the act of one ignorant or unwilling.

This distinction by *Themistius* is fully illustrated *You have made a difference betwixt an Injury, a Fault, and a Misfortune; although you neither study* Plato, *nor read* Aristotle, *yet you put their Doctrine in practice; for you have not thought them worthy of equal punishment, who from the beginning perswaded the War, and who afterward were carried with the stream, and who at last submitted to him, that now seemed to have the highest Power, the first you condemned, the next you chastised, the last you pitied.* Most certain, to spare Captives or Prisoners of War, is a command of Goodness and Equity, and in Histories they are often commended, who when too great a number prove burthensome or dangerous, chose rather to let them all go than to stay them, or detain them, though for Ransoms, as in the last *Flemish* Wars with *England.* So for the same causes, they that strike or yield up themselves are not to be slain (though there is no Provision made by Covenant) In Towns besieged it was observed by the *Romans,* before the *Ram* had smitten the Wall, *Cæsar* * denounceth to the *Aduatici,* he would save their City, if before the *Ram* had touched the Wall, they yielded, which is still in use in weak Places, before the great Guns are fired, in strong places, before an Assault is made upon the Walls †; and at Sea, by firing one or two Guns, or hanging out the Bloody Flag, according as the Instructions are, however, till there be an absolute yielding or quarter cried, by the *Law of Arms,* as well as the abovementioned Article, every Commander and Soldier is to do

scientiâ malè agit, non infælix, sed injustus And *Cicero* hath a Saying out of *Demosthenes,* We must shew compassion to those whom Fortune, not their own Deeds, have made miserable.

Scipio Æmilianus at the Overthrow of *Carthage,* proclaim'd that they should fly that would *Polybius, vide Tacitus Annal.* 12.

Vide Serran. in reb Franc. 1 *& Hen.* 23. *Thucyd lib* * *Cæsar lib* 2. *de bello Gallico* † *Dinant* in *Germany* being taken by Assault, the Town was razed and burnt, and the Prisoners all

put to Death.
*Phil. Comin.
lib. 2. cap.* 1.
do his utmoſt to take, fire, kill, and endamage the Enemy, or whatſoever may tend
thereunto.

XVI. By the *Law of Arms,* he deſerves
puniſhment who doth not keep off force that
is offered to his Fellow Soldier; and though
it hath been conceived, if there be manifeſt
danger, that he is not bound to cóme into his
I will defend
my Compa-
nion at the
hazard of my
own Blood,
and partake
in his danger.
Senec. de Ben.
2 15
Relief, for ſuch Commander may prefer the
lives in his own Ship before thoſe in another,
yet that ſuffices not; for every Soldier by the
Law of Arms is not only bound to defend,
but alſo to aſſiſt and relieve his Companion:
Now Companions are in two reſpects, either
thoſe that are in actual ſervice with ſuch Soldiers, or thoſe that are not, but only committed to their Protection or Convoy, which
are to be defended and guarded at the ſame
peril and charge that a fellow Soldier is, and
therefore all Ships that are committed to Convoy and Guard,

Artic 13.
*Every Perſon in the Fleet, who through Cow-
ardice, Negligence, or Diſaffection, ſhall forbear
to purſue the Chace of an Enemy, Pirate, or Rebel,
beaten or flying, or ſhall not relieve or aſſiſt a
known Friend in view to the utmoſt of his Power,
ſhall ſuffer Death.*

*Etiam hujus
rei in feris i-
mago quædam*
Leo in Adul-
teræ pœnam
conſurgit
*Plin Hiſt
Nat.* 8. 16.
Protection of Convoys by the *Laws of Nations,* is of a great Utility to a Kingdom or
State; therefore when Violence is offered to
thoſe Ships under Convoy, they are not ſaid
to be done to them, but to thoſe Ships of
War under whoſe Guard they paſs; and therefore when Violence is offered to ſuch, publick Revenge is let in, according to that of
*Tacitus, He ſhould provide for their Security by
a juſt Revenge.* Now that ſuch Ships may
not

not fuffer Wrong from their Invaders, two ways may be taken by their Convoys. Firft, by deftroying him or them that fhall have attempted and committed any hoftile Act againft any thing under their Protection, fecondly, by all ways imaginable endeavour the weakening his or their Force, that he or they may not be able to do any other or further Hurt; therefore there is no doubt but Vindication to thefe Ends is within the Bounds of Equity, though this is no more than private, yet if he refpect the bare Law of Nature, abftract from Laws Divine and Human, and from all not neceffary Accidents to things, it is not unlawful, whether the Satisfaction or Revenge is taken by Convoy Ships themfelves, or the wronged ones under his or their Guard or Protection, feeing it is confentaneous to Nature, that Man fhould receive Aid from Man, and in this Senfe may be admitted that faying of *Cicero, The Law of Nature is that which comes not from Opinion, but innate Virtue:* Among the Examples of it is placed *Vindication,* which he oppofes to Favour, and that none might doubt how much he would have underftood by that name, he defines Vindication, *whereby, by defending or revenging, we keep off Force and Contumely from us and ours, who ought to be dear unto us, and whereby we punish Offences.*

Now thofe Ships that are not under Convoy, but engaged in Fight, are faithfully to be relieved, and therefore if a Squadron fhall happen to be over-charged and diftreffed, the next Squadron or Ships are to make towards their Relief and affiftance upon a Signal given them. Again, Ships that are difabled by lofs

of Mafts, fhot under Water, or the like, fo
as they be in danger of finking or taking,
the diftreffed Ships generally make a Sign by
Waft of their *Jack* and *Enfigns*, and thofe
next to them are bound to their Relief : But
yet this does not always hold place ; for if
the diftreffed Ship is not in probability of
finking, or otherwife encompaffed with the
Enemy, the Reliever is not to ftay under pretence of fecuring them, but ought to follow
his Leader and the Battle, leaving fuch lame
Ships to the Sternmoft of the Fleet, it being
an undoubted Maxim, *That nothing but beating the Body of the Enemy can effectually fecure
fuch difabled Ships*

XVII. It is not enough that Men behave
themfelves valiantly in the beating of an
Enemy, for that is not all, but the reducing
of them into a condition to render right either
for Damage done, or to render that which is
right, which can't well be done without
bringing him to Exigences and Straits, and
therefore if the Enemy, Pirate, or Rebel be

Artic. 14. beaten, *None, through Cowardice, Negligence,
or Difaffection, ought to forbear the Purfuit,*
But that is to *and thofe of them flying ; nor ought fuch, either*
be underftood *through Cowardice, Negligence or Difaffection,*
as in the 12th *forbear the Affiftance of a known Friend in view,*
§. of this *to their utmoft Power,* the Breach of which
Chapter. fubjects the Offenders to the Pains of Death,
or at leaft fuch Punifhment as a *Court Martial*
fhall think fit.

Empires are got by Arms, and propagated
by Victory ; and by the *Laws of War,* they
that have overcome, fhould govern thofe they
have fubdued. Hence it is, that Generals
having compleated a Conqueft in a juft War,
and

and in chase or otherwise have taken the Ships
or *Goods* of the *Enemy*, have absolute Power
over the Lives, Eftates, Ships and things that
they by Force of Arms have acquired by the
Laws of Nations.

But yet in fuch Conquefts where the reeking Sword knows no Law, that is, they are
done *impunè*, without Punifhment, (becaufe *Tacit 3. An-*
co-active Judges do grant them their Au- *nal Pompeius*
thority) yet fuch Power may be exorbitant *gravior reme-*
from that Rule of Right called *Virtue*; and *dits quam de-*
though by the *Law of War* Captives may be *licta erant.*
flain, yet what Law forbids not, Modefty
prohibits to be done. Hence it is, that *Generals*
do often reftrain that Power of killing; for
though fuch Prifoners of War do fight for
the Maintainance of an unjuft Caufe, and
although the War is begun by a folemn Manner, yet all Acts that have their rife from
thence, are unjuft by internal Injuftice, fo that
they who knowingly do perfift in fighting,
* yet ought they not always to be flain, ac- *Grot. de Jure*
cording to that of *Seneca*, *Cruel are they,* fays *Belli ac Pacis,*
he, † *that have Caufe of Punifhment, but have l 3. c. 10. §*
no meafure.* For he that in punifhing goes † 2 *de Clem.*
further than is meet, is the fecond Author of *cap. 4.*
Injury, and the principal Reafon why Mercy
is often fhewed, is, for that Soldiers of Fortune offend not out of any Hatred or Cruelty
but out of Duty.

XVIII. Again, *Generals* in the Meafure of
killing, look commonly no further than the
Deftruction of thofe who by Force of Arms
oppofe them, and though Ships or Cities are
taken by Affault, the which by the Laws of
War, fubjects every individual to the Mercy
of the Conqueror, yet Children, Women,

old Men, Priests, Scholars, and Husband-
men are to be spared; the first by the Law
of Nature, according to that of *Camillus : We*
have Arms, says he, *not against that Age which*
even in taking Cities is spared, but against arm-
ed Man : And this is the Law of Arms
amongst good Men; by which we are to note,
that by the Words *good Men,* as is observed,
we mean the Law of Nature, for strictly by
the Law of Arms, the Slayers of them are
without Punishment.

In Vita Ca-
milli Liv lib
1, & 5.

Grotius, lib.
3. cap 11.
who observes,
that many
Pretences may be found out against Men of mature Age, but against
Infants, Calumny itself can find nothing to say, as being clearly Innocents.

Now that which hath always place in Children that have not attained the use of Reason,
for the most part prevails with Women; that
is, unless they have committed something
peculiarly to be avenged, or do usurp manly
Offices, as flinging of Stones from the Walls,
pouring down burning Pitch, Brimstone, and
the like bituminous Stuff, firing of Guns,
and the like, for it is a Sex that hath nothing
to do with the Sword, that are capable of
that Clemency.

Herod in Vi-
ta Maximin
fol 417.

The like for Old Men, who, *Papinius* observes, are not to be slain, so for Ministers
of sacred things, even barbarous Nations have
had them in Reverence and Preservation, as
the *Philistines,* Enemies of the *Jews,* did to
the *College of Prophets,* to whom they did no
Harm. And with those Priests are justly
equalled in this Respect, they that have chosen a like kind of Life, as *Monks* and *Peni-*
tents, whom therefore as well as Priests, the
Canons following in natural Equity will have
spared :

Papin nullis
violabilis ar-
mis Turba se-
nes. Vid D.
loco

1 Sam v. 5.
and 1 Sam
xix. 18

spared: To thefe are defervedly added thofe *2d Inftit.* 58.
that give themfelves to the ftudy of good
Learning and Sciences ufeful to Mankind,
be it in *Univerfities,* or other publick *Schools*
or *Colleges.* But yet if any of thefe be taken
in actual Service, they then may receive the
common Fate of others. So our King *Richard* the Firft, having taken the Martial Bifhop
of *Beauvais* Prifoner, received a Letter from
the *Pope,* that he fhould no longer detain in
Cuftody his dear Son; the King fent the *Pope*
back the Armour wherein he was taken, with
the Words of *Jacob*'s Sons to their Father,
See whether or no this be the Coat of thy Son

To thefe are added Tradefmen, fo likewife *Leg execut C.*
Merchants, which is not only to be under- *quæ res pign.*
ftood of them that ftay for a time in the Enemy's Quarters, but of perpetual Subjects;
for their Life hath nothing to do with Arms, *Vide 2 Inftit.*
and under that Name are alfo contained other *58 &*
Workmen and Artificers, whofe Gain loves *Trin 21 E. 1.*
not War but Peace. *Rot 127.*

Again, Captives, and thofe that yield, are
not to be flain, for to fpare fuch *is a Command of Goodnefs and Equity,* fays *Seneca*;
however it may fo come to pafs, that though *De Benefic. 5.*
the military Power may exempt a Prifoner of *cap. 18.*
War from the Execution of the Sword, yet
it may be out of their Power to exempt or
difcharge a Delinquent or Traitor from the
Execution of the Magiftrate, as if the Fleet
were prepared, and the War principally begun for the Suppreffion of fuch; and the Reafon of this is, if it fhould be in the Power
of one Soldier, who takes a Traitor Prifoner
upon fuch Terms, it would *pari ratione* be in
the Power of all to pardon, not that the Ar-

T 3 ticle

*Libertinum in-
gratum in pri-
stinam redigit
servitutem.*
Fortescue,
cap 46.

ticle hath no effect, for the Traitor is by that
freed from the immediate Execution of the
Sword: Sure it is, that if the yielding be in
aperto prælio, methinks absolute Pardon is
implicitly in the Contract: However this is
undeniable, that having yielded himself Pri-
soner of War, if he escape, he forever loses
the Benefit of the Promise Nor are Hostages
to be destroyed, according to that of *Scipio,*

Liv lib 28.
The same
saith *Julian*
in *Nicetas.*

who said: *He would not shew his Displeasure
on harmless Hostages, but upon those that had
revolted, and that he would not take Revenge
of the unarmed, but of the armed Enemy.* 'Tis
very true by the Law of Arms, if the Contract be broke for which they became Hosta-

Grot. lib 3.
cap 11

ges, they may be slain, that is, the Slayer is
without Punishment: But yet some conceive
the Slayer is not without Sin, for that no such
Contract can take away any Man's Life; that
is, I suppose, an Innocent's Life; but without Controversy, if those that become Hostages be, or were before, in the number of
grievous Delinquents, or if afterwards he
hath broken his Faith given by him in a great
Matter, the Punishment of such may be free
from Injury.

XIX. Where Offences are of that nature
as they may seem worthy of Death, as Mutiny, and the like, &c it will be a Point of
Mercy, because of the multitude of them, to
remit extreme Right, according to that of

2 *de Ira cap*
10 *Quicquid
multispeccatur
multum est
Magis monen-
ao quam mi-
nando, sic enim*

*Seneca The Severity of a General shews itself
against Particulars, but Pardon is necessary
when the whole Army is revolting · What takes
away Anger from a wise Man? the multitude
of Transgressors.* Hence it was, that casting
of

of * Lots was introduced, that too many agendum *eſt* might not be ſubjected to puniſhment. *cum multitudine peccantium, ſeveritas autem exercenda eſt in peccata paucorum. Vide* Gailium de Pace publ. *lib.* 11 *cap.* 9, 36.

Vide Grot. *lib.* 3. *cap.* 11. §. 17.

However, all Nations have generally made it a ſtanding Rule in the Puniſhment of Mutineers, as near as poſſible to hunt out the Authors, and make them Examples †. † *Victor de Jure Belli. n.* 55. *lib.* 2.

And therefore by the 14th Article. *If when Action, or any Service ſhall be commanded, any Perſon ſhall preſume to delay or diſcourage the ſaid Action or Service, upon pretence of Arrears of Wages, or upon any pretence whatſoever, he ſhall ſuffer Death, or ſuch other Puniſhment, as from the Nature and Degree of the Offence a Court Martial ſhall deem him to deſerve;* and indeed the ſame ought to be without Mercy, by how much the more they may raiſe a Mutiny at a time when there is nothing expected but an Action, and the ſhewing the moſt obſequious Duty that poſſibly may be; the Breach of which may occaſion the Damage of the whole Fleet, and being of ſuch dangerous Conſequence, ought to be ſeverely puniſhed *Guſtavus Adolphus,* upon his firſt entrance into *Germany,* perceiving how that many Women followed his Soldiers, ſome being their Wives, and ſome wanting nothing to make them ſo but Marriage, yet moſt paſſing for their Landreſſes (though commonly defiling more than they waſh) the King coming to a great River, after his Men and the Waggons were paſſed over, cauſed the Bridge to be broken down, hoping ſo to be rid of theſe feminine Impediments, but they on a ſudden lift up a panick Shriek which pierced the Skies, and *If* Artic. 14.

T 4　　　　　the

the Soldiers Hearts on the other side of the River, who inftantly fell into Mutiny, vowing not to ftir a Foot further except with Baggage, and that the Women might be fetched over, which was done accordingly, for the King finding this ill Humour fo generally difperfed in his Men, that it was dangerous to purge it all at once, fmiled out his Anger for the prefent, and permitted what he could not amend. So likewife, *If any Perfon fhall endeavour to make any mutinous Affembly upon any Pretence whatfoever, he fhall fuffer Death : And if any Perfon fhall utter any Words of Sedition or Mutiny, he fhall fuffer Death, or fuch other Punifhment as a Court Martial fhall deem him to deferve · And if any Officer, Mariner, or Soldier, fhall behave himfelf with Contempt to his fuperior Officer, fuch fuperior Officer, being in the Execution of his Office, he fhall be punifhed according to the Nature of his Offence by the Judgment of a Court Martial*

If any Perfon fhall conceal any traiterous or mutinous Practice or Defign, he fhall fuffer Death, or fuch other Punifhment as a Court Martial fhall think fit , and if any Perfon fhall conceal any traiterous or mutinous Words fpoken by any, to the Prejudice of his Majefty's Government, or any Words, Practice, or Defign, tending to the Hindrance of the Service, and fhall not forthwith reveal the fame to the commanding Officer, or being prefent at any Mutiny or Sedition, fhall not ufe his utmoft Endeavours to fupprefs the fame, he fhall be punifhed as a Court Martial fhall think he deferves And whereas in any of the Offences committed againft any of the Articles for the Government of any of *His Majefty's* Ships of War, within the narrow.

Seas,

Seas, wherein the Pains of Death are to be inflicted, Execution of such Sentence ought not to be made without leave of the *Lord Admiral*; *this of Mutiny is totally* excepted, for such may be executed immediately.

XX. It is not lawful for Princes or States to make of their Enemies Traitors, or cause *Grotius, l. 3.* them to desert the Service of their Prince, or *c. 1. §.* to bring over their Ships, Ordinance, Provisions, or Arms; for as 'tis not lawful for any Subject to do the same, so neither to tempt him, for he that gives a Cause of sinning to another, sins also himself, but if a Man will voluntarily, without any other Impulse than his own, bring over the Ships or Armies, or desert the Service of his Prince to serve another, this, though a Fault in the Deserter, is not in the Receiver *We receive a Fugitive by* * *Leg. Transf-* *the Law of War,* (saith * *Celsus*) *that is, it is fug de acqu. not against the Law of War to admit him, who rerum dom Po- having deserted his Prince's part, elected his lyb. in excerp Enemy's,* nor are such to be rendered, except 34 *Menander* it shall be agreed, as in the Peace of † *Lewis Protector idem* the Eleventh. However such sort of Game- *nos docet* sters, if caught, are to be severely punished, *†Phil Comin.* and therefore it is provided, *That if any Sea- Artic 16 Captain, Officer, or Seaman, shall betray his Trust, or turn to the Enemy, Pirate, or Rebel, or run away with their Ship or Ordinance, Ammunition, or Provision, to the weakening of the Service, or yield the same up to the Enemy, Pirate or Rebel, they shall be punished with Death;* so likewise, *If any desert the Service or the Em- Artic 17. ployment which they are in on Ship-board, or shall run away, or entice any other so to do, they are subject to the like pain of Death.* And by the Law of Nations, such Deserters that run

away

Tertul. Apol.
9 c. quando
liceat, l 2. in
reos majestatis
& publicos
hostes omnis
homo miles.
Vide Grot. lib
cap. 5. Hutt. 134.
away from their Colours or Fleet before
Peace proclaimed and concluded, all Persons
of that Prince from whom they fled, have a
Right indulged to them to execute publick
Revenge.

Vide Grot. lib 1 cap. 5 Hetley. Rep 235 7 H. 7. cap. 1. 3 H 8.
cap. 5. Hutt. 134.

Liv l 2. c. 3.
§ ult. ad Leg.
Corn. de Sicar.
pun.
XXI. By the Laws of Nations, *Spies* may
be sent to view and survey the Enemy's Force,
Fleet, Station, and make discovery of whatsoever may give Advantage to the Persons
sending, as is mentioned above; but being
deprehended they are put to Death; and
Artic 5.
therefore *all Persons in the nature of Spies,*
bringing or delivering any seducing Letters or
Messages from any Enemy or Rebel, or endea-
vouring to corrupt any Captain, Officer, Mari-
ner, or other in the Fleet, to betray his Trust,
shall be punished with Death, or such other
Punishment as the Court Martial shall impose.

XXII Soldiers and Mariners owe all Respect and Duty to their Superior Officers; and
therefore when they are in Anger they ought
to avoid them, but above all not to quarrel
with, or give them any provoking Language:
And therefore by the Law of Arms, a Soldier
who hath resisted his Captain, willing to chas-
tise him, if he hath laid hold on his Rod, is
cashiered, if he purposely break it, or laid
* Leg. milit.
D. de re milit
Refus Leg mi-
litar cap 15.
Artic 22.
violent Hands upon his Captain, he dies *:
And by the Laws of *England, if any Officer,*
Mariner, Soldier, or other Person in the Fleet,
shall strike any of his superior Officers, or draw,
or offer to draw, or lift up any Weapon against
him, being in the Execution of his Office, on any
Pretence whatsoever, he shall suffer Death; and
if

if any Officer, &c shall presume to quarrel with any of his superior Officers, being in the Execution of his Office, or shall disobey any lawful Command of any of his superior Officers, he shall suffer Death, or such other Punishment, as shall, according to the Nature and Degree of his Offence, be inflicted upon him by the Sentence of a Court Martial.

XXIII And though Mariners and Soldiers may have just cause of Complaint, as that their Victuals or Provisions are not good, yet must they not mutiny or rebel, whereby to distract or confound the whole Crew, but must make a civil and humble Address to their Commander, that the same may be amended; and if the Case be such, that the Commander *Bacon's Max-* cannot redress the same, by going to Port to *im, fol* 17. supply the Exigencies, without Detriment of *Privilegium* the Fleet, (as if ready to engage, or the like) *non valet contra rempubli-* they must, like Men and Soldiers, bear with *cam.* the Extremity, considering that 'tis better that some Men should perish, nay the whole Crew in one Ship, than the whole Fleet; nay, perhaps the whole Kingdom be destroyed: And therefore, *if any Person in the Fleet shall* *Artic* 21. *find Cause of Complaint of the unwholesomeness of the Victuals, or upon other just Ground, he shall quietly make the same known to his Superior or Captain, or Commander in Chief, as the Occasion may deserve, that such present Remedy may be had as the Matter may require; and the said Superior, &c. shall, as far as he is able, cause the same to be presently remedied; and no Person upon any such or other Pretence, shall attempt to stir up any Disturbance, upon pain of such Punishment as a Court Martial shall think fit to inflict, according to the Degree of the Offence.*

XXIV And

Artic. 24.

XXIV. And the Law doth provide, that there *shall be no wasteful Expence of any Powder, Shot, Ammunition, or other Stores in the Fleet, nor any Embezzlement thereof, but the Stores and Provisions shall be carefully preserved, upon pain of such Punishment to be inflicted upon the Offenders, Abettors, Buyers and Receivers (being Persons subject to Naval Discipline) as shall be by a Court Martial found just in that behalf.* In Fights, and when great Fleets are out, there are generally Instructions appointed for all *Masters, Pilots, Ketches, Hoyes,* and *Smacks,* who are to attend the Fleet, and to give them notice of the Roads, Coasts, Sands, Rocks, and the like; and they have particular Stations allotted them, and Orders given, that if they shall find less Water than such a proportion, they then give a Signal as they are directed to give, and continue their Signal till they are answered from the Capital Ships.

But in time of Fight they generally lay away their head from the Fleet, and keep their lead; and if they meet with such a Proportion of Water as is within their Directions, they are to give such Signal as they receive Orders for, and stand off from the danger. *Every Person in the Fleet, who shall unlawfully*

Artic. 25.

burn or set Fire to any Magazine or Store of Powder, or Ship, Boat, Ketch, Hoy or Vessel, or Tackle or Furniture thereunto belonging, not then appertaining to an Enemy, Pirate, or Rebel, shall suffer Death.

XXV. There are other Faults often committed by the Crew, the which the Law does punish. *If any Person in the Fleet shall quar-*

Artic 23

rel or fight with any other Person in the Fleet,

or

or *ufe reproachful or provoking Speeches or Gef-tures, tending to make any Quarrel or Diftur-bance, he fhall fuffer fuch Punifhment as the Offence fhall deferve, and a Court Martial fhall impofe.*

All Murders committed by any Perfon in the Artic 28. *Fleet, fhall be punifhed with Death.*

If any Perfon in the Fleet fhall commit the Artic 29. *unnatural and deteftable Sin of Buggery or Sodomy with Man or Beaft, he fhall be punifhed with Death.*

All Robbery committed by any Perfon in the Artic. 30. *Fleet, fhall be punifhed with Death, or otherwife, as a Court Martial, upon Confideration of Circumftances, fhall find meet.* And when any Perfons have committed any of the Offences particularly mentioned in the *Statute* of 22 *Geo.* 2. *c* 33, or any others, and for the which they fhall be committed.

No Provoft-Martial belonging to the Fleet, Artic 32. *fhall refufe to apprehend any Criminal, whom he fhall be authorized by legal Warrant to apprehend, or to receive or keep any Prifoner committed to his Charge, or wilfully fuffer him to efcape, being once in his Cuftody, or difmifs him without lawful Order, upon pain of fuch Punifhment as a Court Martial fhall deem him to deferve; and all Captains, Officers, and others in the Fleet, fhall do their endeavour to detect, apprehend, and bring to Punifhment all Offenders, and fhall affift the Officers appointed for that Purpofe therein, upon pain of being proceeded againft, and punifhed by a Court Martial, according to the Nature and Degree of the Offence*

Every Perfon being in actual Service and full Artic. 34. *Pay, and part of the Crew in or belonging to any of His Majefty's Ships or Veffels of War,*
who

who shall be guilty of Mutiny, Desertion or Dis-obedience to any lawful Command, in any Part of His Majesty's Dominions on Shore, when in actual Service relative to the Fleet, shall be liable to be tried by a Court Martial, and suffer the like Punishment for every such Offence, as if the same had been committed at Sea on board any of His Majesty's Ships or Vessels of War.

Artic. 35.

If any Person, who shall be in the actual Service and full Pay of his Majesty's Ships and Vessels of War, shall commit upon the Shore, in any Place or Places out of His Majesty's Dominions, any of the Crimes punishable by these Articles and Orders, the Person so offending shall be liable to be tried and punished for the same, in like Manner to all Intents and Purposes, as if the said Crimes had been committed at Sea, on board any of His Majesty's Ships or Vessels of War.

Touching the Punishments that the *Roman Generals* used to their Soldiers, when they were at a *Court Martial* found faulty, they were commonly proportioned according to the Offence committted: Sometimes they were easy, of which sort were those which only branded the Soldier with Disgrace; others were those that came heavy on the Person or Body.   To the first belonged a shameful dis-charging or cashiering a Mariner or Soldier from the Army, and generally looked on as a matter of great Disgrace, which Punishment remains at this day for Offences as well in *England* as in most parts.   A second was by stopping of their Pay; such Soldiers which suffered this kind of mulct, were said to be *Ære diruti*, for that *Æs illud diruebatur in fiscum, non in Militis sacculum*, the which is,
and

Ignominiosa dimissio.

Fraudat sti-pendii. Rosin. Ant Rom l. 10 c. 25.

and may at this day be inflicted, especially
on such as shall wilfully spoil their Arms, and
for the like sort of Offences.   A third was, a
Sentence enjoined on a Soldier to resign up
his Spear; for as those which had atchieved
any Noble Act, were for their greater Ho- *Censio Hasta-*
nour *Hasta pura donati*, so others for their *ria.*
greater Disgrace were inforced to resign up
that Military Weapon of Honour.   A fourth
sort of Punishment was, that the whole *Co-*
hort, which had lost their *Banners* or *Standards*,
either in the Fields or at Sea, were inforced
to eat nothing but Barley-bread, being deprived of their allowance in Wheat, and every
Centurion in that *Cohort* had his Soldier's Belt
or Girdle taken from him, which was no less
Disgrace among them, than the degrading
(among us) one of the *Order of the Garter :*
For petty Faults they generally made them
stand bare-footed before the *General's Pavi- Goodwin An-*
lion, with long Poles of Ten Foot in length *tiq Rom. fol.*
in their Hands, and sometimes in the sight of [127]
the other Soldiers to walk up and down with
Turf, on their Necks, and sometimes carrying a Beam like a Fork upon their Shoulders
round the Town.   The last of their Punishments was, the opening of a Vein, or letting
them Blood in one of their Arms, which generally was inflicted on them who were too hot
and bold.

The great Judgments were, to be beaten
with Rods, which was generally inflicted on
those who had not discharged their Office, in
the sending about that *Table* called *Tessera*,
wherein the Watch-word was written, or those
who had stolen any thing from the Camp, or
that had forsaken to keep Watch, or those
that

that had borne any falfe Witnefs againft their
Fellows, or had abufed their Bodies by Women, or thofe that had been punifhed thrice

Lipf de milit.
Rom. lib 5.
Dialog. 18.
for the fame Fault, fometimes they were fold
for Bond-flaves, beheaded and hanged. But
the laft, which was in their Mutinies, the
Punifhment fell either to Lots, as the Tenth,
Twentieth, and fometimes the Hundreth
Man, who were punifhed with Cudgelling;
and with thefe Punifhments thofe in *England*
have a very near affinity, as cleanfing the
Ship, lofing Pay, ducking in the Water, beaten at the Capfon's-head, hoifted up the main
Yard end with a Shovel at their Back, hanged,
and fhot to Death, and the like.

See 22 *Geo.* 2
c. 33
    XXVI. The *Admiral* may grant Commif-
fions to inferior *Vice-Admirals* or *Commanders
in Chief* of any Squadron of Ships, to affemble *Court-Martials*, confifting of *Commanders*
and *Captains*, for the Trial and Execution
of any of the Offences or Mifdemeanors

37 *H* 6 *fol*
4, 5.
which fhall be committed at Sea; but if one
be attainted before them, the fame works no
corruption of Blood or forfeiture of Lands,
nor can they try any Perfon that is not in
actual Service and Pay in *His Majefty's* Fleet
and Ships of War. But in no cafe where
there is Sentence of Death, can the Execution of the fame be without leave of the *Lord
Admiral*, if the fame be committed within the
narrow Seas Yet this does not extend to Mutiny, for there in that cafe the Party may be
executed prefently.

    All Offences committed in any Voyage be-
yond the narrow Seas, where Sentence of
Death fhall be given upon any of the aforefaid Offences, Execution cannot be awarded

nor

nor done, but by the Order of the Commander in Chief of that-Fleet or Squadron, wherein Sentence of Death was paſſed

XXVII The Judge-Advocate, or his Deputy, hath Power given by the words of the *Statute*, to adminiſter an Oath, in order to the Examination or Trial of any of the Offences mentioned in the *Statute* of 22 *Geo.* 2. *c.* 33. and in his Abſence the *Court Martial* hath Power to appoint any other Perſon to adminiſter an Oath to the ſame purpoſe. This *Statute* enlarges not the Power and Juriſdiction of the *Admiral*, any further than only to the above-mentioned Offences, in any caſe whatſoever, but leaves his Authority as it was before the making of this *Statute* Nor does it give the *Admiral* any other or further Power to enquire and puniſh any of the abovementioned Offences, unleſs the ſame be done upon the main Sea, or in Ships or Veſſels being and hovering in the main Stream of great Rivers, only beneath the Bridges of the ſame Rivers nigh to the Seas, within the Juriſdiction of the *Admiralty*, and in no other place 15 *R.* 2. *cap.* whatſoever 3

XXVIII. As Soldiers and Mariners for the *Stat* 43 *Eliz.* Honour and Safety of the Realm, do daily *cap* 3 & *Vide* expoſe their lives and limbs, ſo the Realm 13, 14 *C* 2. hath likewiſe provided for them, in caſe they *c* 9 7, 8 *W.* ſurvive, and ſhould prove diſabled or unfit 3 *c* 21 2, 3. for Service, a reaſonable and comfortable *A c* 6 whereby Provision Maintenance to keep them, the which the is made for Juſtices of the Peace have power yearly in the Widows their *Eaſter Seſſions* to raiſe by way of a Tax, and Orphans for a weekly relief of maimed Soldiers and Mariners.

The maimed Soldier or Mariner muſt repair to the *Treaſurer* of the County where he was preffed, if he be able to travel; if he be not, then to the *Treafurer* of the County where he was born, or where he laft dwelt by the fpace of three Years; but if he prove unable to travel, then to the *Treafurer* of the County where he lands.

He muft have a Certificate under the chief Commander, or of his Captain, containing the Particulars of his Hurt and Services.

The Allowance to one not having been an Officer, is not to exceed Ten Pounds *per Annum*;

> *Under a Lieutenant* — 15 ⎫
> *A Lieutenant* — — 20 ⎭

Till the Mariner arrives at his proper *Trea-furer*, they are to be relieved from *Treafurer* to *Treafurer*; and when they are provided for, if any of them fhall go a begging or counterfeit Certificates, they fhall fuffer as common Rogues; and lofe their Penfions: Over and above this Provifion, *His Sacred Majefty George the Firft* provided a further Supplement for his maimed Mariners and Soldiers difabled in the Service, which is iffued out at the *Cheft* at *Chatham*, and con-ftantly and duly paid them, and for his Commanders, Officers, and others that ferv-ed abroad, he, of his Royal Bounty, hath given to thofe that bear the Character of War, and purchafe the fame by their Fide-lity and Valour, a pious Bounty called *Smart-Money*, over and above their pay, and laid the Foundation of an *Hofpital* at *Chelfea*, in

See *Stat* 28 Geo. 2 c. 1. his Life-time, which his late Sacred Majefty *George* the Second compleated, and endow-ed, ed, both for Beauty and Magnificence, excelling all in *Christendom*.

Nor must we forget that noble Hospital at *Greenwich*, which for a further Encouragement for Mariners, maimed or worn out with Age, or any other Infirmity, in the Sea Service, our late most glorious Deliverer King *William* the Third, was graciously pleased to give as a Royal Bounty a stately Palace at *Greenwich* for an Hospital, which is since so enlarged as to receive a thousand Seamen, and when compleat will be able to receive five hundred more, which for Statelinefs and Grandeur, I may venture to say, will exceed any thing of its Kind that *Christendom* can produce.

See Stat 7 & 8 W 3 c. 21. S 10 8 & 9 W. 3 c. 23. 12 & 13 W 3 c. 13 2 & 3 An c 6 S 19 4 An c. 12 S. 14. 6 An. c 13 S. 11. 10 An c. 17. S 9. 20. 1 Geo 2 c St. 2 c 9 2 Geo 2 c 7 c 36. S 10 6 Geo 2 c 25 S.

10 8 Geo. 2. c. 29. 11 Geo. 2 c. 30 13 Geo. 2. c 4 S 11 16 18 Geo 2. c. 31 20 Geo 2 c. 24 S 16. 17 22 Geo. 2. c. 52. 25 Geo. 2 c. 42 27 Geo 2 c. 10 S. 7 28 Geo 2 c 22 S 14. 29 Geo 2 c 29. S. 8. 30 Geo. 2. c 26 S 9. 3 Geo. 3. c 16

A very laudable Undertaking must not be omitted, being a generous and voluntary Subfcription by all the Officers of the Navy, allowing Three-pence in the Pound to be deducted out of their Wages for the Maintenance of the Widows and Orphans of such Commiffion and Warrant-Officers, who died since the 30th of *August* 1732, from which time it commences, which his late Majesty King *George* II. was graciously pleased to encourage by the granting his Royal Commiffion, bearing Date the 30th of *August* 1732, by which a comfortable Maintenance is secured by the following Allowance.

Widow of the	Captain	45 *l.* per Annum.
	Lieutenant Master	30
	All other Warrant Officers	20

U 2 The

The greatest assurance of a Fleet is in the prudent Government of the *Admiral*, the greatest weakening of it is by discontent, which generally proceeds from two things, want of good Victuals at Sea, and Pay when come home, these are the poor Mariners *Aqua vitæ*; but want of them is such an *Aqua fortis*, as eats thro' all manner of Duty and Obedience: That Prince that expects to be well served and obeyed, (especially by an *Englishman*) must take care that he suffer not a greater Power in his Fleet than his own, this Commander is Necessity, which breaks Discipline at Sea, and creates Discouragement at Land

Vide Salmuth in Pancir Leg-terum depræd Ca de Triumph D on Halicarnaf. Lb. 5.

XXIX. The Wisdom of the *Romans* was mightily to be commended, in giving of *Triumphs* to their *Generals* after their Return, of which they had various sorts, but the greatest was when the *General* rid in his Chariot, adorned and crowned with the Victorious Laurel, the *Senators* with the best of the *Romans* meeting him, his Soldiers (especially those who by their Valour had purchased Coronets, Chains, and other Ensigns of reward for their Conduct and Courage) following him: But what alas! could these to the more sober represent any other but horror, since the Centers from whence the Lines were drawn, could afford nothing but Death, Slaughter and Desolation on those who had the Souls and Faces of Men, and if it were possible, that the Blood which by their Commissions was drawn from the sides of Mankind, and for which they made those Triumphs, could have been brought to *Rome*, the same was capable of making of a Source great as their *Tiber*, but *Policy* had need of

all

all its Stratagems to confound the Judgment
of a Soldier by exceffive Praifes, Recom-
pences and Triumphs, that fo the Opinion
of Wounds and wooden Legs might raife in
him a greater Efteem of himfelf, than if he
had an entire Body. To allure others, fomething alfo muft be found out handfomely to
cover wounds and affrightments of Death;
and without this *Cæfar* in his Triumph, with
all his Garlands and Mufick, would look but
like a Victim, but what forrow of Heart is
it to fee paffionate Man, a Ray of Divinity,
and the Joy of Angels, fcourged thus with
his own Scorpions? The cholericknefs of
War (whereby the luftful heat of fo many
Hearts is reduced) ftirs up the Lees of *Kingdoms* and *States*, as a Tempeft doth weeds
and flimy fediment from the bottom to the
top of the Sea, which afterwards driven to
the Shore, together with its Foam, there co-
vers Pearls and precious Stones: And tho'
the Cannon fhould feem mad by its continual
firing, and the Sword reeking hot by its daily flaughters, yet no good Man doubts but
they, even they, fhall weather out thofe
Storms, and in the midft of thofe mercilefs
Inftruments find an *inculpata Tutela*, who love
Juftice, exercife Charity, and put their Truft
in the *Great Governor of all things.*

CHAP. XIV.
Of Salutations by Ships of War, and Merchant Men.

I. *Of Salutations paid in all Ages as an undoubted Mark of Sovereignty of this Empire.*

II. *Of those Seas where this Right is to be paid to the King of England's Flag.*

III. *In what manner the King of England holds this Right, and by whom to be paid.*

IV. *Of those that shall neglect or refuse to do the same, how punished and dealt withal.*

V. *Where His Majesty of Great Britain's Ships are to strike their Flag, and where not*

VI. *Of the saluting Ports, Castles, and Forts, how the same is to be done, and on what Terms.*

VII. *Of Ships of War, their saluting their Admiral and Commanders in Chief.*

VIII. *Of Ambassadors, Dukes, Noblemen, and other Persons of Quality, how to be saluted coming aboard and landing.*

IX. *The Admiral of any Foreign Nation, if met withal, how to be saluted and answered.*

X. *Of the Men of War or Ships of Trade of any Foreign Nations, saluting His Majesty's Ships of War, how to be answered.*

XI. *Of the saluting of His Majesty's own Forts and Castles, and when the Salute ceases.*

XII. *Of the Objection that seems to be made against the Necessity of such Salutations.*

XIII. *Why Kingdoms and States attribute the Effects, not the cause of Rights, to prescription.*

XIV. *That Kingdoms and Republicks ought not to be disordered for the Defect of Right, in presumption, and the Objection in the XII §. answered*

XV. *The Inconveniency of War, and the Causes justifying the same.*

XVI. *Of the Causes not justifiable in War*

XVII. *Of Moderation, and the utility of Faith and Peace*

I. IT is evident by what hath been said, that the *British Seas*, before the *Roman Conquest*,

Conqueſt, ever belonged to the *Iſle of Great Britain*, they always claiming and enjoying the ſole Dominion and Sovereignty of the ſame, which afterwards accrued to the *Romans* by Conqueſt, and from them tranſlated with its *Empire* to the ſucceeding *Saxon*, *Daniſh*, and *Norman* Kings, and in the Reigns of thoſe Princes there were always ſome marks of Sovereignty paid, wherein the Right of the ſame was evinced and acknowledged.

II. Now thoſe Seas in which this Salutation or Duty of the Flag are to be paid, are the four circumjacent Seas, in which all Veſſels whatſoever are to pay that Duty, according to the Cuſtom of the ſame, and the Ordinance of King *John*. How far this Right is payable, appears in the Fourth Article in the Peace between *His Majeſty* and the *States-General of the United Provinces*, in theſe words:

———— *That whatever Ships or Veſſels belonging to the ſaid United Provinces, whether Veſſels of War or other, whether ſingle or in Fleets, ſhall meet in any of the Seas from* Cape Finiſterre *to the middle Point of the Land* Van Staten in Norway, *with any Ships or Veſſels belonging to His Majeſty of* Great Britain, *whether thoſe Ships be ſingle or in great number, if they carry His Majeſty of* Great Britain's *Flag or Jack, the aforeſaid* Dutch *Veſſels or Ships ſhall ſtrike their Flag and lower their Top-ſail, in the ſame Manner, and with as much Reſpect as hath at any Time, or in any Place, been formerly practiſed, towards any Ships of His Majeſty of* Great Britain, *or his Predeceſſors, by any Ships of the* States-General, *or their Predeceſſors.*

III. Now His Majeſty holds not this *Salutation* or Reſpect, by virtue of the League of

U 4   the

the Article, but as the fame is a RIGHT inherent to the *Empire of Great Britain*, and therefore in the first part of the Article it is declared in thefe Words

———*That the aforefaid States General of the United-Provinces, in due Acknowledgment on their Part of the King of Great Britain's RIGHT to have his Flag refpected in the Seas hereafter mentioned, fhall and do declare, and agree.* ———

Now this Right extends and fubjects all Nations whatfoever that fhall pafs through thofe Seas, and between thofe Places, meeting with any of His Majefty's Ships of War, bearing his Flag, Jack, or Cognizance of Service, to ftrike their Top-fail, and take in their Flag, in acknowledgment of His *Majefty's* Sovereignty in thofe Seas; and if any fhall refufe to do it, or offer to refift, they may be compelled, *vi, & manu forti,* for His *Majefty's* Honour is by no means to receive the leaft Diminution

Selden Mare Claufum lib 2. cap. 23

IV. If therefore any of His *Majefty's* Subjects fhould be fo negligent or forgetful to pay that Obedience, when it may be done without lofs of the Voyage, they are to be feized on, and brought to the Flag, to anfwer the Contempt, or elfe the *Commander* may remit the Name of the Ship, *Commander* or *Mafter*, as alfo the Place from whence, and the Port to which fhe fhall be bound to the *Admiral*, however, before fhe is difmiffed, fhe muft pay the Charge of the *Shot* that her Negligence or Forgetfulnefs occafioned, and afterwards may be indicted for the fame, and feverely punifhed.

V. In His Majefty's Seas, none of his Ships of War are to ftrike to any, and in no other

Part

Part is any Ship of His Majesty to strike her Flag or Top-sail to any Foreigner, unless such Foreign Ship shall have first struck, or at the same time have struck her Flag or Top-sail to His Majesty's Ships.

VI. But if any of the King of *England*'s Ships of War shall enter into the Harbour of any Foreign Prince or State, or into the Road within shot of Cannon of some Fort or Castle, yet such Respect must be paid, as is usually there expected, and then the *Commander* is to send ashore to inform himself what return they will make to his Salute, and that if he hath received good Assurance, that His Majesty's Ships shall be answered Gun for Gun, the Port is to be saluted, as is usual; but without assurance of being answered by an equal number of Guns, the Port is not to be saluted. And yet in that very respect before the Port is to be saluted, the Captain ought to inform himself, how Flags (of the same quality with that he carries) of other Princes have been saluted there; the which is peremptorily to be insisted on, to be saluted with as great Respect and Advantage as any Flag (of the same quality with the Captains) of any other Prince hath been saluted in that place.

VII. A Captain of a Ship of a second Rate, being neither Admiral, Vice-Admiral, nor Rear-Admiral, at his first coming and saluting his Admiral or Commander in Chief, is to give Eleven Pieces, his Vice-Admiral Nine, and his Rear-Admiral Seven, and the other proportionably less by two, according to their Ranks; but the Commander or Captain of a *Artic. 38.* Ship is not to salute his Admiral or Commander in Chief, after he had done it once,

except

except he hath been abfent from the Flag Two Months:

VIII. When a Ship of the fecond Rate fhall carry any Ambaffador, Duke or Nobleman, at his coming aboard he is to give Eleven Pieces, and at his Landing Fifteen ; and when he fhall carry a Knight, Lady or Gentleman of Quality, at their coming aboard he is to give Seven, and at their Landing Eleven, and the other Ships are to give lefs by two, according to their Ranks and number of Ordinance

IX. When an Admiral of any Foreign Nation is met with, he is to be anfwered with the like Number by all the Ships he fhall falute ; if a Vice-Admiral, the Admiral is to anfwer him with twelve lefs ; but the Vice-Admiral and Rear-Admiral, and as many of the reft as he fhall falute, fhall give him the like Number ; if a Rear-Admiral, then the Admiral and Vice-Admiral to anfwer him with two lefs ; but if he fhall falute the Rear-Admiral or any other, they are to anfwer him in the like Number.

X. When a Man of War or Merchant Man of another Nation, or of our own, falutes any of the King's Ships, he is to be anfwered by two lefs.

XI When any of the Captains of his Majefty's Ships fhall have occafion to falute any of the King's Caftles, he is to give two Guns lefs than they are directed to give upon faluting their Admiral or Commander in Chief, as aforefaid : But this extends only to time of Peace ; for if War is begun, no Guns ought to be fired in Salutes, unlefs to the Ships or Caftles of fome Foreign Prince or State in Amity.

XII. Thofe

XII.-Thofe Duties or Obligations being laid on *Commanders*, they confift of two parts; the one is that antient prefcription, which the *Crown of England* claims by virtue of the Sovereignty of that *Empire*; the other is but that Refpect which is paid as vifible Marks of *Honour* and *Efteem*, either to Kingdoms or Perfons publick or private, to whom thefe feveral Commands are to be obferved; and yet in thefe, which are both innocent and harmlefs of themfelves, we want not thofe, who being empty of all that may be called Good, want not malice to ftart up words, *Wherefore fhould the Lives of Men, even* Chriftian *Men, be expofed to Death and Slaughter for Shadows* (as they call them) *the Right of Salutation* or Compliment being no other in their Opinion.

XIII Admitting therefore that the Evidence of original Compacts and Rights ftand at fuch remote diftances from us, that they are hardly difcernable, and that the principal of Civil Things, as well as Natural, is fought for in a Chaos or Confufion, fo that the Evidence of antient Facts *veftigia nulla retrorfum,* there being no infallible marks of their pre-exiftence (one ftep doth fo confound and obliterate another) and that time itfelf is but an imagination of our own, an intentional, not a real meafure for actions, which pafs away concomitantly with that meafure of time in which they were done, for which reafon we talk of antient Things, but as blind Men do of Colours. Notwithftanding Prefcription is *Coke* on *Littleton, fol 113, 114.* fuppofed by moft to hold out fuch an Evidence, that as they fay, it ought to filence all Counterpleas in all Tribunals, and by the prefent allowance which is indulged to it, it either proves a good, or cleanfes a vitiated

Title;

Title; and hath this Power in the Civil Conftitution of the World, that for Quietnefs fake what it cannot find, we grant it a Power to make.

And if we examine all this ftrictly at the two great Tribunals, the external and the internal, and argue the *Jus* of it, as Statefmen and Lawyers do, we can then raife the Argument of it no higher in the external or temporal Court, than only this —— *That it is very convenient it fhould have the effects of Right, left Properties and Dominion of things fhould be uncertain, and by the apparent negligences of Time Owners fhould be punifhed, and that Controverfies may have a fpeedy end* · States looking more after publick repofe and quiet than after ftrict Virtue; and more after thofe things which are *ad alterum*, than that which concerns a Man's own felf; for, fay they, *The Gods look well enough after their own Injuries* States meddle not fo much with great Prodigalities as in petty Larcenies, *our chief-eft Liberty, Privileges, or Prerogative in this World, confifting only in an uncontroulable Right, which we have to undo ourfelves, if we pleafe* Certainly if we plead at the other *Tribunal*, as confcientious Lawyers, we muft give our ultimate Refolution out of that Law, *Quæ inciditur non ære, fed animis* · Which is not engraved in Tables of Brafs, but in the Tables of our Souls, for the Rule of Law tells us, *Quæ principio vitiantur, ex poft facto reconvalefcant*, and that prefcription or ufucaption (which is but the lapfe of fo much Time) hath the power to make *Wrong a Right*; yea, to change the morality of an Action, and turn Quantity into Quality · Upon the Refult of all which taking for granted, what

thofe

Deorum injuriæ Diis curæ.

those stubborn People do hold, that instead of being a Right, or a certain Cause or Proof of it, it only makes a shadow or an opinion of Right

XIV. And when we have taken those People by the hand, and with eagerness run with them to the very bottom and end of the line, and there find nothing, we are but in *Pompey's* Astonishment, when after his Conquest of *Jerusalem*, when he had with such reverence and curiosity visited the *Sanctum Sanctorum*, and found nothing there but a pair of Candle-sticks and a Chair, in which there was no God sitting, yet for all this Mistake, he would not (as *Josephus* saith) disorder or rob the Temple, which he took by force of Arms, *Machiavel's Discourses, cap* 11 because *the very Opinion of Religion hath something of Religion*, (which made *Jacob* accept of *Laban's* Oath by an *Idol*) so ought not we for defect of giving the Causes of the Inception of Prescription, or of the Right in Prescription disorder a State, or be the occasion of setting of two Nations at Enmity, nay, though in Conscience we are satisfied that it contains but the Opinion or Shadow of Right And as to the involving the Lives of the Innocent, there is no such thing in the matter, for there is not required any thing which they do not owe, nor are they designed to Death, but if the Cause be such, that they that are Innocent must perish, that is, be exposed to Death by their Rulers, because they obstinately will not yield that which is right, but will involve the Lives of their innocent Subjects by Force, to defend that which is wrong, such guilty Governors must answer for the Defect of their own evil Actions On the other hand, there

can

can be no doubt made, but he that hath an undoubted Right, being a Sovereign, the Subjects partake in the same, and the Indignity offered to him, they immediately become Partakers in the Suffering, for the Satisfaction of which they may, yea, are obliged both by the Law of God and Nations to seek Reparation (if their Prince shall command) *vi, & manu forti*, by the Hazard of their Blood and Lives.

XV. On the other hand, as War introduces the greatest of Evils, *viz.* the taking away of Men's Lives, and that which is equivalent to Life; so right Reason and Equity tells us, that it ought not to be undertaken without the greatest Cause, which is the keeping of our Lives, and that without which our Lives cannot be kept; or if they should be kept, yet they would not be of any value to us, seeing there may be a Life worse than Death, even Captivity; wherefore as we are forbidden to go to Law for a little Occasion, so we are not to go to War, but for the greatest. Now those things that are equivalent to a Man's Life, are such to whom *Almighty God* appointed the same equal Punishment as to Murderers, and such were breakers into Houses, breakers of Marriage-fidelity, Publishers of false Religion, and those who rage in unnatural Lusts, and the like.

However, before Men's Persons or Goods are to be invaded by War, one of these three Conditions is requisite

1. Necessity, according to the tacit Contract in the first dividing of Good, as hath been already observed.

2. A Debt.

3. A Man's ill Merits, as when he doth great Wrong, or takes part with those who do it.

Against

Against which if any thing is committed, War may be commenced, nor is the same repugnant to the Laws of Nature; that is, whether the thing may not be done unjustly, which hath a necessary Repugnance to the rational and social Nature; amongst the first Principles of Nature, there's nothing repugnant unto War, on the other hand, there is much in favour of it, for both the end of War, the Conservation of Life and Members, and the keeping and acquiring of things useful unto Life, is most agreeable to those Principles, and if need be, to use Force to that Purpose is not disagreeable; since every living thing hath by the Gift of Nature Strength, to the end it may be able to help and defend itself. Besides, Reason and the Nature of Society, inhibits not all Force, but that which is repugnant to Society, that is, which depriveth another of his Right, for the end of Society is, that every one may enjoy his own; this ought to be, and would have been, though the Dominion and Property of Possessions had not been introduced; for Life, Members and Liberty would yet be proper to every one, and therefore without Injury could not be invaded by another: To make use of what is common, and spend as much as suffices Nature, would be the right of the Occupant, which Right none could without Injury take away. And this is proved by that Battle of *Abraham* with the four Kings, who took Arms without any Commission from G O D, and yet was approved by him, therefore the Law of Nature was his Warrant, whose Wisdom was no less eminent than his Sanctity, even by report of *Heathens*, *Berosus* and *Orpheus*; nor is the same repugnant to the

Ulpian Leg 1. *Sect vim. vi. D de vi, & vi arma.*

Hebrew

Hebrew Law or *Gospel*, as the same is most excellently proved by the *Incomparable Grotius* *.

* Lib 1. cap. 1.

XVI. On the other hand, the Fear of uncertain Danger, as building of Forts, Castles and Ships, and the like, though the former be on Frontiers, the refusing of Wives (when others may be had) the changing of Countries either Barren or Moorish for more fertile or healthful which may justly be done; as in the Case of the old *Germans*, as *Tacitus* relates: So likewise to pretend a Title to a Land, because it was never found out or heard of before; that is, if the same be held by a People that are under a Government; nay, though the Government be wicked or think amiss of G O D, or be of a dull Wit; for Invention is of those things that belong to none; for neither is moral Virtue, or Religion, or Perfection of Under-

Victor. de Ind. rel. 1. n. 31.

standing required to Dominion; but yet if a new Place or Land shall be discovered, in which are People altogether destitute of Reason, such have no Dominion, but out of Charity only is due unto them what is necessary

Victor de Jure Bell, n 5, 6, 7, 8.

for Life; for such are accounted as Infants or Madmen, whose Right or Property is transferred, that is, the use of the same, according to the Law of Nations; in such Cases a charitable War may be commenced

XVII To prevent all the sad Calamities that must inevitably follow the ungoverned Hand in War, Faith must by all Means be laboured for;' for by that, not only every Common-Wealth is conserved, but also that greater Society even of Nations, that once being taken away, then farewel Commerce, for that must be then taken away from Man; for Faith is the most sacred Thing that

is

is feated in the Breaft of Man, and is fo much more religioufly to be kept by the fupreme Rulers of the World, by how much more they are exempted from the Punifhment of their Sins here than other Men : Take away Faith, and then Man to Man would be (as Mr. *Hobbes* obferves) even Wolves ; and the more are Kings to embrace it, firft for Confcience, and then for Faith and Credit fake, upon which depends the Authority of their Government. The Ambaffadors of *Juftinian* addreffed their Speech to *Chofroes* after this manner : *Did not we fee you here with our own Eyes, and pronounce thofe Words in your* Procopius Perfic 2. *Ears, we fhould never have believed that* Chofroes, *the Son of* Cabades, *would bring his Army, and enter forcibly into the* Roman *Bounds, contrary to his Leagues, the only hope left to thofe that are afflicted with War ? For what is this, but to change the Life of Men into the Life of wild Beafts ? Take away Leagues, and there will be eternal Wars, and Wars without end will have this Effect, to put Men befide themfelves, and diveft them of their Nature* If then a fafe Peace may be had, it is well worth the releafing of all or many Injuries, Loffes, and Charges, according to that in *Ariftotle Better it is to yield fome of our Goods to thofe that are more Potent, than contend with them and lofe all*, for the common Chances of War muft be confidered, which if fo, the Scope of the principal Part of this Firft Book may be avoided, and we let into the peaceable Track of Traffick and Commerce.

END of the FIRST BOOK

BOOK II.

CHAP. I.

Of the various Rights and Obligations of Owners and Partners of Ships in Cases private.

I IN the precedent Book having obferved fomething of the Rights of Perfons and of Things in a State of *Nature*, and how neceffarily they came at firft to be appropriated, and how equitably they are now continued in the poffeffion of thofe to whom they are configned by the *donation* of others, by the *Laws of Nations*, and maintained or deftroyed by the equity of thofe various Laws which rule and govern them in reference to Matters *publick*, all which is juftified by the Scripture itfelf · It may not now feem improper to examine the *private caufes* changing the fame, and of the contingencies and advantages that wait on that which we properly call Commerce.

The Great Creator having finifhed his Mighty Work, and given Man that Dominion which he now enjoys, as well over the Fifh in the Seas, as the Beafts in the Field, he was not forgetful of beftowing on him thofe things which were neceffary for the Government and fupport of the fame, creating at the fame time Trees which grow as it were fpontaneoufly into Veffels and Canoos, which wanted nothing but launching forth to render them ufeful for his accommodation, which afterwards he by his Divine Genius (infpired by that Mighty One) finding Materials, hath fince fo compleated and equipped, as to render it the moft beautiful and ftupendous Creature (not improperly fo called) that the whole World can produce, which being not retarded by lett of Winds, or other contingent accidents, fubmits itfelf to plow

X 2   the

the unknown paths of that vaſt Element, to brave all Encounters of Waves and Rocks, to fathom and ſurvey the vaſt immenſities of the very World itſelf, to people, cultivate, and civilize uninhabited and barbarous Regions, and to proclaim to the Univerſe the Wonders of the *Architect*, the Skill of the *Pilot*, and, above all, the Benefits of *Commerce*; ſo that it is no wonder at this day to find Nations contending who ſhould ſurpaſs each other in the Art of Navigation, and to monopolize, if poſſible, the very Commerce and Trade of the World into their hands, and that, all by the means of this moſt excellent Fabrick

Arelin poſt
Joan Faber.
in § item ex-
erci c-. ι um.
3 Inſt. de
c.'hg- q' α e-
q-c.ʃ del.'t.

II Hence it is, that Ships and Veſſels of that kind being originally invented for uſe and profit, not for pleaſure and delight, to plow the Seas, not to lie by the Walls; to ſupply thoſe of the Mountains, as well as thoſe on the Sea Coaſts.

Therefore upon any probable deſign the major part of the Owners may even *againſt the conſent*, though not without the *privity* and knowledge of the reſt, freight out their Veſſel to Sea

If it ſhould ſo fall out that the major part *proteſt* againſt the Voyage, and but one left that is for the Voyage, yet the ſame may be effected by that Party, eſpecially if there be *equality* in Partnerſhip

F.izg-h 19z
Houſton c
Leeds Tri
18 and 19
Geo. 2 B. R. Degrave v Hodger. Paſch 6 An B. R, 1707 L Raym
223 2d Edit 2 L Raym 1285.

But the Admiralty compels them to give Security for her ſafe Return, and the Recognizance may be ſued there

But where two Part-Owners ſent out the Ship, without the Conſent of the third, and ſhe was loſt, the third muſt bear his Proportion

tion of the Loss, because he would have had
his Share of the Profits, if any. 1 *Vern* 297.
But note, in this Case there had been no previous Application to the Admiralty, as there
ought to have been.

The Account of the Voyage settled by a *Vern* 465.
major part of the Part-Owners, binds the rest

As an Encouragement to the Building of
Ships being of that universal Advantage to
the Publick in point of Trade, and Commerce, to contrive and vest the Owners propriety in them, both by the Common Laws
of this Realm, and the Maritime Laws, it is
provided, that in case a Ship be taken away
or the Owners dispossessed, they may maintain
an Action of Trover and Conversion for an 8th,
a 16th, or any other Part or Share of the same.

In an Action on the Case, the Plaintiff de- Tenants in
clared that he was Owner of the 16th part of Common of
a Ship, and the Defendant Owner of another a Ship.
16th Part of the same Ship, and that the Defendant fradulently and deceitfully carried the
said Ship *ad loca transmarina*, and disposed
of her to his own use, by which the Plaintiff
lost his 16th part to his Damage: On not
guilty pleaded, and verdict for the Plaintiff,
it was moved in Arrest of Judgment, that the
Action did not lie, for tho' it be found de-
ceptive, yet this did not help it, if the Action
did not lie on the subject matter, and here
they are Tenants in Common of the Ship,
and by *Littleton* between Tenants in Com- *Litt* § 323.
mon there is not any Remedy, and there can- 1 *Inst.* 199 *b*
not be any fraud between them, because the 200 *a*
Law supposes a trust and confidence betwixt *Salk.* 290,
them, and upon these Reasons Judgment 392.
was given *quod Querens nil capiat per billam*.
Graves against *Sawcer*, *T. Raym.* 15. *Lev.*

29. and 1 *Keble* 38. *Bennington* against *Bennington* 3 *Leon.* 228

Leg. Fin C §. pro Sacro & poss. inst. & D eod.

III. Owners by Law can no ways be obliged to continue their paction or partnership without sundering ; but yet if they will sunder, the *Law Marine* requires some considerations to be performed before they can do so   And therefore if the Ship be newly built, and never yet made a Voyage, or is newly bought, she ought to be subject to one Voyage upon the common out-read and hazard, before any of the Owners shall be heard to sunder and discharge their parts , but by the Laws of *England* the Owners may, before any such Voyage, sell or transmit their Right.

Leg in hoc pararaȝ f convenat pro Sco

Bart. & Paul in Leg hæc distinctio § cum fundum ff locat.

If it falls out that one is so obstinate that his Consent cannot be had, yet the Law will enforce him either to hold, or to sell his proportion , but if he will set no Price, the rest may out-rigg her at their own Costs and Charges, and whatsoever Freight she earns, he is not to have any Share or Benefit in the same   But if such Vessel happens to miscarry or be cast away, the rest must answer him his Part or Proportion in the Vessel

Gloss Leg si ravis & juris in Leg i que para culpe de re unde & Leg arboribus § navis at si frad

But if it should fall out that the major Part of the Owners refuse to set out the Vessel to Sea, there by reason of the unequality they may not be compelled , but then such Vessel is to be valued and sold   The like where part of the Owners become deficient or unable to set her forth to Sea

Leg non aliter F. de usu & hab.

IV   The Master of the Vessel is eligible by the Part-Owners in Proportion, not by the Majority, and he that is most able is to be preferred   The Wisdom of the latter Ages have been such, that few have gone out in that condition, but those that have commonly

had

had Shares or Parts in the same Veſſel. In the preferring therefore of a Maſter, his Ability and Honeſty is to be conſidered, ſince on him reſts the charge not only of the Veſſel, but of the Lading, their very Actions ſubjecting the Owners † to anſwer for all Damage that ſhall be ſuſtained by him or his Mariners, be it in the Port or at Sea, to the Lading or Goods of the Merchant or Laders, and they are made liable as well by the Common Laws * of *England*, as the Law † Marine.

margin: †4 *Inſtit* 146. 18 H. 8 n 58. *2 Keb Rep 866 pl 22 Morſe v Sluc.* † *Nautæ Caup Stab. Leg* 1. *Sect* 3.

V. If the Maſter commits Offences either negligently or wilfully, he ſhall be reſponſible over to his Owners for the Reparation of Damage, ncr are they bound to join, but may ſever and ſue apart as well by the *Common Law* * as the Marine So likewiſe if the Ship hath earned Freight, and part of them receive their parts, the reſt may bring their Action for their Share, without joining with the others.

margin: * *Stanley v. Ayles 3 Keble* 444.

The Defendant and ſeven other Perſons were Proprietors of a Ship, in which Goods were uſually tranſported for hire, and the Plaintiff *onerat* Goods upon the Ship to be carried for Hire, from *London* to *Topſham*, in *Comitatu Devon*, and that the Defendant received them, and undertook to bring them to *Topſham*, but that he not being careful of his Duty, but neglecting it, *tam improvidentur* placed and carried the ſaid Goods, that tho' the Ship ſafely arrived at *Topſham*, yet the Goods were ſpoiled And upon *non culp.* pleaded, the Jury found a ſpecial Verdict, *viz* That the Defendant and ſeven other Perſons were Proprietors and Part-Owners of the Ship, that the Ship had a Maſter *locat* in her by the Part-Owners, who had 60*l.* Wages for every Voyage between *Topſham* and *London*,

margin: Maſters and Owners reſponſible.

den, that the Goods were delivered to the Master, none of the Part-Owners being present, and that there was not any Contract made with them or any of them by the Plaintiff, that the Ship arrived safe to *Topſham*, but the Goods were spoiled   *Et ſi pro Quer' pro Quer' ſi non pro* Def

And two Points were made.

1. If the Proprietors are chargeable no Contract being made with them, and there being a Master that is chargeable in respect of his Wages, according to the Case of *Morſe* and *Slue*, yet *per Holt Ch. Juſtice* clearly, that tho' the Master be chargeable in respect of his Wages, so are the Proprietors in respect of their Freight that they receive for the carriage of the Goods, at the Election of the Plaintiff

2 If the Action lay against the Defendant alone, it appearing that there are other Part-Owners not made Defendants, and held that the Action did not lie against him sole, but ought to have been against all the Part-Owners, for all the Part-Owners are chargeable in respect of the Profit they make by the carriage of the Goods, and that in point of Contract upon their undertaking, be it implied or expreſs, and are not chargeable as Treſpaſſers, for then one might be chargeable alone, but in point of Contract upon their Receipt of the Goods to be carried for hire   Judgment *pro Defen.* as by 3 *Mod.* 321. *Boſon con. Sanford* 3 *Levinz.* 258. where it is with a *Cur. adviſare, mes le Reporter ut audivit* Judgment *pro Defen.*

VI If a Ship be broken up or taken in Pieces, with an intent to convert the same to other

other ufes; if afterwards, upon Advice or *Sacram ff de* change of Mind, fhe be rebuilt with the fame *vei oblig.* Materials, yet this is now another, and not the fame Ship, efpecially if the Keel be ript up oi changed, and the whole Ship be once all taken afunder and rebuilt, theie deter-mines the Partnerfhip *quoad* the Ship But if *Leg. quod in §.* a Ship be ript up in paits, and taken afun-*fin. F. de Leg.* der in parts, and repaired in parts, yet fhe remains ftill the fame Veffel and not another; nay, though fhe hath been fo often repaired, that there remains not one ftick of the origi-nal Fabrick.

VII If a Man fhall repair his Ship with *Leg Mufius ff* Plank or other Materials belonging to another, *de rei vindic.* yet the Ship maintains and keeps her firft Owners

But if a Man take Plank and Mateiials be-*ff lib 6 tit* 1. longing to another, and prepared for the ufe *leg.* 61 of Shipping, and with them build a Ship, the Propeity of the Veffel follows the Owners of the Materials and not the Buildei

But if a Man cut down the Trees of ano-*Leg fiea meis,* thei, or takes Timber oi Planks prepared foi *ff de acq. rei.* the erecting or repairing of a Dwelling-*dom & Leg fi* Houfe, nay, though fome of them are for *convenerit § fi* *quis fic. ff de* Shipping, and builds a Ship, the Property *pign act* follows not the Owners but the Builders.

VIII If a Ship be fold togethei with hei *Leg Marcellus* Tackle, Furniture, Apparel, and all other *in § arma-* her Inftruments thereunto belonging, yet by *menta ff. de* *rei vindica'* thefe Words the Ship's Boat is not conveyed, but that remains ftill in the Owners, fo it is ✝ *Rolls A-* if the Ship be freighted out, and afterwards *bridg* 530 at Sea fhe commits Piracy, the Ship is for-*Bald in Leg.* feited, but the Boat iemains ftill to the *cum proponas* *Cod de Nau-* Owners ✝. *tic è fænore,* *num* 6

And

And though Ballaft is generally ufed in Shipping by thofe Ships that are freighted outwards, in order to bringing home of Goods, yet is not the fame any part of the Furniture of the Veffel; and fo it was adjudged in debt on Bond, The Condition was, that whereas the Plaintiff had bought of the Defendant a Ship, if the Plaintiff fhall enjoy the faid Ship with all the Furniture belonging to the fame, without being difturbed for the Ship or any Furniture appertaining to it, that then, &c. And the cafe fell out to be, that after the fale of the Ship, a Stranger fued the Plaintiff for certain Monies due for Ballaft bought by the Defendant for the fame Ship, in which Suit he obtained Sentence, upon which the Ship was feized, The Queftion was, If Ballaft be Furniture for a Ship or not, it

Lifter's Cafe, *Leon* 46, 47. was refolved that it was not, for though it may be as neceffary as Sails, yet it is not always fo, for fometimes they fail without Ballaft, for the Merchandize itfelf may be fufficient to anfwer that Purpofe

Bingley's Cafe, *Rolls* Abridg *fol* 530 *Dig lib.* 14. *tit* 1 § 17. IX If a Ship commits a Piracy, by reafon of which fhe becomes forfeited, if before feizure fhe be *bona fide* fold, the Property fhall not be queftioned, nor the Owners divefted of the fame.

1 P *Williams* 393, 394 A Mortgagee of a Ship, by Deed, intrufts the Mortgager with the original Bill of Sale, the Mortgager indorfes thereon fubfequent Mortgages or Bills of Sale of feveral Parts of the Ship, the firft Mortgagee acquiefces, he fhall be poftponed.

X If a Mafter fhall take up Monies to mend or victual his Ship where there is no occafion, though generally the Owners fhall anfwer the fact of the Mafter, yet here they fhall shall not, but only the Master. But if there were cause of mending the Ship, though the *Bridgman's Case, Hobart, fol* 11, 12 *Moo.* 918. Master spend the Money another way, yet the Owner and Ship become liable to the satisfaction of the Creditor, for it were very unreasonable that the Creditor should be bound to take upon him the care of repairing the Ship, and supply the Owners Room, which must be so, if it should be necessary for him, to prove that the Money was laid out upon the Ship, so on the other hand, it stands with reason that he be sure that he lends his Money on such an occasion, as whereby the Master's fact may oblige the Owners, which he cannot do otherwise, unless he knows that the Money borrowed was necessary for the repair of the Ship, and therefore if the Ship wanted *Gloss. African super cod leg. & §* some repairs, and far greater and more extravagant Sum was lent than was needful, the Owners shall not be liable for the whole.

The *East-India* Company's Agent in the *Indies* bought a Ship and her Cargo of the Commander, who had no Power to sell her; the Owner had the Value decreed for Ship and Cargo (the Value being found by a Jury) and *Indian* Interest, viz 12 *l per Cent.* *1 P Williams* 395

XI. If a Man gets possession of a Ship having no Title to the same, by the Law Marine, he shall answer such Damage as the Ship in all probability might have earned; and the reason of that is, because the only end of Shipping is the Employment thereof; but if a Warrant be directed out of the *Admiralty* to the *Marshal*, to arrest such a Ship and *Salvo Custodie*, who by force of the same enters into the same Ship, though the Warrant does not mention that the Officer should carry away the Sails of the same Ship, yet he may *Dig lib 6 tit. 1. 62 & lib. 7 tit I 12. § 1 & Papinian on the same Law.*

*Creamer v.
Jockley,
Latch.* 188.
may juftify the taking the fame, for that he cannot *Salvo Cuftodire* the fame Ship, unlefs he carries away the Sails.

XII. A Ship is freighted out, accordingly fhe receives in her Lading purfuant to Agreement, afterwards an Embargo happens, and *Digeft lib* 19.
tit 2. 61.
Scævola on
thefameLaw. the Laden is taken as forfeited, yet the Owners fhall notwithftanding receive Freight, for here is no fault in them, but only in the Merchant.

XIII. In *Aqua dulci* a Ship may become a Deodand, but in the Sea, or in *Aqua falfa*, 3 *Inft fol* 58. being an Arm of the Sea, no Deodand of the Ship or any part of it, though any body be drowned out of it, or otherwife come by their Death in the Ship, becaufe on fuch Waters, Ships and other Veffels are fubject to fuch Dangers upon the raging Waves in refpect of Wind and Tempeft; and this Diverfity all our antient Lawyers do agree in, and it does more *Rot. Parliam*
51 *Ed* 3
num. 73.
1 *R.* 2. *n* 106
4 *R.* 2 *n* 33. efpecially appear in the Parliament Rolls, where upon a Petition it was defired, *That if it fhould happen that any Man or Boy fhould be drowned by a Fall out of any Ship, Boat, or Veffel, they fhould be no Deodands* Whereupon the King, by great Advice with his Judges and Council learned in the Laws, made anfwer, *The Ship, Boat or Veffel, being upon the Sea fhould be adjudged no Deodand, but being upon a frefh River it fhould be a Deodand ——* 1 *H* 5 *n* 35. *but the King will fhew favour* There are abundance of other Petitions upon the like occafion in Parliament

A Ship lying at *Rotherhith*, in the County of *Kent*, near the Shore, to be careened and made clean, it happened that one of the Shipwrights being at work under her at low Water, the Veffel (then leaning afide) fortuned to

turn

turn over the contrary side, by means of which the Shipwright was killed · Upon a Trial at Bar, where the Question was, Whether this Deodand did belong to the Earl of *Salisbury*, who was Lord of the Manor, lying contiguous to the place where the Man was slain, or to the Almoner, as a matter not granted out of the Crown? In that case it was resolved, That the Ship was a Deodand, and the Jury thereupon found a Verdict for the Lord of *Salisbury*, that the same did belong to his Manor.

Mich 29 *Ca.* 2 *in B R.*

I have nothing to add (says that late learned and worthy Judge Sir *Michael Foster*) to what other Writers have said touching Deodands, more than to observe, that as this Forfeiture seemeth to have been originally founded rather in the Superstition of an Age of extreme Ignorance, than in the Principles of sound Reason and true Policy, it hath not of late Years met with great Countenance in *Westminster-Hall*. And when Juries have taken upon them to use a Judgment of Discretion, not strictly within their Province, for reducing the *Quantum* of the Forfeiture, (I wish the Temptation to it was taken out of their way) the Court of *King's Bench* hath refused to interpose in Favour of the Crown or Lord of the Franchise.

It hath frequently interposed its Authority as Sovereign Coroner in this Case, and also in the Case of Suicide, *in favour of the Subject, and to save the Forfeiture*, but will not do it in either Case *to his Prejudice* And herein it proceedeth upon the same Principle of equitable Justice, that the Courts of *Westminster-Hall* constantly do, in refusing to set aside a wrong Verdict given in *Favour* of the Defendant

dant in a Criminal Case, or in an hard Action,
though it is done every Day where a wrong
Verdict goeth against him

In the Case of the King and *Rolfe* Coroner
of *Kent*, which came on in *Mich* and *Hil.*
5 *Geo.* 2. Coroner's Inquest found, that
A B. sitting on his Waggon accidentally fell
to the Ground, and that the Horses drawing
the Waggon forward, one of the fore Wheels
crushed his Head, of which he instantly died,
and then concluded that the Wheel, on which
they set a small Value, *only* moved to his
Death   A Motion was made in behalf of
Mr *Mompesson*, Lord of the Franchise, for
quashing this Inquisition, upon Affidavits
tending to shew, that the Cart and Horses
were equally instrumental; which indeed the
finding of the Jury did sufficiently imply.
But the Court was very clear, that neither this
Court nor the Coroner can oblige the Jury to
conclude otherwise than they have done, and
would not suffer the Affidavits for quashing
the Inquisition to be read.   A like Case came
on in *Mich.* 29 *Geo.* 2. the King against
Drew, Coroner of *Middlesex*. The Coroner's
Jury upon view of the Body of a Person killed by the like Accident, found that one
Wheel of the Waggon *only* moved to the
Death.   The Court, on Motion in behalf of
the Lord of the Franchise, granted a Rule for
shewing Cause, why the Inquisition should not
be quashed for this Misbehaviour of the Jury.
On the Day for shewing Cause, Mr *Hume
Campbel*, Council for the Lord of the Franchise, informed the Court, that upon looking
into Precedents, he was satisfied he could not
support the Rule, and thereupon it was discharged.   The Case of the King and *Rolfe*
was

was mentioned on this occasion, and greatly relied on *Foft* Cr. Law 266, 267

On Importation of prohibited Goods, the *Vide Sid* 421. Ship cannot be seized as forfeit till a Con- *Mod.* 18 demnation in the Exchequer thereon. *Horne* against *Ivy,* 2 *Keble* 604. 1 *Vent.* 47

XIV. Thus Men from their necessity and safety having from hollow Trees, nay Reeds, Twigs and Leather (for such were the rude beginnings of those stupendious things we now admire) advanced the Art to that degree, as to render it now the most useful thing extant; and as the Mathematicks, Astronomy and other Sciences have added to its security, so have succeeding Ages, from time to time, provided Privileges and Laws, by which it hath always been regulated and governed, the which upon all Occasions, and in all Courts, have generally had a genuine Construction as near as might be to the Marine Customs; and therefore at this Day, if a Ship be taken away, or the Owners dispossest, they may maintain an Action of Trover and Conversion for an eighth or sixteenth part of the same, as well by the Common Laws of this Kingdom, as the Law Marine, and they need not join with the rest of their Owners.

XV. Upon an Information *tam quam,* Ship Naturagrounded upon the Act of Navigation, for lized. importing Goods in a Foreign Ship contrary to that Act, The Question was, whether or not, if a Foreign Ship naturalized by the new Act, being a Prize taken in the late War with *Holland,* be afterwards sold to a Foreigner, who sells her again to an *English* Man, whether or no the Oath must be taken again according to the Act? *Per Curiam* it need not, because

that

that the Ship was once lawfully naturalized. *Hardres* 511. *Martin* againſt *Verdue.*

XVI. Stat. 4th and 5th *Will.* and *Ma. cap.* 15. §. 14. All Perſons who by way of Inſu-rance, or otherwiſe, ſhall undertake to deli-ver any Goods imported from beyond Sea, without paying the Duties payable for the ſame, or any prohibited Goods, ſhall for-feit 500 *l.*

§. 15

And all who ſhall agree to pay any Money, for the inſuring or conveying any Goods im-ported without paying the Duties, or any prohibited Goods, or ſhall receive ſuch pro-hibited Goods, or ſuch other Goods before the Duties are paid, knowing thereof, ſhall alſo forfeit for every Offence 500 *l.*

§. 16.

And if the Inſurer or Manager of ſuch Fraud be the Diſcoverer, he ſhall not only keep the Inſurance Money given him, and be diſcharged of the Penalties to which he is liable, but ſhall have one half of the Penalties impoſed upon the Parties making ſuch Inſurance or receiving the Goods as aforeſaid: And in caſe no diſcovery be made by the Inſurer, and the Party in-ſured ſhall make diſcovery thereof, he ſhall recover back his *Præmium,* and have one Moiety of the Forfeitures impoſed upon the Inſurer, and be diſcharged of thoſe impoſed upon himſelf.

§ 17

The ſaid Penalties and Forfeitures to be re-coverable according to the Courſe of the Ex-chequer.

§ 18
*Tra. Cb. xi
Se. ult.*

No Penalty to be recoverable, unleſs pro-ſecuted within 12 Months after the Fact com-mitted

CHAP.

CHAP. II.

Masters of Ships, their Action considered in reference to Cases private and publick.

I *A Master or Skipper his condition considered, in reference to his Interest and Authority generally The Master only liable to Deviation and Barretry.*

II *If Goods be lost or imbezzled, or any other detriment happens in a Port, who shall answer. Master chargeable to pay the Duty of weighage.*

III. *The Duty of* Masters of Ships, *as if they shall set Sail after an Embargo, who shall answer?*

IV *Of Faults ascribed to him before departure in tempestuous Weather, staying in Port, &c.*

V *Over-charging or over-lading the Ship above the Birth-mark, or receipt of such Persons on Ship-board as may hazard the Lading*

VI *Of Lading aboard in the Ships of Enemies, his own proving disabled.*

VII *Of shipping Goods elsewhere than at the publick Ports or Keys, and the taking in prohibited Goods.*

VIII *Of wearing unlawful Colours or Flags, and of yielding up his Ship cowardly, if assaulted, where liable, and where excused.*

IX. *Of carrying fictitious Coquets and Papers, and refusing payment of Customs and Duties*

X *Of setting Sail with insufficient Tackle, and of taking in and delivering out with the like, and of his Charge of Goods till safely delivered*

XI *Of departing without giving notice to the Customer.*

XII *Of Faults committed by Master and Skipper at Sea*

XIII *Rules in Law in the charging him for reparation of damage. Infant Master of a Ship sueable in the Admiralty, for wasting or spoiling Goods*

XIV *Of the Power and Authority that the Master hath in disposing, hypothecating or pledging the Ship, Furniture and Lading*

XV. *Where Masters are disabled, though in necessity, to impawn the Vessel*

XVI. *Where they may dispose of Vessel and Lading, and where not.*

XVII. *What Vessels and Mariners the Master must have for importing in or exporting out of His Majesty's Plantations in* Asia, Africa, *and* America

XVIII. *What Ships may go from Port to Port in* England.

XIX. *Ships not to import the Goods of any Country, but of that from whence they are brought.*

XX. *What time the Master shall be coming up after arrived at* Gravesend, *or at any other Port within the Realm, in order to his discharge*

XXI. *Of going from Port to Port within the Realm how provided*

XXII *Of Goods prohibited to be imported from the* Netherlands *or* Germany *in any Ships whatsoever.*

1. A Master of a Ship is more than one, who, for his knowledge in *Navigation*, fidelity and discretion, hath the Government of the Ship committed to his care and management; and by the *Common Law*, (by which Properties are to be guided,) he hath no Property either general or special, by the constituting of him a Master, yet the Law looks upon him as an *Officer*, who must render and give an account for the whole charge, when once committed to his care and custody, and upon failure to render satisfaction · And therefore if misfortunes happen, if they be either through negligence, wilfulness, or ignorance of himself or his Mariners, he must be responsible.

Leg 1 de Exerat d̄d. Hob 11. Bridgman's Case Moor 918.

In Chancery. A Master of a Ship, so appointed by B. Owner, treats with the Plaintiff to take the Ship to Freight for 80 Tuns to sail from *London* to *Falmouth*, and so from thence to *Barcelona*, without altering the Voyage, and there

there to unlade at a certain Rate *per* Tun.
And to perform this the Master obliges the
Ship and what was therein, valued at 300 *l.*
and accordingly a Charter-party was made and
sealed between the Master and the Merchant;
but the Owners of the Ship were no Parties
thereunto The Master deviates and commits Barretry, and the Merchant in effect,
loses his Voyage and Goods, for the Merchandize, being Fish, came not till *Lent* was
past, and were rotten. The Merchant's Factor thereupon sueth the Master in the Court
of Admiralty at *Barcelona,* and upon an Appeal to a higher Court in *Spain,* hath Sentence
against the Master and the Ship, which coming to his Hands (*viz.* the Merchant's Hands)
the Owner brings an Action of Trover for
the Ship; the Master sues in Chancery to
stop this Suit, and another Suit brought for
the Owner for Freight, claiming deductions
out of both, for his Damages sustained by
the Master, for the breach of the Articles by
the Master, for if the Owner gives Authority
to the Master to contract he shall bear the
loss, but in Case of Bottomry after a Voyage
begun, the Master cannot oblige the Owner
beyond the Value of the Ship. But this Case
is on Contract.

Lord-Chancellor *Nottingham.* The Charter-Party values the Ship at a certain rate,
and you shall not oblige the Owners farther,
and that only with relation to the Freight,
not to the value of the Ship, the Master is
liable to the Deviation and Barretry, but not
the Owners, else Masters should be Owners
of all mens Ships and Estate, *Mich* 29.
Ca. 2.

But

2 Vern 643.

But where the Master of the Ship took Beef, Sails, &c on Credit, and failed, the Owners were obliged to pay , and not allowed to defend themselves by insisting that the Master was liable only, and that they had given him Money to pay the Plaintiff   He is but their Servant, and where he buys they are liable, and continue so if he has not paid the Creditor, though they gave him Money for that Purpose

II. If the fault be committed in any Port, Haven, River, or Creek, or any other place which is *infra Corpus Comitatûs*, the *Common Law* shall have Jurisdiction to answer the party damnified, and not the *Admiralty* ; but if the same be committed *super altum mare*, the Admiralty shall have Jurisdiction of the same, yet if it be on a place where there is *divisum imperium*, then according to the Flux or Reflux the Admiralty may challenge , the other of Common Right belonging to the *Common Law*

Vide 5 Co 107. Mo 891, 916.

L Raymond 272

The *Common Law* is the over-ruling Jurisdiction in this Realm ; and they are to intitle themselves well who would draw a thing out of it.

And therefore so soon as Merchandizes and other Commodities are put aboard the Ship, whether she be riding in Port, Haven, or any other part of the Seas, he that is *Exercitor Navis* is chargeable therewith , and if the same be there lost or purloined, or sustain any damage, hurt or loss, whether in the Haven or Port before, or upon the Seas after she is in her Voyage, whether it be by Mariners, or by any other through their permission, he that is *Exercitor Navis* must answer the damage,

F Nav. crap
J h les 1.
Sea 2, 3, 6, 7

mage, for that the very lading of the Goods aboard the Ship, does subject the Master to answer the same And with this agrees the *Common Law*, where it was adjudged, That Goods being sent aboard a Ship, and the Master having signed his Bills of Lading for the same, the Goods were stowed, and in the night divers Persons, under the pretence that they were Press-masters, entered the Ship and robbed her of those Goods, the Merchant brought an Action at the *Common Law* against the Master, and the Question was, Whether he should answer for the same, for it was alledged on his part, That there was no default or negligence in him, for he had a sufficient guard, the Goods were all locked up under Hatches, the Thieves came as *Press-Masters*, and by force robbed the Ship, and that the same was *vis major* †, and that he could not have prevented the same And lastly, That though he was called Master or *Exercitor Navis*, yet he had no share in the Ship, and was but in the Nature of a Servant, acting for a Salary. But notwithstanding it was adjudged for the Plaintiff, for at his peril he must see that all things be forth-coming that are delivered to him, let what accident soever happen, (the act of God, or an Enemy, perils and dangers of the Seas only excepted) but for Fire, Thieves and the like, he must answer, and is in the nature of a * Common Carrier; and that though he receives a Salary, yet he is a known and publick Officer, and one that the Law looks upon to answer, and the Plaintiff hath his Election to charge either Master or Owners, or both at his pleasure, but can have but one Satisfaction.

Mod. 85.
T Raym 220.
1 *Ven.* 190,
238
2 *Keb.* 866.
3 *Keb* 72,
112, 132,
135.

† The which the Civil Law does sometimes allow.

* *Rey* 105
F N B 104 *b.*
1 *Inst* 89
4 *Co* 84 *a.*
Mo 876
Hob 17, 18.
Poph 178,
179
Cro Jac 188,
189, 330, 331.
If *Salk.* 388.

Y 3

1 Sid. 36. Debet Exercitor omnium nautarum suorum, sive liberi sint sive servi, factum præstare, nec immerito factum eorum præstat, cum ipse eos suo periculo adhibuerit : Sed non alias præstat quam si in ipsa nave damnum datum sit, cæterum si extra navim, licet à nautis, non præstabit. Naut. Caup Stabilit. Leg 1 Sect. 7 debet Exercitor

Eod Leg debet Exercitor. If a Mafter fhall receive Goods at the Wharf or Key, or fhall fend his Boat for the fame, and they happen to be loft, he fhall likewife anfwer both by the Marine Law and the *Common Law*

Mayor & Com de London againft Hunt.

Error of a Judgment in B R. in Affumpfit brought by the Mayor and Commonalty againft *Hunt*, where they declared of a Cuftom, That they and their Predeceffors, Majors, &c had of every Mafter of a Ship 8 *s. per* Tun for every Tun of Cheefe brought from any place in *England* to the Port of *London, ab oriente de London-Bridge*, in the name of Weighage , and that the Defendant being Mafter of a Ship, had brought to the Port of *London* fo many Tuns, which at that rate came to fo much, which he hath not paid, upon *non Affumpfit*, Verdict and Judgment for the Plaintiff. Upon which *Hunt* the Defendant brought a Writ of Error, and two Errors were affigned. 1. That the Action did not lie againft the Mafter, but that the Duty was due from the Merchants, Owners of the Goods ; but the Judgment was affirmed, for that the Mafter is intrufted with the Goods, and hath a Recompence from the Merchants for bringing the Goods, and is refponfible for them, and therefore fhall be charged for the Duty ; and it would be infinite to fearch for the Owners of the feveral Goods, which are all in the Cuftody of the Mafter

Master who brought them into Port, and therefore he shall be charged   *3. Levinz 37*

III. If Goods be laden aboard, and after *Digest lib 9.* an Embargo or Restraint from the Prince or *tit. 2. Leg 61.* State comes forth, and then he breaks Ground, or endeavours to sail away, if any damage accrues, he must be responsible for the same. The reason is, because his Freight is due and must be paid, nay, although the very Goods be seized as *bona contrabandos*

A Ship was hired to *J. S.* in *England* to *2 Vern 242.* freight at 3 *l* 10 *s per* Tun to *Bourdeaux*, then an Embargo is laid, she afterwards proceeds to *Bourdeaux*, the Master, not discovering his first Agreement, agrees with the Correspondents there of *J. S* to allow him 6 *l.* 10 *s per* Tun, upon this last Agreement he recovered at Law, and Equity would not relieve, because the Performance of the first Agreement was hindered by the Embargo.

IV He must not sail in tempestuous Weather, nor put forth to Sea without having first consulted with his Company *, nor must ** Leg. Oleron,* he stay in Port or Harbour without just cause *Judg. 2.* when a fair wind invites his departure.

V. He must not over-charge or lade his Ship above the Birth-mark, or take into his Ship any Person of an obscure and unknown Condition, without Letters of safe Conduct. *Stat 18 H 6.*

VI. Nor ought he to lade any of his Mer- *cap 8* chant's Goods aboard any of the King's Ene- *Lib ult ad* mies Ships (admitting his own Vessel leaky or *Leg. Rhod &* disabled) without Letters of safe Conduct; *Leg quum proponas C de* otherwise the same may be made Prize, and *Naut. fœnor* he must answer the Damage that follows the *Stat. 4 H 4.* Action *20*

Nor shall he come or sneak into the Creeks *Stat 15 H. 6.* or other places, when laden homewards, but *cap 8*

into

into the King's great Ports, (unless he be
driven in by Tempest) for otherwise he forfeits to the King all the Merchandize, and
therefore must answer

1 El. c. 11 §
2.
13, 14 C 2
c 11 § 14
19 El cap 9.
1,2 P & M 5
1 Jac cap 25.
12 Car 2 cap
18.

VII Nor ought he to ship any Merchandizes, but only at the *Publick* Ports and
Keys

He must not lade any prohibited or unlawful Goods, whereby the whole *Cargo* may be
in danger of Confiscation, or at least subject
to seizure or surreption.

He may not set sail without able and
sufficient Mariners both for quality and
number

By 5 G 2 *ch* 20 Masters of Vessels out-
ward-bound are not to receive on board their
Gunpowder, either as Merchandize or Ammunition (the King's Service excepted) before they be at, over-against, or below *Black-
Wall*, on forfeiture of 5 *l* for every 50 *lb.*
Weight, &c

By the same Act, the Masters of Ships coming into the *Thames* shall land their Powder
before their Arrival at *Black-Wall*, or within
twenty-four Hours, if Weather permit, after
they come to anchor there, or at the Place
of unloading, forfeiture as in foregoing
Section

Keeping Guns shotted, firing a Gun above
Blackwall before Sun-rising or after Sun-set-
ting, are also prohibited by the same Act,
but under smaller Penalties, *viz* A Gun
shotted 5 *s* a Gun fired 10 *s.* melting Pitch
there on board is liable to a Penalty of 5 *l.*

Search may be made by an Elder-Brother
of *Trinity-House*, impowered under the Corporation Seal, and not permitting him to
make due search is liable to a Penalty of 5 *l* ·

VIII,

VIII. He may not use any unlawful Colours, Enfigns, Pendants, Jacks or *Flags* *, whereby his Ship or Lading may incur a Seizure, or the Cargo receive any detriment or damage

He muft not fuffer the Lading to be ftoln or imbezzled, if the fame be, he muft be refponfible, unlefs it be where there is *vis major*, as if he be affaulted at Sea either by Enemies, Ships of Reprize, or Pirates, there, if no fault or negligence was in him, but that he performed the part of an honeft, faithful, and valiant man, he fhall be excufed Yet it hath been adjudged, That if a Merchantman lies in a Port or Haven, and a Pirate, Sea-Rover, or other Thieves enter her and over-power her Men, and then rob her, yet the Mafter muft be refponfible; but if an Enemy enter and commit the depredation, there the Mafter is excufed   2 *Keble* 866, 3 *Keb* 72, 112, 132, 135

IX He muft not carry any counterfeit Coquets or other fictitious and colourable Ship-papers to involve the Goods of the Innocent with the Nocent

Nor muft he refufe the payment of the juft and ordinary Duties and Port-charges, Cuftoms and Imports, to the hazard of any part of his Lading, yet if he offers that which is juft and pertains to pay, then he is excufed

X He muft not fet fail with infufficient Rigging or Tackle, or with other or fewer Cables than is ufual and requifite, refpect being had to the burden of the Veffel And if any damage happens by the delivery of the Goods into the Lighter, as that the Ropes break, and the like, there he muft anfwer, but

[marginal notes]
* Proclamation *Sept* 25 *An* 26 *Car* 2. *Per Leg. quum proponas ad Leg Rhod D Leg in fin. & Leg fi vendita peric rei vend & Leg.* 5 & 6. *Naut. Caup.* 1 *Ven.* 190, 238 *Raymond* 220. 1 *Mod* 85 2 *Levinz* 69.

13 *R* 2 *cap* 9. *Leg* 1 *Cod de Navib non excufand*

Secund fin Leg. ultad Leg quum proponas C d. Naut fœnor. Leg Oleron 21. *Per Leg. quant de pub*

but if the Lighter comes to the Wharf or Key, and then in taking up the Goods, the Rope breaks, the Master is excused, and the Wharfinger is liable.

If fine Goods, or the like, are put into a close Lighter, and to be conveyed from the Ship to the Key, it is usual there, that the Master send a competent number of his Mariners to look to the Merchandize, if then any of the Goods are lost and imbezzled, the Master is responsible *, and not the Wharfinger; but if such Goods are to be sent aboard a Ship, there the Wharfinger, at his Peril, must take care the same be preserved

*Pasch 26 Car ru'd at Guild-Hall by L C J. Hale.

XI After his Arrival at Port, he ought to see that the Ship be well moored and anchored; and after reladed, not to depart or set sail till he hath been cleared, for if any damage happens by reason of any fault or negligence in him or his Mariners, whereby the Merchant or the Lading receives any damage, he must answer the same

18 Eliz cap 9
14 Car 2.
cap. 11.

XII. And as the Law ascribes these things and many more to him as faults, when committed by him or his Mariners in Ports, so there are other things which the Law looks upon to be as faults in him in his Voyage, when done

As if he deviates in his course without just cause, or steers a dangerous and unusual way, when he may have a more secure passage, though to avoid illegal impositions, he may somewhat change his course, nor may he sail by places infested with Pirates, Enemies, or other places notoriously known to be unsafe, nor engage his Vessel among Rocks or remarkable Sands, being thereto necessitated by violence

Digest. l. cum in deb to F. de Probat

Lib 1 Cod de Navibus non excusard.

violence of Wind and Weather, or deluded by false Lights.

The Master shall not be answerable for the Contracts of their Mariners, but they may be detained for their Crimes

XIII. By the Marine Law, he that will charge a Master with a fault, as in relation to his Duty, must not think that a general charge is sufficient in Law, but he ought to assign and specify the very fault wherewith he is so charged

So he that will infer, that such or such a sad disaster hath happened or been occasioned by reason of some fault in the Mariners, must not only prove the fault itself, but must also prove that that fault did dispose to such a sad event, or that such a misfortune could not have happened without such a fault precedent.

If an Infant being Master of a Ship, by Contract with another, take upon him to bring certain Goods from *St. Christophers* to *England*, and there to deliver them, but de-delivers them not according to agreement, but wastes and consumes them, he may be sued in the Admiral Court altho' he be an Infant, for this Suit is but in Nature of a Detinue or a Trover and Conversion at the Common Law, and a Prohibition denied for that Cause. *Furnes* against *Smith*. 1 *Rolls Abr* 530

Infant Master of a Ship, liable to be sued in the Admiralty

XIV. When Voyages are undertaken, the Master is there placed in by the Owners, and they ought to make good the Master's fact and deed, † and therefore as the whole care and charge of Ship and Goods are committed to the Master, it is the prudence of the Owners to be careful who they will admit Commander of their Ship, since their actions sub-ject

† *Receepit salvum fore, utrum si in navim res missæ et assignatæ sint, anet si non sint et assigna-*

sæ, hoc tamen
ipso quod in na-
vi missæ sint,
receptæ viden-
tur, & omni-
um recepit cu-
stodiam quæ in
navum illata
sunt, & fact-
um non solum
rautarumpræ-
stare debet, sed
& rectorum
F Nautæ
Caup Stab.
Leg 1. Sect
recepit.

ject them to answer the damage, or whatever other Act he shall do in reference to this Imploy, and therefore he can freight out the Vessel, take in Goods and Passengers, mend and furnish the Ship, and to that effect, if need be, in a strange Country he may borrow Money, with Advice of his Mariners, upon some of the Tackle, or sell some of the Merchandize. If part of the Goods shall be sold in such necessity, the highest price that the remainder are sold for, must be answered and paid to the Merchant, after which the Merchant must pay for the Freight of those Goods as well as for the remainder, *Leg Oleron.* 1. But if the Ship in the Voyage happens to be cast away, then only shall be tendered the price that the Goods were bought for

By the *Common Law*, the Master of a Ship could not impawn the Ship or Goods, for any Property either general or special was not in him, nor is such power given unto him by the constituting of him a Master

Leg Oleron.
c 22
Hob. 11, 12.
Latch 252
Nor 95
Plo 918
Leg Oleron
c. 1 12
Sav 34 pl 7

Yet the *Common Law* hath held the Law of *Oleron* reasonable, That if a Ship be at Sea and takes leak, or otherwise want Victuals or other Necessaries, whereby either herself be in danger, or the Voyage may be defeated, that in such case of necessity the Master may impawn for money or other things, to relieve such extremities, by imploying the same to that end, and therefore he being the Person trusted with the Ship and Voyage, may therefore reasonably be thought to have that power

Lex Mercator
102, 122

given to him implicitly, rather than to see the whole lost

A Ship put into *Boston* in *New-England*, and there the Master took up Necessaries, and gave a Bill of Sale by way of Hypothecation,

cation, and there being a Suit againſt the Ship and Owners to compel Repayment, a Prohibition was prayed, whereupon the Court held, that the Maſter could not by his contract make the Owners perſonally liable to a Suit, and therefore granted a Prohibition as to them, but refuſed it as to the Ship, for the Maſter can have no credit but upon giving ſecurity by Hypothecation And that it was unreaſonable for them to prevent the Court of Admiralty's giving a Remedy, when they could give none themſelves *Salk 35 pl 9. 6 Mod. 79 11 Mod 30. L Raymond, 982 S. C.*

But a Maſter, for any debt of his own, cannot impawn or hypothecate the Ship, &c for the ſame is no ways liable, but in caſe of neceſſity for the relief and compleating of the Voyage. *L Raymond, 984 S C*

Nor can he ſell or diſpoſe of the ſame without an Authority or Licence from the Owners, and when he does impawn or hypothecate the Veſſel or Furniture, he ought to have the conſent and advice of his Mariners *1 Siderf 453 Vid 1 Rolls Abr 530 pl 2*

A Ship being repaired, &c. in the *Thames,* is not liable, but the Owners *Peer Williams 367 See L. Raymond 152, 806.*

XV. And where the Ship is well engaged, ſhe is for ever obliged, and the Owners are concluded thereby till Redemption

But in regard Maſters might not be tempted to engage the Owners, or infetter them with ſuch ſort of obligations, but where there is very apparent cauſe and neceſſity, they ſeldom ſuffer, any to go Skipper or Maſter, but he that hath a ſhare or part in her, ſo that if Monies or Proviſions be taken up, he muſt bear his equal ſhare and proportion with the reſt.

Nor

Judgment, O-
leron, cap. 22. Nor can the Master on every case of necessity impawn the Vessel or Furniture; for if she
be freighted, and he and the Owners are to
join in the laying in of the Provisions for the
Voyage, and perhaps he wants money, (a
great sign of Necessity) yet can he not impawn the Vessel or Furniture, any other or
further than for his own part or share in her,
the which he may transfer and grant, as a
Man may do an eighth or fifth part in Lands
or Houses: But such obligation of the Vessel
must be in Foreign parts, or Places where
the Calamity or Necessity is universal on the
Vessel, that will oblige all the Owners

L Raymond
577, 578. Where a Ship was hypothecated at *Amster-*
dam, the Party was allowed to sue in the Admiralty here.

XVI. If the Vessel happens afterwards to
be wrecked or cast away, and the Mariners
by their great Pains and Care recover some of
the Ruins and Lading, the Master in that
Case may pledge the same, the Product of
which he may distribute amongst his distressed
Mariners, in order to the carrying them home
Judgment, O-
leron., cap 3 to their own Country: But if the Mariners
no way contributed to the Salvage, then their
Reward is sunk and lost with the Vessel.
And if there be any considerable part of the
Lading preserved, he ought not to dismiss
the Mariners, till Advice from the Laders or
Freighters; for otherwise perchance he may
be made liable

If Merchants freight a Vessel at their own
Charges, and set her to Sea, and she happens
afterwards to be Weather-bound, the Master
Leg Oleron
cap 22. may impawn either the Ship or Lading at his
Pleasure, or at least such as he could conve-
niently raise Monies on, rather than see the
whole

whole Voyage loft. And if he cannot pawn the Lading, he may fell the fame, that is, fo much as is neceffary; in all which Cafes his Act obliges.

However, Orders and Inftructions are as carefully to be looked upon and followed as the Magnet.

XVII. He is not to import into, or export out of any the *Englifh* Plantations in *Afia*, *Africa*, or *America*, but in *Englifh* or *Irifh* Veffels, or of the Veffels built and belonging to that Country, Ifland, Plantation, or Territory; the Mafter and three-fourths of the Mariners to be *Englifh*, upon forfeiture of Ship and Goods; and if otherwife, they are to be looked upon as Prize, and may be feized by any of the King's Officers and Commanders, and to be divided as Prizes, according to the Orders and Rules of the Sea

All Goods of the Growth of his Majefty's Plantations are not to be imported into *England*, *Ireland*, or *Wales*, Ifland of *Jerfey* or *Guernfey*, but in fuch Veffels as truly belong to Owners that are of *England, Ireland, Wales, Jerfey* or *Guernfey*, and three-fourths at leaft of the Mariners are to be *Englifh*, upon forfeiture of Ship and Goods

The Goods and Wares of thofe Plantations, and brought in fuch manner as aforefaid, muft be brought from thofe very Countries of their feveral Productions and Growths, or from the Ports where they are ufually fhipped out, on forfeiture of Ships and Goods

XVIII. No Ship to go from Port to Port in *England, Ireland, Wales, Jerfey,* or *Guernfey,* or *Berwick,* unlefs the Owners are Denizens or Naturalized, and the Mafter and three-fourths to be *Englifh*

The like provifion on the like penalty is for Goods of Mufcovy, and of the Dominions and Territories of the Czar So likewife of Currants belonging to the Ottoman Territories or Dominions. Note, Cafes of ficknefs, death, captivity, falve the Claufe as to Mariners.

That is thofe that do not belong to Englifh, Irifh, Welfh, or thofe of Jerfey, or Guern-

All *fey,*

All Owners muſt ſwear that their Veſſels or Ships are their own proper Ships and Veſſels, and that no Foreigner hath any Share or Part in her, and muſt enter the ſame; and that ſhe was bought for a valuable Conſideration, *Bona fide.*

XIX. Nor to bring in any Goods from any Place, but what are of the Growth of that very Country, or thoſe Places which uſually are for the firſt ſhipping, on pain of forfeiture of their Veſſel and Furniture

This doth not extend ſo far, but that Maſters may take in Goods in any part of the *Levant* or *Streights*, although they are not of the very Growth of the Place, ſo that they be imported in *Engliſh* Ships, three-fourths *Engliſh* Mariners. So likewiſe thoſe Ships that are for *India* in any of thoſe Seas to the Southward and Eaſtward of the *Cape of Good-Hope*, although the Ports are not the Places of their very Growth

12 *Car* 2. *cap* 18.

Any People of *England* may import (the Maſter and Mariners three-fourths *Engliſh*) any Goods or Wares from *Spain*, *Portugal*, *Azores*, *Madura*, or *Canary* Iſlands, nay in Ships that are not *Engliſh* built, Bullion may be imported, ſo likewiſe in thoſe that are taken by way of Prize, *Bona fide*

But Sugars, Tobacco, Cottons, Ginger, Indicoes, Fuſtick, or any other dying Wood of the Growth of his Majeſty's Plantations, to be ſhipped, carried or conveyed from any of the *Engliſh* Plantations, are to be carried to no Place in the World, but are to come directly for *England*, *Ireland*, *Wales*, or *Berwick*, upon pain of forfeiture of Ship and Goods, and the Maſter is to give Bond with one Security in 1000 *l* if the Ship be under the burden

den of 100 Tuns, and 2000 *l* if above, that upon Lading he brings his Ship directly into *England, Ireland, Wales* or *Berwick,* (the danger of the Seas excepted) so likewise they are to do the same for the Ships that shall go from the Plantations, to the Governor of such Plantation, upon forfeiture of the Ship and Goods.

By 3 *Geo* 2 *c* 28. Rice is permitted to be carried South of *Cape Finesterre* without first coming to *Great-Britain*

XX When the Master shall arrive at *Gravesend,* he shall not be above three Days coming from thence to the Place of Discharge, nor is he to touch at any Key or Wharf till he comes to *Chester*'s Key, unless hindered by contrary Winds, or Draught of Water, or other just Impediment to be allowed by the Officers· And likewise he or his Purser are there to make Oath of the Burden, Contents and Lading of his Ship, and of the Marks, Number, Contents, and Qualities of every Parcel of Goods therein laden, to the best of his Knowledge, also where and in what Port she took in her Lading, and what Country built, and how manned, who was Master during the Voyage, and who the Owners, and in Out-Ports must come up to the Place of unlading, as the condition of the Port requires, and make Entries, on pain of 100 *l* 12 *Car* 2, *c* 18

Nor is such a Master to lade aboard any Goods outwards to any Place whatsoever, without entering the Ship at the Custom-House, her Captain, Master, Burden, Guns, Ammunition, and to what Place she intends, and before Departure to bring in a Note under his Hand of every Merchant that shall have laid aboard any Goods, together with the Marks and Numbers of such Goods, and be sworn as to the same, on pain of 100 *l*

No Captain, Master, Purser of any of His Majesty's Ships of War, shall unlade any Goods before Entry made, on pain of 100 *l.*

Note, There is a List of all Foreign built Ships in the Exchequer No Foreign Ship, not built in any of His Majesty's Dominions of *Asia, Africa,* or *America,* after *Octob* 1, 1662, and expresly named in the List, shall enjoy the Privileges of a Ship belonging to *England* or *Ireland,* although owned and manned by *English,* except only such as are taken by way of Reprize, and Condemnation made in the Admiralty as lawful Prize None but *English* and *Irish* Subjects in the Plantations are to be accounted *English.*

XXI. If the Master shall have Freight from Port to Port within the Realm, he ought to have Warrant for the same, on pain of Forfeiture of the Goods, and he is to take forth a Cocquet, and become bound to go to such Port designed for, and to return a Certificate from the chief Officers of that Port where the same is designed for, and discharged within six Months from the date of the Cocquet

XXII. But from the *Netherlands* or *Germany,* there may not be imported any sort of Wines (other than Rhenish) Spicery, Grocery, Tobacco, Pot-ashes, Pitch, Tar, Salt, Rosin, Deal-boards, hard Timber, Oil, or Olives, in any manner of Ships whatsoever

It might not seem impertinent, that this latter Part which is abridged, in reference to Matters publick, should be inserted, for that sometimes it may happen, that an honest and well meaning Master or Skipper might innocently

cently involve and hazard the Loſs of his Ship, by committing Acts againſt Laws poſitive and prohibitory, and though Maſters and Mariners, *qua tales*, be not ſo exquiſite, as to know all that does belong to their Duties, or at leaſt that which the Law lays incumbent on their Shoulders, yet for that moſt of them have ſome ſmall glimmerings of the ſame, ſuch Hints in Matters publick as well as private, may not only be of ſome Advantage to them, but alſo to Merchants, who always, upon the Miſcarriages of the Maſters, prove the greateſt Sufferers, the Offenders, for the moſt part, proving not ſufficiently ſolvent

CHAP.

CHAP. III.

Of Mariners, their several Offices and Immunities, and of Barretry committed by them.

XVIII *Of*

XVIII. *Of Caution or fore-warning where the same shall excuse the Master.*

XIX. *Where the Master shall be liable, notwithstanding such Caution.*

1 THE Persons ordinary for sailing in Ships have divers Denominations: The first, which is the Master, known to us and by most Nations both now and of old, and especially by the *Roman* Laws, *Navicu-* *Leg. 1. &* *larius* or *Magister Navis*, in *English* rendered *passim ad Leg.* Master, or *Exercitor Navis*, in the *Teutonick* *Rhod & lib.* Skipper, by the *Grecians*, *Navarchus* or *Nau-* *1 parag 2.* *clerus*, by the *Italians*, *Patrono*. But this is *Naut. Caup.* only to those Vessels that are Ships of Burden and of Carriage, for to Ships of War the principal there is commonly called Commander or Captain The next in order of Office to the Master, is he who directs the Ship in the Course of her Voyage, by the *French* called *Pilote*, by the *English* and *Flemming*, *Steersman*; by the *Romans*, *Gubernator*; by the *Italians*, *Nochiero Pilotto* and *Navarchus*, as *Gerettus* writes The third is esteemed the Master's Mate or Companion, chiefly if the Master be Steersman himself, of old by the *Grecians* and *Romans* called *Proreta*, his *Vid. Leg. Con-* Charge is to command all before the Mast. *sol.*

His Successor in order is the Carpenter or Shipwright, by those two Nations of old called *Naupegus* by the latter, by the first *Cala-* *phates* From the Loins of one of that Rank sprang that great Emperor *Michael*, sirnamed *Calaphates*, who denied not to own the Quality of his Father among his Regal Titles *The Father* The very Name of *Chalaphate* the *Venetian* and *was of Phla-* *Italian* still use to this Day. *gonia, as Eg-* *natius Volate-* The next who succeeds in order, is, he who *ranus ob-* bears the Charge of the Ship's Boat, by the *serves, lib. 23.*

Italians

Italians called *Brachiere*, by the *Græcians* and *Romans*, *Carabita*, from *Carabus*, which denotes the Boat of a Ship

The fixth in order, especially in Ships of Burden, is the Clerk or *Purser*, by the *Italians* called *Scrivano*, whose Duty is the registering and keeping the Accounts of all received in or delivered out of the Ship, for all other Goods that are not by him entered or taken into charge, if they happen to be cast overboard in a Storm, or are stolen or imbezzled, the Mafter anfwers them not, there being no Obligation on him by Law for the fame; his Duty is to unlade by Day, not Night.

Il Confolato Stat 14 Car 2 cap 11

The feventh a moft neceffary Officer, as long as there are aboard Bellies, sharp Stomachs and Provifion, called the *Cook*

The eighth is the Ship's Boy, who keeps her continually in Harbours, called of old by the *Græcians*, *Nauphilakes*, by the *Italians*, *Guardino* · Thefe Perfons are diftinct in Offices and Names, and are likewife diftinguifhed in their Hires and Wages, the reft of the Crew are under the common Name of Mariners, by the *Romans* called *Nautæ*, but the *Tarpollians*, or thofe Youths or Boys that are Apprentices, obliged to the moft fervile Duties in the Ship, were of old called *Mefonautæ*.

Budæus ad Leg 1 Naut. Caup. tot.

Mafters of Ships, &c obliged to take Apprentices.

By Stat 2 and 3 *An. c* 6 *Sect* 8 " Every Mafter or Owner of a Ship from thirty to forty Tons burden, fhall be (1) obliged to take one Apprentice, and one more for the next

(1) By Stat 4 *Ann c* 19 *Sect* 16 " No Mafter fhall be obliged to take any fuch Apprentice under thirteen Years of Age, or who fhall not appear to be fitly qualified, both as to Health and Strength of Body for that Service."

fifty

fifty Ton, and one more for every hundred
Ton Ship shall exceed the Burden of an hundred
Ton, on pain of forfeiting 10 *l.* to the
Poor of the Parish from whence such Boy was
bound "

By *Sect.* 1. " It shall be lawful for two
Justices, and for the head Officers in Corporations,
and for the Church-wardens and
Overseers of the several Parishes or Townships,
with the Consent of such Justices or
head Officers, to bind and put out any Boy
of the Age of ten Years or upwards, or who
shall be chargeable, or who shall beg for Alms,
to be an Apprentice to the Sea Service, to
any *Subject,* being Master or Owner of any
Ship or Vessel, until he shall attain the Age
of twenty-one Years

The Boy's Age shall be inserted in the Indenture,
being truly taken from a Copy of the
Entry in the Register Book (where it can be
had) which Copy shall be given and attested
without Fee · And where no such Entry can
be found, two Justices, and such head Officers,
shall, as fully as they can inform themselves
of such Boy's Age, and from such Information
insert the same in the Indentures *id.*

By *Sect.* 2 " And the Church-wardens
and Overseers shall pay down to the Master,
at the Time of the Binding, the Sum of fifty
Shillings for Cloathing and Bedding, and the
Charges by this Act appointed, shall be allowed
on their Accompts "

By *Sect.* 5 " The Church-wardens and Overseers
shall send the Indentures to the Collector
of the Customs at the Port whereunto the
Master belongeth, who shall enter the Indenture
in a Book, and make an Indorfement

Z 4   upon

Parish Boys
may be put
out Apprentices
for the
Sea Service
to Masters
Ships, &c.

Boy's Age to
be inserted in
the Indenture

Church-wardens
to
pay down
50s for Boy's
necessary
Cloathing,
&c and be
allowed the
same in Accompt

Apprentice's
Indentures to
be sent to the
Collector at
the Port
where unto

his Master be-upon the Indenture of the Registry thereof,
longs. Col- subscribed by him without Fee; and if he
lector to enter shall neglect or refuse to enter such Inden-
same *gratis* tures, and indorse the same, or make false
Entries, he shall forfeit five Pounds to the
Poor of the Parish from whence such Boy was
bound."

Inrolment   The Indentures of Persons binding themselves Apprentices to Mariners, are to be inrolled in the next Corporate Town 3 *Lev.
Rep.* 389 5 *Eliz. c* 4. *Sect* 29

How Ap-   By *Sect* 10. " Such Apprentice shall be
prentices conveyed to the Port to which his Master be-
shall be con-longeth, by the Church-wardens and Over-
veyed to the seers, or their Agents, and the Charges
Port to which thereof shall be (1) paid as by the Vagrant
their Masters Act 11 and 12 *W* 3 *c* 19
belong

The Counter-   By *Sect.* 11 " The Counterpart of the
parts of their Indenture shall be sealed and executed by the
Indentures to Master, and attested by the Collector of the
be transmit-Port, and the Constable or other Officer who
ted to the carries the Apprentice; which Officer shall
Church-war-transmit such Counterpart to the Church-wardens, &c dens and Overseers of the Place from whence
the Apprentice was bound "

Parish Boys   By *Sect* 6 " Every Person to whom any
bound Ap-poor Parish Boy shall be put Apprentice by
prentices the *43 Eliz.* may with the Consent of two
may be turn-Justices dwelling near the Parish where such
ed over to the poor Boy was bound, or with the like Con-
Sea Service sent of the chief Officer in a Corporation, at
the Request of the Master, his Executors,
Administrators or Assigns, by Indenture assign over such poor Boy Apprentice to any

(1) That is to say, out of the Goal and Marshalsea
Money, which, by 12 *Geo.* 2. *c* 19 is directed to be
paid out of the General County Rate *Burn.* 65

Master

Master or Owner of a Ship or Vessel, using the Sea Service, during the remaining Time of his Apprenticeship "

By 4 *An. c* 19. *Sect.* 16. " If the Master Master dying. shall die during the Term, his Widow, or his Executor or Administrator may assign over such Apprentice to any other Master who hath not his Complement of Apprentices "

By 2 and 3 *An c.* 6 *Sect.* 5 " The Col- Lord Admi- lector or his Deputy shall transmit a Certifi- ral to grant cate under his hand to the Commissioners of Protections from being the Admiralty, containing the Name and impressed till Age of such Apprentice, and to what Ship 18, *gratis* he belongs, and on Receipt of such Certifi- cate, a Protection shall be made and given *gratis* to such Apprentice, till he attain the age of eighteen Years "

By *Sect* 15 " Every Person who shall Persons vo- voluntarily bind himself Apprentice to the luntarily Sea Service, shall not be impressed for three binding Years from the Date of his Indentures, which themselves Indentures shall be registered, and Certificates Apprentices to the Sea thereof given and transmitted by the Collec- Service, not tor as aforesaid, on Receipt of which Cer- to be impres- tificate, Protections shall be made and given sed for three for the first three Years without Fee " Years In- dentures to be registered, and Protections given for said three Years.

By 4 *An c* 19 *Sect* 17 " No Person of No Appren- the Age of 18 Years shall have any Protec- tice to the tion from being impressed, who shall have Sea Service of been in any Sea Service, before he bound 18 Years old himself Apprentice " exempt from the Queen's Service at Sea.

By 13 *Geo* 2. *c* 17 *Sect* 3 " Every Per- Lord High- son not having before used the Sea, who shall Admiral, &c. bind himself Apprentice to serve at Sea, to grant Pro- shall be exempted from being impressed for tections to Persons ex- three empted from

being impref-
fed without
Fee. three Years, and the Commiffioners of the Admiralty on due proof of the Circumftances, fhall grant (1) Protection accordingly without Fee."

When im-
preffed, the
Mafter to
have the Wa-
ges of able
Seamen for
them. By 2 and 3 *An. c.* 6 *Sect.* 17. " When fuch voluntary Apprentice fhall be impreffed or voluntarily enter into the King's Service, the Owner or Mafter, his Executors, Adminiftrators or Affigns, fhall be intitled to able Seamens Wages, for fuch of the Apprentices, as fhall upon due Examination be found qualified for the fame notwithftanding (2) their Indentures of Apprenticefhip "

Exempted
from the 6 d
a Month to
Greenwich
Hofpital, un-
til 18 Years
old. By *Sect* 7 " Such poor Boys bound out, or affigned over, to the Sea Service, until they fhall attain to the age of 18 Years, fhall be exempted from the Payment of 6 *d.* a Month to *Greenwich Hofpital.*"

Mafter to en-
ter his Ap-
prentices on
clearing out By *Sect* 9 " Every Mafter fo obliged to take fuch Apprentice, fhall after his arrival into any Port aforefaid, and before he clears out of fuch Port, give an account in writing under his hand, to the Collector, containing the Names and number of fuch Apprentices as are then remaining in his Service "

Officer to in-
fert on the
Cocquet the
Number of
Men and Boys
on board By *Sect.* 14. " Every Cuftom-houfe Officer fhall infert at the bottom of their Cocquets, the Number of Men and Boys on board their refpective Ships at their going out, defcribing the Apprentices by their Names, Ages, and Dates of their Indentures, for which no Fee fhall be taken."

(1) *Note,* by 2 G 3 *c* 15 *Sect* 22, 23, 24, 25 " Maf-" ters, Apprentices, Mariners and others imployed in fifhing Veffels upon the Coafts, are exempted, during fuch their Imployment, from being impreffed "

(2) Is it not the Indenture of Apprenticefhip, and that only, which gives the Mafter a Right to the Wages of his Apprentice ?

By

By *Sect.* 13 " The Collector in the Port shall keep a Register, containing the number and burden of all Ships belonging to the Port, together with the Masters or Owners Names, and also the Names of all such Apprentices in such Ship, and from what Parishes and Places they were sent, and shall transmit (*gratis*) true Copies thereof signed by him, to the quarter Sessions, or to such Towns Corporate, Parishes, or Places, when and so often as he shall be reasonably required so to do, and every Collector refusing or neglecting to send such Copy, shall forfeit five Pounds to the Poor of the Parish from whence such Boy was bound "

Registry to be kept in the Ports by the Collector, and transmit a Copy thereof to the Quarter Sessions, &c. gratis.

Penalty.

By *Sect* 12. " Two Justices near the Port, and Mayors of Towns Corporate, in or near adjoining to such Port, to which such Ship or Vessel shall at any time arrive, may determine all Complaints of ill usage from the Master to such Apprentice, and also of all such as shall voluntarily put themselves Apprentices to the Sea Service, and make such order therein as they are now enabled by Law to do, in other Cases between Masters and Apprentices "

Justices to determine Differences between Masters and Apprentices

By *Sect* 18 " All the Penalties aforesaid shall, by Warrant of two Justices of the County, City, or Town Corporate, be levied by Distress and Sale."

Penalties and Forfeitures how to be levied.

By Stat. 2 *Geo* 2. *c.* 36 *Sect* 1. " It shall not be lawful for any Master of a Ship bound beyond the Seas, to carry any Mariner, except his Apprentices, from the Port where he was shipt, to proceed on any Voyage beyond the Seas, without first coming to an Agreement with such Mariners for their Wages,

No Masters of Ships to proceed on a Voyage without agreeing with the Mariners for Wages in Writing.

Wages, which Agreement shall be made in writing, declaring what Wages each Seaman is to have for so long Time as they shall ship themselves for, and also to express in the Agreement the Voyage for which such Seaman was shipt; and if any such Master shall carry **Apprentices excepted** out any Mariner, except his Apprentice, upon any Voyage beyond the Seas, without first entering into such Agreement, and he and they signing the same, he shall forfeit 5 *l.* **On Forfeiture of 5 *l* for each Mariner.** for every such Mariner, to the use of *Greenwich Hospital*, to be recovered on Information on the Oath of one Witness, before one Justice of Peace, who is required to issue his Warrant to bring before him such Master; and in case he refuses to pay the Forfeiture, to grant his Warrant to levy by Distress and Sale of Goods, and if no Distress can be found, to commit him to the common Goal till he pay the same."

Seamen to sign Agreements, which are to be conclusive. By *Sect.* 2 " If any Seaman Ship himself on board any Merchant Vessel on an intended Voyage for Parts beyond the Seas, he shall be obliged to sign such Agreement within three Days after he shall have entered himself, which Agreement shall be conclusive to all Parties for the Time contracted for "

Wages forfeited by Desertion. By *Sect* 3 " If any Seaman shall desert, or refuse to proceed on the Voyage, or shall desert in Parts beyond the Seas, after he shall have signed such Contract, he shall forfeit to the Owners of the Ship, the Wages due to him at the Time of his Deserting, or refusing to proceed on the Voyage "

Justices may commit Deserters to House of Correction By *Sect* 4 " If any Seaman shall desert, or absent himself from the Ship, after he hath signed a Contract, upon Application made to any Justice of Peace by the Master or other Person having charge of the Ship, it shall
be

be lawful for such Justice to issue his Warrant to apprehend such Seaman, and, if he shall refuse to proceed on the Voyage, and shall not give a sufficient reason for such refusal, to the satisfaction of the Justice, to commit him to the House of Correction, to be kept to hard Labour, not exceeding 30 Days, nor less than 14"

By *Sect.* 5 " If any Seaman shall absent himself from the Vessel to which he belongs, without leave of the Master or other chief Officer having charge of such Ship, he shall for every Day's absence, forfeit two Days Pay to the use of *Greenwich Hospital*"

Penalty of Mariners absenting from Ship without leave.

By *Sect.* 6. " If any Seaman, not entering into the Service of His Majesty, shall leave the Vessel to which he belongs, before he shall have a Discharge in writing from the Master or other Person having the charge of such Vessel, he shall forfeit one Month's Pay."

Of leaving the Ship after arrival, and before Discharge.

By *Sect.* 7. " On the arrival of any Vessel in *Great Britain* from Parts beyond the Seas, the Master shall pay the Seamen their Wages, if demanded, in thirty Days after the Vessel's being entered at the Custom-house (except where a Covenant shall be entered into to the contrary) or at the Time the said Seamen shall be Discharged, which shall first happen, deducting out of the Wages the Penalties by this Act imposed, under Penalty of paying to such Seamen that shall be unpaid, 20 *s*. over and above the Wages, to be recovered as the Wages may be recovered, and such Payment of Wages shall be good in Law, notwithstanding any Action, Bill of Sale, Attachment or Incumbrance whatsoever "

Wages to be paid in 30 Days after arrival.

By *Sect.* 8 " No Seaman, by signing such Contract, shall be deprived of using any

Means

Means for the Recovery of Wages, which
he may now lawfully use; and where it shall
be neceffary that the Contract in Writing
fhould be produced in Court, no Obligation
fhall lie on any Seaman to produce the fame,
but on the Mafter or Owner of the Ship; and
no Seaman fhall fail in any Action or Procefs
for recovery of Wages, for want of fuch Contract being produced."

By *Sect* 9 " The Mafters or Owners of
Ships fhall have Power to deduct out of the
Wages of any Seaman all Penalties incurred
by this Act, and to enter them in a Book,
and to make Oath, if required, to the Truth
thereof; which Book fhall be figned by the
Mafter and two principal Officers belonging
to fuch Ship, fetting forth, that the Penalties
contained in fuch Book are the whole Penalties
ftopt from any Seaman during the Voyage;
which Penalties (except the Forfeitures of
Wages to the Owners, on the Defertion of any
Seaman, or on refufing to proceed on the
Voyage) fhall go to the ufe of *Greenwich
Hofpital*, to be paid and accompted for by
the Mafters of Ships coming from beyond
the Seas, to the fame Officer at any Port,
who collects the 6 *d* per Month, which Officer fhall have Power to adminifter an Oath
to every Mafter touching the Truth of fuch
Penalties."

By *Sect*. 10 " If any Mafters or Owners
of Ships fhall deduct out of the Wages of
any Seaman, any of the Penalt es by the Act
directed to the Ufe of *Greenwich Hofpital*,
and fhall not pay the Money to fome Officer
who collects the 6 *d* per Month in the Port
where the Deduction fhall be made, w thin
three Months after fuch Deduction, they fhall
forfeit

forfeit treble the Value to the use of the Hospital, which, together with the Money deducted, shall be recovered by the same Means as the Penalties for not duly paying the 6 d. per Month."

By *Sect.* 11. " This Act shall be a Public Act." Public Act

By *Sect* 13. " Nothing in this Act shall debar any Seaman from entering into the Service of his Majesty, nor shall such Seaman for such Entry forfeit the Wages due to him during his Service in such Merchant Ship, nor shall such Entry be deemed a Desertion " Act not to debar Seamen from entering into the King's Service,

By Stat 2 *Geo* 3 *c.* 31 " This Act is perpetuated and extended to his Majesty's Colonies in *America*, the Penalties there, to *Greenwich Hospital*, to be paid to such Person as the Commissioners of the Admiralty shall direct: Master deducting, and not paying the same in three Months, shall forfeit treble to the said Hospital " 2 *Burn.* 423. perpetuated and extended to *America.*

See Stat 31 *Geo.* 2. *Sect.* 16.

II The Master hath the supreme Rule on Ship-board, and by that Means his Power and Authority is by Law much countenanced, especially in the keeping his Crew in Peace so long as they eat his Bread; and if a *Mariner* shall happen to be bruised or hurt in doing his Duty and Service, the Master * is to take Care that he be carefully looked after, in order to the procuring his Recovery; and if it be occasioned by the Miscarriage of another on Ship-board, he may refund the Damage out of his Wages, but still remembring who gave the first Assault * *Per Leg Oleron, cap* 6. *Per Leg. de exerc act & l in fin Naut Caus*

If it happens that the Master commands his Boat to be manned out, and it so happens that the same is out of order, or unfit to take the Sea, the Tews or other Accoutrements being impotent, if the *Mariners* happen to be drowned, the Master is to repay by the Law *Marine* one whole Year's Hire to the Heirs of the Drowned   Therefore Masters ought carefully to view and see that the Boat be fit for Men to trust their Lives in, upon his Command

If a *Mariner* shall commit a Fault, and the Master shall lift up the Towel three times before any *Mariner*, and he shall not submit, the Master at the next Place of Land may discharge him; and if he refuseth to go ashore, he shall lose half his Wages, and all his Goods

Per Leg Oleron, cap 14. within the Ship   If the *Mariner* shall submit, and the Master will not receive the same, he shall have his whole Wages; or if the *Mariner* shall depart the Ship on the Master's Command, and the Master happens not to take another, if any Damage happens to Ship or Goods, the Master must answer

Per Leg. Oleron, cap 13 *& per Leg Denmarc* III. *Mariners* must help one another at the Sea and in Port; if any refuse, upon the Oaths of his Fellows, he loseth his Wages   None of the Crew must or ought to leave the Ship, without Leave of the Master, when she comes to a Port, or rides at Anchor, but always constantly to wait upon her till they are discharged, or have leave, at least half to be left on Ship-board.

Leg retro ce Reg jur & Leg plerumque de in jus vos. A *Mariner* may not carry out of the Ship above one Meal's Meat, but Drink not a drop; and when on Ship board, ought not to be there arrested for Debt, but only so much of his Wages in the hands of the Master attached   Yet this is doubted, if it be not on a sworn Debt, that is, a Judgment or Sentence, or a Penalty to the King.

They

They ought not to depart from on Ship-board when once admitted into their full Pay (which is always when they break Ground) without Licence of the Master, and before they may so do, they are to leave a sufficient number to guard the Ship and Decks.

See the several Acts of the 7th and 8th *William* III *cap.* 21. Intituled an Act for the Increase and Encouragement of Seamen; and of the 8th and 9th of the same King, *cap.* 23 Intituled an Act for the further Increase and Encouragement of Seamen, for registring of Seamen, and providing for their Widows and Children in such manner as therein is mentioned, too large to be recited here

By Stat 9 *Ann ch.* 21. the Registring of Seamen is repealed.

IV If the Ship breaks Ground, and is set sail, if after she arrives at her desired Port, their full Pay continues till she returns, nor may they in any wise depart from on Shipboard without Leave or Licence of the Master, if they do, and any Disaster happens, they must answer　Yet at such Port if the *Leg Oleron, cap 5.* Vessel be well moored and anchored with two Cables, they may go without leave, yet so as they leave a sufficient number behind to guard the Decks: But then their return must be in due Season, for if they make longer stay, they must make Satisfaction

V If *Mariners* get drunk and wound one another, they are not to be cured at the Charge of the Master or Ship, for such Accidents are not done in the Service of the Ship・But if any of the *Mariners* be any ways wounded, or do become ill in the Service of the Ship, he is to be provided for at the Charges of the Ship, and if he be so ill as *Leg Oleron,* not fit to travel, he is to be left afhore, and Care to be taken that he hath all Accommodations of Humanity adminiftered to him: And if the Ship is ready for a Departure, fhe is not to ftay for him; if he recover, he is to have his full Wages, deducting the Mafter's Charges which he laid out for him

Leg. Oleron, cap. 11.   VI. In Cafe of Storm, if Goods are caft over-board for lightening the Ship, the Oaths of the *Mariners*, fwearing that it was done for the Prefervation of the Veffel and the reft of the Lading, fhall difcharge the Mafter.

So Goods damnified at Sea, are cleared by the Oath of the Mafter and *Mariners*, by the Laws of *Oleron*.

Leg Oleron, cap 13.   To affault the Mafter on Ship-board, is a Crime that fubjects the *Mariner*'s Hand to be cut off, unlefs he redeems it at 5 *Solz*

VII. If a Ship happens to he feized on for Debt, or otherwife to become forfeited, the *Confolat. del. mare.*   *Mariners* muft receive their Wages, unlefs in fome Cafes where their Wages are forfeited as well as the Ship; or if they have Letters of Marque, and inftead of that they commit Piracy, by reafon of which there becomes a *Rolls's A-bridg. 530.*   Forfeiture of all. But Lading of prohibited Goods aboard a Ship, as Wool, and the like, though it fubjects the Veffel to a Forfeiture, yet it difables not the *Mariner* of his Wages; for the *Mariners* having honeftly performed their Parts, the Ship is tacitly obliged for their Wages. But if the Ship perifhes at Sea, they lofe their Wages, and the Owners their Freight. And this being the Marine Cuftom, is allowed by the *Common Law* as well as the *Civil Law*

If fhe comes to her firft delivering Port they have Wages till then: If loft afterwards, they

they only lose those subsequent Wages. L. *Raym* 631 *Q* this, and see L. *Raym.* 739. where they lost part of their first Wages

VIII The Courts at *Westminster* have been very favourable to *Mariners* in order to the suing for Wages, for at the *Common Law* they cannot join, but must sue all distinct and apart for their Wages.

Yet in the Admiralty they may all join, *1 Vent* 146 and the Courts at *Westminster* will not grant 343 *2 Vent.* a Prohibition And so it was ruled, where one 181 *Jones* † a Master of a Ship was sentenced in *2 Keble* 779. the Admiralty for Wages at the Suit of poor † *Winch* Rep 8. *Mariners*, a Prohibition being prayed upon a Suggestion that the Contract was made at Land, and not *super altum Mare*, the Court denied it, for that he came too late, Sentence being given below against him Yet if the *Mariners* had only libelled, and there had been no Sentence, and the Defendant had prayed a Prohibition, as above, the Court would have denied it. This hath been, and is usually done

It was by meer Indulgence that Mariners were permitted to sue in the Admiralty for their Wages · And this Indulgence was, be- *Salk* 33 *pl* cause the Remedy in the Admiralty was the 4 easier and better, easier because they must sever here, whereas they may join there; and better, because the Ship itself is answerable; but it is expresly against the Statute, tho' now *Communis Error facit Jus* The first in- stance of it is in *Winch.* 8 Yet it was never allowed the Master should sue there, nor is *Com Rep* 74. it reasonable where he commenceth the Voy- *Carth* 518 age as Master, for tho' the Mariners contract upon the Credit of the Ship, the Master doth

A a 2 contract

contract on the Credit of the Owners. L.
Raym. 397. *ad idem.*

Salk 33 *pl* 5. But yet the Mate may fue in the Admiralty
for his Wages, becaufe he contracts with the
Mafter, as the reft of the Mariners do.
L *Raym.* 632, *ad idem.*

Sitwell & al.
Owners of a
Ship, verf
Love & al
Mich. 27 *Car*
in B R. But the Court will be very well informed,
that the Libel is for *Mariners* Wages, for
fome who work Carpenters work, and fuch
like Labour, aboard a Ship in a Haven or
Port within the Realm, which is *infra Corpus
Comitatûs*, (notwithftanding thofe great and ingenious Objections againft it) and muft be tried
by the *Common Law*, and not elfewhere, will
libel under that Cloak for *Mariners* Wages.
But the Court in that Cafe will grant a Prohibition. And fo it was done in the like Cafes.

But if a Ship rides at Anchor in the Sea,
and the Mafter fends his Boat afhore for Victuals or other Provifions for the Ship, and
accordingly the *Providore* or Slop-feller does
Latch. fol 11 bring Victuals and Provifions aboard, in that
Cafe if the Contract be made there, it muft be
fued for in the Admiralty   But if the Goods
are by the Purfer or *Mariners* contracted for
at Land, they muft fue at *Common Law*

But a Suit in the Admiralty for Seamens
Wages grown due in the River, tho' no Voyage made, was not prohibited L *Raym* 1044.

Nor tho' made by Writing at Land; or
even by Deed. (*Q.* of this laft Point) L.
Raym 1206

The Mafter cannot fue in the Admiralty
for his Wages   L. *Raym* 576

Mafter of a Ship prohibited to fue the
Part-Owners in the Admiralty for Seamens
Wages which he had paid; for that Privilege
and

and Indulgence to Seamen is perfonal, and cannot be transferred. *Fortef Rep.* 230

IX If Goods are fo imbezzled, or fo dam- *This Doc-*
nified that the Ship's Crew muft anfwer, the *trine cited,*
Owners and Mafter muft deduct the fame out *L Raym.*
of their Freight to the Merchants, and the Maf- *650.*
ter out of the Wages of the *Mariners*, for tho'
Freight is the Mother of Wages, fo is it the
very Father of Damage, for before the *Mari-*
ner can claim his Wages out of what the Ship
hath earned, the Ship muft be acquitted from
the Damage that the Merchant hath fuftained
by the Negligence or Fault of the *Mariners*:
And the Reafon is, for that as the Goods are
obliged to anfwer the Freight, fo the Freight
and Ship is tacitly obliged to clear the Damage; which being done, the *Mariners* are *Leg. Oleron.*
then let in to their Wages.

X. If a Mariner be hired, and he deferts
the Service before the Voyage ended, by the
Law Marine he lofes his Wages And the
fame Cuftom at *Common Law* pleaded, it
hath been conceived will bar him

If a *Mariner* fhall commit any wilful or
negligent Fault, by reafon of which the Mafter, Owners, or the Ship anfwers Damage
to the Merchant, an Action lies well againft
him

In a Suit for Mariners Wages 'twas agreed, *1 Sid. 236.*
That if the Ship do not return, but perifhes by
Tempeft, Enemy, Fire, *&c* the Mariners
fhall lofe their Wages, for if the Mariners
fhall have their Wages in thefe Cafes, they
will not ufe their beft Endeavours, nor hazard
their Lives to preferve the Ship, *1 Sid.* 179.
But if the Ship unlade, they fhall have their
Wages, in the Cafe of *Culleneal v Mico,*
Keb. Rep. 831.

If

If a Seaman be preffed, he fhall have his Wages *pro ratâ* L. *Raym* 1211

XI. If a *Mariner* takes up Monies or Cloaths, and the fame is entered in the Purfer's Book, by the Cuftom *Marine* it is a Difcount or a Receipt of fo much of their Wages as the fame amounts to, and in an Action brought by them for their Wages, the fame fhall be allowed, and is not accounted mutual, the one to bring his Action for the Cloaths, and the other for his Wages.

Pafch 27 Car. in B R Pidgeon ad fect Argee per L. C. J. Hale Leg Oleron, c 13.

XII. A Mafter of a Ship may give moderate and due Correction to his *Mariners*, and if they bring an Action againft him, he may juftify the fame at the *Common Law*, and by the Law of *Oleron*, if a *Mariner* fhall affault the Mafter, he is to pay 5 *Solz*, or lofe his Hand.

Mariners after they have unladen the Ship, if they demand their Wages, and there be any Intention of their Departure, the Mafter may detain a reafonable Proportion of the fame till they bring back the Ship, or give Caution to ferve out the whole Voyage

Per Leg. Oleron, c. 18

XIII *Barretry* of the *Mariners* is a Difeafe fo epidemical on Ship-board, that it is very rare for a Mafter, be his Induftry never fo great, to prevent it, a Span of Villany on Ship-board foon fpreads out to a Cloud, for no other Caufe, but of that circular Encouragement that one knavifh *Mariner* gives another

Juft de ob jua ex dilect § Fin

However, the Law does in fuch Cafes impute *Offences* and *Faults* committed by them to be *Negligences* in the Mafter; and were it otherwife, the Merchant would be in a very dangerous Condition

Pafch 11 Jac in B. R Hern verfus Smith

The Reafons why they ought to be refponfible, are, for that the *Mariners* are of his own chufing, and under his Correction and Government,

vernment, and know no other Superior on Roll's A-
Ship-board but himself; and if they are faulty bridg.
he may correct and punish them, and justify 533.
the same by Law   And likewise if the Fact
is apparently proved against them, may re-
imburse himself out of their Wages.

XIV. And therefore in all Cases wherefo- *Naut Caup*
ever the Merchant loads aboard any Goods or *Stab. Leg* 1.
Merchandize, if they be Loft, Imbezzled, or § 3, 6, & 7.
any other ways Damnified, he must be re- 1 *Ven* 190,
238
sponsible for them , for the very lading them *Raym* 220.
aboard makes them liable, and that as well 1 *Mod* 85
by the *Common Law* as the *Law Marine*   2 *Lev* 69.

XV. Nay, if his *Mariners* go with the *Glof fupereod*
Ship-Boat to the Key or Wharf to fetch Goods *Sect verb &*
on Ship-board, if once they have taken Charge *factum.*
of them, the Master becomes immediately
responsible, if they Steal, Lose, Damnify or
Imbezzle them

XVI. The antienteft Record that is found
extant, is that in *Edward* the Third's Time,
where one brought an Action of Trefpafs
against the Mafter for the Imbezzlement by
his *Mariners* of twenty-two Pieces of Gold,
Bow, Sheaf of Arrows, Sword, and other
things ; and adjudged he should answer.   And
for that the same is or may be of great Moment, accept of a Tranfcript of the Record,
as the same was certified into *Chancery*, in order to have it fent into the *King's Bench*, to
enable the Plaintiff to bring an Action upon
the same Judgment in any Place in *England,*
where he could meet with the Defendant.

" V Enerabili in Chrifto Patri Domino J. *Brevia Regis*
Dei gratia Wygorn' Epifcopo Domi- *in Turre Lon-*
ni Regi3 Ed. Cancellario vel ejus locum te- *don Trin An-*
nenti fu humiles & devoti, Robertus Gyene, *no 24 E. 3 n.*
45. Briftol.

A a 4   Major

Major Ville Briftol, Edwardus Blankeit, & Johannes de Caftle-acre Ballivi libertatum ejufdem Ville, falutem cum omni reverentia & honore. De tenore & Recordi & procef-fus loquele que fuit coram nobis in Cur' Domini Regis ibidem fine brevi inter Hen. Pilk & Jurdanum Venore Magiftrum Navis vocat la Graciane de Bayone in pl'ito tranf-grefs' prout per breve Domini Regis nobis directum fuit vobis inde certificatur, fub fi-gillis noftris vobis fi placit mittimus in hiis fcriptis. Ad placit' *Tolls* tent' ibidem die Martis prox' poft Feftum *Epiphaniæ* Domini anno Regni Regis nunc 24 Hen Pilk quer' opt' fe verfus Jurdanum Venore Magiftrum Navis vocat' la Graciane de Bayone de pl'ito tranfgrefs' per' pl' &c. & unde quer', quod fecundum legem & confuetudinem de *OLE-RON* unufquifq, Magifter Navis tenetur ref-pondere de quacunque tranfgrefs' per fervien-tes fuos in eadem fact', & Johannes de Rule & Barcolet de Bornes fervientes predicti Jur-dani Magiftri Navis predicte die Mercur. prox' ante Feftum omnium Sanctorum Anno Regni predicti Regis Ed. 23. in Mari juxta Britan in eadem navi de Johanne de Cornub' fervient' predict' 22 libr' in auro, arcus, fagit' glad & al' bona & catalla ad valenc'. 40 *l.* ceperunt & afportaverunt injufte, &c. ad dampnum predict' Hen. 60 *l* & fi predictus Jurdanus hoc velit dedicere, predict Hen. paratus eft verificare, &c. Et predictus Jur-danus venit & dicit quod lex de *Oleron* talis eft quod fi aliqua bona & catalla Magiftro alicujus Navis liberata funt cuftodiend', unde idem Magifter pro eifdem vel pro aliqua alia re in eadem navi facta manucap' illo modo Magifter Navis tenetur refpondere, non alio modo,

modo, & fup' hoc petit Judicium. Et predict Hen. dicit, quod unufquifque Magifter
tenetur refpondere de quacunque tranfgreſ-
fione per fervientes fuos in Navi fua fact' &
petit Judicium fimiliter. Et fup' hoc predict' partes habent diem hic die Sabbati prox'
poft Feftum fci Hillarii prox' futur' ad audiend' Judicium fuum, &c Ad quem diem
predicte partes venerunt & petierunt Judicium
fuum, &c. Et recitat Recordo & proceffu
predictis in plena Curia coram Majore &
Bailivis & aliis probis hominibus Ville & Ma-
giftris & Marinariis, vifum fuit Curiee, quod
unufquifq, Magifter Navis tenetur refpondere
de quacunque tranfgreffione per fervientes
fuos in Navi fua facta Ideo confideratum
eft, quod predict' Hen recuperet dampna *The Judg-*
fua 40 *l.* verfus predict' Jurdanum per Cur *ment in this*
taxat' & nihilominus idem Jurdanus tranf- *cording to*
greffione predicta in mifericordia " *Law, and*
ought not to

have been a *capiatur ,* for it is not fuch a Trefpaſs as the King is entitled to a Fine, *Vide Cro Jac* 224. *Yelv* 162 *Beedle verfus Morris.*
Coke's Entries, *fol* 347

XVII. The Mafter fubject to anfwer Damage, is to be underftood in all fuch Cafes
where the Lading was brought aboard either
by his Confent or his Purfer's , for any other, *Leg in fin.*
or fuch as fhall be fecretly brought in, not *Naut Caup.*
being entered in the Purfer's Book, or in the *per leg itaque*
Bills of Lading, the Mafter is not obliged to *de furtis.*
fee forth-coming, unlefs it be fuch Goods as
the Parties bring into the Ship about them,
as Clothes, Money, and the like, as above,
thofe things being feldom entered, yet moft
commonly thofe that are vifible, the Mafter
by Law is refponfible for

XVIII. So likewife if a Mafter forewarn a *Eod Leg. in*
Paffenger to keep his Goods, and that he will *fin Naut*
no *Caup & per*

leg. itaque de ead. edict. Bart & Jason in leg. non solum.

no ways take Care of them, and if they be loft or purloined by the Crew, he will not be obliged to fee them forth-coming; the Mafter is not there held refponfible in Cafe of a Lofs, efpecially if there be any thing of Agreement thereunto

§ *mortem de non oper.*

XIX. But if Goods fhall be fent aboard a Ship, and the Mafter fhall appoint a Cabbin for the fame, and deliver the Key to the Lader, and tell him he will not be refponfible if a Lofs happens; yet if the Goods are ftole, he muft notwithftanding make Satisfaction: By the *Common Law* it fhall bind an Innkeeper. *Mo.* 78.

8 *Coke* 33. a *Mo.* 158. *Salk.* 18.

But if the Inn-keeper defires his Gueft to put his Goods in fuch a Chamber under Lock and Key, &c and then he will warrant, otherwife not, and the Gueft leaves them in an outer Court, where they are ftole, &c. the Inn-keeper fhall not be charged.

Note, That Goods once delivered to a Mafter, the Cargo is not fubject to be attached in his Hands, nor can any Cuftom whatfoever fupport the fame; for they are in Law as it were bailed to the Ship, until the

Mich. 27 Car 2. *per* Lord Chief Juftice Hale.

Freight and all other Charges are paid And very much doubted, whether an Attachment can be made in *London* of any Goods at all lying on Ship-board in the River of *Thames,* (which, though the Port of *London*) notwithftanding Freight and all other Charges are paid off.

Hill 8 *Annæ in Chancery.* 2 *Eq. Caf. Abr.* 98. *pl.* 1

Commiffioners of Bankrupt iffued a Warrant to feize Goods of the Bankrupt on board two Ships in *Topfham Bay* in *Devonfhire,* the Goods were configned to Perfons in *Holland,* who had not paid the Bankrupt for them: The Mafters refufed to deliver the Goods, not-

notwithstanding the Warrant; which occasioned the Commissioners coming to demand the Goods, which still were refused.

Sir *Peter King* moved for an Order upon the Masters for their Contempt

The Court at first greatly doubted, whether they can make an Order in Aid and Assistance of the Warrant of the Commissioners of Bankrupt, the Statute having vested a large Power in them, besides, the Persons to whom the Goods are consigned, would be indebted to the Creditors of the Bankrupt, which Creditors may recover by the Law of *Holland*.

Sir *Peter King*. We shall rather lose the Goods, than follow them into *Holland*.

Lord Chancellor Cowper. Their refusing to deliver the Goods upon the Warrant, is no Contempt to this Court, tho' the Commissioners act under a Commission under the Broad Seal. I remember the Queen was applied to, to lay an Embargo upon a Ship in the like Case, but denied; because an Embargo would have affected other Goods in the Ship. The Masters in this present Case have some Colour to detain the Goods; for upon a Delivery of them, they may be disappointed of Freight, and the Assignees of the Commission must stand in the same Place as the Bankrupt, and be subject to his Contract

But however, an Order was made upon the Masters to deliver the Goods upon Payment of the Freight Money, and the Masters to be indemnified by the Creditors, against a Bill of Lading, which was sent to the Consignees.

CHAP.

CHAP. IV.

Of Freight, Charter-parties, and De-morage.

I. *The various ways that Ships may be freighted at this Day.*

II. *The antient way of Freighting.*

III. *How the same is governed upon the various Contracts, and of Accidents happening to Masters or Laders preventing the Voyage.*

IV. *Of Agreements parol and in Writing, how construed by the Common Law; what it is.*

V. *Of Ships laded and unladed before the Voyage begun, their becoming disabled, viz. perish in the Voyage before the same is compleated*

VI *Of Ships Departure considered in reference to Freight and Damage.*

VII. *Of Freight arising on Trading Voyages, and lost by contingent Actions, considered by the Common Law, and the Law Marine*

VIII *Of Freight becoming due upon the various ways of Contract, or general where none was agreed for.*

IX *Of Faults arising from the Freighters, and of the Decease of the Ship in reference to Freight.*

X. *Faults of Masters arising from taking in Goods more than were contracted for, and of being forced into Ports in his Passage.*

XI *Passengers dying, the Ship's Title to their Goods and Concerns.*

XII *The Ship in construction of Law how far liable to Freight.*

XIII *Ships taken and retaken in War, whether the same destroys the Contract*

XIV. *Goods become lost without Fault of the Ship, whether Freight becomes due.*

XV. *Of Freight contracted with Persons deficient.*

XVI. *Of Ships contracted for by the Month, to be paid at the Arrival at a Port, Ship is cast away, the Goods saved. Whether the Freight ought to be paid.*

XVII,

XVII. *Covenant mutual in a Charter-party, shall not be pleaded the one against the other Plea that answers to Part only is ill. Covenant therein by several, yet brought against one only Covenant by several &* quemlibet eorum, *may be brought against one only.*

I. IN the *Freighting* of Ships, respect is always had to the Ship itself, or else to a certain Part thereof.

Again, the Merchants either Freight her by the *Month*, or the *entire* Voyage, or by the *Tun*; for it is one thing to Freight a Ship, and another thing to take certain *Tunage* to Freight.

So also it is one thing to be a Cape-Merchant, another to be an under Freighter.

II. There was of old another way of Freighting; which was, when the Merchant agreed with the Master for a Sum certain to convey his Goods ensured against all Peril; such were to be responsible if any Detriment or Loss happened, but that is now become obsolete. *21 E 3. Cotton's Records, 63.*

III. *Freight* is governed generally by the Contract, and varies according to the Agreement, reduced generally into a Writing, commonly called a *Charter-party*, executed between the Owners and Merchant, or the Master in the Behalf of himself and Owners, or himself and the Merchant, or between them all; or else is Parol *Naut. eaup Stab &c Leg. 1 § quancunque vim. Si quis navem conduxerit, instrumenta consignata sunto. Pekieus com. ad Leg Rhod Art 20*

The Master or Owners generally covenant to provide a *Pilot* and all other Officers and *Mariners*, and all other things necessary for the Voyage, and for the taking in and delivering out of the Lading

If there be an Agreement and *Earnest*, but no Writing, if the same be broke off by the Merchant, he loseth his *Earnest*, but if *Per Leg. Naval Rhod Art 19.*

the

the Owners or Master repent, they lose double the *Earnest*.

Cro. Car. 383.   But by the *Common Law* of *England*, the Party damnified may bring his Action of the Case, and recover all Damages on the Agreement

Per Leg item § Si in Leg. loca.   If a time be appointed by the *Charty-party*, and either the Ship is not ready to take in, or the Merchant not ready to lade aboard, the Parties are at Liberty, and the Party Damnified hath his Remedy against the other by Action, to recompence the Detriment.

If Part of the Lading be on Ship-board, and it happens some Misfortune may overtake the Merchant, that he hath not his full Lading aboard at the time, the Master is at Liberty to contract with another, and shall have Freight by way of Damage for the time that those Goods were aboard after the time limited; for such Agreements being of a Conditional nature Precedent, a Failure, as to a compleat Lading, will determine the same, unless afterwards *affirmed by Consent*   And though it be no Prudence for every Merchant or every Master to depart from the Contract, if it should so fall out, that the Agreement as to the Lading is not performed according to Promise, ('seldom or ever done if any Part be aboard) yet it is the highest Justice, that Ships and Masters should not be Infettered, but Free; for otherwise by the bare lading of a Cask or Bale, they might be defeated of the Opportunity of Passage or Season of the Year.

Cro. Car 383. 3 *Lev. no* 283 *Per Leg fi ex corduct & Leg fuit in fundus & Leg.*   So on the other hand, if the Vessel is not ready, the Merchant may ship aboard in another Vessel the Remainder of his Goods, and discharge the first Skipper, and recover Damages against the Master or Owners for the rest   This is grounded upon the like Reason as the former.   And

And therefore by the *Law Marine*, Chance, or some other notorious Neceffity, will excufe the *Mafter*; but then he lofeth his Freight till fuch time as he *breaks ground*, and till then he fuftains the Lofs of the Ship

But if the Fault be in the Merchant, he then muft anfwer the Mafter and the Ship's Damage, or elfe be liable to entertain the Ship's *Crew* ten Days at his own Charge; but if after that, then the full Freight: And if any Damage happens afterwards, the Merchant muft run the Rifque of that, and not the Mafter or Owners. (a) But by the *Common Law*, fo long as the Mafter hath the Goods on Ship-board, he muft fee them forthcoming

IV. *Charter-parties* have always, by the *Common Law*, had a genuine Conftruction as near as may be, and according to the Intention and Defign, and not according to the literal Senfe of Traders, or thofe that Merchandize by Sea, yet they muft be regularly pleaded; and therefore in an Action of Covenant on an Indenture dated 9 *Oct* 38 *El.* wherein was recited, Whereas by Indenture of *Charter-party* dated *Sep.* 8. 38 *Eliz.* between the Plaintiff and *Francis Cherry*, the Plaintiff having hired of him a Ship, for a Voyage to *Dantzick*, upon taking Ship it was agreed between them, that the Ship fhould be laden with Corn at *Dantzick,* and to fail to *Leghorn.* Now by the faid Indenture, in Confideration the Plaintiff had agreed, that the Defendant fhould have the Moiety of Corn, *quod tunc fuit*, or afterwards fhould be laden in theShip during the faid Voyage, the Defendant covenanted to pay the Moiety of the Money

for

hæc diftinctio.
Per Leg Oleron cap 21

Art 25 Legem Naval Art 29 eod.
(a) 1 *Mod* 85.
Raym 220.
1 *Ven.* 190, 238.
2 *Keb.* 866.
3*Keb.*72,112, 135.

for the said Corn, *quod tunc fuit*, or afterwards should be laden. &c. and alledgeth *in facto*, that Oct 9. 38 *Eliz.* the Ship was laden with 60 Lasts of Corn, and for not Performance of this Covenant the Action was brought, the Defendant pleaded that the Deed was sealed and delivered Oct. 28. 38 *Eliz & quod ad tunc vel postea* there was not any Corn laden there, and traverseth the Delivery Oct. 9. or at any time afterwards before the 28 Oct 38 *Eliz.* And it was adjudged upon Demurrer, That in regard the Plaintiff declared upon a Deed, dated Oct 9 38 *Eliz.* it shall be intended to have its Essence and Delivery at that time, and no other; and if he should confess it to be delivered at any other time, it would be a Departure from his Declaration, and the Word *tunc* is referred to the Delivery, and not to the Date, and if it were delivered ten Months after the Date, he should not have the Benefit of the Corn laden before the Delivery And therefore the Defendant was adjudged not to be charged with paying for any Corn before the Delivery of the Deed, the Words of the Deed being, that he should pay for the Corn then laden, &c. which (*then*) is referred to the time of the Essence of the Deed by the Delivery, and not to the Date.

Cro. Ja 263.
Osley v. Sir
Baptist Hicks.

3 Bulst. 152.
1 Ro 312

Atkinson did contract with *Buckle* for the Carriage of 100 Quarters of Barley, and did promise to deliver unto him the 100 Quarters of Barley, a Ship-board at *Barton* Haven, in the County of *York*, to carry them for him, and for the Carriage thereof did promise to pay to him so much, and *Buckle* promised to carry the same for him, and accordingly brought his Ship to the said Haven, expect-

ing

ing there the Delivery of the 100 Quarters of Barley, but *Atkinson* came not to deliver the same to him, whereupon *Buckle* brought his Action of the Case upon the Promise, and upon *non Assumpsit* pleaded had a Verdict and Judgment, which was affirmed upon a Writ of Error.

Charter-party (*Charta partita*, i e a Deed of Writing divided) is all one in the Civil Law, with an Indenture at the Common Law. It settles the Agreement and Bills of Lading, the Contents of the Cargo, and binds the Master to deliver them well conditioned at the place of Discharge, according to the Contents of the Charter-party or Agreement, and for Performance, the Master obliges Himself, Ship, Tackle, and Furniture, to see the same done and performed.

Covenant upon a Charter-party between *Bolton* Owner, and *Lee* and *Morgan* Merchants, Freighters of a Ship, by which *Bolton* put to Freight the Ship in a Voyage to *Guiney* at 48 *l. per Mensem*, and there was a mutual Covenant between the Parties *& quemlibet eorum modo sequente*, and then divers Covenants follow concerning the Ship's Tackle and Performance of the Voyage ; and then a Covenant for the Payment of the Freight (*viz*) when the Ship arrived at *Guiney*, the Freight then due was upon Notice to be paid in *England*, and when she arrived in *England* the Residue from the time of the last Payment was to be paid. And saith, that at such a time the Ship arrived, and that 6 Months and 10 Days were then past, which came to so much, whereof Notice was given, and that after such a time the Ship arrived at *England*, and that the Freight for 6 Months,

Covenant inter A of the one Part, and B and C on the other, & quemlibet eorum, and the Action brought against one only, and well

from the time of the last Payment, and the Freight came to 287 *l.* 4 *s.* and that the Defendant had not paid any of the Sums, upon which the Defendant demurred And took these Exceptions to the Declaration:

Tarrsley 154
Salk 393.
pl. 2.

1. For this that the Action is brought against one of the Defendants only, omitting the other, *fed non allocatur,* the Covenant being between them *& quemlibet eorum* is joint and several of every Part.

2. For that it appears upon Computation, the Plaintiff demanded more upon the first Breach than is due by 30 *s.* and less than is due upon the second by 16 *s.* and tho' that the first may be cured by the Jurors finding less, or by the Plaintiff's releasing the Overplus, yet where he demands less than his due, it is incurable, and cited several Books there quoted for that purpose in Assumpsit, where, as in this Case, only Damages are to be recovered; and on the other Part was cited, *Cro. Jack.* 498. *Pemberton v. Shelton,* & 529. *Parker v. Curson & uxor,* see 2 *Levinz* 4. *Hulme & Sambers,* & 2 *Vent* 129. *Welby & Philips* *Hale* Chief Justice took a Difference between this Case or Covenant, and Debt, and held, that after Verdict it had been cured without Question, but upon Demurrer there may be some Doubt, the Demurrer being general, but had the Demurrer been special it had been ill, and ruled Judgment, *pro Quer.* 2 *Levinz* 56. & 3 *Keble* 39. & 50. *Bolton* and *Lee.*

If Goods are fully laded aboard, and the Ship hath *broke Ground,* the Merchant on Consideration afterwards resolves not on the *Adventure,* but will unlade again, by the *Law Marine* the Freight is due.

And

And if the Ship in her Voyage becomes *unable* without the Master's Fault, or that the Master or Ship be arrested by some Prince or State in her Voyage, the Master may either *mend his Ship, or Freight another.* *Judg Oleron. Leg ult. ad. Rhod.*

But if the Merchant will not agree to the same, then the *Freight* becomes due for so much as the Ship hath *earned*, for otherwise the Master is liable for all Damages that shall happen. And therefore if that Ship, to which the Goods were tranflated, perifhed, the Master fhall anfwer; but if both the Ships perifh, then he is difcharged *Digeft Paulus, l 14 c 2. §. 10.*

But if there be extreme Neceffity, as that the Ship is in a finking Condition, and an empty Ship is paffing by, or at hand, he may tranflate the Goods; and if that Ship fink or perifhes, he is there excufed · But then it muft be apparent that that Ship feemed *probable* and *fufficient.*

VI. If a fet time be fixed and agreed upon between the Merchant and the Mafter, wherein to begin and finifh his Voyage, it may not be altered by the *Supra Cargo*, without fpecial Commiffion for that Purpofe. *Leg qui Romæ § Callimachus, ff ae verb obl.*

If a Mafter fhall weigh Anchor, and ftand out to his Voyage after the time covenanted or agreed on for his Départute, if any Damage happens at Sea after that time, he fhall refund and make good all fuch Misfortune · Yet if a *Charter-party* is made, that the Plaintiff fhall fail from *London* to *Lisbon* with the firft Wind and Opportunity, &c in Confideration of which the Merchant did covenant to pay fo much for Freight, the Ship departs not with the firft Wind and Opportunity, yet afterwards *breaks Ground,* and arrives at

B b 2   her

Popham. 161
Palm 398.
Latch. 12 49.
her Port, the Freight in this Cafe is become due; for there is nothing can bar the Ship of her Freight but the not Departure, for only that in Law is traverfable, being material to avoid the Payment of Freight, but to fay the Ship did not depart with the next-Wind, is but a Circumftance which in ftrictnefs of Law is not traverfable.

Argl. Alex &
Jafon in dict
§ Callima-
chus
If it be agreed, that the Mafter fhall fail from *London* to *Leghorn* in two Months, and Freight accordingly is agreed on, if he be-gins the Voyage within the two Months, tho' he does not arrive at *Leghorn* within the time, yet the Freight is become due.

2 Vern 210.
Where the *Eaft-India Company* by Charter-party might keep the Ship a long time in *In-dia*, and did fo keep her until fhe was unfit for Service, and could not come Home; they were obliged in *Chancery* to pay the Damage; tho' by the perufing of the Charter-party it was payable at the Return of the Ship.

2 Vern 212
So where no Freight was to be paid for the Cargo outwards but Freight for the Cargo homewards; and the Factor abroad had no Goods to load her homewards, Payment of the Freight was decreed.

2 Vern 727
So though the Officers and Mariners gave Bond not to demand Wages unlefs the Ship returned to *London*, fhe arrived at a deliver-ing Port, and afterwards was taken by the Enemy. They had their Wages to the de-livering Port

Leg Pelega.
ff. de pœnis &
Leg li de
Sep vio.
VII. If the Ship is freighted from one Port to another Port, and thence to a third, fourth, and fo home to the Port from whence fhe firft failed, (commonly called a *Trading Voyage*) this is all but one and the fame Voy-age,

age, fo as it be in Conformity to the *Charter-party*.

A Merchant agrees with a Mafter, that if he carries his Goods to fuch a Port, he will then pay him fuch a Sum, in the Voyage the Ship is affaulted, entered and robbed by Pirates, and part of her Lading taken forth, and afterwards the Remainder is brought to the Port of Difcharge, yet the Sum agreed upon is not become due, for the Agreement is not by the Mafter performed.

Trin. 9. Jac in C. B Rot. 638 Bright verfus Cooper, 1. Brownl. 21.

But by the *Civil Law* this is *vis major* or *cafus fortuitus*, there being no Default in the Mafter or his Mariners, and the fame is a Danger or Peril of the Sea, which if not in Naval Agreements expreffed, yet is naturally implied: For moft certain, had thofe Goods, which the Pirates carried away in ftrefs of Weather, *Navis levandæ caufa*, been thrown over-board, the fame would not have made a Difability as to the Receipt of the Sum agreed on, for by both the *Common Law* and the *Law Marine*, the Act of God, or that of an Enemy, fhall no ways work a Wrong in Actions private.

1 Co 97 Shelley's Cafe. Reginer and Fogaffa's Cafe. Plowden Com 1. But a Pirate is not an Enemy. Vide Chap. Piracy.

VIII. If a Ship be freighted by the Tun, and fhe is full laden according to the *Charter-party*, the Freight is to be paid for the whole; otherwife but for fo many Tun as the Lading amounted to

If Freight be contracted for the lading of certain Cattle, or the like, from *Dublin* to *Weft-Chefter*, if fome of them happen to die before the Ship's Arrival at *Weft-Chefter*, the whole Freight is become due as well for the Dead as the Living *.

Leg fi quis Cod. de juftit. & fubftit

* *Arg. Leg.*

But if the Freight be contracted for the tranfporting them, if Death happens, there arifeth

fcioff de ann. legat & leg. illis libert .

B b 3

fin ff de condit
& demon.
Arg. 7.

† *Leg. qui ope-*
ra, & Leg. si
edes § cum
quidam & §.
si. ff. locati
Leg. sed &
addes in § Si
quis mulierem
ff. locat.

ariseth due no more Freight than only for such as are living, at the Ship's Arrival at her Port of Discharge, and not for the Dead †.

If the Cattle or Slaves are sent aboard, and no Agreement is made either for lading or transporting them, but generally, then Freight shall be paid as well for the Dead as the Living.

If Freight be contracted for the transporting of Women, and they happen in the Voyage to be delivered of Children on Shipboard, no Freight becomes due for the Infants.

There are 3
Bills of lading
generally
made, the
one to be sent
over Sea to
him whom
the Goods are
consigned to,
the other for
the Master,
and the last
for the Mer-
chant or
Lader.

The *Charter-party* does settle the Agreement, and the Bills of Lading the Contents of the Cargo, and binds the Master to deliver them well conditioned at the Place of Discharge, according to the Contents of the *Charter-party* or Agreement, and for Performance, the Master obliges Himself, Ship, Tackle and Furniture to see the same done and performed.

If Goods are sent aboard, generally the Freight must be according to Freight for the like accustomed Voyages

If a Ship shall be freighted and named to be of such a Burden, and being freighted by the Tun shall be found less, there shall no more be paid than only by the Tun for all such Goods as were laded aboard.

If a Ship be freighted for two hundred Tuns or thereabouts, the addition of *thereabouts* is commonly reduced to be within five Tun, more or less, as the Moiety of the number *Ten*, whereof the whole number is compounded.

If

If a Ship be freighted by the great, and the Burden of it not expreſſed, yet the Sum certain is to be paid.

Chaſe & Jones
verſ Lovering
Styles
220

IX. If the Ship, by reaſon of any Fault ariſing from the Freighter, as lading aboard prohibited or unlawful Commodities, occaſions a Detention, or otherwiſe impedes the Ship's Voyage, he ſhall anſwer the Freight contracted and agreed for.

Leg. penult. §
9. *F. de locat.*

If a Ship be freighted *out* and *in*, there ariſes due for Freight, nothing, till the whole Voyage be performed: So that if the Ship die, or is caſt away coming-home, the Freight outwards, as well as inwards becomes loſt.

Trin 9. Jac.
B. R. Bright.
verſ Cowper,
Brownlow,
1 *part 21.*

13th *July*, 1680, in Chancery, a Part-Owner of a Ship ſued the other Owners, for his Share of the Freight of the Ship which finiſhed her Voyage; but the other Owners ſet her out, and the Complainant would not join with them in ſetting her out, or in the Charge thereof, whereupon the other Owners complained in the Admiralty, and by Order there, the other Owners gave Security, That if the Ship periſhed in the Voyage, to make good to the Plaintiff his Share, or to that effect; in ſuch a Caſe, by the Law Marine, and Courſe of the Admiralty, the Plaintiff was to have no Share of the Freight It was referred to Sir *Lionel Jenkins* to certify the Courſe of the Admiralty, who certified accordingly, and that it was ſo in all places, for otherwiſe there would be no Navigation, whereupon the Plaintiff's Bill was diſmiſt See more of Freight, and the Incidents thereunto, *Lex Mercatoria* 100

X If a Maſter freights out his Ship, and afterwards ſecretly takes in other Goods unknown to the firſt Laders, by the Law Ma-

Leg. Oleron.
Leg. Naval.
Rhod. Art. 2.

rine

rine he loses his Freight; and if it should so fall out, that any of the Freighter's Goods should for Safety of the Ship be cast overboard, the rest shall not become subject to the Average, but the Master must make good that out of his own Purse: But if the Goods are brought into the Ship secretly against his Knowledge, it is otherwise, and Goods so brought in, the same may be subjected to what Freight the Master thinks fitting

Consol. del Mer.

If the Ship puts into any other Port than what she was freighted to, the Master shall answer Damage to the Merchant, but if forced in by Storm or by Enemy, or Pirates, he then must sail to the Port conditioned at his own Costs

Leg. Oleron.

Generally the touching at several Ports by Agreement, imports not a Diversity, but a Voyage entire

Rule

XI If Passengers having Goods, happen to die on Ship-board, the Master is to *inventory* their Concerns, and the same may keep a Year, and if none claim the same, the Master becomes Proprietor defeasable But the Bedding and Furniture of the Parties become the Master's and his Mates, and the Cloathing are to be brought to the *Ship-Mast-Head*, and there praised and distributed amongst the *Crew*, as a Reward for their Care of seeing the Body put into the Sea.

Leg. Corsolat. del Merc.

The Captain died leaving Money on board, the Mate became Captain, and improved the Money: He shall, on Allowance for his Care in the Management of it, account for the Profits, and not for the Interest only

1 P. Will. 140

XII The Lading of the Ship in Construction of Law, is *tacitly* obliged for the Freight, the same being, in Point of Payment, preferred

Bald in leg certi juris ir 4 2 in verb.

ferred before any other Debts to which the *Quid ergo Cod.* Goods so laden are liable, though such Debts, *locat* as to time, were *precedent* to the Freight, for the Goods remain as it were bailed for the same : Nor can they be *attatched* in the Master's Hands, though vulgarly it is conceived otherwise.

Ships deserve *Wages* like unto a Labourer; and therefore in the Eye of the Law, the Actions touching the same, are generally construed favourably for the Ship and her Ow- *Stanley versus* ners : And therefore if four Part-Owners of *Ayles by Hale,* five, shall make up their Accounts with the 3 *Keble* 444. Freighters, and receive their Proportions, yet the fifth Man may sue singly by himself without joining with the rest, and this as well by the *Common Law* as the *Law Marine.*

XIII A Ship in her Voyage happens to be taken by an Enemy, aftewards in Battle is re-taken by another Ship in Amity, and Restitution is made, and she proceeds on in her Voyage, the Contract is not determined, though the taking by the Enemy divested the 7 *R. 2 Sta-* Property out of the Owners, yet by the Law *tham* Abridg. of War that Possession was defeasable, and 54 being recovered in Battle afterwards, the *In Jure Posli-* Owners became re-invested. So the Contract, *minii leg re-* by Fiction of Law, became as if she never *tor. & leg. in* had been taken, and so the entire Freight be- *bello,* § 1. comes due.

Covenant by a Charter-party, that the Ship shall return within the River of *Thames* by a certain time (*periculis & casualitatibus Marium, Anglicè,* Dangers of the Sea, *exceptis*) and after in the Voyage, and within the time of the Return, the Ship was taken upon the Sea, *per homines bellicosos modo guerrino arraiatos,* to the Covenantor unknown, *&c. & abinde*

abinde huc uſque detenta fuit by them, *per quod* he could not return within the River of *Thames* within the time mentioned in the Covenant. Reſolved this Impediment was within the Exception, for theſe Words intend as well any Danger upon the Sea by Pirates and Men of War, as Dangers of the Sea by Shipwreck, Tempeſt, or the like. *Pickering* and *Barkley, Stiles* 132. *&* 2 *Roll*'s Abridg. 248.

Boyce v. Cole, Hill. 26, 27 *Car.* 2. *B. R.*

XIV. If Freight be taken for 100 Tuns of Wine, and twenty of them leak out, ſo that there is not above eight Inches from the Buge upwards, yet the Freight becomes due: One Reaſon is, becauſe from that Gage the King becomes entitled to Cuſtom; but if they be under eight Inches, by ſome it is conceived to be then in the Election of the Freighters to fling them up to the Maſter for Freight, and the Merchant is diſcharged But moſt conceive otherwiſe; for if all had leaked out, (if there was no Fault in the Maſter) there is no Reaſon the Ship ſhould loſe her Freight; for the Freight ariſes from the Tunnage taken, and if the Leakage was occaſioned through Storm, the ſame perhaps may come into an Average Beſides, in *Bourdeaux* the Maſter ſtows not the Goods, but the particular Officers appointed for that Purpoſe, *quod nota.* Perhaps a ſpecial Convention may alter the Caſe.

When ſuch Misfortune happens, the Inſured commonly transfer thoſe Goods over to the Aſſurors,

Moſt certain, if a Ship, freighted by the Great, be caſt away, the Freight vaniſhes; but if by the Tun or Pieces of Commodity, and ſhe happens to be caſt away, afterwards Part is ſaved, doubted whether *pro rata* ſhe ought not to be anſwered her Freight.

who take them towards Satisfaction of what they pay by Virtue of their Subſcriptions.

Debt

Debt upon a Charter-party upon a Penalty, the Covenant was to pay so much *per* Tun for Freight, and Breach was assigned in *non* Payment, for so many Tun and an Hogshead, which came to so much. Upon Demurrer, 'twas held the Declaration was ill, for the Covenant is only to pay so much *per* Tun; *aliter* if it had been to pay *secundam ratam* of so much *per* Tun. *Roe* against *Barns.* 2 Levinz 124. 3 *Keble* 421.

Yelv. 134.

XV. If a Merchant takes Freight by contracting with a Mariner that is not a Master, if Loss happens, he must be contented to sit down without any Remedy against the Owners; but perhaps such a Mariner for such an Act may subject himself to an Action.

But if there be a Fault committed by a Mariner which was hired, or put in by the Master or Owners; there for Reparation the Owners become liable

4 Inst. 146.

XVI. The Master is not bound to answer Freight to the Owners for Passengers, if they are found to be unable to pay.

Johannes Locunus, l. 3. c. 8.

If Ship by *Charter-party* reciting to be of the Burden of 200 Tuns is taken to Freight for a Sum certain, to be paid at her Return, the Sum certain is to be paid, though the Ship amounts not to that Burden

If a Ship is freighted after the Rate of 20 *l.* for every Month that she shall be out, to be paid after arrival at the Port of *London*; the Ship is cast away coming up from the *Downs*, but the Lading is all preserved, yet the Freight is become due. For the Money arises due monthly by the Contract, and the Place mentioned is only to shew where Payment is to be made, for the Ship deserves Wages like a Mariner who serveth by the Month;

and

and though he dies in the Voyage, yet his Executors are to be anfwered *pro rata.* Befides, the Freight becomes due by intendment on the Delivery or bringing up of the Commodities to the Port of *London,* and not of the Ship.

Bulftr. 176.
Inft 204. a
Dy. 76. a.
2 *Band.* 350.
If a Man freights a Ship out, and covenants that the Ship with the firft Wind and Opportunity fhould fail out of that Port to *Cales,* and the Freighter covenants that he for the Freight of all the Premiffes would pay unto the Mafter 184 *l. pro tota tranfretatione omnium premiffarum,* if the Mafter doth not aver that the Ship did arrive at the Port of *Cales,* he cannot maintain an Action againft the Freighter.

If the Mafter enters into a *Charter-party* for himfelf and Owners, the Mafter in that cafe may releafe the Freighters without advifing with the Owners; but if the Owners let out to Freight fuch a Ship, whereof *J. S.* is Mafter, though the Mafter covenant in the fame *Charter-party* and fubfcribes, yet his Releafe in that cafe will not bind the Owners, but the Owners Releafe on the other hand will conclude the Mafter. And the reafon is, for that the Mafter is not made a proper Party to the Indenture. And fo it was ruled, where an *Indenture* of *Charter-party* was made between *Scudamore* and other Owners of the good Ship called the *B.* whereof *Robert Pitman* was Mafter on the one Part, and *Vandenftene* on the other Part, in which Indenture the Plaintiff did covenant with the faid *Vandenftene* and *Robert Pitman,* and bound themfelves to the Plaintiff and *Robert Pitman* for Performance of Covenants in 600 *l.* and the Conclufion of the Indenture was, ——*In witnefs witness whereof* the said *Robert Pitman* put his Hand and Seal, and delivered the same; in an Action of Covenant for not performing certain Covenants in this Indenture, the Defendant pleaded the Release of *Pitman*, whereupon the Plaintiff demurred And it was adjudged, That the Release of *Pitman* did not bar the Plaintiff, because he was no Party to the Indenture; and the Diversity in that case was taken and agreed between an Indenture reciprocal between Parties on the one side, and Parties on the other side, as that was, for there no Bond, Covenant or Grant can be made to or with any that is not Party to the Deed, but where the Deed indented is not reciprocal, but is without a *Between &c* as *Omnibus Christi fidelibus, &c* there a Bond, Covenant or Grant may be made to divers several Persons.

Cro. Eliz 56. *Scudamore & al' v Pitman.* *Trin* 29 *Eliz in B. R.* cited in 2 *Inst.* 673 2 *Levinz* 74. *Cook & Child,* 3 *Levinz* 138 *Gilby versus Copley.* *que semble contra.*

If an Indenture of *Charter-party* be made between *A* and *B*. Owners of a Ship of the one Part, and *C*. and *D* Merchants of the other Part, and *A*. only seals the Deed of the one Part, and *C* and *D*. of the other Part; but in the Indenture it is mentioned that *A* and *B*. covenant with *C*. and *D*. and *C* and *D*. covenant with *A*. *B*. in this Case *A*. and *B*. may join in an Action against *C*. and *D*. tho' that *B*. never sealed the Deed, for he is a Party to the Deed, and *C*. and *D*. have sealed the other Part to *B*. as well as to *A*. *Clement* against *Henley*, 2 *Rolls Abr.* 22.

XVII. Covenant upon a *Charter-party*, by which the Master of the Ship covenants to sail with the first fair Wind to *Barcelona*, and that the Mariners shall attend with a Boat to relade the Ship, and then to return with the first fair Wind to *London*, and to unlade and deliver

Covenants mutual shall not be pleaded one against the other.

deliver the Goods, and the Merchants covenant to pay so much for Freight, and so much for Demurage every Day, the Master brought his Action for the Freight and Demurage, and declares that he sailed such a Day with the first fair Wind, and upon all the other Points. The Defendant, *quoad* the Freight, that the Ship did not return directly to *London*, but went to *Alicant* and *Tangier*, and made divers Deviations, and by these Delays the Goods were spoiled, and as to the Demurage, that this was occasioned by the Negligence of the Mariners in not attending with the Boat to relade the Ship, to which the Plaintiff demurred, and *per Curiam pro Quer.* for that the Covenants are mutual and reciprocal, upon which each shall have his Action against the other, but shall not plead the Breach of one in bar of another, for perhaps the Damage of the one side and of the other are not equal. 3 *Levinz* 41. *Cole contra Shallet.* Sir *Tho. Jones* 216. *Showers* against *Cudmore.*

Plea that answers to Part only is ill.
Cro El. 268
pl 3 330 pl
10 433, 434
Cro Jac 27
1 Sand 27, 28.
2 Sand. 127.
Lutw 1492
Ploud. 138.

In Covenant the Plaintiff declared, that he covenanted to sail with a Ship to D. in *Ireland*, and there to take 280 Men of the Defendant's, and to carry them to *Jamaica*, and the Defendant covenanted to have the 280 Men there ready, and to pay for their Carriage 5 *l.* for each Man, and that the Defendant had not the 280 Men ready, but that he had 180, which he took on board, and carried them, but that the Defendant had not paid for them; the Defendant pleaded that he had the 280 Men ready, and tendered to the Plaintiff, who refused to receive them, but said nothing as to the carrying of the 180 Men, nor to the Payment for them, and for that it was not a Plea to all, Judgment was given for the Plaintiff upon Demurrer, 1 *Levinz* 16 1 *Keble* 100.

C H A P.

CHAP V.

Of Wreck.

I. IN matters of *Wreck*, there is, as it were, a Contract between them which have lost their Goods by such Misfortune, and them upon whose Lands the Goods and Merchandize are driven, that the same be restored to them or those that claim under them. And therefore by the *Civil Law*, it is precisely forbid, that no Man shall meddle with such Goods as are wreckt, and such as are proved to have stolen any thing thereout, are holden

Leg. ne quid ff. de incendio, ruina & naufragio.

for

Leg. 44. D. de
acq. rer dom.
for Robbers, for that such Goods being cast
on Land and recovered out of the Sea, remain still his who was the Owner thereof, and
descend upon his Successor; neither Escheat
to the King, neither to any other to whom
the King hath granted such Royal Privilege.

The reason why the Laws were so strictly
declared by the *Romans*, was, for that by the
Laws of *Rhodes*, if any Ship had become
Wreck, though all the Persons were saved
and alive, yet the Ship and Goods became
seizable by the Lord. But the same being
barbarous, was afterwards repealed and abrogated.

The Emperor *Constantine* the Great says,
in this Case, if any Ship at any time by any
Shipwreck be driven to the Shore, or touch
Leg 1. lib 11.
C. de Naufrag.
at any Land, *Let the Owner have it, and let
not my Exchequer meddle with it. For what
Right hath my Exchequer in another Man's Calamity, so that it should hunt after Gain in such
a woful Case as this is?*

And yet if no Kindred appear within a
Year and a Day, or, appearing, prove not
the Goods shipwrecked to be theirs, the Goods
come to the *Exchequer*, even by that Law:
So much that Law condemns Carelessness,
which is written, *vigilantibus & non dormien-
tibus, &c.* And with this agree the Laws of
Oleron and the Laws of this Land, as taken
out of those Imperial Laws, in that Point, as
is conceived.

*Leg 1. in pr.
de incend ruin
leg. 1r eam cum
auth seq de
furt. Leg 3
in fin de in-
cend ruin.
naufrag*
II. The *Civil Law* was ever so curious
and careful to preserve the Goods of such
miserable Persons, that if any should steal
such, they should pay four-fold to the Owner,
if pursued within a Year and a Day, and as
much to the *Prince* or his *Admiral*. So careful

ful were they, and so exact in requiring Restitution, that the very stealing of a Nail, or
the Worth thereof, obliged the Thief to the
Restitution of all the remaining Goods   And
by the Emperor *Antonius* it was made a Law
for such sort of Men, that they should be
battened and banished for three Years, but *Leg pedibus*
that was for only those of a high and honour- *cod*
able Rank. But those that were Base and Ig-
noble, should be scourged and sent to the
Gallies or Metal M.nes   *Arg leg. suc-*
                                             cularn de Ex-
And the preventing of Help to such ship-   *trod. crim.*
wreckt Persons, was punished with the same
Suffering as a Murderer

The like for those that put forth any treacherous Lanthorn or Light, with Intention
to subject others to Danger or Shipwreck,
these were punished with Death

And though no Harm happens, yet he may
be punished. Hence it is, that Fishers are *Per leg incend-*
forbidden to fish with Lights in the Night, *rum nausi ag*
for fear of betraying Sailors   *Leg nepiscator.*
                                             And here I
cannot omit the great and pious Care that his Majesty hath had, in
his Directions about Light-Houses and Lanthorns, and other special
Sea-marks; but more especially in his erecting, at his own Princely
Charge, that most Excellent Light-House near *Goldson* by *Yarmouth*,
which, both for Height, Curiosity and Form, is not inferior to, if
not excelling, all, or most, in Christendom.

III And as the Emperor, and other maritime Kingdoms, had in some sort abrogated
and repealed that cruel Law, and subjected
the Violaters to Punishment for the Inhumanity offered to such distressed Persons, so our
famous King *Richard*, returning from the
Holy War, in his own Experience at Sea, became sensible of the Miseries which Merchants
and Mariners at Sea underwent, their Lives
being always within few Inches, often within

an Hair's Breadth of Death; and having Consideration of their Calamities and diftreffed
State in his Voyage, refolved to revoke that
Law, and at *Oleron* in the Bay of *Aquitain*
(then part of his Dominions, as Sovereign
Lord of the Ocean, and all thofe Maritime
Kingdoms) did there, amongst other good
Marine Laws, declare, *That if any Perfon or
living Thing efcaped out of any wrecked Ship to
Land, it fhould not be Wreck or confifcated to
him or his Succeffor, as it was before, though
all the Men efcaped alive.* For before that,
both in *England* and in * *Normandy*, the †
Crown was entitled to fhipwreckt Goods, and
the King *Jure Gentium* (indeed according to
the *Rhodian* Law) became Heir unto them,
which otherwife *Jure naturali* were conceived
to be *in bonis nullius*, pertaining to no Owner:
But now that Valiant and Religious Prince
refolved no longer to embrace fo cruel a Prerogative, by the ftripping the diftreffed Mariners of thofe Rags of their Eftates, which
the Mercy and Modefty of the Waves and
Winds had left them, and therefore in the
Month of *October* at *Meffana*, in the Prefence
of many Archbifhops, and Bifhops, and
others, he then for ever quitted the Royal
Claim to Wrecks, which afterwards was declared and publifhed at *Oleron* in his own
Territories; fo that if any Man out of the
Ship came alive to Shore, the Property of the
fhipwreckt Goods were ftill preferved to the
Owner. Which Royal Condefcention was fo
enlarged by our fucceeding Kings, *That if a
Man, Dog, or Cat efcapes alive out of the Ship,
neither the Ship or other Veffel, nor any thing
therein, fhall be adjudged* Wreck, *but the Goods
fhall be faved and kept by the* Sheriff, Coroners,

* *Bracton, lib 2. cap. 5*
† *Cuftuma Norman. c 17.*

Roger Hoveden in the latter part of his Annals, fol. 678. Joan. Brompton Chron. Coll fol 1887

or

or the King's Bailiffs, and delivered to the Inhabitants of the Town where the Goods are found; so that if any, within a Year and a Day, *Weſtm* 1 *c* 4. ſue for thoſe Goods, and after prove that they 3 *E* 1 were his at the time of the Shipwreck, they ſhall be reſtored to him without delay. But if not, they ſhall be ſeized by the ſaid Sheriff, Coroners, 2 *Inſt.* 166. or Bailiffs for the King's uſe; and ſhall be delivered to the Inhabitants of the Town, who ſhall anſwer before the Juſtices for the Wreck belonging to the King. But this good Law extends not to Pi- *Per Leg Ole-* rates, Robbers, Sea Rovers, Turks, or other *ron, cap* 47. Enemies to the Catholick Faith.

Where the *Wreck* belongs to another, he ſhall have it in like manner, and if any be attained to have done otherwiſe, he ſhall ſuffer Impriſonment, make Fine to the *King*, and yield Damage alſo

If a Bailiff do it, and it be diſallowed by his Lord, the Bailiff ſhall anſwer for it if he hath wherewithal; but if not, the Lord ſhall deliver his Bailiff's Body to the King.

IV. If the Ship periſhes only, and the *Leg* 37 *Na-* Goods are ſafe, in that Caſe the Goods ought *val Rhod &* to pay a Proportion of a fifth or tenth Penny, 40 according to the eaſy or difficult Winning or Saving of the ſaid Goods Rich Goods, as Gold, and Silver, and Silk, pay leſs than Goods of great Weight and Cumber, being in leſs Danger, unleſs it were a Wreck going into a Port, which the Skipper was not bound for, there *è contra*, then the Skipper is not to be conſidered

Goods may be retained for Payment of *L Raym* 393. Salvage   2 *Salk* 654

But if the Ship and Goods periſh in the Sea, *pl* 2 *Sec* 2 *Barnard B. R.* and the Owners do totally forſake her, and 407 ſo ſhe becomes a meer *Derelict*, in that Caſe

the firſt Poſſeſſor that recovers her, or any
part of her Lading, gains a *Property:* And
this according to the Laws of Nations, *as is
that given for loſt, whereof there is no Hopes of
Recovery,* like a Lamb in the Paws of a Lion.
And the incomparable *Ulpian* compares ſuch
a *Derelition* to a Man that knows his own
Goods to be by another Man detained, and,
makes no Claim unto them in a long time;
unleſs ſome Cauſe do manifeſtly appear, ſeems
to do it to no other purpoſe, but to ſhew that
he is willing to renounce them, and this is it
what *Ulpian* elſewhere intends, where he ſaith,
that a Houſe poſſeſſed for a long time by
another, and no Claim made, nor Rent
demanded for it, ſeems to be deſerted by the
right Owner.

To exact Intereſt long ſince due, ſaith the
good Emperor *Antonius, is hardly juſt; for
the not demanding it in ſo long a ſpace, makes it
probable that thou wert willing to remit it, and
that by not ſo much as demanding it, thy purpoſe was to make thyſelf the more Beloved and
Honoured, and thy Debtor the more Thankful.*

Now that Silence ſhould be of ſuch a force
as to juſtify our Preſumption of a *Derelition,* two things are requiſite; Firſt, That
he that is ſilent knows that he hath a Right;
for him that knows it not, Silence cannot prejudice. Secondly, That his Silence be free
and voluntary, and not occaſioned by Fear,
or any other ſuch Cauſe; and the true Reaſon is, that it is hardly poſſible, that in a long
time a Man ſhould not by ſome Means or
other arrive at the Knowledge of his own
Right, Time daily adminiſtring Occaſions to
the Diſcovery of Truth.

But

But becaufe that Time, which exceeds the Memory of Man, is in a moral Senfe infinite, therefore if Claim be not made with *a reafonable time* to a thing out of Poffeffion, it is a fufficient Prefumption that it *is forfaken*, un- *Grotius, lib 2.* lefs fome very ftrong Reafons be brought to *cap 4 §. 5,6.* the contrary; and therefore the Recovery of the Plate near the *Bahama* Rocks, loft near fifty Years before by the *Spaniard*, became moft apparently a Derelict, and free not only for the Undertakers to recover and poffefs, *Duke of Albe-* but to keep as a Property juftly acquired by *marle & al.* them, as well by the Laws of Nations, as the *in Anno 1687.* *Civil Law*

By Stat 3 *Geo* c. 13. *Sect* 6. (continued to 25th of *March*, 1778. by Stat 4 *Geo* 3. *c*. 12. *Sect*. 1.) The Lord Warden of the Cinque Ports fhall nominate under his Hand and Seal three or more Perfons in each of the Cinque Ports, two ancient Towns and their Members, to adjuft any Difference relating to Salvage, between the Mafter of any Ship that has in bad Weather been forced from her Anchor and Cable, and the Perfons bring them afhore: And if any Veffel be forced from her Cables and Anchors by Extremity of Weather, and leave the fame in any Roads within the Jurifdiction of the Cinque Ports, and the Salvage cannot be adjufted between the Perfons concerned, the fame fhall be determined in twelve Hours, by any one or more of the Perfons appointed as aforefaid

V. The *King* fhall have Wreck of the Sea, *17 E 2 c. 1* Whales, and great Sturgeons taken in the Sea, and elfewhere throughout the whole Realm, except in Places privileged by the *King*

Alfo.

Ld. Raym
474 2 Mod.
259
Ld. Raym
473.

Also Wreck may be claimed by Prescription; and the Lord High Admiral possibly may have it by Prescription.

A Grant of Wreck to the Lord High Admiral as appertaining to his Office, will not pass Wreck belonging to the King's Manor by Prescription.

Sir Henry Constable's Case,
5 Coke 107.

VI. By the Grant of Wreck will pass *Flotsam*, *Jetsam*, and *Lagan*, when they are cast upon the Land, but if they are not cast upon the Land, the Admiral hath Jurisdiction, and not the *Common Law*, and they cannot be said Wreck.

5 Co 106 a
5 Co 106. b

Wreccum Maris, are such Goods only as are cast and left upon the Land by the Sea.

Flotsam, is when a Ship is sunk, or otherwise perished, and the Goods float upon the Sea

Ibid.

Jetsam, is when the Ship is in Danger to be sunk, and for lightning the Ship the Goods are cast into the Sea, notwithstanding which the Ship perisheth.

Ibid

Lagan vel Ligan, is when the Goods being heavy, are cast into the Sea before the Ship perishes, which by the Prudence of the Master or Mariners, who have an Intent to save them so sunk, as that they may come at them again; in order to which they fasten a Buoy, or other light Matter, that they may signify to them where they lie, if Providence should bring them in a Condition to retake them, *& dicitur Ligar à ligando*.

Bracton, lib.
3 c 2

F N B 122
46 E 3 15.
Antb Omnis
peregrini comm a de suc-
cessoribus acq.
per Leg Oloron
5 Coke 107.

The King shall have *Flotsam*, *Jetsam* and *Lagan*, when the Ship perisheth, or when the Owners of the Goods are not known, but when the Ship perishes not, *è contra*

A Man may have *Flotsam* and *Jetsam* by the King's Grant, and may have *Flotsam*
within

within the high and low Water-mark by Pre-
fcription, as it appears by thofe of the Weft- *2 Inftit 167.*
Countries, who prefcribe to have Wreck in *Leg 8 D de*
the Sea; fo far as they may fee a *Humber* *jactu.*
Barrel

VII If the Ship be ready to perifh, and
all the Men therein, for Safeguard of their
Lives, leave the Ship, and after the forfaken
Ship perifhes, if any of the Men be faved and
come to Land, the Goods are not loft.

A Ship on the Sea was purfued by Enemies,
the Men therein for Safeguard of their Lives,
forfake the Ship, the Enemies take the Ship,
and fpoils her of her Goods and Tackle, and
turn her to Sea, by ftrefs of Weather fhe is *5 R 2 pro.*
caft on Land, where it happened her Men *Willielmo Fifh-*
arrived. It was refolved by all the Judges of *lake Co 2 Inft.*
England, that the Ship was no Wreck, nor *f. 167 Leg.*
loft. *43. § 11.*
D de furt
VIII. If Goods are caft up as a Wreck, *Pl Com 466.*
and it falls out they be *bona peritura,* the Sheriff may fell them within the Year, and the
Sale is good, but he muft account to the true
Owners.

Owners claiming the Wreck, muft make *F N B. fol.*
their Proof by their Marks or Cocquets, by the *112 c* The
Book of Cuftoms, or by the Teftimony of ho- Year and Day
neft Men; and if the Wreck belongs to the counted from
King, the Party may fue out a Commiffion to the Seizure,
hear and determine, and that by the Oaths of *2 Inft 168.*
twelve Men; or elfe he may bring his Action *5 Co 107 b.*
at Law, and make out his Proof by *Verdict,* *1 Keb 657.*
but fuch Action muft be brought *within the*
Year and Day

Note, *Flotfam, Jetfam* and *Lagan,* are *5 Co. 126. b.*
Goods on or in the Sea, and belong to the
King, who by Charter hath granted them to
the Lord Admiral

IX.

Left unre-
folved in *Moor*
fol. 224. But
fince adjudg-
ed in C B.
upon a fpecial
Verdictfound
at *St Edmund's*
Bury.
Shephard v.
Gofnold, Hill.
23, 24 *Car* 2.
Rott. 615.
Vaughan,
159.

IX. If Goods were wrecked on the Shore; and the Lord having Power, takes them, he fhall not pay Cuftom, neither by the *Common Law* nor by the *Statute*, for at the *Common Law*, wrecked Goods could not be charged with Cuftom, becaufe at the *Common Law* all *Wreck* was wholly the King's, and he could not have a fmall Duty of Cuftom out of that which was all his own, and by *Weftm* 1. where wrecked Goods belonged more to another than to the King, he fhall have it in like manner, that is, as the King hath his.

Now Goods that are chargeable with Cuftom, according to the Act of *Tunnage and Poundage*, muft have thefe Properties

12 *Car.* 2. c 4.

1. They muft be Goods which fhall come or be brought into the Ports or Places of the Kingdom.

2. They muft come or be brought into fuch *Ports* or *Places*, as *Merchandize* that is for Sale, and to that end; for there can be no other Conception of *Goods* brought as *Merchandize*

3. They muft come and be brought as *Merchandize*, and for Sale by the King's natural born Subjects, or by Strangers and Aliens, as diftinguifhed from the natural Subjects

4. The Duty payable to the King, is to be meafured by the Quality of him that imports the Commodity, that is, if the Importer be a natural Subject, he pays lefs to the King; and if an Alien, more.

5 All thofe Goods charged with the Duty by the *Statute*, fo to come, or be brought into Ports or Places of the Kingdom, are to be foreign, as of the Growth of *France*, the *Levant, Spain, Portugal, Germany*, &c.

Whence

Whence it follows, 1. That Goods of foreign Growth, and which by their kind are to pay Duty, if they shall come or be brought into the Ports or Places of the Kingdom, neither by the King's natural born Subjects, nor by Aliens, they are not chargeable with the Duties mentioned in the Act.

2. If they are not brought into the Ports and Places of the Kingdom, as Merchandize, *viz.* for Sale, they are not chargeable with the Duty , but Wines or other Goods coming or brought into the *Realm* as *Wreck*, are neither brought into the Kingdom by any of the King's *Natural born Subjects*, nor by any *Strangers*, but by the Wind and Sea, for such Goods want a Proprietor until the Law appoints one.

3. *Wrecked Goods* are not brought into the Kingdom being cast on Shore, as Merchandize, *viz.* for Sale , but are as all other the native Goods of the Kingdom, indifferent in themselves, for Sale or other Use at the Pleasure of the Proprietor.

4 All Goods foreign or domestick are, in their Nature, capable to be Merchandize, that is, to be sold; but it follows not thence, that wheresoever they are brought into the Kingdom, they are brought as Merchandize, and to be sold, and should pay Custom , for they are transferred from Place to Place, more for other Uses than for Sale.

5. All Goods charged with the Duty of the Act, must be propriated by a Merchant *Natural born*, or Merchant *Alien*, and the greater or less Duty is to be paid, as the Proprietor is an Alien or Native Merchant , but wrecked Goods are not the Goods of any Merchant *Natural born*, *Alien* or *Denizen*, whereby the
Duty

Duty payable fhould be either demanded, diftinguifhed, or paid : Therefore a Duty impoffible to be known, can be no Duty, for Civilly *what cannot be known to be, is as that which is not.*

6. All Goods fubject to the Duty of Tunnage and Poundage, may be forfeited by the Difobedience and Mifbehaviour of the Merchant-Proprietor, or thofe trufted by him, as *unfhipping before Payment, or lawfully tendering or agreeing for*, &c. But wrecked Goods cannot be imported into any Creek or Place of the Realm by way of Merchandize, and unfhipped to be laid on Land; for if fo imported and unfhipped to be laid on Land, it is no Wreck, and therefore are not Goods forfeitable by the Mifbehaviour of any within the Act, and confequently not Goods intended to be charged with the Duties by the Act.

Goods drowned or loft in paffing a Ferry, a great River, or an Arm of the Sea, are not to be faid to be exported, though they be carried to Sea; but Goods exported are fuch as are conveyed to Sea in Ships or other Naval Carriages of Man's Artifice; and by like Reafon, Goods imported muft not be Goods imported by the Wind, Water, or fuch inanimate Means, but in Ships, Veffels, and other Conveyances ufed by reafonable Agents, as Merchants, Mariners, Sailors, &c Whence it may be concluded, that Goods or Merchandize imported within the Meaning of the Act, can only be fuch as are imported with Deliberation, and by reafonable *Agents*, not cafually and without Reafon, and therefore wrecked Goods are no Goods imported within the Intention of the Act, and confequently not to anfwer the King's Duties, for Goods,

as

as Goods, cannot Offend, Forfeit, Unlade, pay Duties, or the like, but Men whose Goods they are: And wrecked Goods have no Owners to do those Offices, when the Act requires they should be done; therefore the Act intended not to charge the Duty upon such Goods.

Per Holt, C. J. That Wreck shall not pay Custom, has never been made a Doubt since the Case in *Vaughan* 159. of *Shephard v. Gosnold*. L. Raym 388. The same Point (including *Flotsam*) resolved by both Courts, viz. C. B. and then B R. on Error brought. L. *Raym*. 501. 502.

The Admirals of *England*, *ut magnus Admirallus Angliæ, Hiberniæ, Walliæ, ac Dominorum & Insularum earundem, Villæ Calisiæ & Merchiarum ejusdem, necnon Gasconiæ, Aquitaniæ, elassium & Marium dictorum Regnorum Angliæ præfectus generalis, &c.* which are the words of their Patents used at this Day, do claim all Wrecks arising from any of those Places, by virtue of their Grants. The very Words of the L. *Howard*'s Patent, in 28 *Eliz* in *Rot*. *Admir*. m. 10.

And yet in the like Case, in all Circumstances, between *Power* and Sir *William Portman*, *Hill* 6. *William Com B. Rot.* 1431. where the Judges, and more particularly Justice *Treby*, seemed to be of Opinion, that Goods wrecked, or Flotsam, should pay Custom

X King *Edward* the Second, in the first Year of his Reign, by his Charter, granted the Castle of *Carisbrook*, with all the Lands and Tenements in the *Isle of Wight*, formerly belonging to *Isabella Fortibus*, Countess of *Albemarle*, to his great Favourite *Peter de Gaveston*, and *Margaret* his Wife, and the Heirs of their two Bodies begotten (together with sundry other Castles and Lands) and commanded 1 E. 2. m. 6. num. 6.

commanded *Nicholas de Bosco* to put him into actual Possession; and likewise commanded *Robert de Sanson*, Keeper of the Forest of *Parkhurst* in that Isle, to be Intendent to them for the Farm he had granted him for Life, for the Custody thereof, which being afterwards soon reseized into the King's Hands, he granted this Castle with all its Services, and all his Lands in that Isle, to *Edward* his Son and his Heirs Kings of *England*, and afterwards, for the ascertaining what did of Right belong to the same Castle, an Inquisition went out, by which it was found, *inter alia, qd' wreckum Maris pertinens ad dictum Castrum valet per Ann. 4 s.*

Pat. 20. E. 2. n. 10. intus pro Edvardo filio Regis

So that, by the general Patent of the Admiral, will not pass the Wreck of this Isle, without special Words granted in the Patent.

Inquisit de An. 47 H 3. n 32.

Note, If the Wreck happened, or was occasioned by reason of any Fault or Negligence in the Master or Mariners, the Master must make good the Loss; but if the same was occasioned by the Act of God, to avoid an Enemy or Pirate, and the like, there he shall be excused.

Leg. 3 § 1. D. Naut caup St lib. 1. §. 4 D. de obl. & act. leg. 26 § 6. D. mand Quia vis major providentiam & industriam humanam superat, nisi culpa casum praecesserit.

Persons convicted of plundering shipwrecked Goods, &c.

By Stat 26 *Geo.* 2. *c.* 19. *Sect.* 1 If any Person plunder, steal, take away, or destroy any Goods or Effects, from or belonging to any Ship or Vessel of his Majesty's Subjects, or others, being in Distress, wrecked, lost, stranded, or cast on Shore, in any Part of his Majesty's Dominions (whether any living Creature be on board such Vessel or not) or any of the Furniture, Tackle, Apparel, Provision, or part of such Vessel; or beat or wound with intent to kill, or otherwise wilfully obstruct

ſtruct the Eſcape of any Perſon endeavouring to ſave his Life from ſuch Ship, or the Wreck thereof, or put out any falſe Light with intention to bring unto Danger, ſuch Perſon ſo offending ſhall be deemed guilty of Felony, and being convicted, ſhall ſuffer Death as in Caſes of Felony, without Benefit of Clergy.

Or of obſtructing the Eſcape of any Perſon from a Wreck, or of putting out falſe Lights, to ſuffer Death without Clergy.

By *Sect.* 2. When Goods or Effects of ſmall Value be ſtranded, loſt, or caſt on Shore, and be ſtolen without Circumſtances of Cruelty or Violence, it ſhall be lawful for any Perſon to proſecute for ſuch Offence by way of Indictment for Petit Larceny ; and the Offenders being convicted, ſhall ſuffer ſuch Puniſhment as in Caſes of Petit Larceny.

Where Goods of ſmall Value ſhall be ſtolen without any Circumſtances of Cruelty, the Offender may be indicted of Petit Larceny.

By *Sect.* 3. It ſhall be lawful for any Juſtice of Peace, upon Information upon Oath, of any Part of the Cargo or Effects belonging to any Ship loſt or ſtranded upon or near the Coaſts aforeſaid, being unlawfully carried away, or concealed in any Houſe or Place, or of ſome reaſonable Suſpicion thereof, to iſſue his Warrant for the ſearching of ſuch Houſe or Place, as in other Caſes of ſtolen Goods, and if the ſame be found in ſuch Houſe or Place, or in the Cuſtody of any Perſon, not legally authorized or intitled to keep the ſame, and the Owner or Occupier of ſuch Houſe or Place, or the Perſon in whoſe Cuſtody the ſame be found, ſhall not upon Demand deliver the ſame to the Owner, or to ſuch Perſon as ſhall be authorized to demand the ſame ; or ſhall not give a good Account, to the Satisfaction of the Juſtice, how he became poſſeſſed thereof, ſuch Juſtice, upon proof of ſuch Refuſal, ſhall commit

Juſtices upon Information of ſhipwrecked Goods being ſtolen or concealed, to iſſue ſearch Warrants.

And the Perſons in whoſe Cuſtody the Goods ſhall be found, not giving a ſatisfactory Anſwer, to be committed for 6 Months,

commit the Offender to the common Goal for fix Months, or until he have paid to fuch Owner, or to the Perfon authorized to receive the fame, treble the Value of the Goods unlawfully detained.

By *Sect.* 4. If any Perfon offer to Sale any Goods or Effects belonging to any Ship, loft, ftranded, or caft on Shore, and unlawfully taken away, or fufpected fo to have been, it fhall be lawful for the Perfon to whom the fame be fo offered for Sale, or any Officer of the Cuftoms or Excife, or any Conftable, or other Peace Officer, to ftop and feize the faid Goods and Effects; and he fhall carry the fame, or give Notice of fuch Seizure, to fome Juftice of Peace; and if the Perfon who offered the faid Goods to Sale, or fome other Perfon on his Behalf, appear not before the faid Juftice, within ten Days next after fuch Seizure, and make out the Property of the faid Goods to be in him, or in the Perfon by whom he was employed to fell the fame, the faid Goods fhall, by Order of the Juftice, be delivered over to or for the Ufe of the rightful Owner, upon Payment of a reafonable Reward for fuch Seizure, (to be afcertained by the Juftice) to the Perfon who feized the fame, and fuch Juftice fhall commit the Perfon who fo offered the faid Goods to Sale, to the common Goal for fix Months, or until he have paid to fuch lawful Owner, or to the Perfon authorized to receive the fame, treble the Value of the Goods fo unlawfully offered to Sale.

By *Sect.* 5 In cafe any Perfon not employed by the Mafter, Mariners or Owners, or other Perfons lawfully authorized, in the Salvage of any Ship, or the Cargo or Provifion thereof,

thereof, in the Abfence of Perfons fo employed or authorized, fave any fuch Ship or Effects, and caufe the fame to be carried, for the Benefit of the Owners, into any Port, or to any near adjoining Cuftom-Houfe, or other Place of fafe Cuftody, giving Notice to fome Juftice of Peace, Magiftrate, or Cuftom-Houfe or Excife Officer, or difcover to any fuch Magiftrate or Officer, where any fuch Effects are wrongfully bought, fold, or concealed, fuch Perfon fhall be entitled to a reafonable Reward, to be paid by the Mafters or Owners of fuch Veffels or Goods, and to be adjufted in cafe of Difagreement, in like Manner as the Salvage is to be adjufted and paid by 12 *Ann* Stat. 2. *cap.* 18. or in the manner herein after prefcribed.

Port, &c for the Benefit of the Owners, and give Notice thereof;

or who fhall difcover where fuch Goods are concealed, intitled to the Reward.

And the Quantum in cafe of Difagreement is to be adjufted according to 12 Ann. St. 2. c 18.

By *Sect.* 6. For the better afcertaining the Salvage to be paid in purfuance of this Act, and the Act before-mentioned, and for putting them in Execution, the Juftice of the Peace, Mayor, Bailiff, Collector of the Cuftoms, or chief Conftable, neareft to the Place where any Ship or Goods be ftranded or caft away, fhall forthwith give public Notice for a Meeting to be held as foon as poffible of the Sheriff or his Deputy, the Juftices of the Peace, Mayors, or other chief Magiftrates of Towns Corporate, Coroners, and Commiffioners of the Land-Tax, or any five or more of them, who are to give Aid in the Execution of this and the faid former Act, and to employ proper Perfons for the faving of Ships in Diftrefs, and fuch Ships and Effects as be ftranded or caft away, and alfo to examine Perfons upon Oath concerning the fame,

Where any Veffel or Effects fhall be ftranded, public Notice to be given for a Meeting of the Sheriff, Juftices, and Magiftrates, &c. who are to aid in faving the Veffel and Goods, &c.

and to adjuft the Salvage.

or

or the Salvage thereof, and to adjust the *Quantum* of such Salvage, and distribute the same among the Persons concerned in such

4 s. a Day allowed for their Attendance.

Salvage, in case of Disagreement; and every such Sheriff, Justice of Peace, Mayor, chief Magistrate, Coroner, Lord of a Manor, Under-Sheriff, or Commissioner of the Land-Tax, acting at such Meeting, shall be paid 4 *s.* a Day for his Expences out of the Effects saved

If the Salvage be not paid, the Officer of the Customs may raise the same by a Bill of Sale of the Vessel or Cargo, which may be redeemed, upon Payment of Principal and Interest.

By *Sect.* 7. If the Charges and Rewards for Salvage, directed to be paid by 12 *Ann. Stat.* 2 *cap.* 18. and by this Act, be not paid, or sufficient Security given for the same, within forty Days, it shall be lawful for the Officer of the Customs concerned in such Salvage, to borrow Money sufficient to pay such Charges and Rewards, or any part thereof then unpaid or not secured, upon one or more Bills of Sale, under his Hand and Seal, of the Ship or Cargo saved, or such part thereof as is sufficient, redeemable upon Payment of the Sum so borrowed, and Interest after the Rate of Four *per Cent. per Annum.*

Where Oath shall be made of Plunder or Theft, or of breaking a Ship, contrary to 12 Ann. St. 2. c 18. And the Examination shall be delivered to the Clerk of of the Peace, he is to prosecute the Offender;

By *Sect.* 8. If Oath be made before any Magistrate lawfully impowered to take the same, of any such Plunder or Theft, and the Examination in Writing thereupon taken, be delivered to the Clerk of the Peace of the County or Division wherein such Fact is committed, or to his Deputy; or if Oath be made before any such Magistrate of the breaking any Ship, contrary to the 12 *Ann. Stat.* 2. *cap.* 18 and the Examination in Writing thereupon taken, be delivered to such Clerk of the Peace, or his Deputy; such Clerk of the Peace shall cause the Offender to be prosecuted for the same, either in the County

where

where the Fact is committed, or in any County next adjoining, in which adjoining County any Indictment may be laid by any other Prosecutor, and if the Fact be committed in *Wales*, then the Prosecution shall be carried on in the next adjoining *English* County, and the Charges of such Prosecutions by the Clerk of the Peace shall be paid by the Treasurer of the County or Division where the Fact is committed, to such Amount, as the Justices of the Peace in their Sessions order, and if such Clerk of the Peace neglect to carry on such Prosecution, he shall forfeit 100 *l* for every such Offence, to any Person who shall sue for the same by Action of Debt, &c. in any Court of Record at *Westminster*, in which no Essoin, &c shall be allowed.

and the Charges to be paid by the Treasurer of the County.

Clerk of the Peace neglecting to prosecute, forfeits 100 l.

By *Sect*. 9 The Commissioners of the Land Tax, the Deputy Sheriff, the Coroner, and the Officers of Excise in each County, Riding, and Division, shall be the proper Officers for putting in Execution this Act, and 12 *Ann.* *St* 2 *cap* 18. with those therein named for that Purpose.

Officers for putting this and 12 Ann. St 2 c 18 in Execution.

By *Sect* 10. The Lord Warden of the Cinque Ports, and the Lieutenant of *Dover Castle*, and the Deputy Warden of the Cinque Ports, and the Judge official, and Commissary of the Court of Admiralty of the Cinque Ports, two ancient Towns, and the Members thereof, and every of them, and every other Person appointed by the Lord Warden of the Cinque Ports, pursuant to 3 *Geo cap* 13. shall be the Persons to put in Execution, within the Jurisdiction of the Cinque Ports, two ancient Towns and their Members, all the Powers given by this Act, and the 12 *Ann.* *St.* 2 *cap* 18. and the 4 *Geo. cap* 12.

Officers for putting this and 12 Ann in Execution within the Liberty of the Cinque Ports, &c

Persons convicted of affaulting any Magiftrate, or Officer, &c in the Salvage of any Veffel or Goods, to be tranfported for feven Years.

By *Sect.* 11. If any Sheriff, or his Deputy, Juftice of Peace, Mayor, or other Magiftrate, Lord of a Manor, Commiffioner of the Land-Tax, Chief Conftable, or Petty Conftable, or other Peace Officer, or any Cuftom-houfe or Excife Officer, or other Perfon lawfully authorized, be affaulted, beaten, and wounded, for the Exercife of his Duty, in the Salvage of any Ship in Diftrefs, or of any Ship or Goods ftranded, wrecked, or caft on Shore, or lying under Water, in any of his Majefty's Dominions, any Perfon fo affaulting, beating, and wounding, fhall upon Conviction, by Indictment at the Affizes, or General Goal Delivery, or at the General or Quarter Seffions for the County or Divifion where fuch Offence is committed, be tranfported for feven Years to fome of his Majefty's Colonies in *America*, and be fubject to fuch Punifhment, in cafe of Return before that Time, as other Perfons under Sentence of Tranfportation.

Juftices in the Abfence of the Sheriff may take a fufficient Force to reprefs Violence, &c. Perfons impowered to give Orders, where any fhall be affembled in cafe of a Shipwreck, &c

By *Sect.* 12. It fhall be lawful for any Juftice of Peace, in cafe of Need, and in the Abfence of the High Sheriff, to take fufficient Power of the County, to reprefs all unjuft Violence, and to enforce the Execution of this Act

By *Sect.* 13. All Perfons fo affembled to fave any Ship or Goods fhall conform in the firft Place to the Orders of the Mafter or other Officers or Owners, or other Perfons employed by them, and for want of their Prefence or Directions, to the Orders of the Perfons authorized by this Act, or 12 *Ann.* St 2. *cap* 18 in the following Subordination, as any of them happen to be prefent, *viz.* in the firft Place, to the Orders of any Officer

of

of the Cuftoms, then of any Officer of the
Excife, then of the Sheriff or his Deputy,
then of any Juftice of Peace, then of the
Mayor or Chief Magiftrate of any Corporation, then of the Coroner, then of any Commiffioners of the Land-Tax, then of any
Chief Conftable, then of any Petty Conftable, or other Peace Officer · And any Perfon acting wilfully contrary to fuch Orders,
fhall forfeit any Sum not exceeding 5 *l.* to
be levied by Warrant of one Juftice of Peace;
and in cafe of Non-payment, the Offender fhall
be committed to the Houfe of Correction, for
any Time not exceeding three Months.

*Perfons act-
ing contrary
to Orders,
forfeit 5 l.*

By *Sect.* 14 This Act fhall not prejudice
his Majefty, or any Grantee of the Crown,
or any Lord of Manor, or other Perfon in
any Right to any Wreck, or Goods which
are *Flotfam, Jetfam,* or *Lagan*

*Rights of the
Crown, &c.
referved.*

By *Sect.* 15 The Officer of the Cuftoms,
who acts in the preferving of any Ship in
Diftiefs, or the Cargo, fhall, as foon as may
be, caufe all Perfons belonging to the faid
Ship, and others who can give any Account
thereof, or of the Cargo, to be examined
upon Oath before fome Juftice of the Peace,
as to the Name or Defcription of the Ship,
and the Names of the Mafter or Chief Officer
and Owners thereof, and of the Cargo, and
of the Ports from or to which the faid Ship
was bound, and the Occafion of the faid
Ship's Diftiefs, which Examination the faid
Juftices are to take in Writing, and they
fhall deliver a Copy thereof, together with a
Copy of the Account of the Goods, to the
faid Officer of the Cuftoms, who fhall forthwith tranfmit the fame to the Secretary of
the

*Examination
on Oath to be
taken of the
Ship's Name,
Cargo and
Owners, &c.*

*And Copy to
be tranfmit-
ted to the Se-
cretary of the
Admiralty
and publifh-
ed in the Ga-
zette.*

the Admiralty; who shall publish in the next *London Gazette*, so much thereof as is necessary for the Information of Persons interested.

By *Sect.* 16 The 12 *Ann.* St 2. *cap.* 18.

The Acts 12 *Ann* St. 2 c 18. and 4 *Geo. c.* 12 to be in Force where not altered by this Act.

and the 4 *Geo cap.* 12 shall remain in Force, save only so far as the same are altered by this Act.

Not to extend to *Scotland*.

By *Sect.* 18 Nothing in this Act shall extend to *Scotland*.

END of the FIRST VOLUME.

Ex W.E.F.
P2/2/.04

Lightning Source UK Ltd.
Milton Keynes UK
UKHW030633190219
337610UK00005B/221/P

9 781170 022863